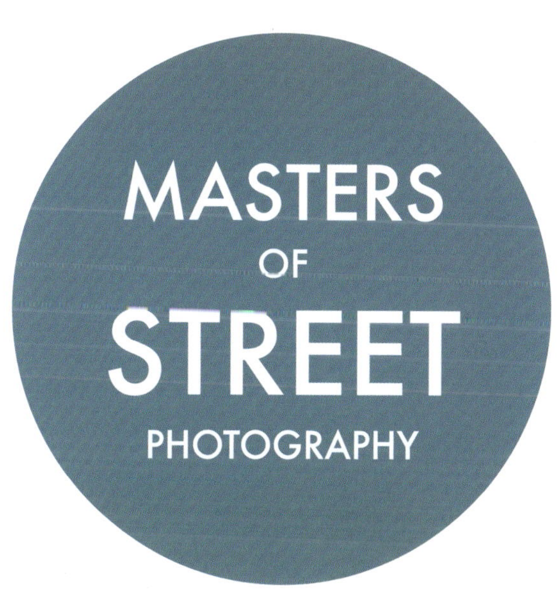

MASTERS
OF
STREET
PHOTOGRAPHY

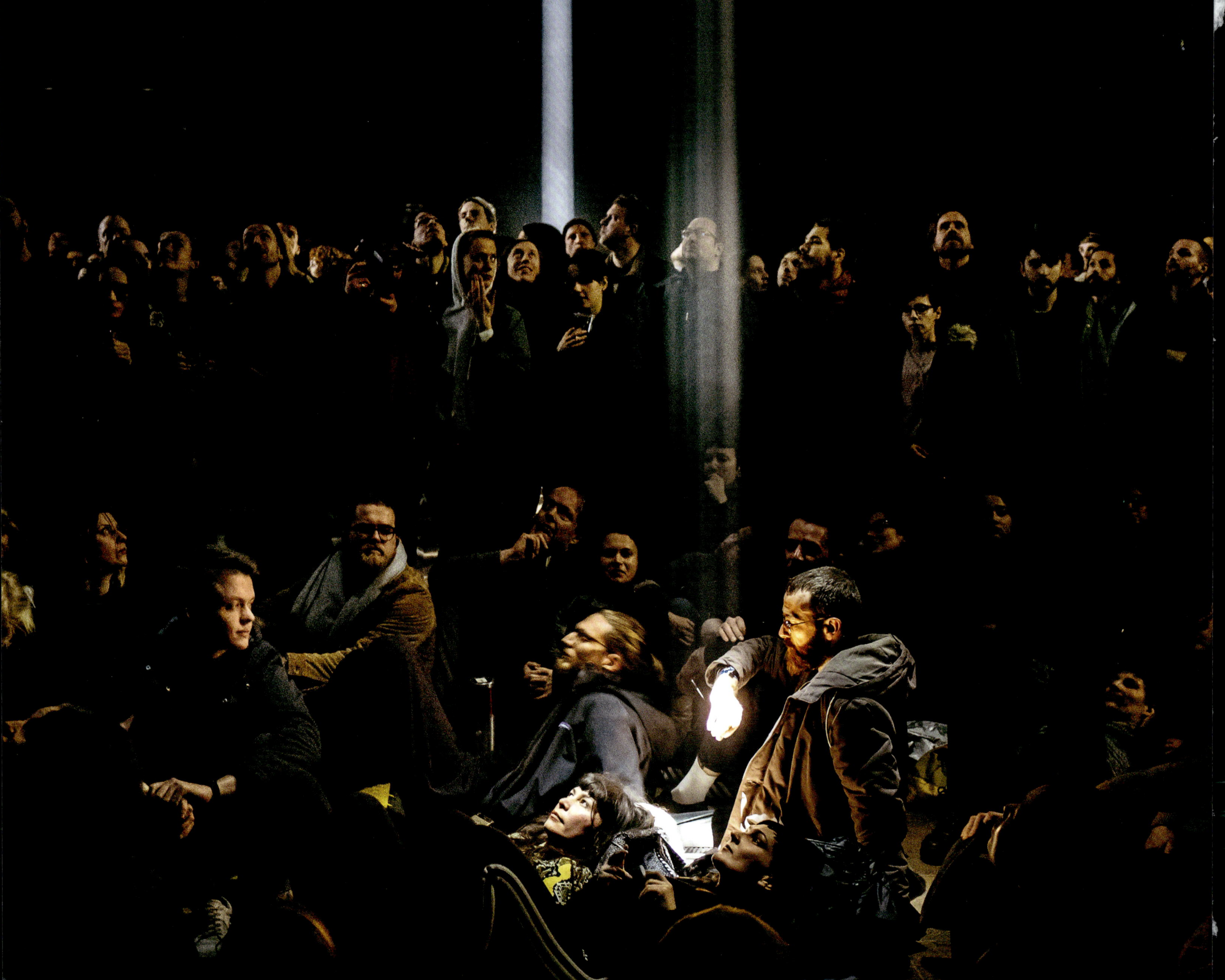

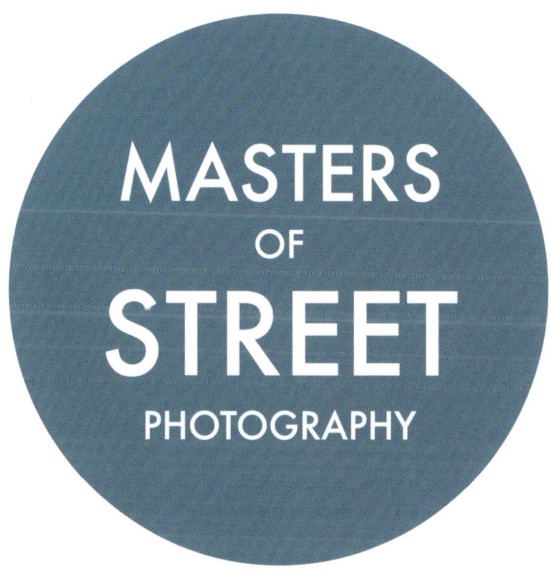

CONSULTANT EDITOR: ROB YARHAM

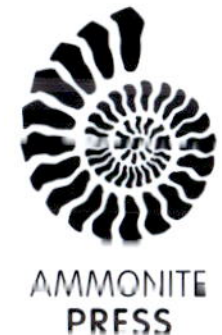

First published 2019 by
Ammonite Press
an imprint of Guild of Master Craftsman Publications Ltd
Castle Place, 166 High Street, Lewes, East Sussex, BN7 1XU,
United Kingdom
www.ammonitepress.com

Reprinted 2021

ISBN 978 1 78145 360 5

Publisher: Jonathan Bailey
Design Manager: Robin Shields
Editor: Rob Yarham
Researcher: Anna Evans

Color reproduction by GMC Reprographics
Printed and bound in China

Front cover image: Copyright © Sally Davies
Title page image: Copyright © Martin U Waltz

CONTENTS

INTRODUCTION

Street photography can be a difficult discipline to define. While we can easily
point to a reportage, landscape, nature, travel, fashion, or portrait photograph,
street photography is harder to pin down. Is it only taken on the street, in an urban
environment? Is it always candid and unposed? Must it include people, and use only
natural lighting? Should it only be shot using a dedicated camera? Or can any, or all,
of these unofficial rules be broken? What exactly is street photography?

Well, we know it when we see it.

Today, when we live in a world saturated by images—images that record, entertain,
inform, and promote—street photography may seem to have lost its distinctiveness,
or even relevance. A huge and increasing number of photographs are now made by
ourselves of ourselves, mostly using our smartphones, as we restlessly share our
daily lives on social media. Among this pictorial stream of consciousness that floods
our eyes and brain, have photographs become simply visual noise? Or can they
continue to have meaning?

It is also a world where the private and public have become blurred, and full of
contradictions. Although we distrust governments having access to the details
of our daily lives, we consciously allow many corporations—especially in tech and
social media—to plunder information on who we are and how we live. And while we
are happy to share our own smartphone photos with the world through the internet,
street photographers find themselves increasingly restricted in what, who, and where
they can shoot in public places. When faced with all these creative, social, and even

MARTIN LUTHER KING DAY PARADE, LOS
ANGELES, CALIFORNIA, 2016, FROM
THE SERIES *AMERICANS PARADE*

GEORGE GEORGIOU

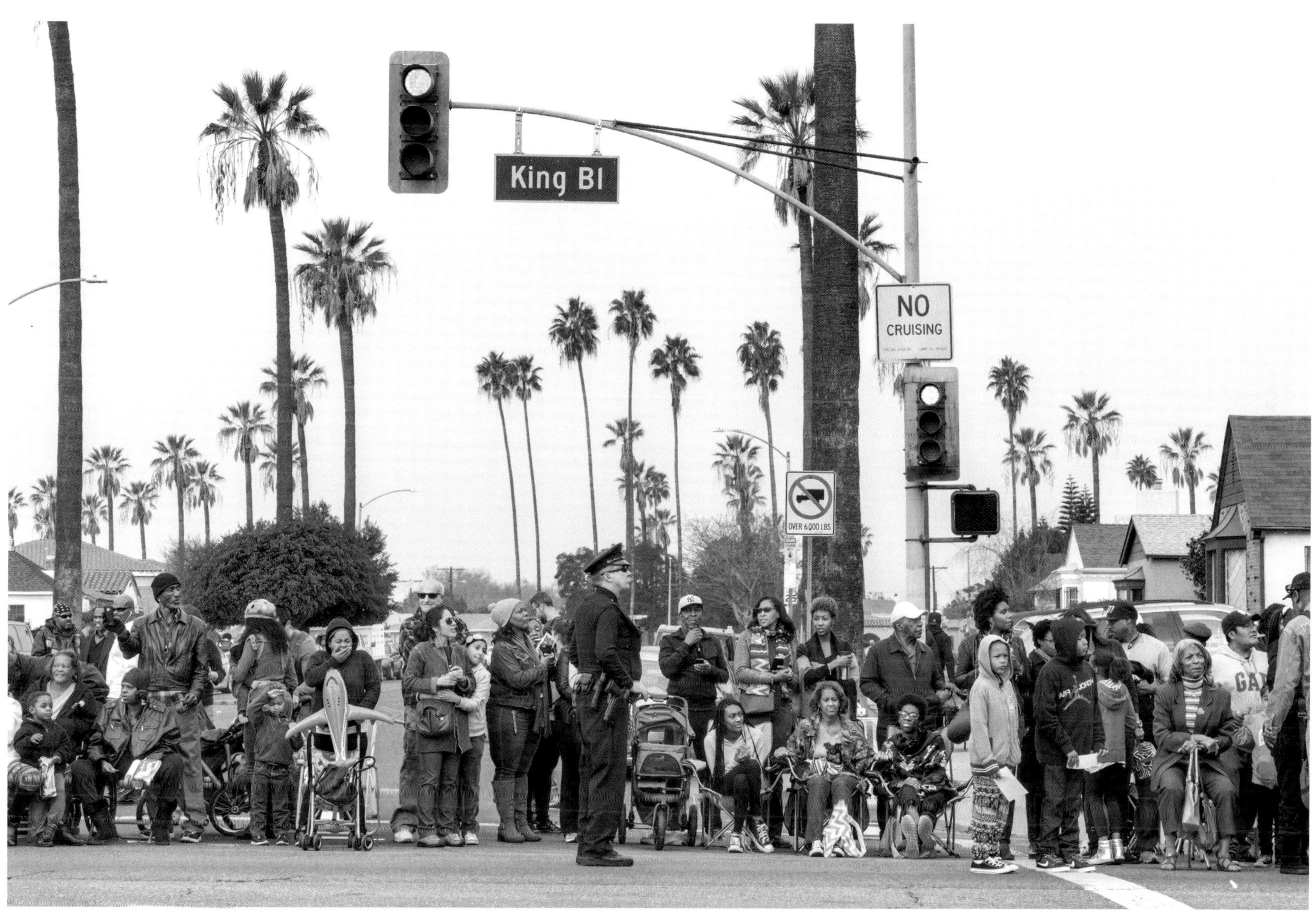
King Bl
NO
CRUISING
OVER 6,000 LBS

legal challenges, can street photography survive? Can it still say something valid, important, or even new? So perhaps the more important question we should pose is why do we still need street photography?

All this seems a long way from Eugène Atget's images of old Paris, carefully crafted using a large, glass dry plate camera from 1897. Atget set out to photograph a city disappearing in the face of modern urbanization, capturing mostly old buildings and quirky details, but also people on the streets. He wanted to record a way of life for posterity, and unwittingly influenced a range of subsequent artists—from the Surrealists, including photographer Man Ray, to many famous street photographers who would follow. From such melancholic acts of nostalgia was born a vibrant, influential, ever-changing art form.

Later on, street photography became associated with the concept of "the decisive moment," as famously set out by Henri Cartier-Bresson in his 1952 book of the same name. Cartier-Bresson explained that: "Photography is the simultaneous recognition, in a fraction of a second, of the significance of an event as well as of a precise organization of forms which give that event its proper expression." But street photography has moved on. Cartier-Bresson's formal compositions are timeless, but also of their time. Since then, street photographers have sought out meaning in imperfection, dissonance, confrontation, harsh lighting, uncompromising crops, bright colors, and jolting juxtapositions—experimenting in order to capture not just a moment, but its emotional and social context.

As you will see from the masters we feature in this book, street photography is still very much a vibrant and evolving art form today, yielding many different and fresh approaches to capturing images of real life. In showcasing the work of some of its best practitioners, we've set out to offer a snapshot of the world of contemporary street photography, showing that it continues to move beyond the restrictive definitions of the past. We've included brief interviews with each photographer that explore the technical and creative possibilities of the discipline, and provide some inspiration for those looking to master street photography themselves along the way. In doing so, we find that street photography is not only relevant, but still has plenty to say.

Like Atget, today's masters of street photography capture the everyday lives of people and the small details of where and how they live. Their art records our society and asks questions about it, arguably making that art more relevant and poignant than many other forms of contemporary photography.

But whether recording how we live, capturing moments or forms, or raising questions about how and why we live together, street photography cannot be complete if it does not engage the viewer, if it does not connect with us on an emotional level. In the words of British photographer Don McCullin: "Photography isn't about seeing, it's about feeling. If I don't have some kind of feeling for what I'm shooting, how can I expect the person who looks at it to feel anything?"

You'll see that many of the photographers featured in this book say similar things about the importance of connecting with their subjects and expressing the emotion of a moment. And their images will certainly make you feel something—they are moving, saddening, amusing, uplifting, intriguing, and thought-provoking.

This is what raises great street photography above so much of the everyday mass of imagery we encounter: it does more than freeze a moment of daily life, it creates an emotional connection with people we don't know—it makes us feel something for them, about them, and with them. And in doing so it captures a wider truth that is revealed in that moment—it tells us something about each other, and also ourselves. Street photography brings us closer together, and in these times that seems more relevant and more important than ever.

Street photography is about life. And we know life, or at least understand it a little better, when we see it.

Rob Yarham

ECLIPSE, 1911, BY EUGÈNE ATGET

This early street photograph by Atget records a solar eclipse in 1911 through the reaction of those witnessing it from a Paris boulevard. As with all great street images, it captures an intriguing moment in time while begging questions of the viewer. Without any background knowledge, one immediately asks what the crowd are looking at. Even with the historical facts to hand, it makes one wonder at the consequences of staring at the sun through raised hands and improvised optical devices. Discovering the raised figure (center-left) looking not at the sun but at Atget, one also begins to wonder whether perhaps the photographer organized a reconstruction of the event. Critic Walter Benjamin, in 1936, noted how Atget's compositions looked uncannily like the "scene of a crime."

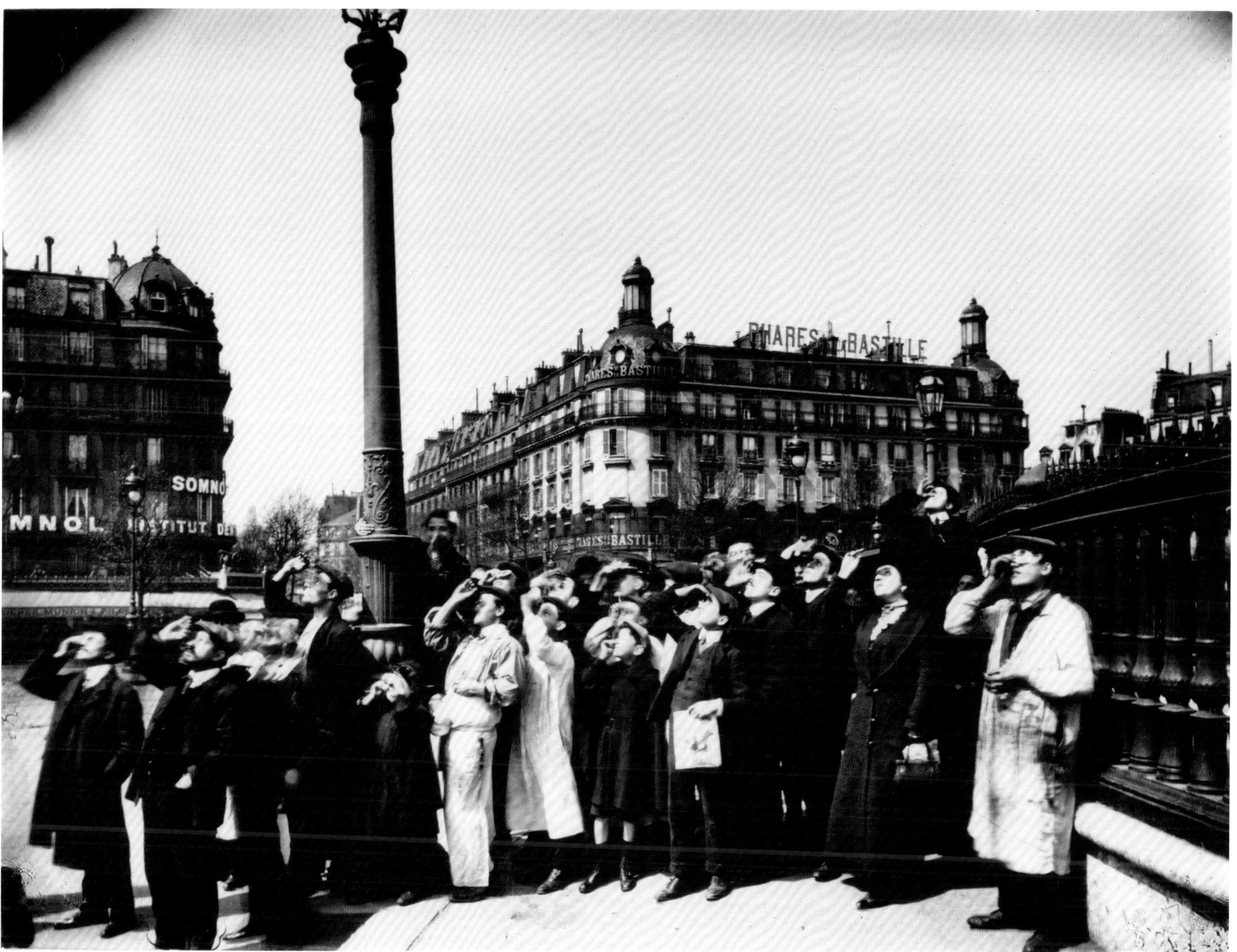

THE BRAGDON BROTHERS

Gavin and Gareth Bragdon are two brothers who originally came from New Hampshire, in the United States. They moved to Scotland in 2009, and a few years later picked up photography. Soon after, they came across street photography, which opened up a creative outlet for both of them at a time when they badly needed one: they had hit a wall with playing music, and had dabbled with various other mediums. Street photography was a way for the brothers to both generate work and express themselves using everyday surroundings. This was important for them, given that they were quite poor and other creative avenues were often out of reach. All of a sudden, things they would otherwise have ignored took on a new weight and potential.

Gavin and Gareth began using off-camera flash initially as a means of bypassing the bad Scottish weather and very short winter days, but they quickly started to use flash as a creative tool in its own right. The brothers studied photography for five years, and graduated with a BA in photography from Edinburgh College in 2017; they now work under the moniker The Bragdon Brothers and collaborate on street and documentary projects and commissions.

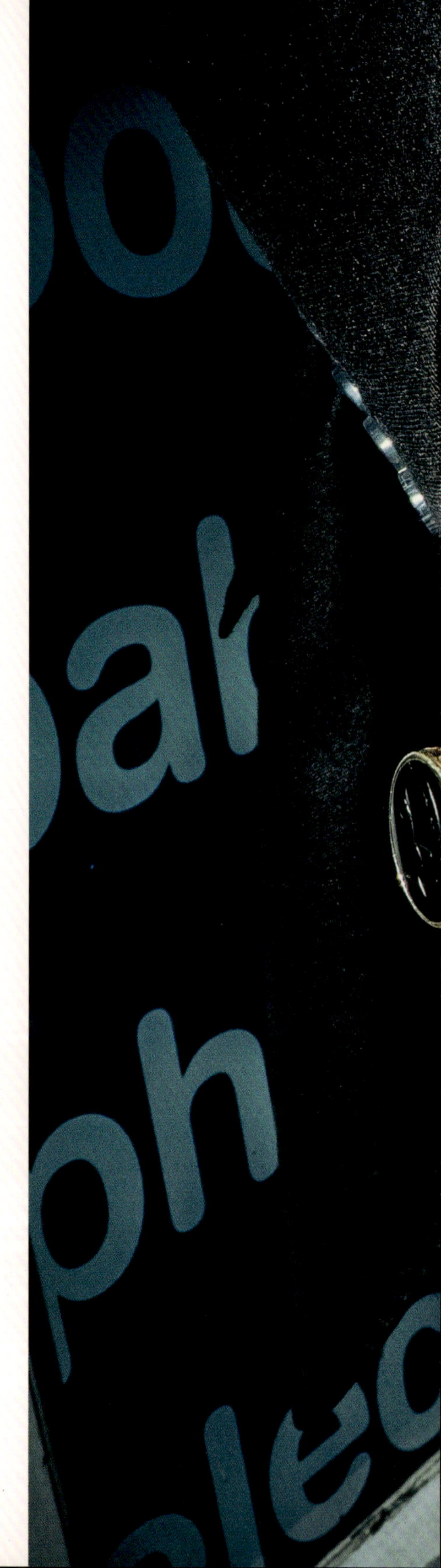

RINGS

This was taken around the time of the Scottish independence referendum in 2014. The Orange Order came into Edinburgh to have a big anti-independence march. I saw this guy with these fantastic rings, and although I really, really disagree with his beliefs and politics, I decided to ask him if I could take a photo of his rings. I very rarely ask permission for a photo, but there was no way I would have got this candidly. I love the details on the rings (you can see George and the dragon on one and, next to it, King Billy, which is like the Orange Order's version of Jesus), and the cigar sticking out. It's small details like these that make the story in the single frame a photograph gives you.

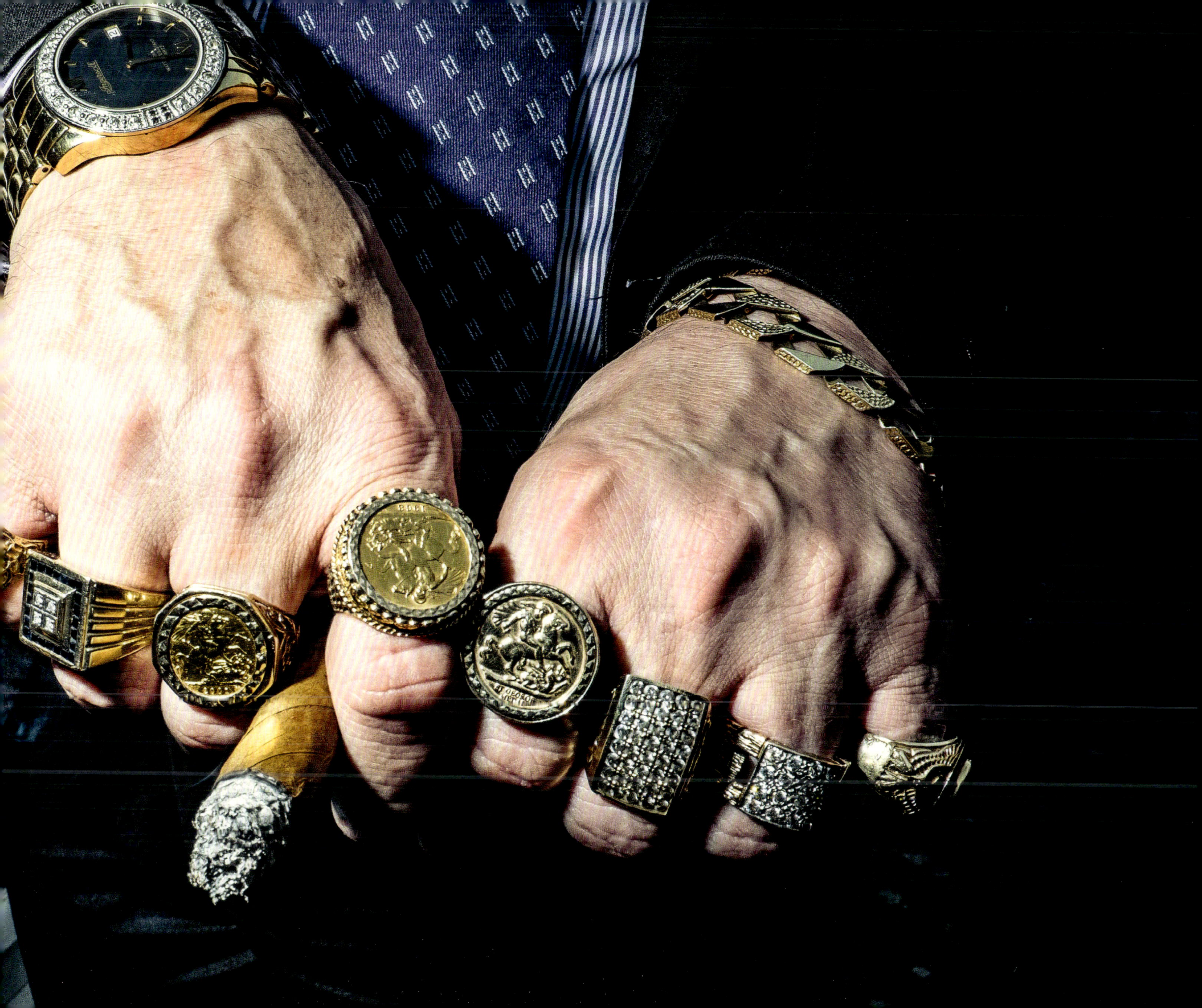

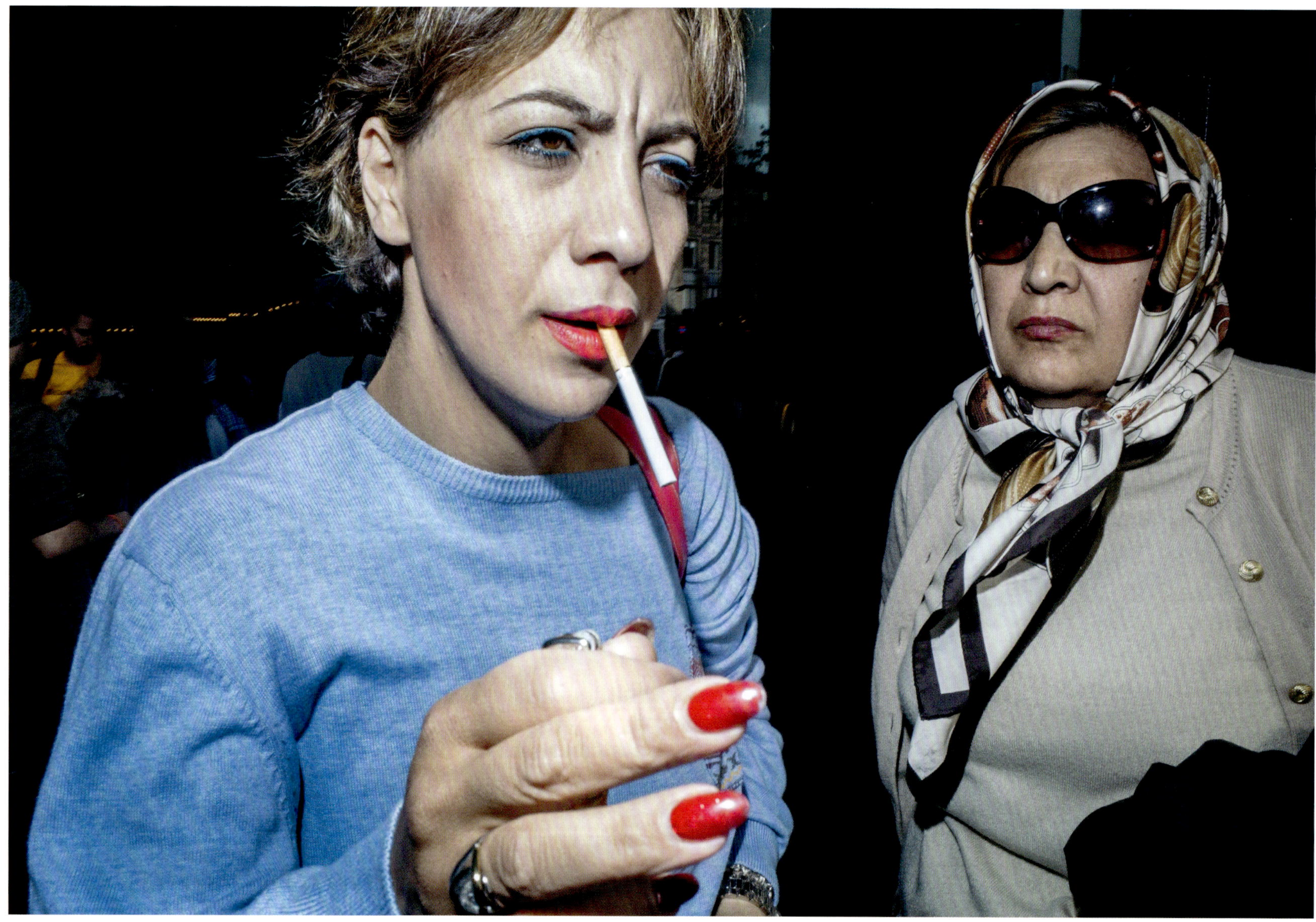

EDINBURGH (2015)

For whatever reason, it seems incredibly hard to get a proper photo of someone smoking—people always seem to put their hands down as soon as you get in range, and what would have made the photograph disappears. It's as if they sense someone is about to take their photo, or maybe it's just pure coincidence? I don't know. Either way, I got lucky with this one.

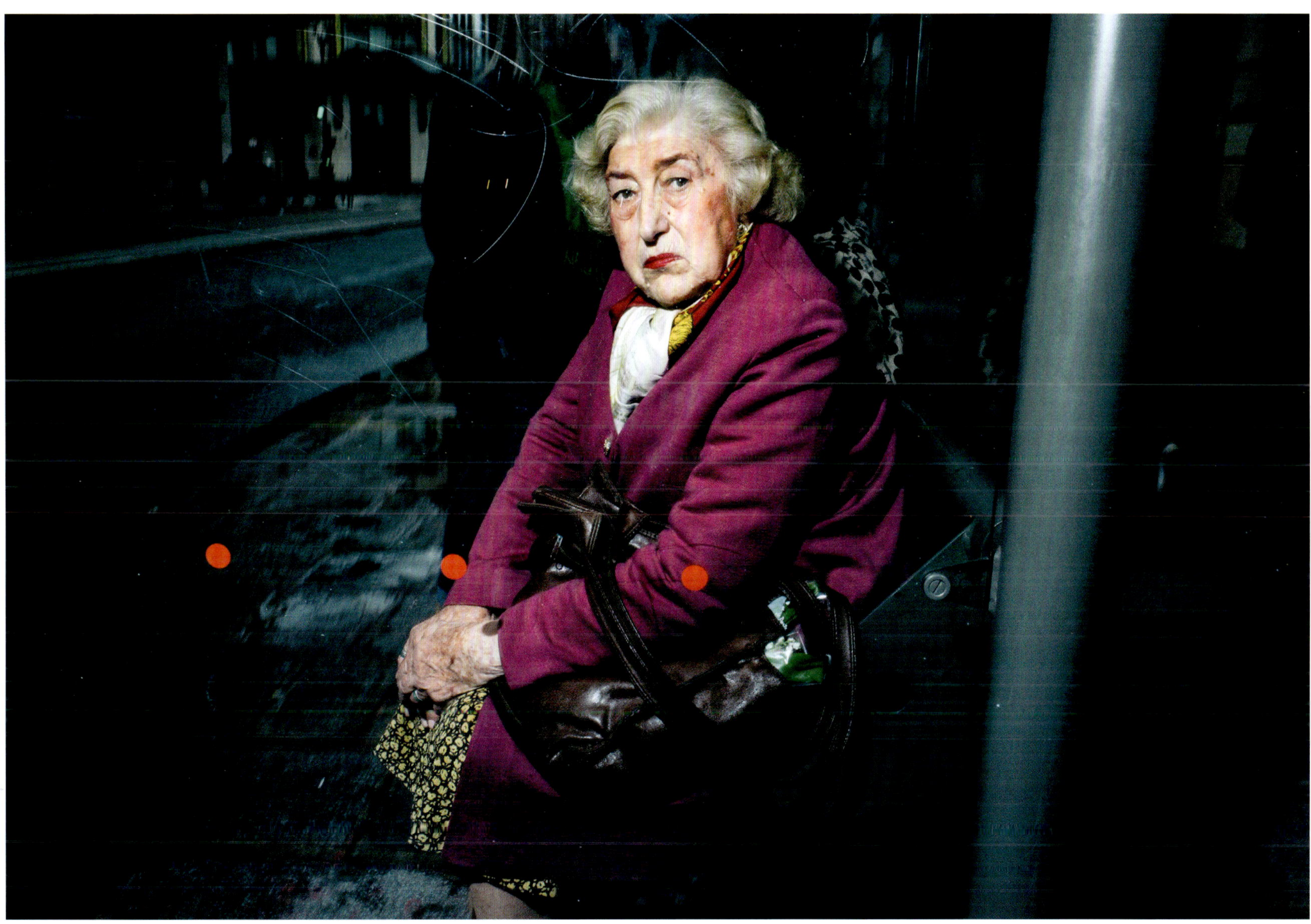

BUS STOP

I saw this lady as I was walking down the Rue de Rivoli in Paris. She looked like someone from another time, and I mean that in a good way—very classical, dignified. After I took the shot, I complimented her, and she just smiled.

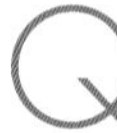

Q
+
A

How do you both work together?

We both shoot in a similar way, and often at the same time and place, so our work tends to complement each other's. That means that when it comes to putting our pictures together, the set becomes stronger than the sum of its parts. We are able to bounce ideas off each other and learn from one another, so it's a productive and creative relationship.

Who or what have been the biggest creative influences in your work?

Before we get to the obvious flash-using photographers like Bruce Gilden, Martin Parr, or Mark Cohen, the surrealism of, say, Trent Parke and the experimental photography of the magazine *Provoke* were big influences. Even non-street photographers, such as Guy Bourdin, have had an impact on us. We've also been influenced by movies and television, especially sci-fi and horror—this might seem surprising, given the point of street photography is to capture everyday reality, but the atmosphere and unsettling oddness of those genres affect our work on at least a subconscious level.

What do you think makes a great street photograph?

A great street photograph is about all the elements somehow coming together, even if—to paraphrase Gary Winogrand—it's on the "edge of failure." The photo should be able to draw your eye graphically and at the same time evoke an emotional response—it has to have what Roland Barthes called "punctum." This applies to whatever genre or technique is being used. You might be able to explain in words why you like a good photograph, but still not be able to put your finger on why it really hits you. It just does.

What techniques do you use to capture your subjects?

We use different techniques depending on what sort of image we want out of the subject. For example, in many of our photos we get very close to the subject, have them fill the frame, and use flash at an angle for more dramatic lighting. Other techniques might include doing something like putting the camera on P mode on a high ISO and having it expose for the ambient light, and setting the flash off, which causes the subject to be a bit overexposed and unusual. You experiment and try to find different ways to make interesting images.

"The photo should be able to draw your eye graphically and at the same time evoke an emotional response—it has to have what Roland Barthes called 'punctum.'"

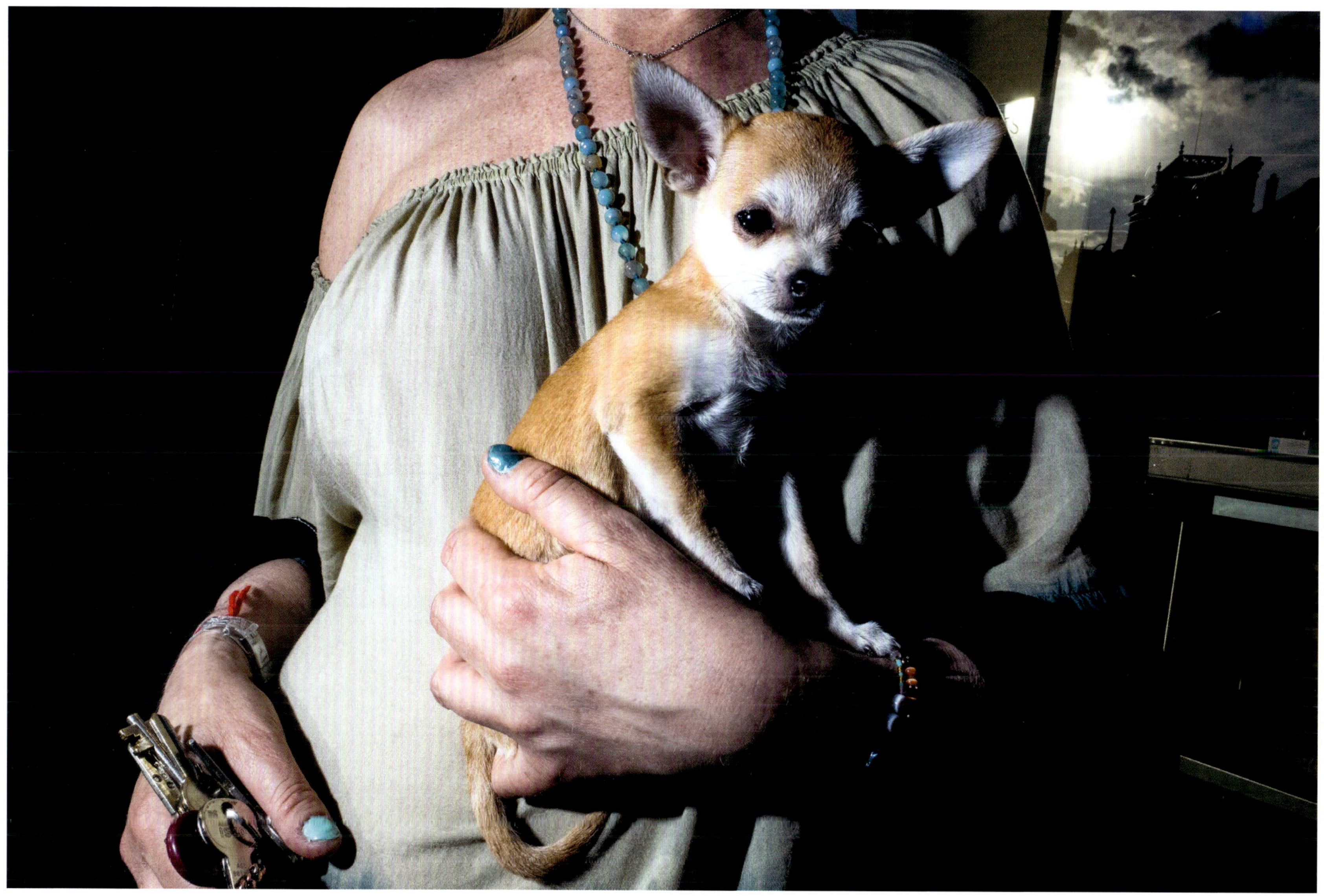

PARIS (2017)

I caught this along the Rue de Rivoli after teaching a workshop. I was going to try and go for a candid capture and shoot without asking, but for whatever reason I asked her first, which I don't usually do. The lady isn't candid, but the dog is.

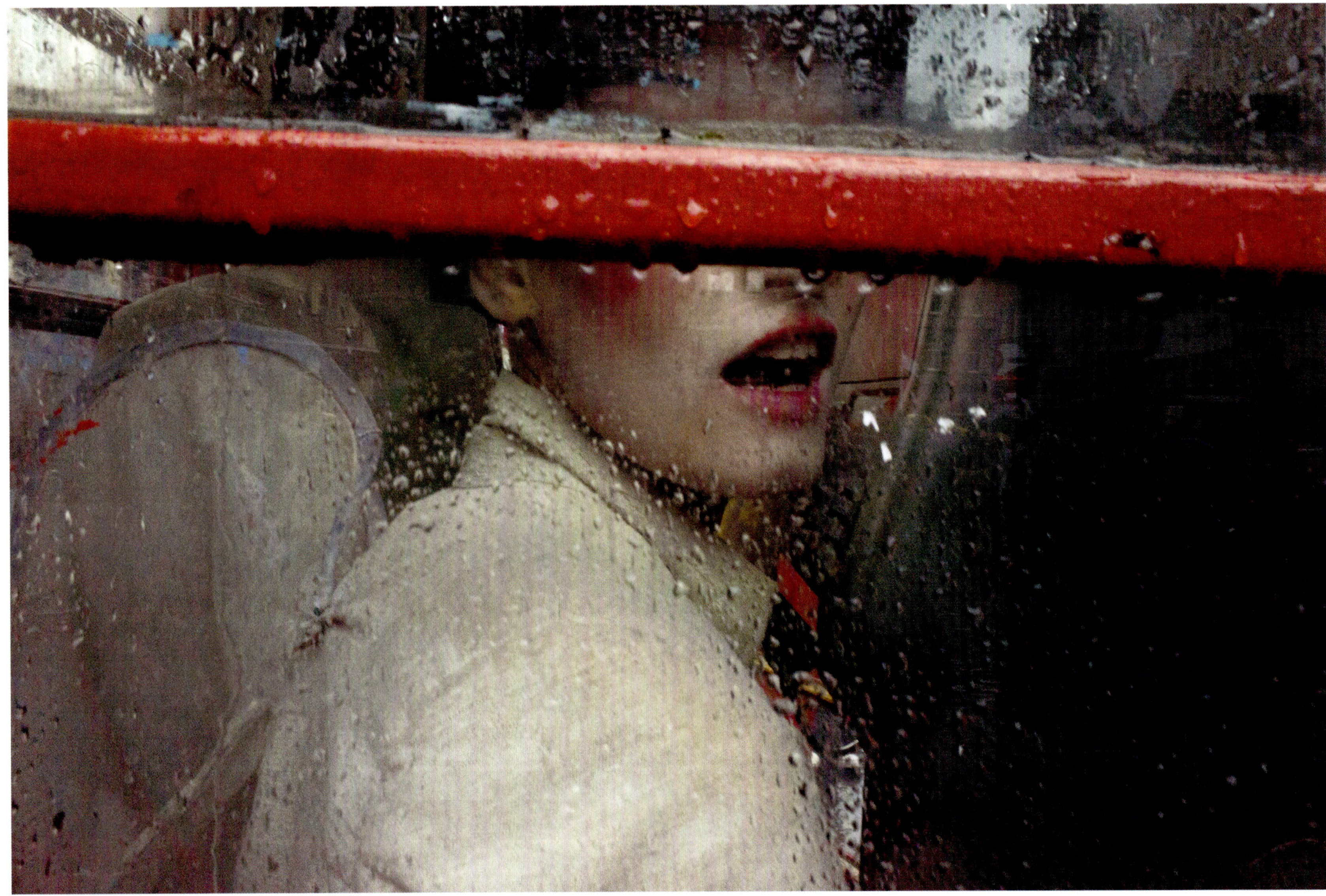

RED

This person was inside a red telephone box. I knew this was going to be a picture before I even lifted the camera up. I lined the frame up perfectly and waited for the subject to turn and face me. I raised the camera and hit the shutter button, but the flash didn't go off and the LCD screen showed black. I thought I'd lost a photo because the flash had not gone off—I was so angry! When I got home, I decided to take a look anyway, and raised the exposure three stops. The image was there after all, and because of the underexposure it came out looking almost like a watercolor. I would not have got these colors if the flash had gone off, so the photo ultimately ended up being much better. Sometimes equipment malfunctions are a photographer's best friend.

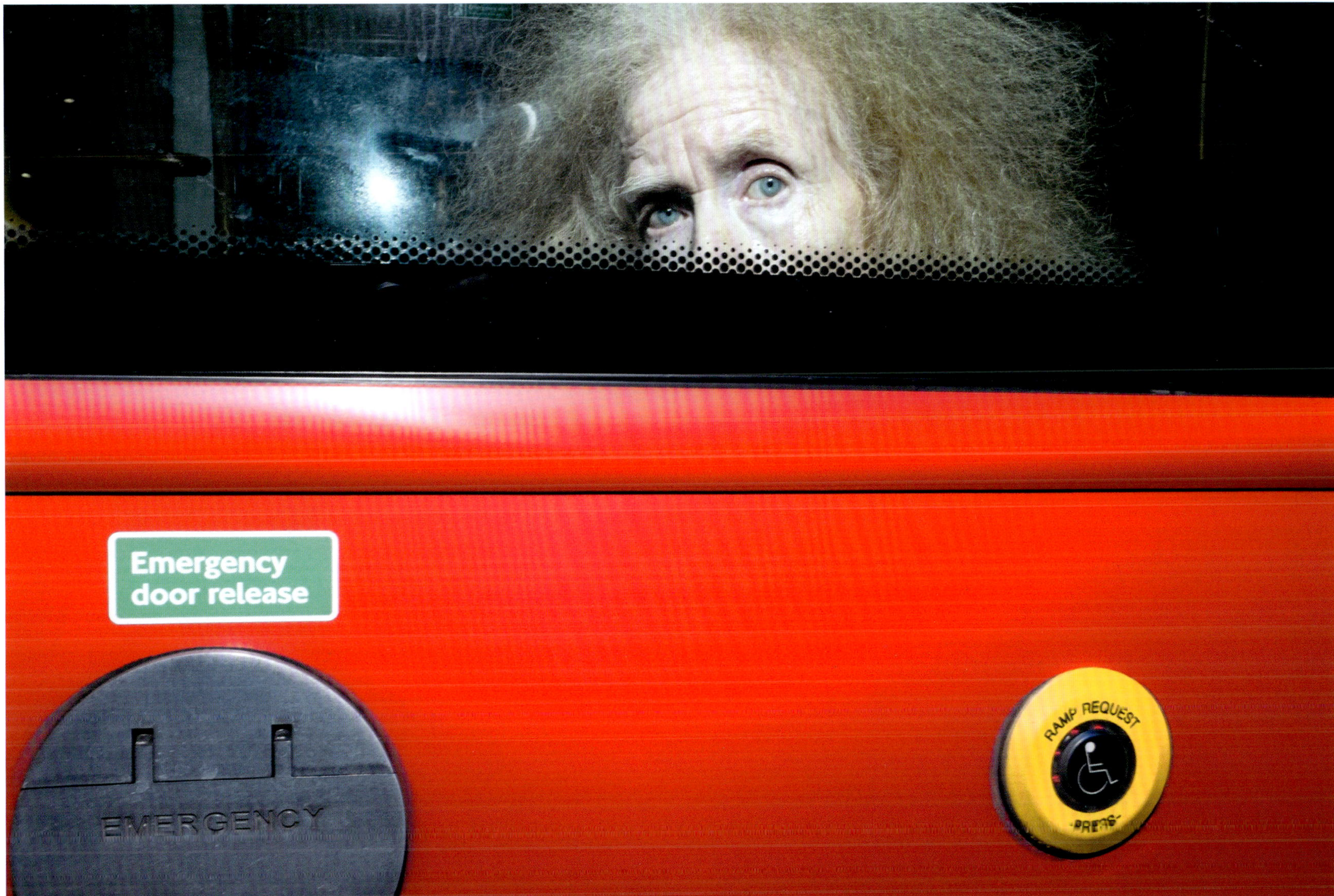

LONDON (2016)

I was in London when a bus pulled up, and I could see this shock of hair popping over the window. It was in the middle of the street, so I was deliberating for a bit, but then just let instinct take over—the instinct that says there's a picture here and I should just do it. I've missed quite a few pictures not listening to that. This time I listened and got a shot I was very happy with.

Q + A

You use flash a great deal, which helps create these theatrical, uncompromising portraits—what do you like so much about this style?

Originally, flash for us was a practical means of getting around the often dull and dark weather in this part of the world; if we had grown as photographers in somewhere sunnier we maybe wouldn't use it so much, but who knows? Either way, it creates a punchy look that we happen to like, bringing out contrast and colors. It can also create something surreal. We don't want to just create a two-dimensional carbon copy of what we pointed the camera at—we want the photograph to show its own version of the world that's a little bit different from what we see with our own eyes. Sometimes that can be done with how natural light hits a subject in a particular time and place, or how you framed it, or it can be done with flash.

What technical challenges do you face when using flash like this?

There are always going to be things such as getting the exposure right. You need to think about the camera and flash settings versus the ambient light, so you don't blow things out too much or underexpose. Of course, your distance from the subject is important as well—you need to make sure you are as far away or as close as you need to be. All this has to come together in a millisecond, so you have to act so fast to capture the photo.

Do you ever feel you are invading a person's privacy?

We don't feel we are invading a person's privacy any more than any other street photographer. Sure, there's always a small element of that, but that comes with the territory and, of course, we are working in a public space. We do make sure that we balance out getting the photos we want without overstepping any boundaries. We get the odd negative reaction here and there, but most of the time people are alright about it. You would be surprised at the number of people who have no idea we took their photo, even when we use flash.

What tips would you give to those who wish to master street photography?

We would say, more than anything, consume good work from others, whether it's from Magnum or curated groups on Instagram, Flickr, or whatever. See what can be done with a photograph: how weird, intricate, simple, sublime, or inexplicable a street photo can be. I think a lot of people don't really dig and look at that stuff. They just see the basics on Instagram, like photos of strangers walking, and think that's what street photography is. So, they don't grow. You should always push yourself to grow and challenge yourself as a photographer.

"We don't want to just create a two-dimensional carbon copy of what we pointed the camera at—we want the photograph to show its own version of the world."

TECHNICAL INFORMATION

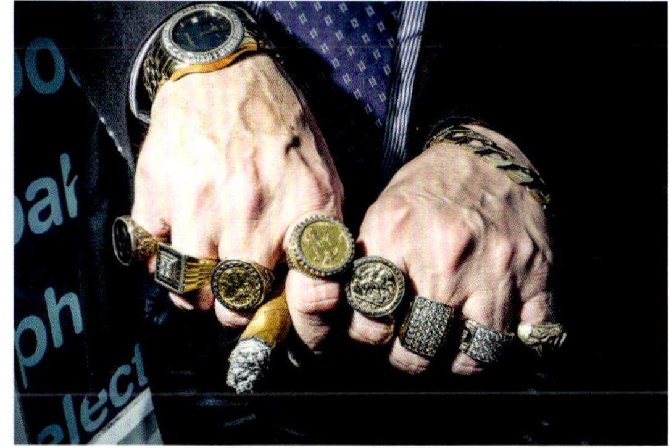

RINGS
EDINBURGH, SCOTLAND, UK

Camera: Fujifilm X100S
Lens/Focal length: 23mm f/2 (35mm equivalent: 35mm)
Aperture: f/16
Shutter speed: 1/250 sec.
ISO: 500

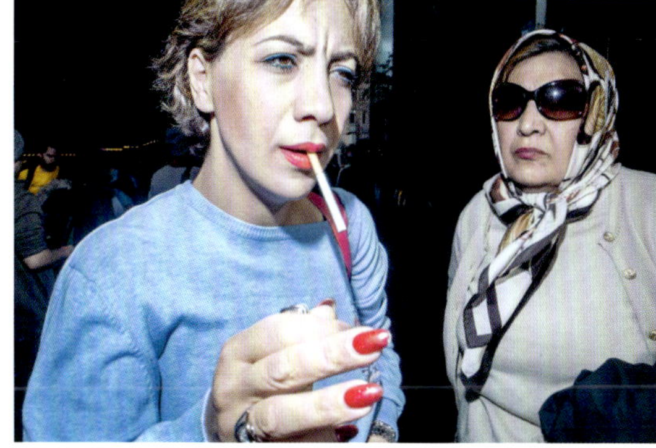

EDINBURGH (2015)
EDINBURGH, SCOTLAND, UK

Camera: Ricoh GR
Lens/Focal length: 18.3mm f/2.8 (35mm equivalent: 28mm)
Aperture: f/16
Shutter speed: 1/320 sec.
ISO: 400

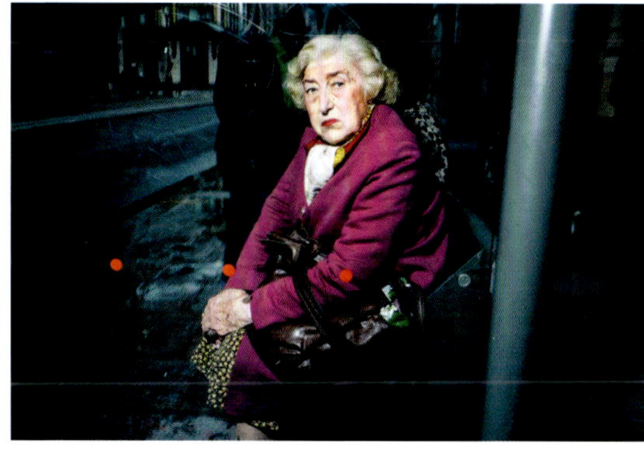

BUS STOP
PARIS, FRANCE

Camera: Ricoh GR
Lens/Focal length: 18.3mm f/2.8 (35mm equivalent: 28mm)
Aperture: f/16
Shutter speed: 1/160 sec.
ISO: 400

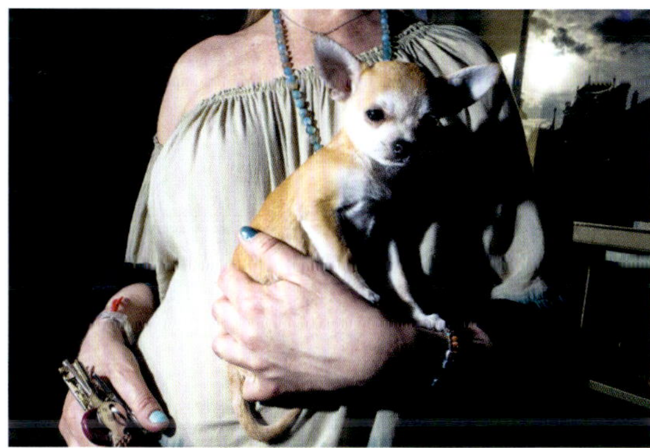

PARIS (2017)
PARIS, FRANCE

Camera: Ricoh GRII
Lens/Focal length: 18.3mm f/2.8 (35mm equivalent: 28mm)
Aperture: f/16
Shutter speed: 1/640 sec.
ISO: 400

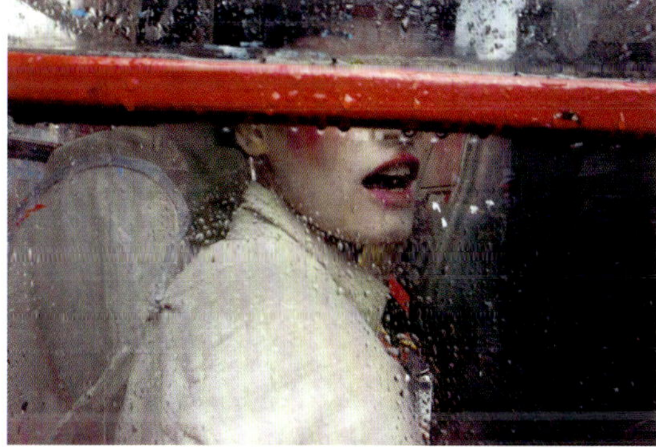

RED
EDINBURGH, SCOTLAND, UK

Camera: Ricoh GR
Lens/Focal length: 18.3mm f/2.8 (35mm equivalent: 28mm)
Aperture: f/16
Shutter speed: 1/160 sec.
ISO: 400

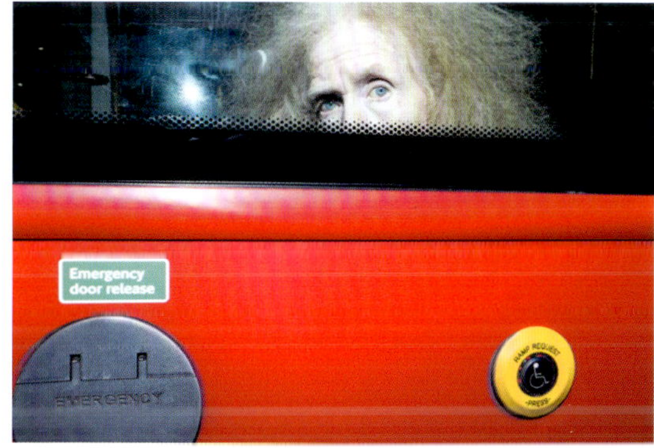

LONDON (2016)
LONDON, UK

Camera: Fujifilm X100S
Lens/Focal length: 23mm f/2 (35mm equivalent: 35mm)
Aperture: f/16
Shutter speed: 1/320 sec.
ISO: 400

MELISSA BREYER

With classical training in studio art and a Masters degree in Museum Studies, Melissa Breyer began making photographs when she stopped making paintings. Thinking that it would be a good way to continue creating images, she bought an old Nikon camera and taught herself how to use it. She started by taking photos of strangers when traveling, and whenever she was back in New York City she would continue taking what she called "travel photos at home," not knowing that there was such a thing as street photography.

Years later, Melissa discovered street photography on social media, and started sharing images she had been taking with her phone. Now she uses both digital and analog cameras to capture scenes of the city and its beautiful inhabitants. With influences ranging from fairy tales and vintage photography to the novels of Edith Wharton, she aims for a timeless feel with a focus on "quiet moments." Her photos are both a document of the city and its people, and also a glimpse into how she sees the world. Her award-winning work has been exhibited around the globe and has been featured in national and international publications.

UNTITLED, FROM *THE WATCHWOMEN* (2015)

I love layers and making abstractions with what's on hand, so when I saw a restaurant with a vertical slatted shutter, and a woman working inside, I thought I could make something work. I loved the simplicity of the interior and the waitress's beautiful, thoughtful face and easy grace.

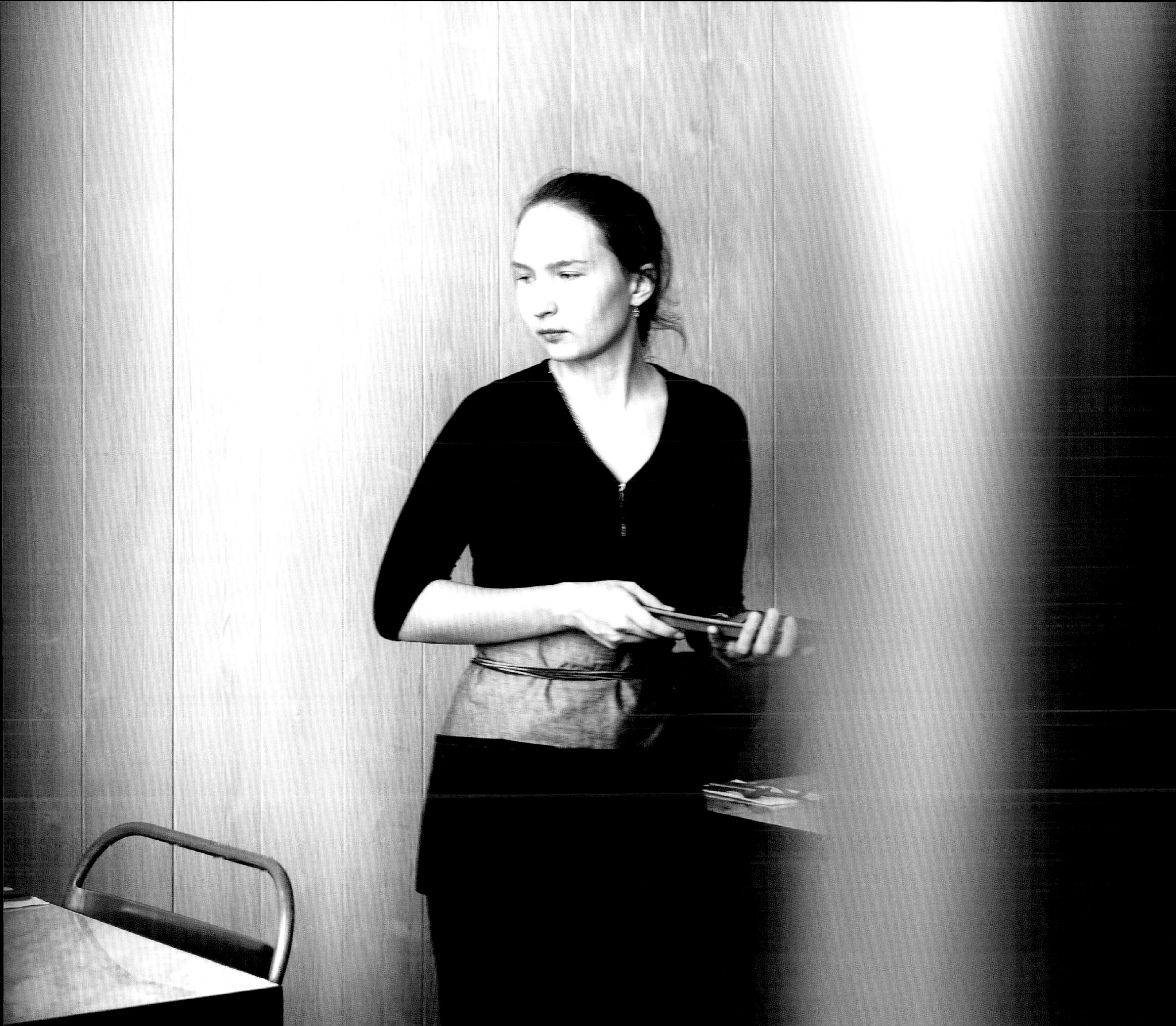

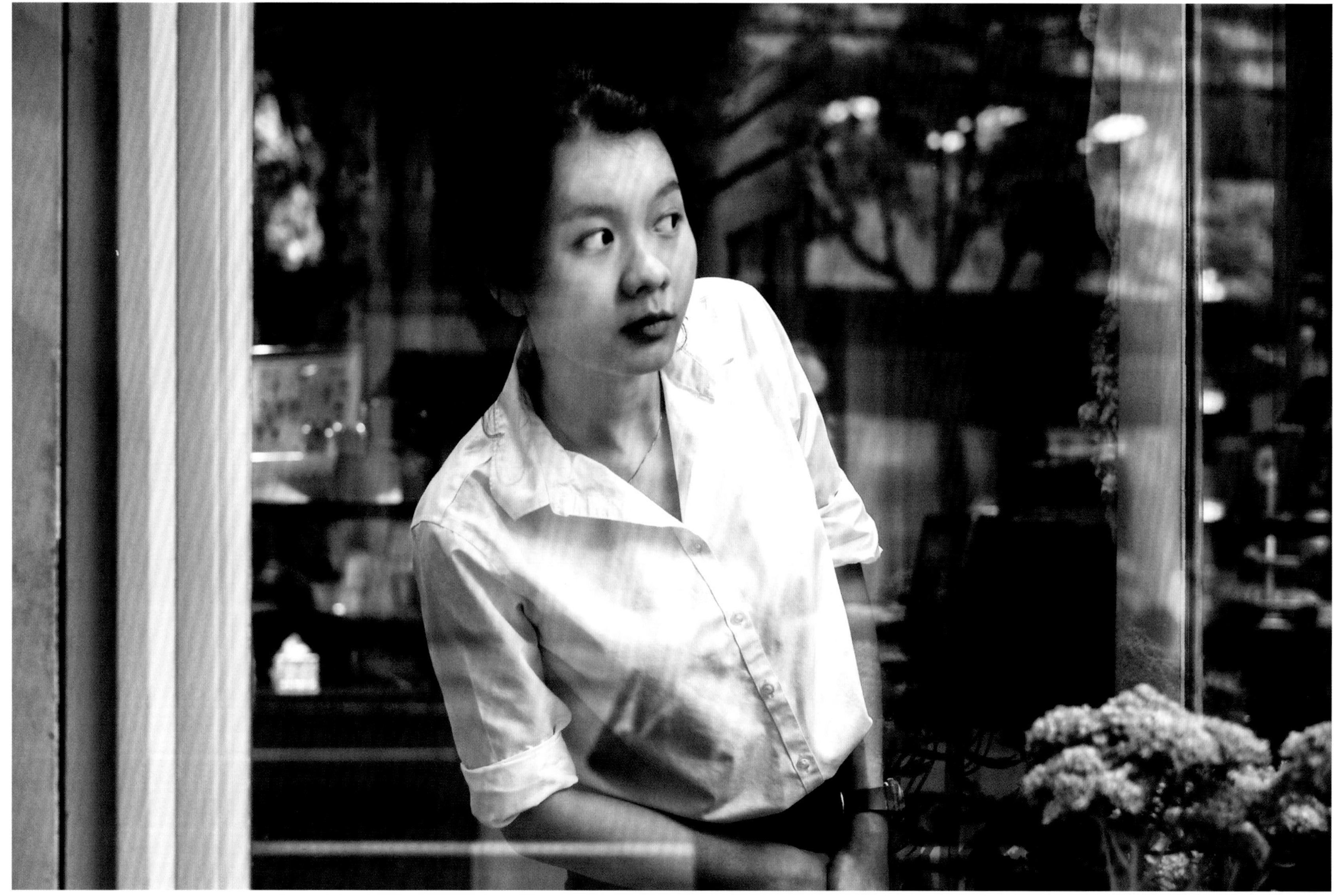

UNTITLED, FROM *THE WATCHWOMEN* (2015)

This was one of those photos that happens right before your eyes. I was walking by and saw the woman deeper in the restaurant and thought maybe I could catch a shot on the fly. As I was raising my camera she walked up to the window, oblivious to me, and peered out. I clicked—pure luck!

UNTITLED, FROM
THE WATCHWOMEN (2013)

I've always been drawn to the neon sign at this bakery near my home, and when I saw this apparition from the past daydreaming as she was cleaning, I was struck by the beauty of the scene. It was in the morning and I was out running, but I slipped my phone from my pocket and took the shot. A more rigorous camera might have taken a more precise shot, but the quality afforded by the phone seems suited to the feel of the photograph.

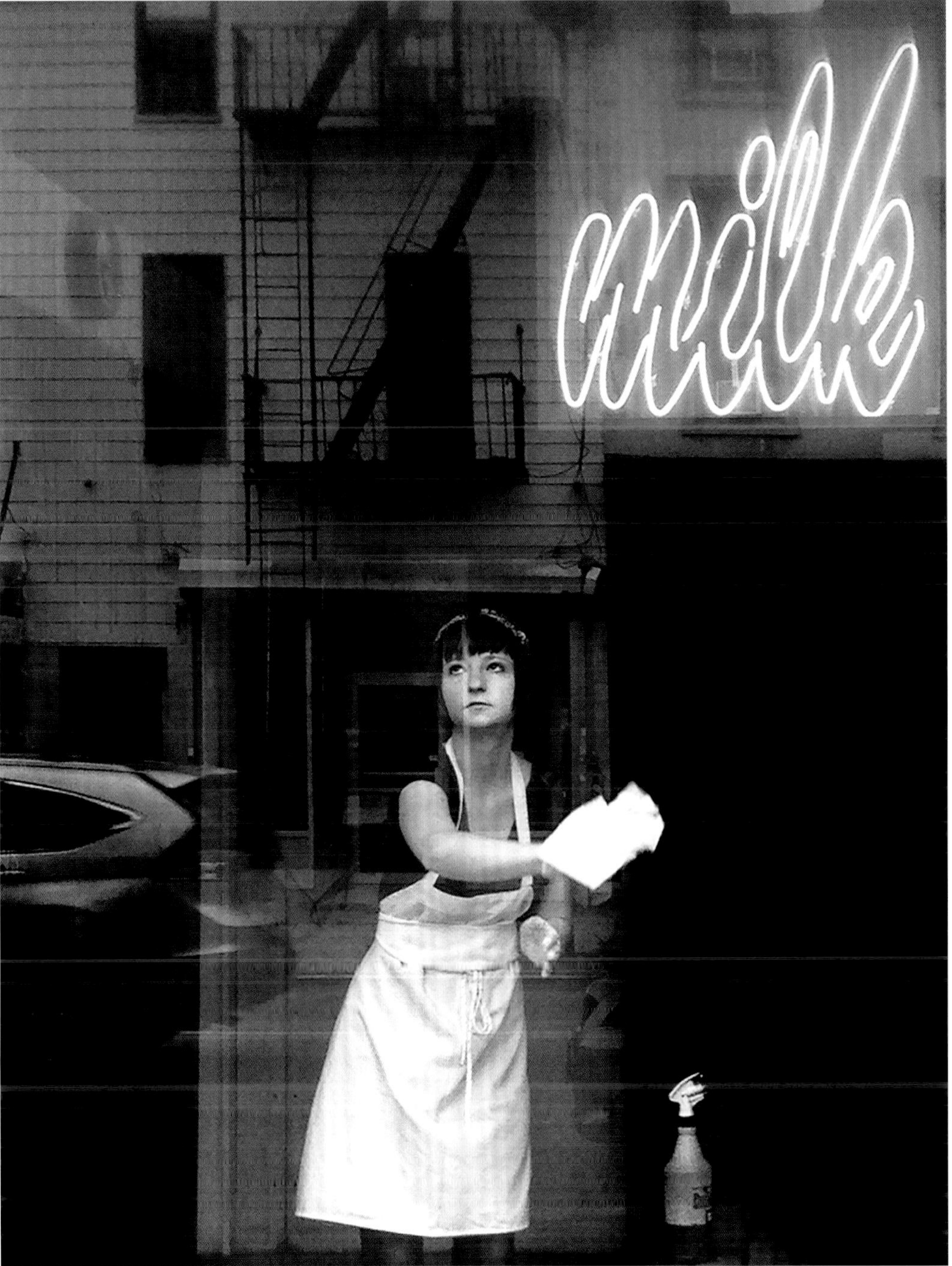

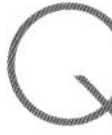

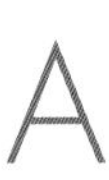

What kinds of subjects attract you?

I'm often drawn initially to an environment—a spot that resonates with me, based on my mood. Maybe it's bright, maybe it has interesting shadows or a steam vent, maybe there are reflections. The city is a favorite subject in itself because it's so important in setting the stage, and because the city is gorgeous and surreal, a beautifully gritty fairy tale. The dynamics of a certain location often dictate what kind of people I will be drawn to in that moment. In general, unlike street photographers who are documenting a current timestamp of the city, I love classic subjects—people who somehow transcend time. Stripped of the signs of the era, the photos become more of a documentation of the person themselves, an attempt to reveal glimpses of an inner life. It is also the reason why I predominantly show people in black and white—color can be such a scene-stealer, but black and white allows for an elegance that lets a subject be the star of the show.

What drew you to portraying waitresses in your famous The Watchwomen series?

Several lifetimes ago, I left California and tumbled into New York City, landing a job at a little restaurant in the West Village. I gave people plates of food, poured them wine, and attended to the tasks of service; and in the calm moments in-between, allowed my mind to wander in thought. My daydreams rambled from paintings I wanted to make to imagined conversations yet to be had, and everything in between. The reveries were a wonderful way to fill in the empty spaces during my work hours. Now, all these years later, whenever I see women working in restaurants lost in thought, I'm reminded of those freewheeling daydreams. I wonder, what are they thinking about? What are their stories? My imagination begins creating narratives for them. These women are so much more than their jobs and I see their grace and dignity even in the smallest of gestures. I love the idea of freezing the frame—to silence the clatter of plates and stop the setting of a table—to pluck them out of their roles as waitresses for a split second and to present them as players in any number of different storylines.

Is it important to empathize with your subjects?

For me, absolutely. It's empathy that keeps street photos straight—if we empathize with our subjects, we can show them in a context that feels right and, most importantly to me, we can show their dignity. We owe that to them since they unwittingly serve as our models. In a way, street photographers are thieves, with stolen glimpses and purloined portraits of passersby. The only way to feel okay about that is to make sure we are doing it with integrity—and it feels like empathy helps to ensure that. I think it's pretty easy to tell when a street photographer is lacking in empathy—and those photographs feel superficial to me, sometimes even mean. They say more about the photographer than the subject, and I never want my photos to be like that.

How important is it to tell a story in street photography?

The greatest marvel to me about this genre is that there are, for example, millions of people in New York City—and each one has their own vast collection of stories. The hot dog vendor, the Rockette, the taxi driver, the college student, the stockbroker—they have places they came from and places they go home to every night… so many histories, so many memories. It's pretty overwhelming to consider. We can't know all of their stories, but we can create our own for them, and that's beautiful to me. It's interactive. But I don't feel like it's the street photographer's role to necessarily create a set story in an image—to do so feels like we're foisting a false narrative on the subject. I think it's more of the street photographer's role to set the stage, introduce the subject, and let the viewers create their own plotlines. The more fluid the potential is for narratives, the more chance that a viewer will create a story that resonates for them, and that's where the magic happens.

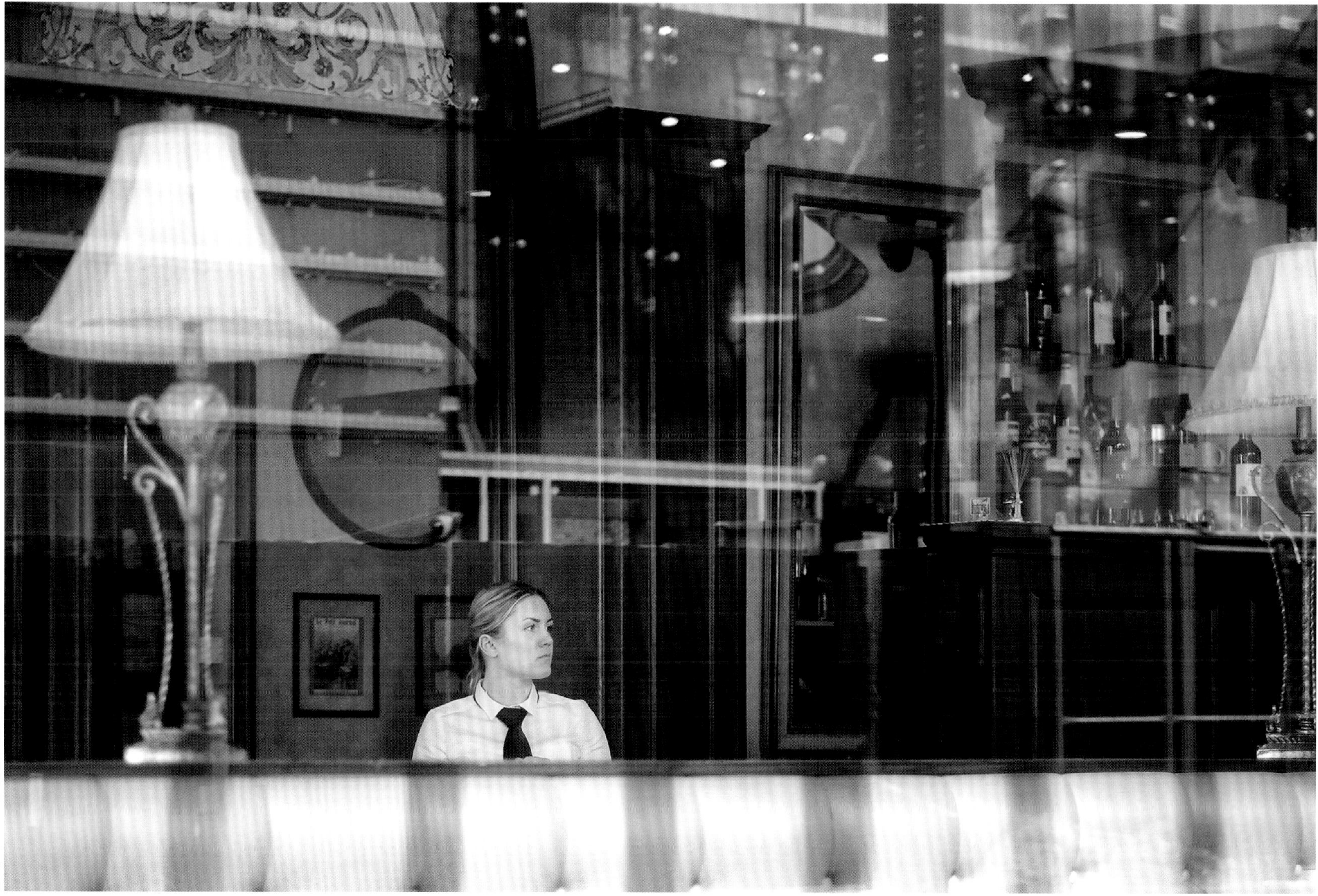

UNTITLED, FROM *THE WATCHWOMEN* (2016)

I have a soft spot for reflections, but they're tricky because, all too often, the scene they reflect is of ugly cars and construction sites. When I saw how the light was hitting this waitress's face and the pretty restaurant behind her, I just hoped that the reflection would add rather than distract. There is definitely a lot going on here, but she has so much presence that she doesn't get lost.

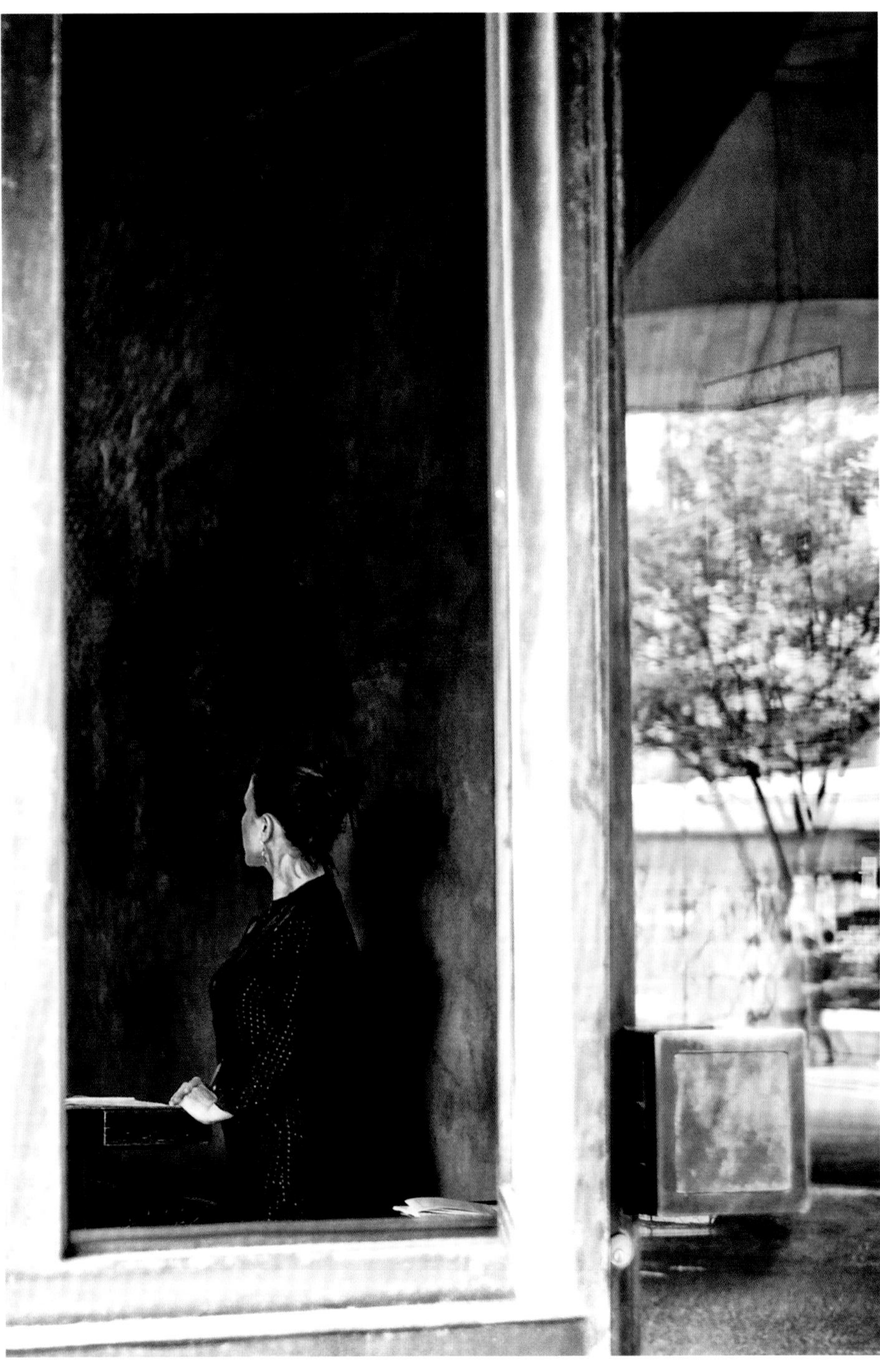

UNTITLED, FROM *THE WATCHWOMEN* (2015)

The light was so beautiful the afternoon this photo was taken, and I could see how it was illuminating the textured wall through the open window. I often scope out shots even when nobody is there, it's just satisfying to see a pretty scene in the camera. I was doing that, and then the woman came back to her spot. I didn't really want to take a photo of someone's back, but when she settled into her great posture and became lost in thought, I saw that it was lovely.

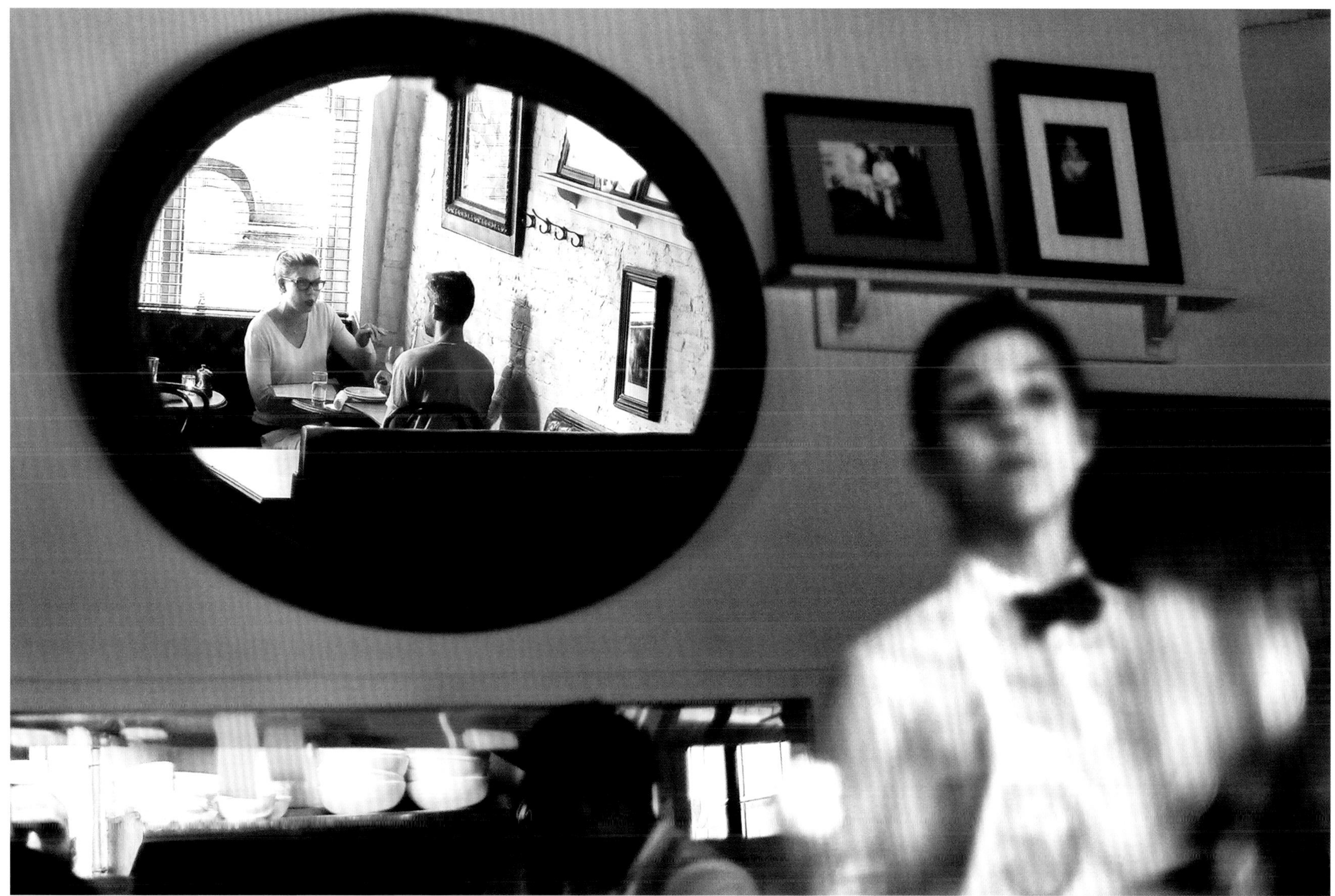

UNTITLED, FROM *THE WATCHWOMEN* (2015)

I was sitting at the bar of a local restaurant waiting for my dinner companion, and was transfixed by how the mirror lined up with the framed images and appeared to be a magically moving photograph. I wanted to include the mirror and the scene it was showing along with a waitress, as I thought it would be a bit more dynamic than the quieter restaurant shots I was making at the time. This is the only photograph in the series that clearly shows customers along with the server.

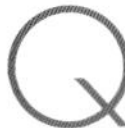

Q
+
A

Do you prefer to blend into the background when shooting people?

The waitresses were not aware of me, or at least as far as I know. I tried to shoot them quickly, or from angles that weren't very obvious. In general, when I'm out shooting I do not want to be seen. My goal isn't to have photos of people reacting to a photographer—that's too easy. I want to show people in their beautiful, quiet moments. I want to show people doing what they do, not show them looking at me.

What do you find the greatest technical challenge in shooting street portraits?

I don't find a lot of challenge in actually taking photos on the street—I guess, if anything, it's in getting a focus that I like. I am always instinctively adjusting the aperture and ISO when shooting digitally—as soon I enter a new set of conditions my fingers get to work without me even thinking about it. But focus is specific and I do miss shots. I think the greatest challenge I have, in terms of tech, is in my conflicted feelings for digital versus analog. I am completely smitten with film. Nothing is more satisfying than the "clunk" of a rangefinder doing its job when the shutter release is pressed; nothing is more sensuous than the idea of the actual light of a scene soaking into film. It is so true, a profound record— observations physically preserved like fleeting fossils. It is magic. But then life is busy and digital is immediate. There is no developing and printing and scanning, just a quick card in the computer and a parade of photos appears. I would love to be the person out on the street with gorgeously impractical vintage cameras, but the lure of digital in this breakneck-speed world is hard for me to deny.

How much of yourself, your history, and your imagination go into your street photography?

It's funny. The obvious answer would be that a classical training in painting has been the biggest influence. I painted portraits of imaginary people and enlightenment scientists, so it would make perfect sense. But I never, ever think of painting when I'm out shooting. What I think about is books. Perhaps an education in drawing and painting may be working behind the scenes to inform how I see lines and light, but the content of it all, the mood, is from the written word. I was pretty obsessed with Edith Wharton for a long time, and her language and portrayal of New York City kind of haunt me. She created such a dynamic tension between the opulence of the gilded age in the city and the restrictions placed on the spirit, mostly women's, because of society's expectations. A heady mix of splendor and repression. The way she described the inner lives of her characters is something I'd love to be able to do with photographs. Often I feel like I am walking around in a Victorian novel when I'm roaming the streets, and there's a sense of wistfulness that is constant, even if I am a chronically happy person.

What is your favorite choice of camera and why?

I have been shooting digital with a Fuji X-Pro1 for years now, paired with a Fuji 35mm f/1.4 lens. I started with film and resisted digital for a long time, until I started taking photos with my iPhone, which was the gateway camera to digital for me. The Fuji was my first serious digital camera, and we bonded immediately. I was drawn to it initially because I liked that one didn't need to get lost in a menu to access its functions. I want to be able to intuitively use my hands to make adjustments with dials and buttons, rather than having to scroll through a screen. It feels great in my hands and I love how it renders images. For film I use a Leica M7. I know this model is the black sheep of the family to a lot of Leica aficionados, but I love it. It has automatic exposure which can be very helpful when I'm out on the street and doing everything else manually. I don't have gear lust, but Leicas are just such beautiful machines and everything about the M7 feels amazing—the weight, the solidity, the mechanics, the sounds that it emits, it's just beautiful and such a pleasure to shoot with.

"Nothing is more sensuous than the idea of the actual light of a scene soaking into film."

TECHNICAL INFORMATION

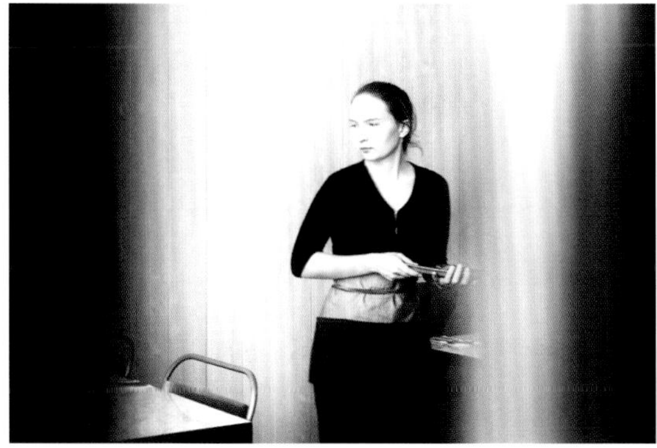

UNTITLED,
FROM *THE WATCHWOMEN* (2015)
BROOKLYN, NEW YORK, USA

Camera: Fujifilm X-Pro1
Lens/Focal length: Fujifilm 35mm f/1.4 (35mm equivalent: 53mm)
Aperture: f/2.2
Shutter speed: 1/150 sec.
ISO: 400

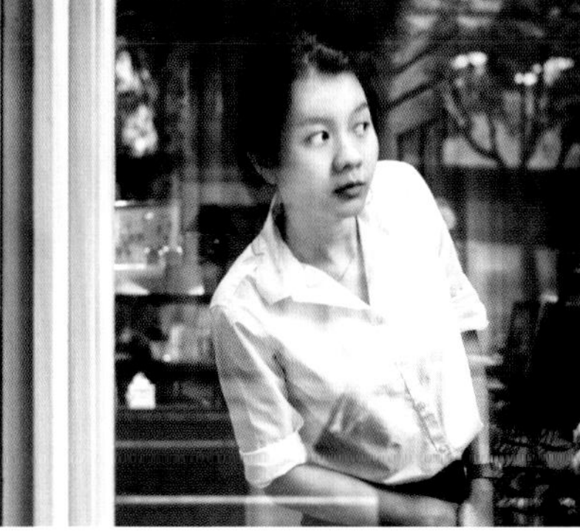

UNTITLED,
FROM *THE WATCHWOMEN* (2015)
NEW YORK CITY, NEW YORK, USA

Camera: Fujifilm X-Pro1
Lens/Focal length: Fujifilm 35mm f/1.4 (35mm equivalent: 53mm)
Aperture: f/2.5
Shutter speed: 1/160 sec.
ISO: 400

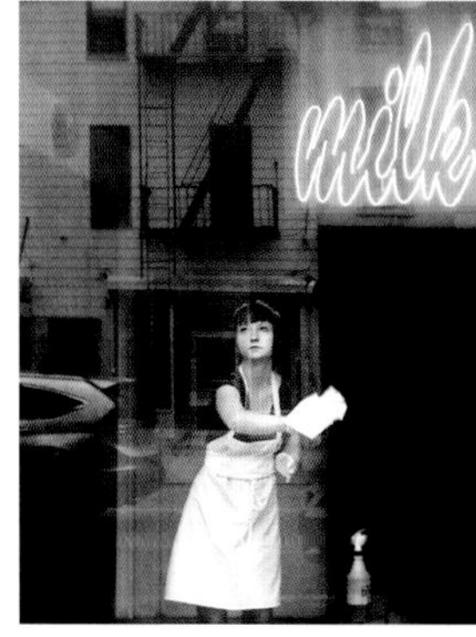

UNTITLED,
FROM *THE WATCHWOMEN* (2013)
BROOKLYN, NEW YORK, USA

Camera: iPhone

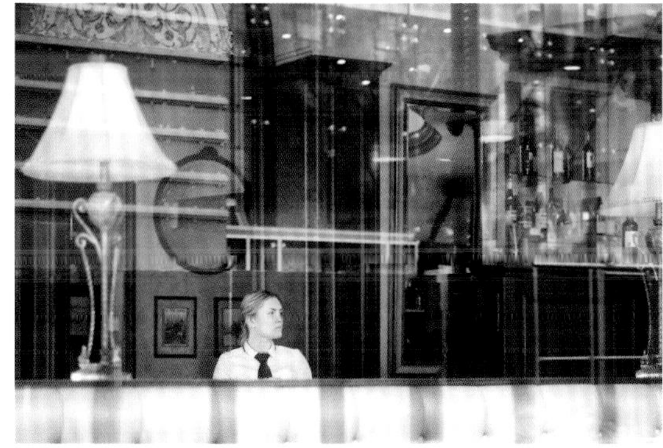

UNTITLED,
FROM *THE WATCHWOMEN* (2016)
NEW YORK CITY, NEW YORK, USA

Camera: Fujifilm X-Pro1
Lens/Focal length: Fujifilm 35mm f/1.4 (35mm equivalent: 53mm)
Aperture: f/1.4
Shutter speed: 1/320 sec.
ISO: 400

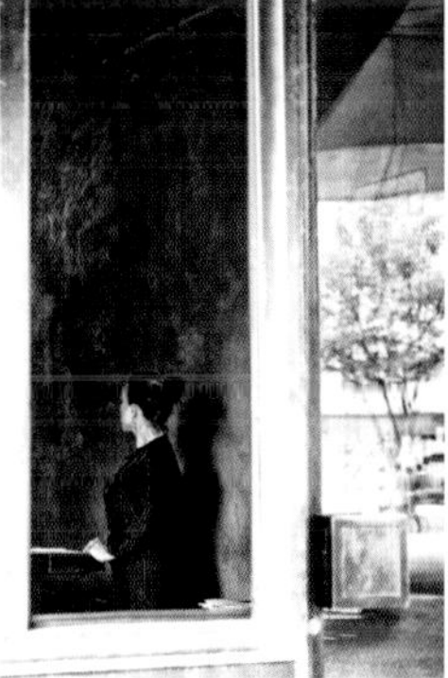

UNTITLED,
FROM *THE WATCHWOMEN* (2015)
NEW YORK CITY, NEW YORK, USA

Camera: Fujifilm X-Pro1
Lens/Focal length: Fujifilm 35mm f/1.4 (35mm equivalent: 53mm)
Aperture: f/1.4
Shutter speed: 1/17 sec.
ISO: 500

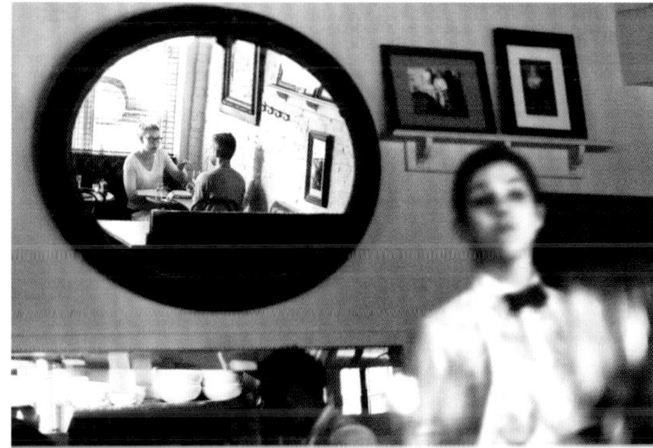

UNTITLED,
FROM *THE WATCHWOMEN* (2015)
BROOKLYN, NEW YORK, USA

Camera: Fujifilm X-Pro1
Lens/Focal length: Fujifilm 35mm f/1.4 (35mm equivalent: 53mm)
Aperture: f/1.4
Shutter speed: 1/65 sec.
ISO: 250

GIACOMO BRUNELLI

Giacomo Brunelli was born in Perugia, Italy, and now lives in London. He graduated with a degree in International Communications in 2002. During his time at university, he picked up his father's camera, a 1960s Japanese Miranda Sensomat, and has been using it ever since. Giacomo is self-taught and started by photographing the animals where he lived, and has since become fascinated by street photography. He still creates his images in the darkroom, where he crafts his limited-edition prints by hand. His high-contrast, mysterious, and powerful images explore the issues of alienation, privacy, and modern urban life.

Giacomo has won the Sony World Photography Award, the Gran Prix Lodz (Poland), and the Magenta Foundation's Flash Forward 2009. His images have been featured in many publications around the world, including the *Guardian* (UK), *Harper's Magazine* (USA), *European Photography* (Germany), *B&W* (USA), and *Creative Review* (UK). His work is in the collection of The Museum of Fine Arts Houston (USA), The New Art Gallery Walsall (UK), Kiyosato Museum of Photographic Arts (Japan), and Portland Art Museum (USA). His publications include *The Animals* (2008), *Eternal London* (2014), and *Self-Portraits* (2017).

UNTITLED

Hamburg's nickname is "The Venice of the North" due to the Elbe river and the city's many canals and bridges. The bridge in this picture is a beautiful iron structure and, as I wanted to have it in my project, I started to shoot around the area of Speicherstadt, the largest warehouse district in the world. The man in the image was walking toward me and I took a shot looking upward as I knelt on the ground.

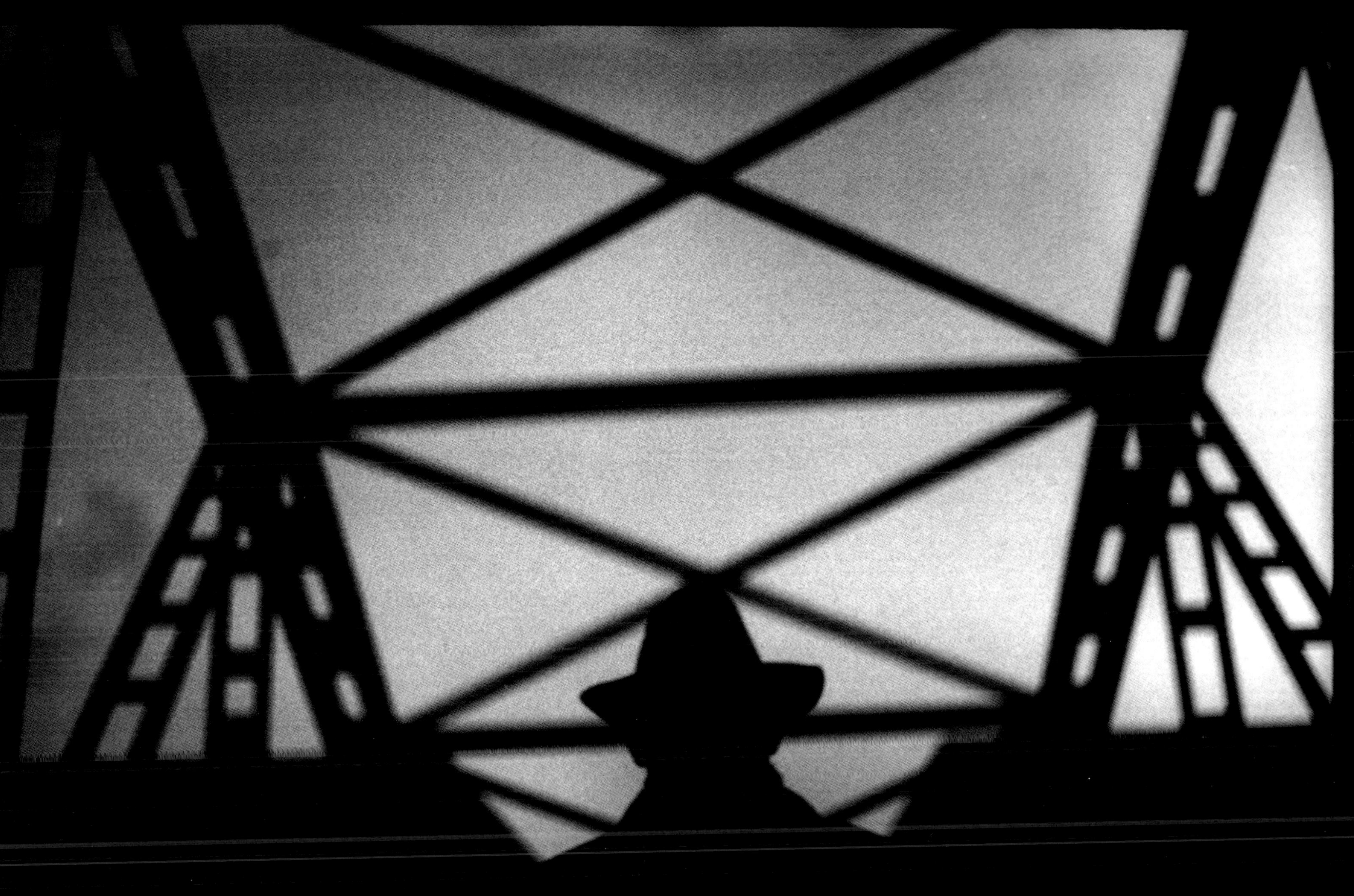

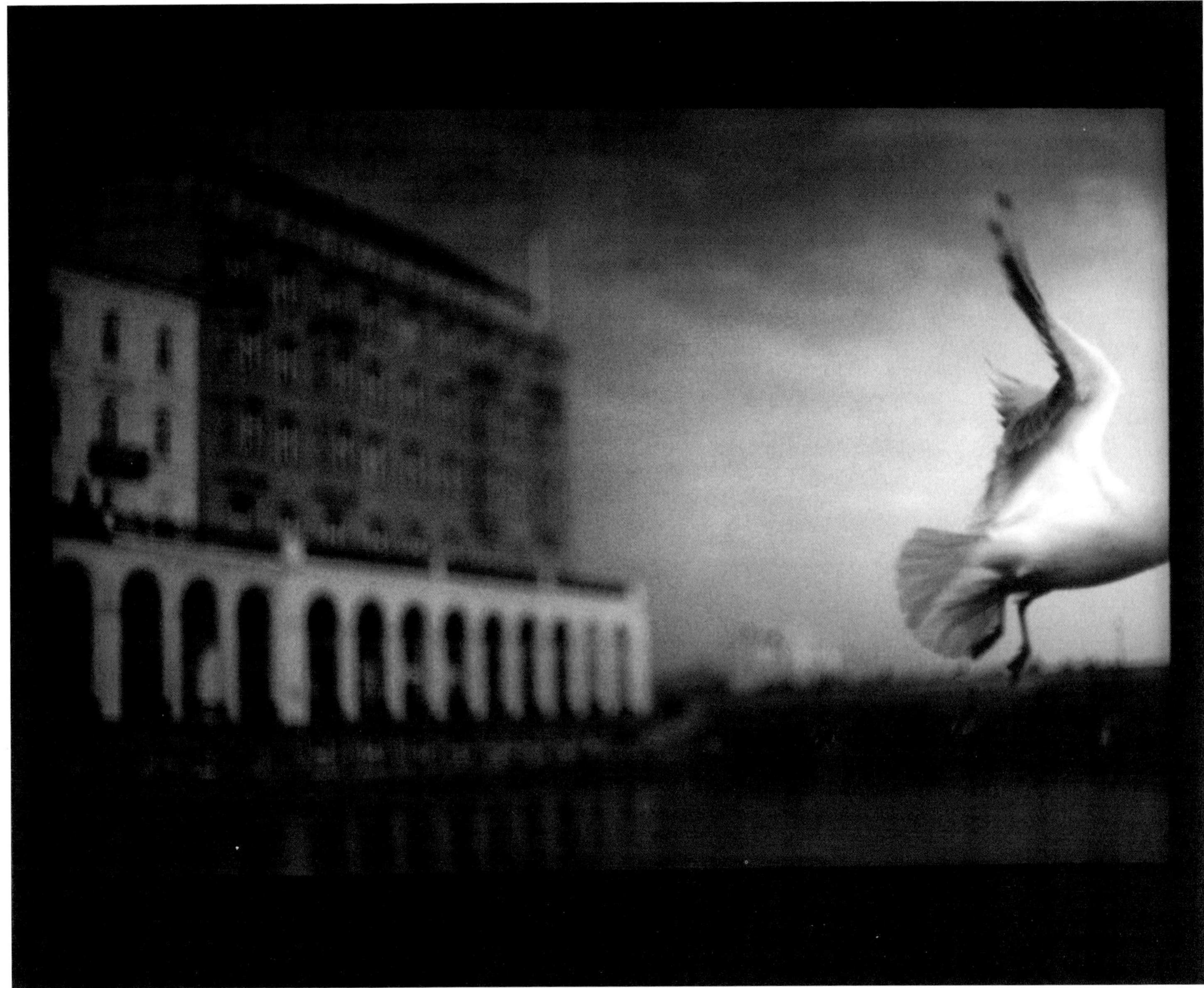

UNTITLED

This image was taken in the main square of Hamburg, where many birds fly around.
The arcade in the background reminded me of St Mark's Square in Venice, and I
wanted to have a moving subject against that fixed backdrop.

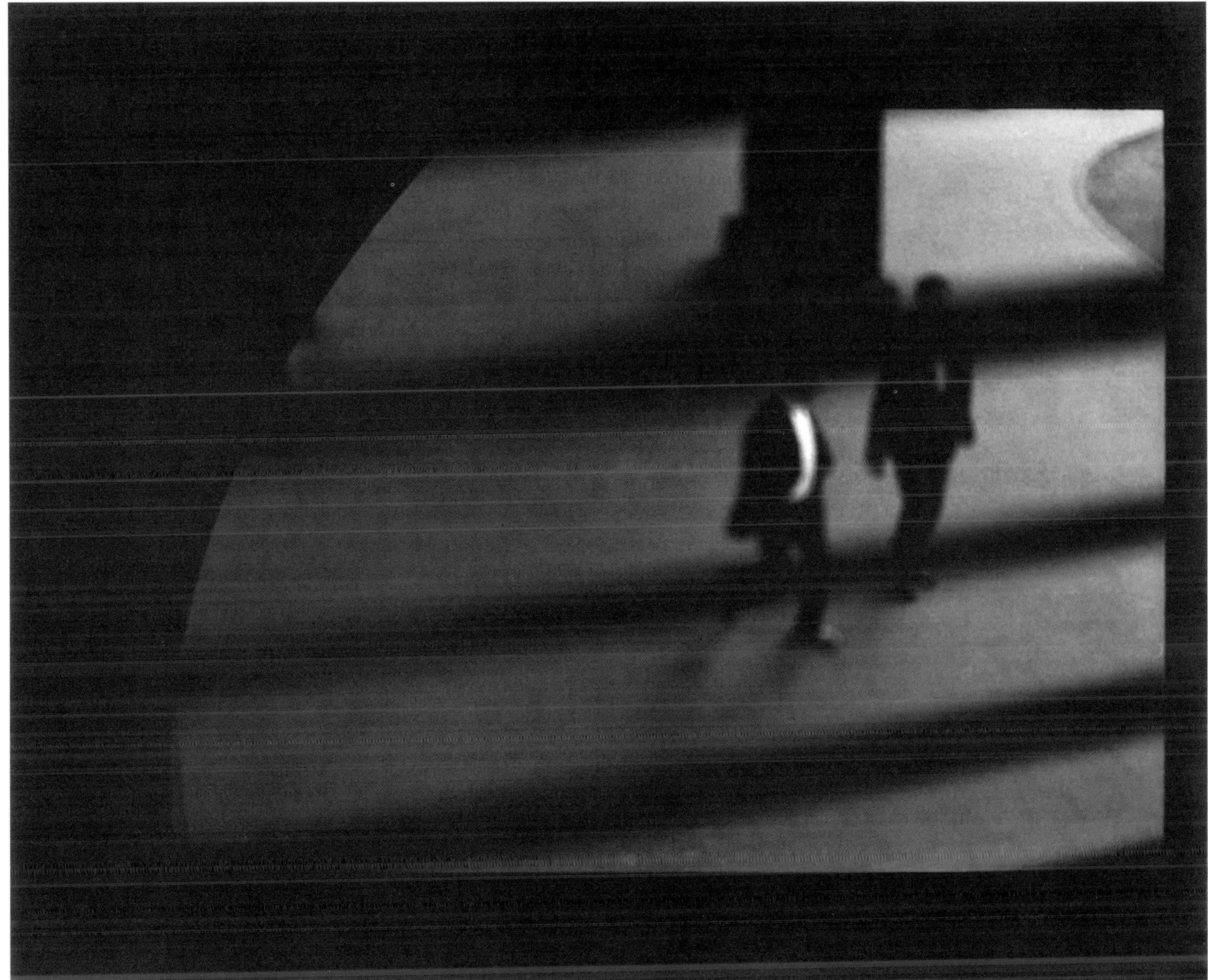

UNTITLED

Hamburg's many bridges are a constant presence and they characterize the city landscape more than anything else. While photographing on one of them, I noticed two men walking on the street below and decided to use the railing to frame the image and give it a film noir look.

Q + A

In much of your work, you use a very low angle of view—why is this?

This is a very interesting question because it actually deals with my equipment. When I started photography, mostly shooting animals, I was using my father's camera—a 1960s Japanese Miranda Sensomat 35mm camera. Five or six years later, I discovered a vertical viewfinder that fitted the camera, so I could look through it from above—as you can with a six-by-six camera, for instance. That intrigued me, because it gave me a fresh view of the world. I then did my London project with the new viewfinder, as well as my pet portrait series. This type of viewfinder enables me to hold the camera at waist level, giving me this low-angle perspective that I like, as well as helping me to be more discreet when shooting on the street. So, over the years, my creative vision has adapted to the equipment.

We don't often see people's faces in your images—is this deliberate?

I do this without being aware of it, really. But I suppose, if I think about it, I don't like including contemporary faces of people because I always like my images to have a timeless feeling. Faces can tell you a lot about a place and time, and these sorts of contemporary details would hurt my vision of the images I'm trying to create. When I look for an interesting picture, I'm probably drawn to a particular person by the type of raincoat, jacket, or hat they're wearing, so the subject becomes less of a recognizable figure. This makes my images more graphic, more iconic, and more mysterious, and open to interpretation, I think.

Why are silhouettes of people so prominent in your work?

Again, when I see the image in my mind, I tend to see the silhouette first. Then I start to follow people, most of the time from behind, and I start to imagine how they might react to my presence. When they become aware of me, then they start to act, in a way— sometimes they get annoyed, because they don't like to be followed, so they become anxious. This is one way that I like to find an image, by making people feel uneasy—it's part of the chase, if you like. I suppose I started my photography by stalking animals, and it's become an important part of my art, a sort of fieldcraft—following people, predicting their reactions, and capturing them at the right moment. In this way, the subjects become characters, as it were, and I can imagine them in my own stories. I like that sort of ambiguity, so the images become like films noirs, in a way.

You often include animals in your street shots—what attracts you to them as subjects?

I've always loved animals. I grew up in the countryside in Umbria in Italy, so I was surrounded by cats, dogs, and pigeons. So, when I first picked up a camera, I looked for animals to photograph—they were easy to find and very close to me. I photographed animals for six or seven years, and when I moved to cities, such as London and New York, it was only natural that I was drawn to them there as well. I'm fascinated by the shapes and forms they make, and feel they complement the urban landscape.

UNTITLED

While shooting in the center of the city of Hamburg, I noticed a woman wearing white shoes standing on a mosaic pavement and took a quick single shot from behind. I enjoyed printing it, as the film has detail but at the same time is a mysterious image as well.

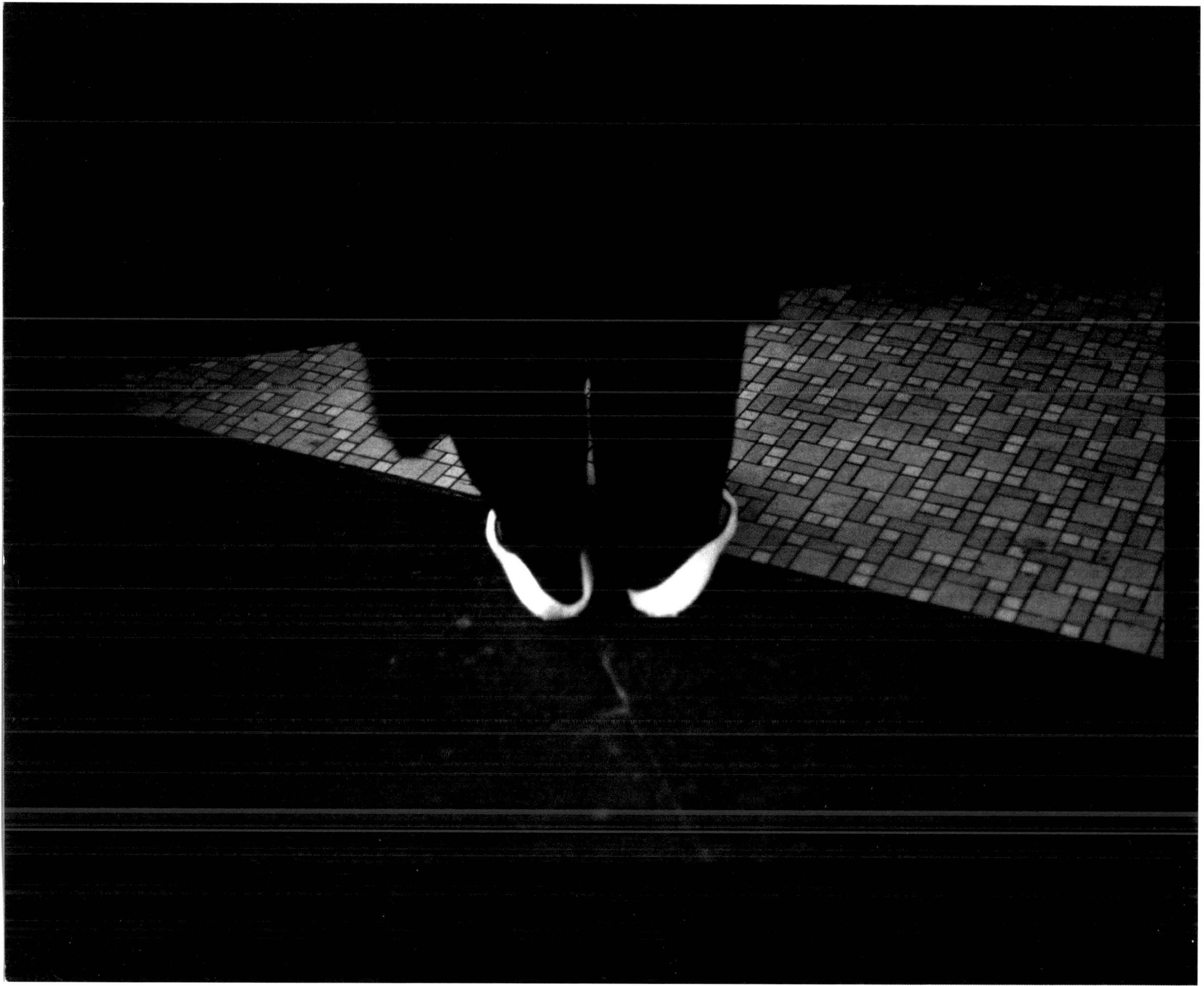

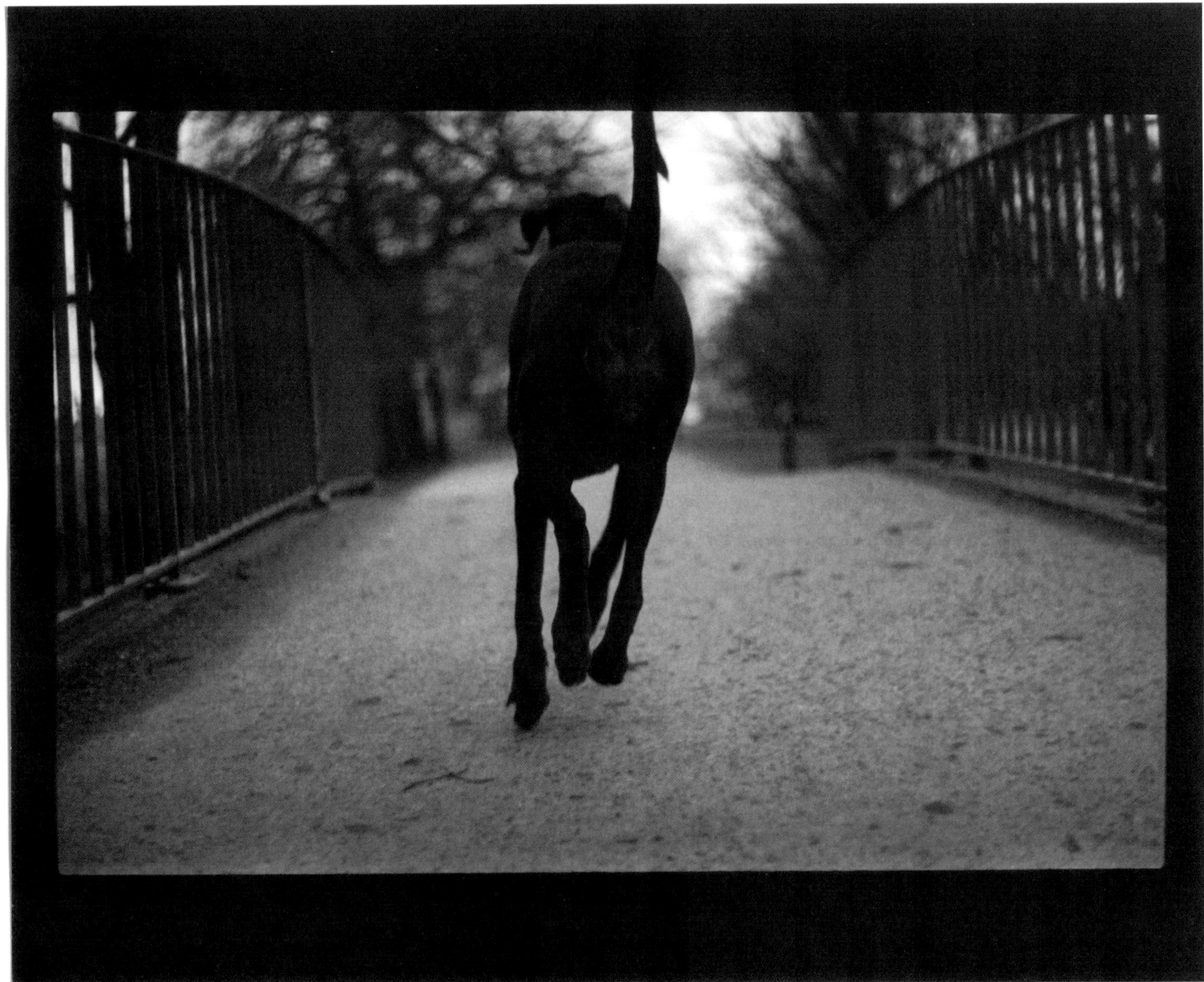

UNTITLED

While walking in Hamburg's Planten un Blomen ("plants and flowers") urban park,
I noticed a big, black dog that was jumping around the park, so I decided to follow
it and managed to catch an on-the-fly shot of it from behind.

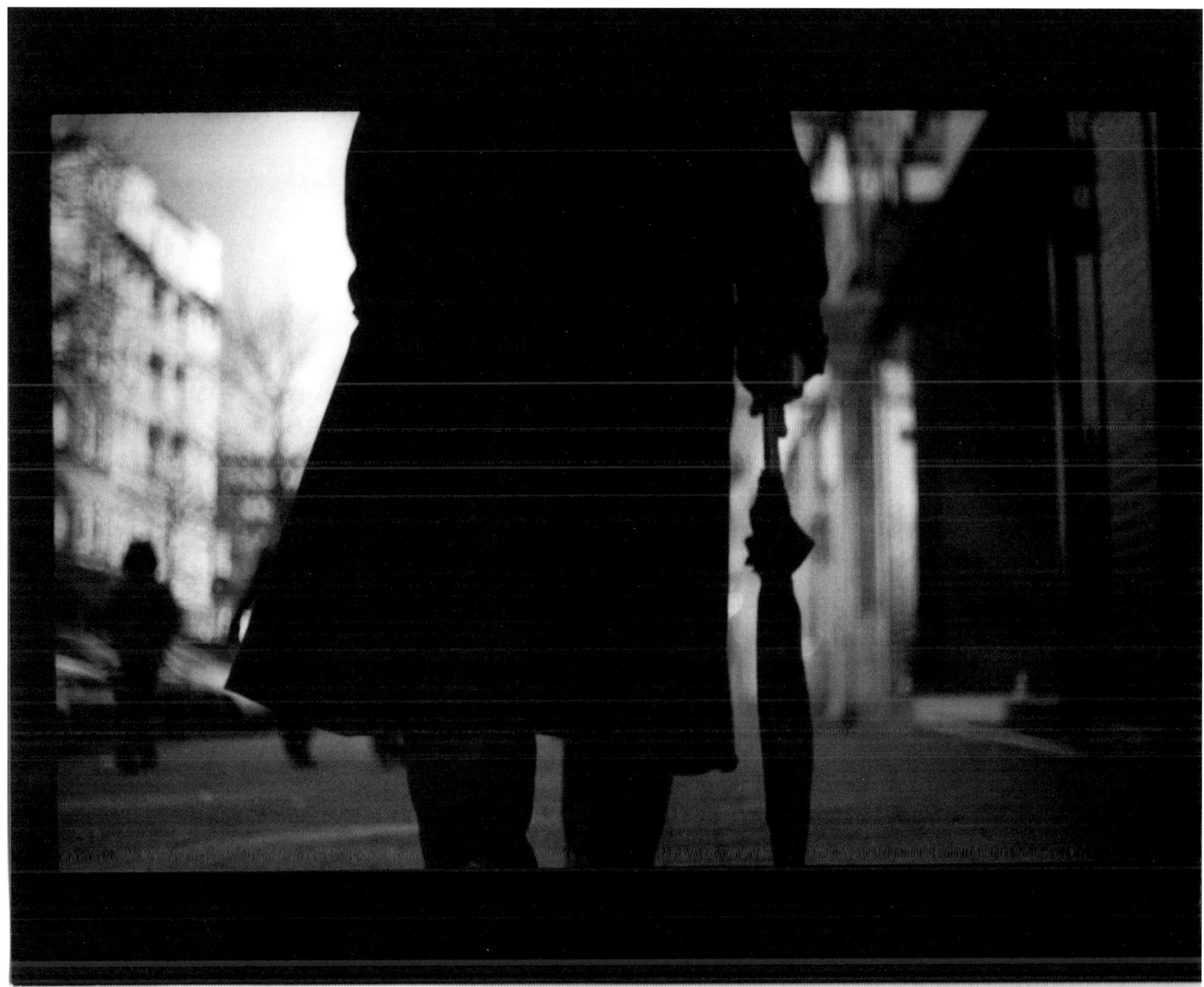

UNTITLED

Sometimes, I just like following people from behind to take pictures of them. On this rainy day, I saw this man in a raincoat leaning on his umbrella; I took six close-up pictures, using the city buildings as the background.

Q
+
A

You have used film ever since you started taking photographs—why do you prefer it?

I've never been tempted to use a digital camera at all. It's both the film camera itself as an object that I like, and the final product that the whole process creates. A print created in this way is such a wonderful tactile object that you can hold in your hand. I love being able to craft a print and then see it hanging in a gallery. Also, when I'm out in the street using a film camera, changing the roll becomes a very important part of the creative process for me. When I'm running out of frames, it makes me pay extra attention to what I'm photographing, and once I've changed a roll of film I often come up with a fresh set of ideas. Even the fact that I use an old camera, which sometimes goes wrong, creates an anxiety and an extra challenge that I have to work with. I believe that helps me creatively in the field as well.

What sort of techniques do you use to create the distinctive look of your images?

I never studied photography formally, but I've always used a darkroom. I like the idea of being an artisan—it's an extension of my aesthetic. My approach is very basic. I use Kodak Tri-X 400 black and white film—I've learned over the years that the right kind of film as a starting point is very important. It allows me to give the density that I want to my images. I have to make compromises in the darkroom when I'm creating a print. I try to get my subjects in focus in the camera, but I'm also trying to create high contrast in order to achieve the silhouettes I want when I'm printing. I also use a fiber-based paper for printing, which softens the images. Together, these techniques create the look to the prints that I like.

Street photography can be intrusive—do you ever feel you are invading a person's privacy?

Most of the time, I don't think I'm being very intrusive, myself, when I photograph people. I never touch them, or do anything inappropriate, and most of my subjects don't even realize that I'm photographing them, especially when it's noisy on the street—as in New York or London—and they can't hear the shutter on my camera. But I do think street photography can invade someone's privacy, yes—it can be like someone bumping into you as you walk. As a photographer, when I follow people, I have this need I feel inside me—I want to get the picture I want, no matter what. I only use a 50mm lens, so I do have to get quite close to the subject for my pictures. But it's part of a bigger plan, if you like, part of my art—it's for what I do. So when I look at the images I've taken, the pleasure that I get from capturing the image I want is enough to justify that brief moment of invading someone's privacy.

What tips would you give to anyone looking to master street photography?

Firstly, it's very important to be out on the street as much as you can—people don't realize how much you have to work to improve. The more you shoot, and the more images you produce, the more you learn. From my point of view, I've been a printer for a while, and that has taught me a lot about what I have to look for when I compose a picture, such as the tonality of the grays across an image. Also, the editing process is crucial. For instance, out of the 40 rolls I might typically shoot during a project, I would select about 15 to 20 images to be shown and exhibited. I could show 40 different stories, but it is important to be very selective and only pick the narratives that say what I want.

"Even the fact that I use an old camera, which sometimes goes wrong, creates an anxiety and an extra challenge that I have to work with. I believe that helps me creatively in the field."

TECHNICAL INFORMATION

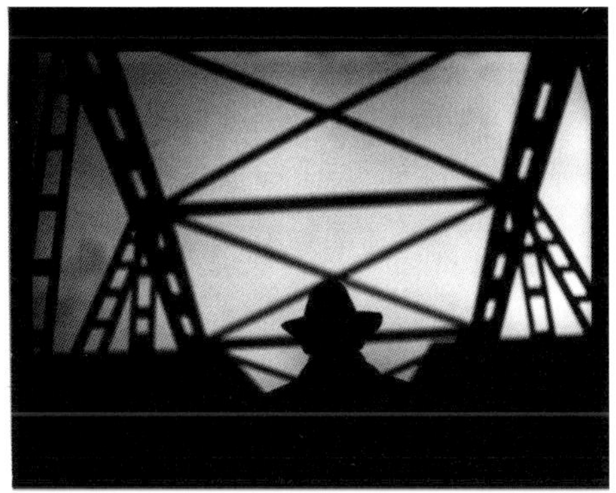

UNTITLED
HAMBURG, GERMANY

Camera: Miranda Sensomat RE
Lens/Focal length: 50mm f/1.8
Aperture: f/1.8
Shutter speed: Unrecorded
Film: Kodak Tri-X 400

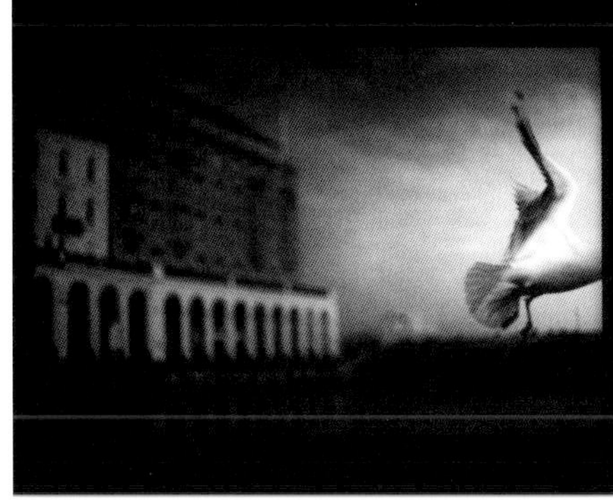

UNTITLED
HAMBURG, GERMANY

Camera: Miranda Sensomat RE
Lens/Focal length: 50mm f/1.8
Aperture: f/1.8
Shutter speed: Unrecorded
Film: Kodak Tri-X 400

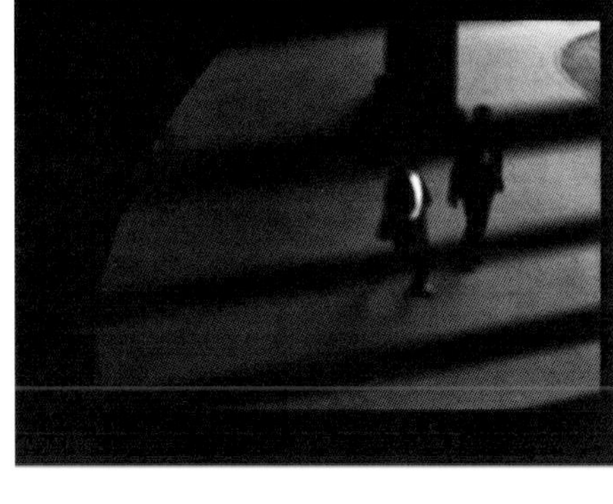

UNTITLED
HAMBURG, GERMANY

Camera: Miranda Sensomat RE
Lens/Focal length: 50mm f/1.8
Aperture: f/1.8
Shutter speed: Unrecorded
Film: Kodak Tri-X 400

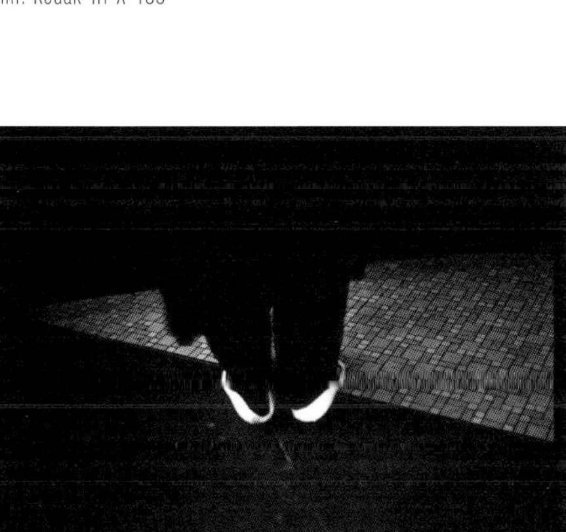

UNTITLED
HAMBURG, GERMANY

Camera: Miranda Sensomat RE
Lens/Focal length: 50mm f/1.8
Aperture: f/1.8
Shutter speed: Unrecorded
Film: Kodak Tri-X 400

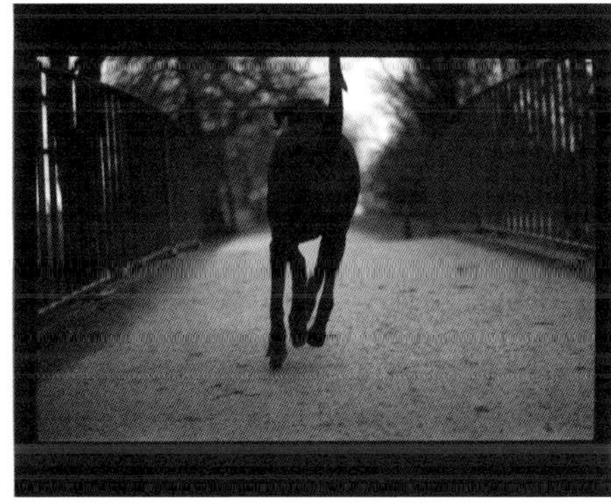

UNTITLED
HAMBURG, GERMANY

Camera: Miranda Sensomat RE
Lens/Focal length: 50mm f/1.8
Aperture: f/1.8
Shutter speed: Unrecorded
Film: Kodak Tri-X 400

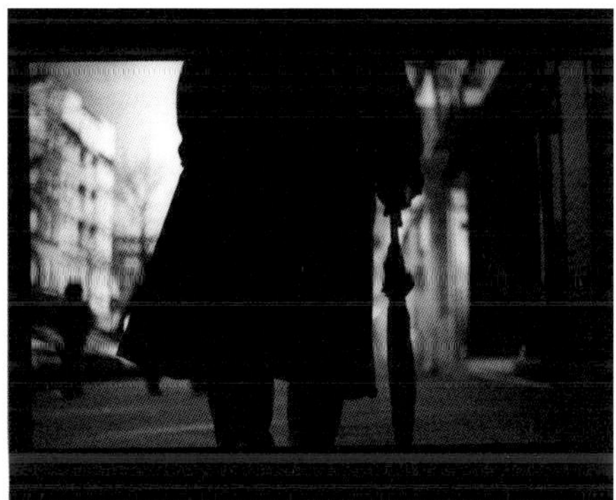

UNTITLED
HAMBURG, GERMANY

Camera: Miranda Sensomat RE
Lens/Focal length: 50mm f/1.8
Aperture: f/1.8
Shutter speed: Unrecorded
Film: Kodak Tri-X 400

PAUL BURGESS

Paul Burgess has spent many years working in television, editing and directing documentaries for a host of international broadcasters, including the BBC, ARTE, and PBS. As a result, he's traveled extensively and enjoyed the challenge of making films and telling stories. But photography has always been his private passion, with its ability to tell a story with a single shot, capturing a moment, a feeling, a personality. Paul also loves the freedom of being able to work alone—just him and his camera; no big crews or anxious producers to deal with.

While Paul's film and video work is often created for a broadcaster or a client, his photography is just for himself. It allows him to explore other areas of his creativity and other modes of expression. At times, his documentary "sensibility" motivates him to look for gritty realism—to capture urban decay and the plight of people in poverty. But he also looks to capture the chaos, weirdness, and poetry of the urban landscape; to take pictures that appeal more to the heart than the head. While documentaries are about realism—explaining and revealing the truth behind the headlines—Paul looks for mystery and enigma with his street photography, through images that raise questions. He doesn't feel the need to provide answers or clarity. Paul believes the best images are ones that are not just pleasing to look at, but also stimulate the imagination or the emotions of the viewer.

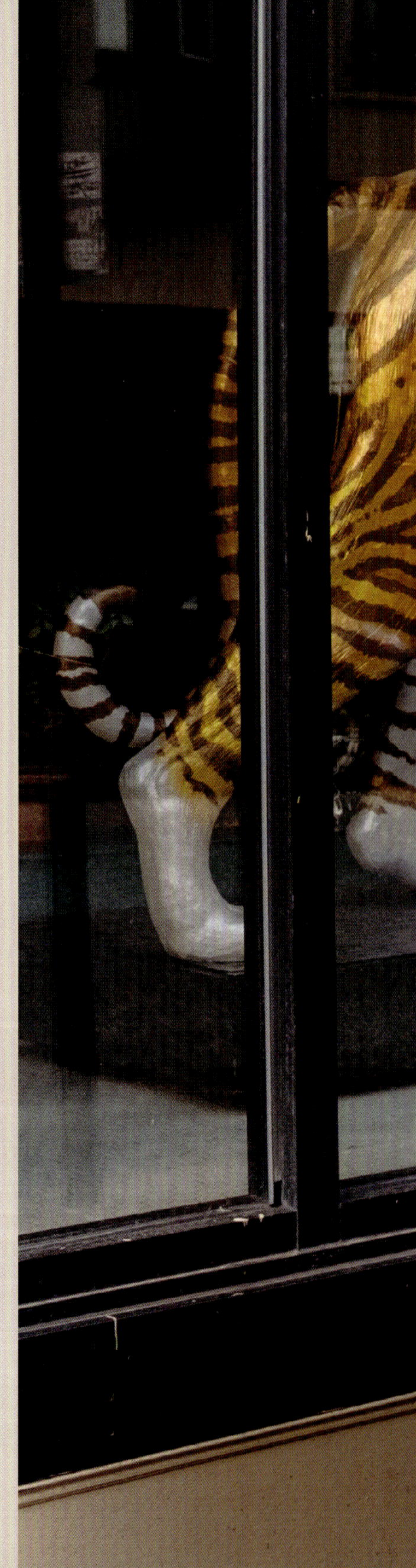

UNTITLED

This was a happy accident. I saw the man running toward the shop and I could see that there was a statue of a tiger in the window. The man was bare-chested, so there was something animal-like about him as well—it's "the urban jungle," and I like the humor in it. My camera was hanging by my side and I didn't have time to adjust the settings or even look through the viewfinder—I just shot a couple of frames from the hip and by some miracle I got this picture. It was very underexposed, but as I was shooting Raw I was able to get an image out of it.

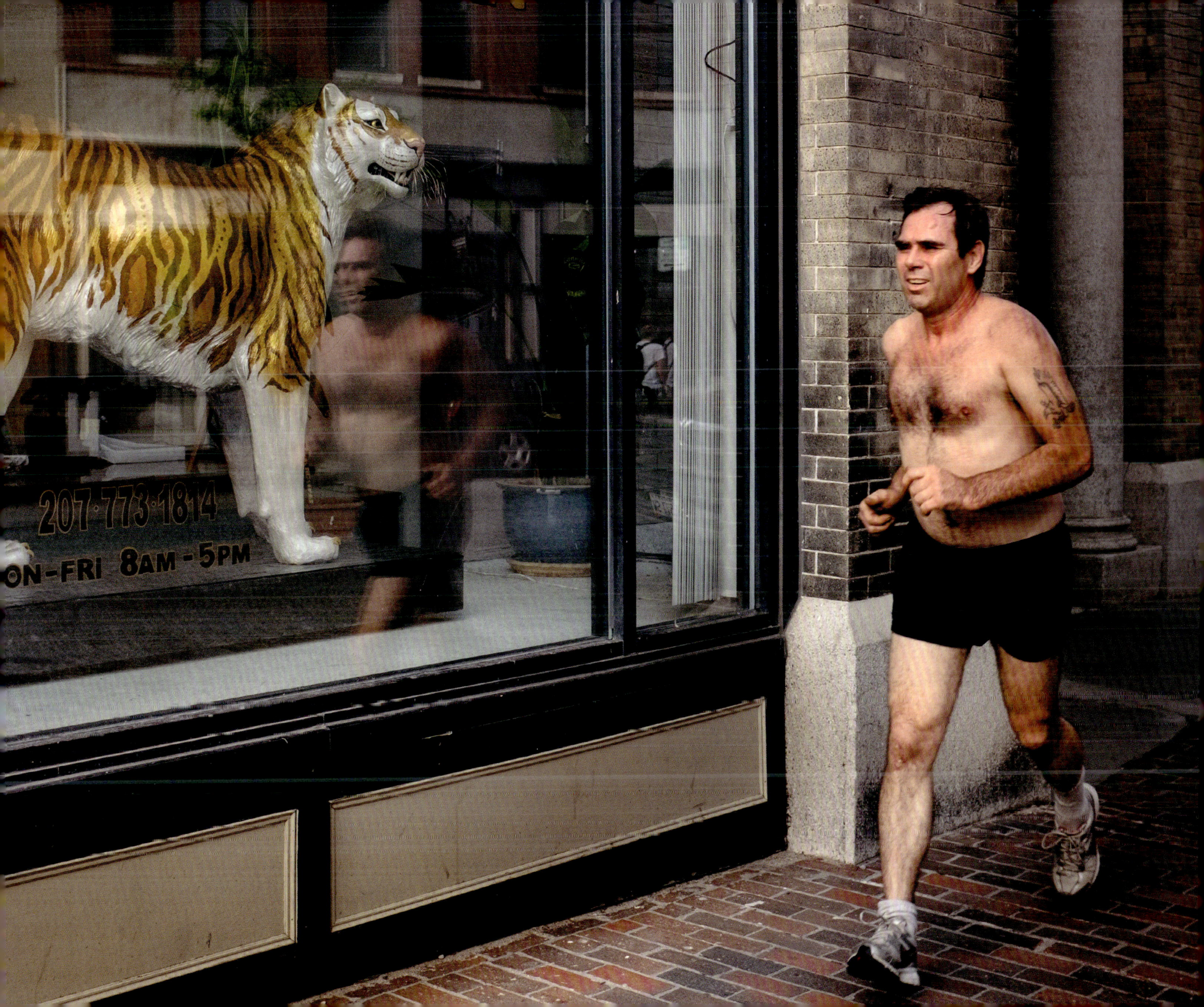

207·773·1814
ON-FRI 8AM-5PM

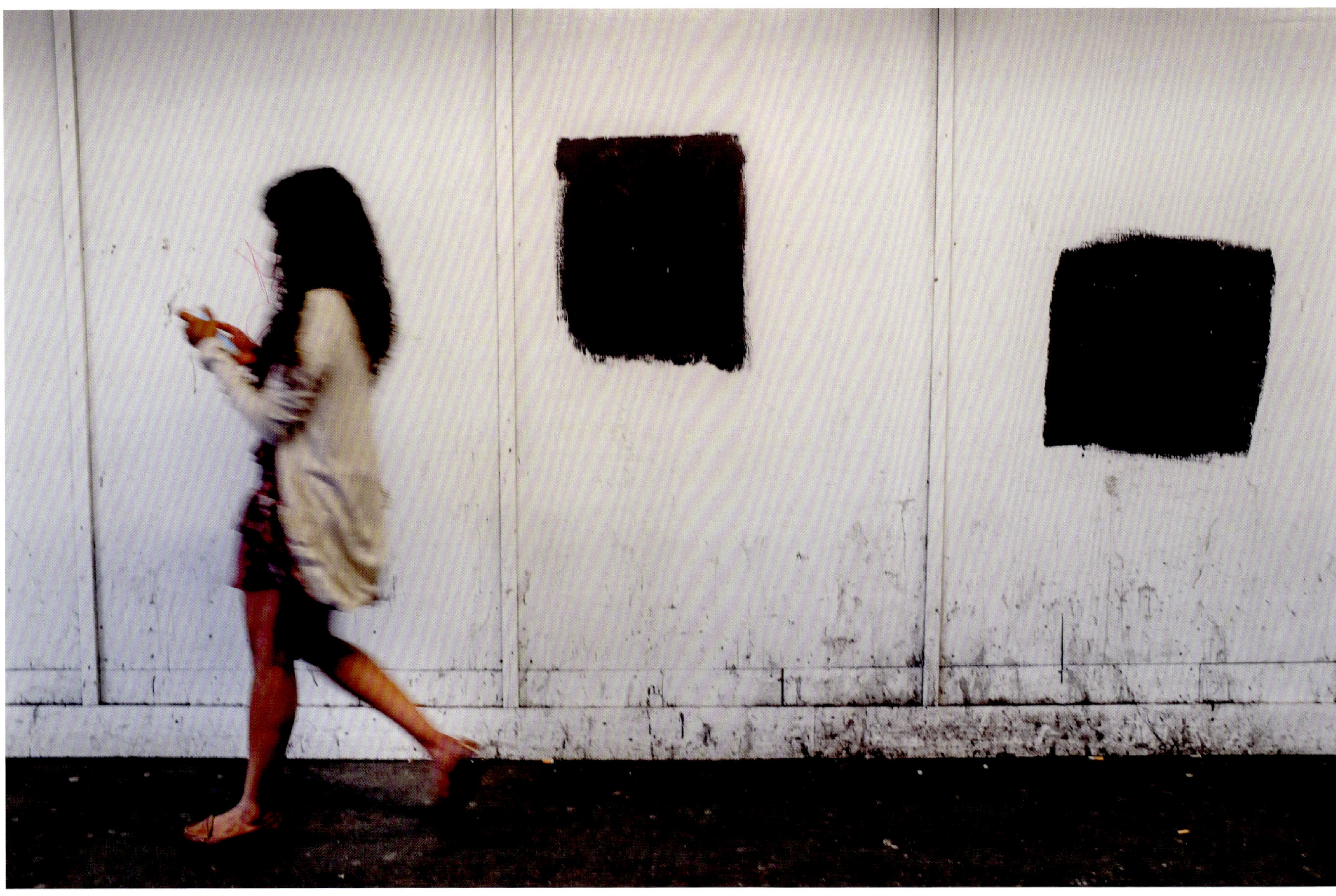

UNTITLED

This was an instinctive shot. I was standing on the corner waiting for someone—I saw the woman passing and just grabbed the camera. She's slightly out of focus but it doesn't really matter, because she's moving. It's quite an urban image—she's on her phone, the wall is dirty and spattered—and it's hard to put a finger on why it works. I like the symmetry of the three sections within the image separating the two black-painted blocks and the woman. The image seems to combine the static and the moving; I think it just has a simple visual poetry that draws you in.

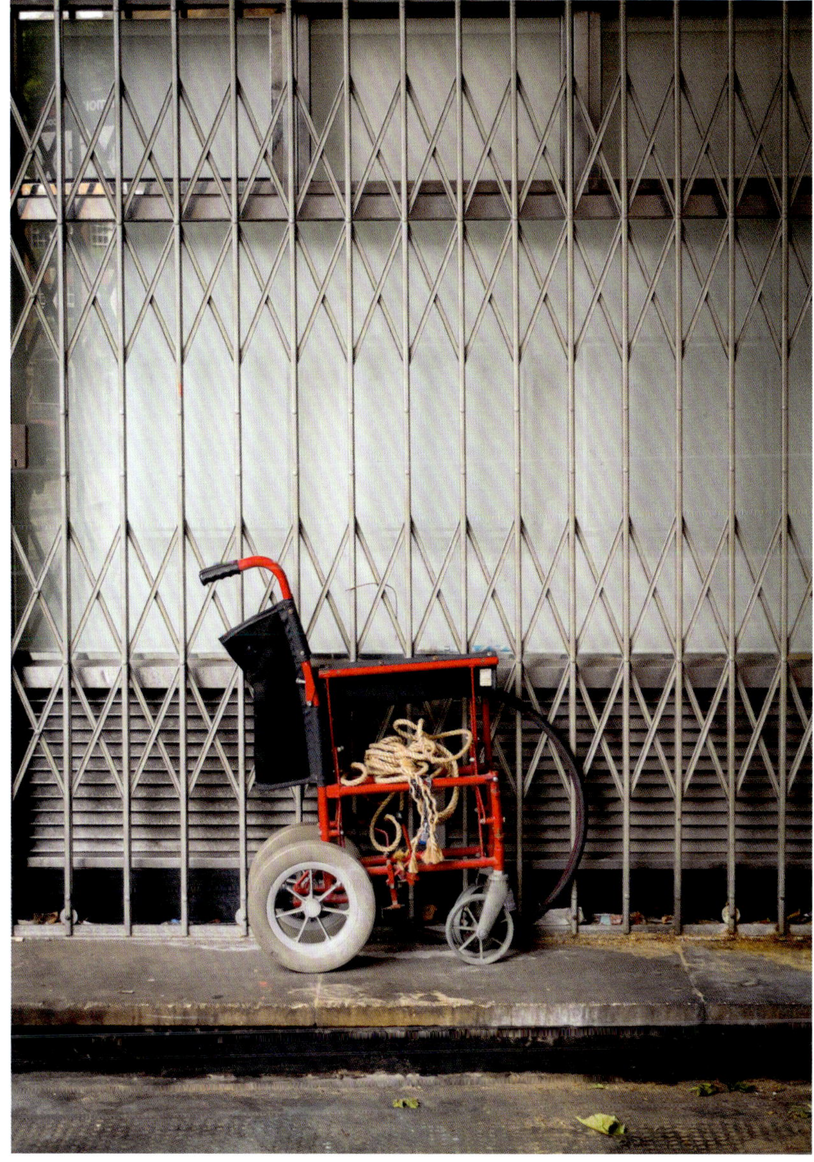

UNTITLED

I like this image on so many levels — the flush of color, and again the unexpectedness of it. You're asking why there's an abandoned wheelchair here, with a bunch of rope, left parked in front of a gate. There are all these lines and textures, as well as the color. It's a puzzle within a puzzle.

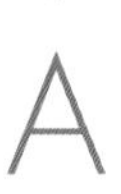

How did you get started in street photography?

I was given my first camera, a Kodak Instamatic, when I was about seven years old, and I loved it. I became a keen photographer and built a darkroom at home, enjoying the magic of processing and printing my own photos. I made of lot of portraits and family pictures. Then in my late twenties I spent time in Egypt and India where I was exposed to wonderful, new, and unfamiliar cultures. I was inspired to grab my camera and capture the chaotic and colorful street life that was all around me. It was that unfamiliarity—the culture shock compared to where I'd come from—that made me want to take pictures. So I took my camera out on the streets with me, and became more observant and more mindful as I walked around. My camera helped me to engage in the world, particularly the cityscape, in a more emotional way. I began to see the visual poetry everywhere I looked. Cities like London, where I live, are full of surreal juxtapositions, accidental abstract art, unintended sculptures, eccentric characters, and life in all its forms. It's fast-paced and changes in front of your eyes. While I still enjoy taking landscape shots and portraits, street photography is for me the most challenging and exciting kind of photography that I do.

What are you looking for when composing an image?

I'm trying to make sense out of chaos. There's all this craziness and confusion—people rushing everywhere, colors, lights, shapes—and if I can find a composition where the elements come together in a visually pleasing and satisfying way, then I'm happy. I'll look for lines that coincide, an interesting juxtaposition, a fortuitous coincidence of things. You want to make an image that makes sense on its own, on its own terms, that works even if it's separated from its context. It's hard to describe—which is why it's an image and not a piece of writing. But usually I'm looking for a composition that's not too cluttered, and shows the beauty, poetry, or hyper-reality of the city. Sometimes, I see an image coming into view, as different elements are converging in front of me, so I rush to get into position. It's very hit and miss, though, and if it works, it's a happy accident. At other times, I spend much longer trying to compose something akin to an abstract painting out of the colors and shapes that I find in the urban landscape. Even if there aren't people around, and even if there isn't much going on, you can find other ways to make images.

What makes an image become a "favorite" for you?

It's when an image has its own internal chemistry; when those elements come together in a poetic and aesthetically pleasing way. It might be a combination of the subject and the background, or one color that stands out as an element. Generally, a favorite image will make me feel something. It will bring out a reaction or an emotion—it might be a melancholy feeling, but often you don't quite know what it is. Other times an image will make me smile. You want to get some sort of feeling from it, even if it's just "Wow, that's great!" I do try to take photographs—like the one of the young woman passing the blocks of black paint on the wall—that communicate something, even if at first I don't know exactly what the image is saying, or if it will work. A good street photograph captures something that can't be put into words.

Light is important in your work—do you prefer particular times of day or types of lighting?

Like many photographers, I love the golden light and long shadows at the end of the day. There's this phrase— "the suffering of light" (from the line by Goethe, "Colors are the deeds and suffering of light," and the title of Alex Webb's book)—that "dying" light that has a magic about it. Having said that, because my photography has to fit in around other things that I do, I will go out at different times of the day, and sometimes the harsh midday sunlight, crashing across the street, can make a shot very special. You get those interesting shapes and shadows, which can result in more striking and intense photographs—but it also makes taking pictures more challenging because of the intense contrast between very bright light and very dark shadows. Lighting is very important to me, but I'm not fixated on one particular kind of light—you have to adapt to the lighting in different situations. If there isn't much light available, then maybe I'll look for a close-up, where it's really about the detail in a shot. I'm more concerned about overexposing the shot, so I will tend to stop down to avoid losing detail in the light areas—I don't mind as much if some detail is lost in the shadows. I almost invariably shoot Raw, which gives you a little more flexibility, but it's important to remember to readjust the exposure after each shot. You've got to try to find an exposure that captures the scene as you want it.

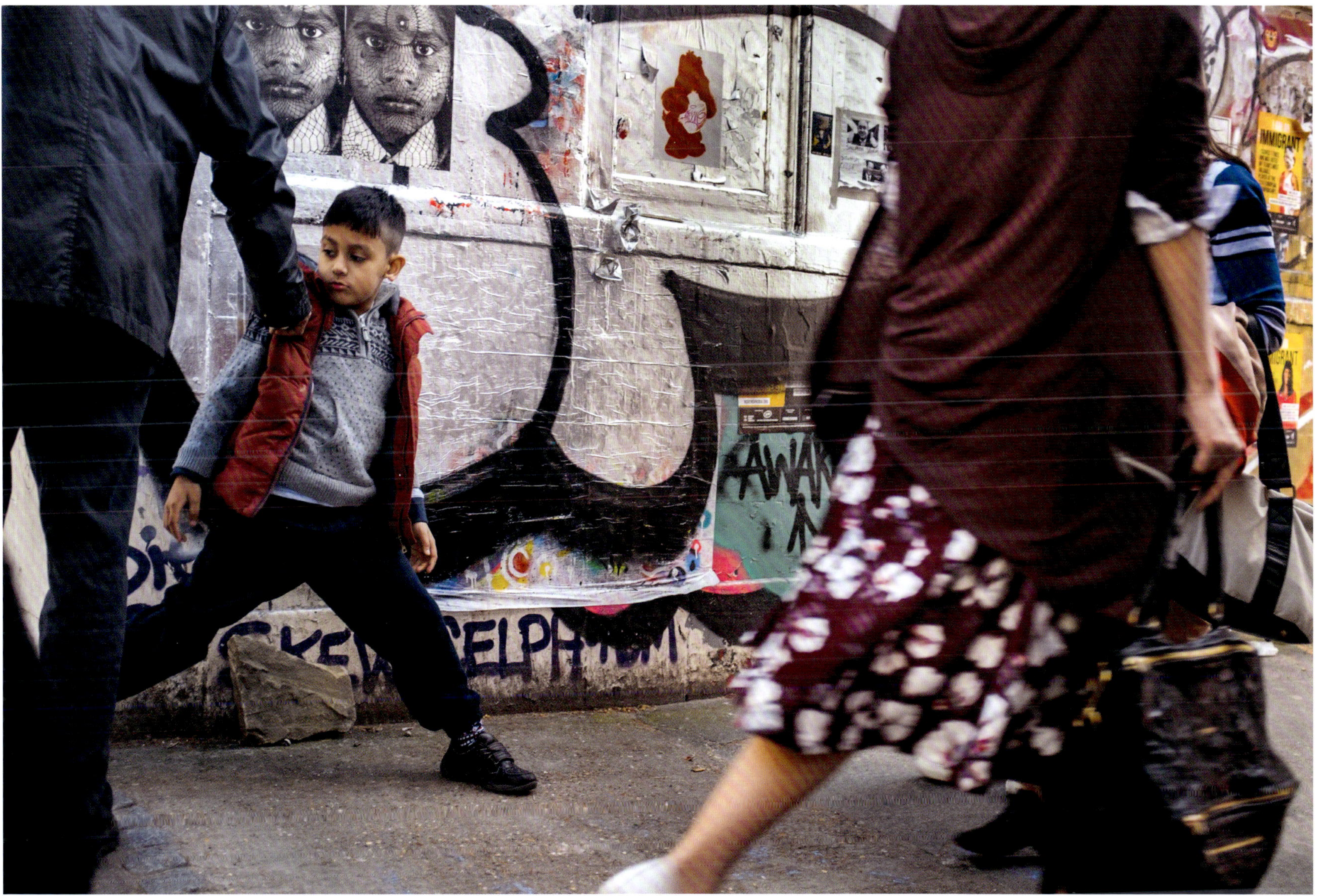

UNTITLED

There's a lot going on in this frame. There's drama (you feel that poor boy is being treated roughly), but there's also movement and dynamism. I saw this scene out of the corner of my eye, while I was walking in the opposite direction. I swung around and took the picture, very quickly and instinctively. When I looked at it afterward, I loved the way the triangular shape of the boy's legs is mirrored by the woman's leg as she walks past. The face of the boy adds to the drama—he's the only one whose face is seen, while the three other people in the picture are obscured. Beside the boy's foot, the graffiti on the wall subliminally almost reads "h-e-l-p," and that's a happy coincidence of things coming together. The more you look at it, the more you see.

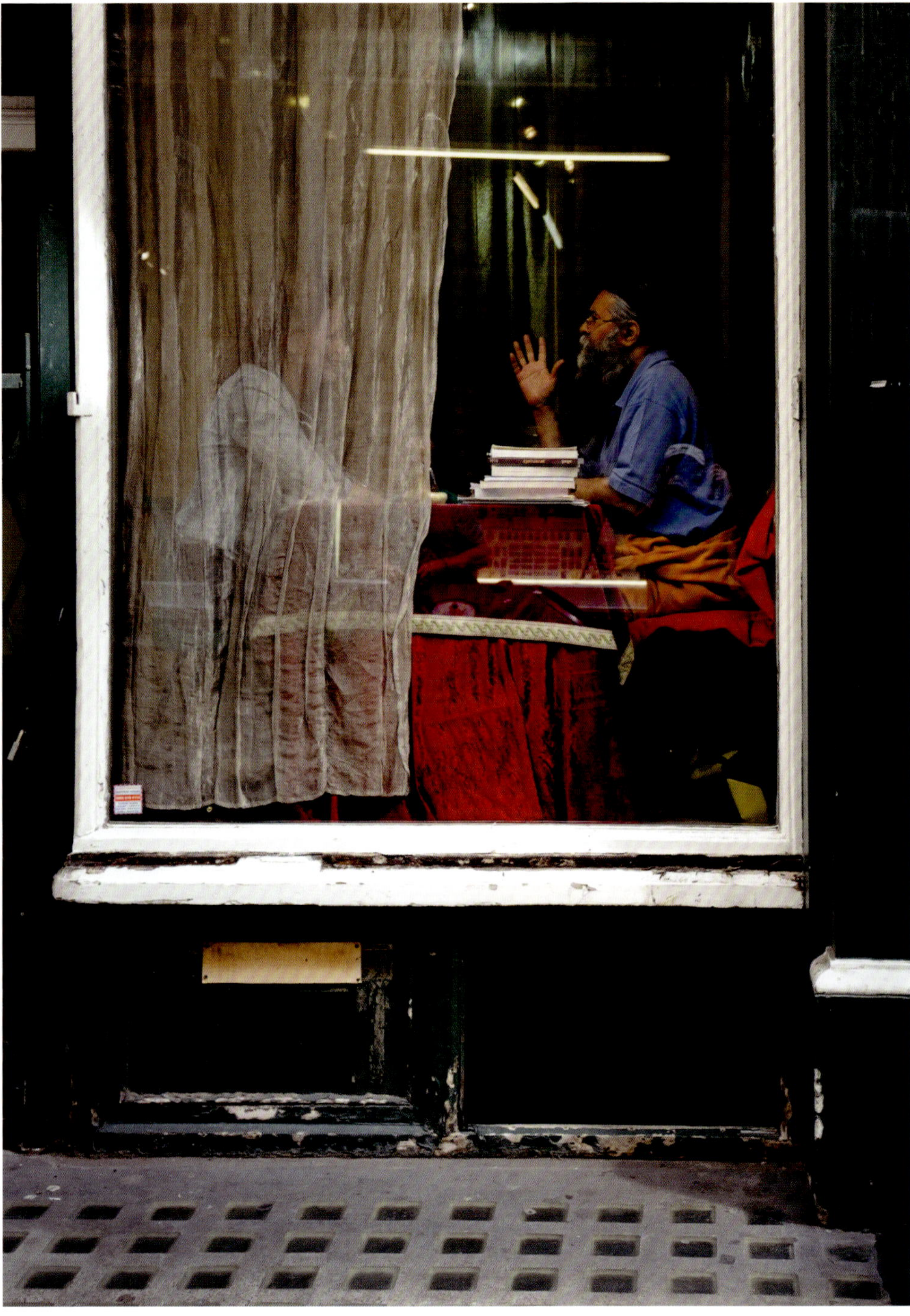

UNTITLED

I like the narrative in this image—it's like a frozen frame from a movie. The couple are in mid-conversation, the man is very expressive with his hands, and you can just see the woman he's talking to, behind the curtain. They're both framed by the window, and then there's this division in the image—this line between them. It's intriguing, and you wonder what their story is. There's also the lovely strong color—the red of the tablecloth and chair, contrasting with the darker green outside.

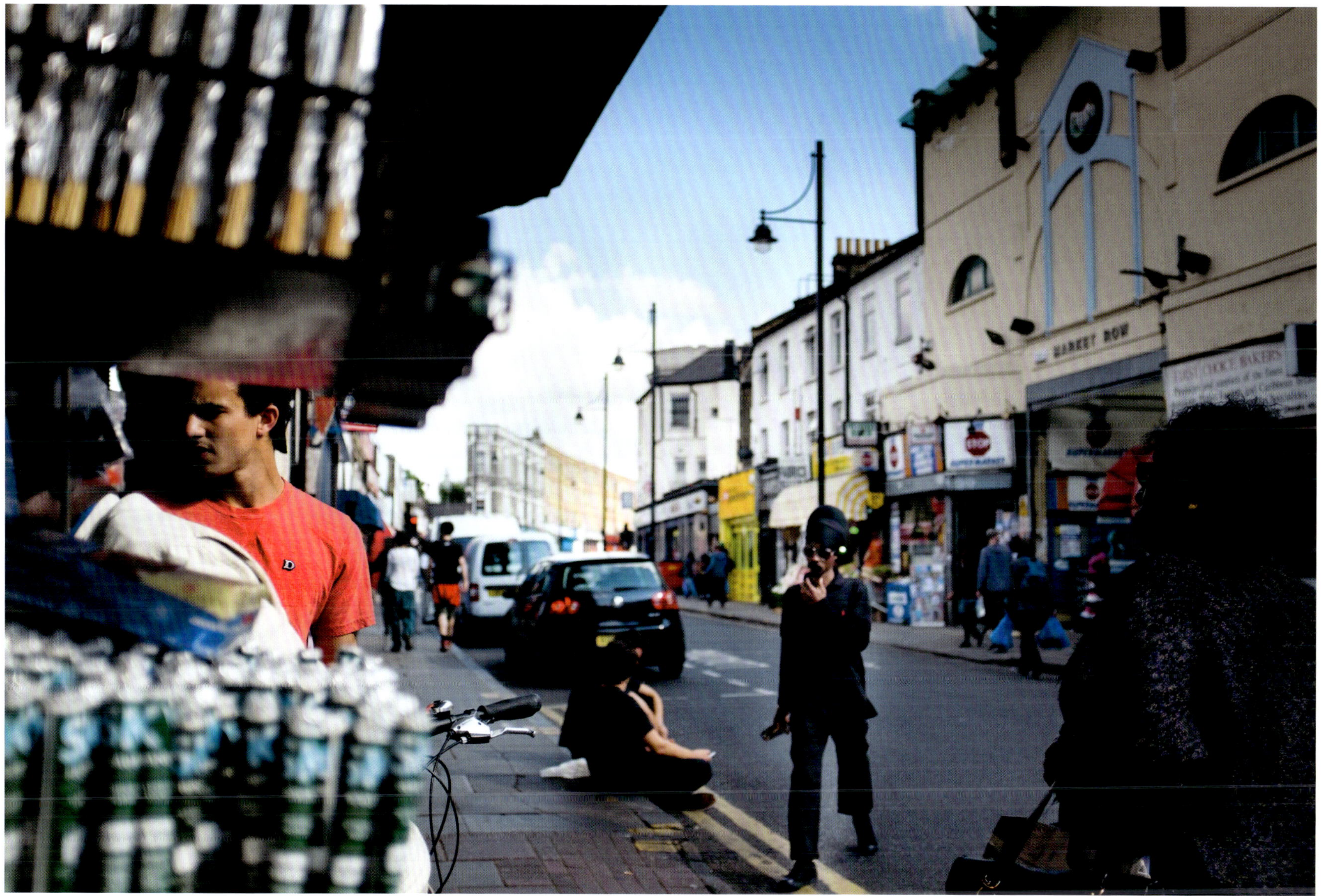

UNTITLED

This was taken in Brixton, London. I liked the movement and color, and the juxtaposition of elements in the composition. There's a triangular formation with the man in the vivid red t-shirt on the left, the man purposefully crossing in the middle, and the woman coming in to frame from the right, which gives the image a kind of drama and pulls you into the frame.

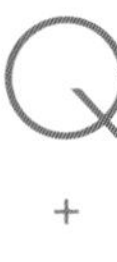

Q + A

People, although ever-present in some form or other, seem almost peripheral in your images—is this a deliberate choice?

I actually spend a lot of time making portraits—it's something I like to do, and I'm endlessly fascinated by the human face. However, with my street photography I'm trying to capture the poetry of the city—I suppose I'm making a portrait of the city. Rather than focusing on any one individual, I'm looking for the combination of elements—people in motion, architecture, graffiti, cars, smoke, litter, advertising, street furniture, abandoned objects, and all the other ephemera of a city. The city has a life of its own, and people are one part of that. That's the difference. I'm not putting people at the very center, because there's so much more to the city. Occasionally, I'm drawn to details, texture, and fabric, such as torn posters or an abandoned object; it's all part of the surrealism of the city. When you find these objects placed against random backgrounds and put a frame around them and photograph them, you are making your own surreal or abstract image.

Your photographs have a particular look. Do you use any specific post-processing techniques?

I always shoot digitally and in color, as you can always convert pictures to black and white afterward, which is something I sometimes do. Photographically I tend to think in color. I'm also partial to a high-contrast look—and I'm not afraid to tweak the images to bring out certain elements. I'm not someone who believes you take a picture and that's it—photographers have been changing the look of a picture and correcting it in the darkroom for years. At the end of the day, it's the final image that's important. I do try to achieve a particular "look," with a richness and a warmth. Color is very emotive. Warmer, richer colors can definitely help create a more emotional connection to the image. I've been using Lightroom for years, which I really love, and there are times when I spend ages trying to get that right look—as I see it. But it's trial and error.

Street photography can be intrusive—do you ever feel you are invading a person's privacy?

Yes, I'm very conscious of this. These days, there is a lot of suspicion and some people are worried about images of themselves appearing on the internet. It's important to be careful, and to take people's concerns seriously. If I want to take a stranger's portrait, I'll ask permission first and spend time explaining to people what I'm doing, so as to put them at ease. A friendly approach goes a long way. I'll give people my card and offer to email them the photos if they want. If somebody doesn't want their picture taken, that's no problem, I'll walk away. But it's not always possible to ask permission in advance when it's a candid, on-the-spot photograph. It's important to be bold and take the photograph anyway. But if, having done so, somebody in the image expresses concern, I will always try to engage with them and reassure them. If they're really unhappy, I'll delete the photo.

What tips would you give to those who wish to master street photography?

Be bold and be patient. Some days you spend hours on the street and take hundreds of pictures but nothing really works. Other days, you might get three great shots in the first hour. It's a journey with no specific destination, so be prepared to go with the flow.

"With my street photography I'm trying to capture the poetry of the city—I suppose I'm making a portrait of the city."

TECHNICAL INFORMATION

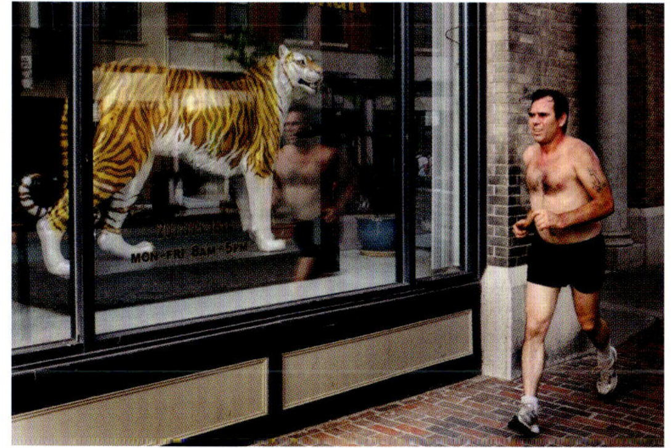

UNTITLED
PORTLAND, MAINE, USA

Camera: Fujifilm X100S
Lens/Focal length: 23mm f/2 (35mm equivalent: 35mm)
Aperture: f/4
Shutter speed: 1/250 sec.
ISO: 200

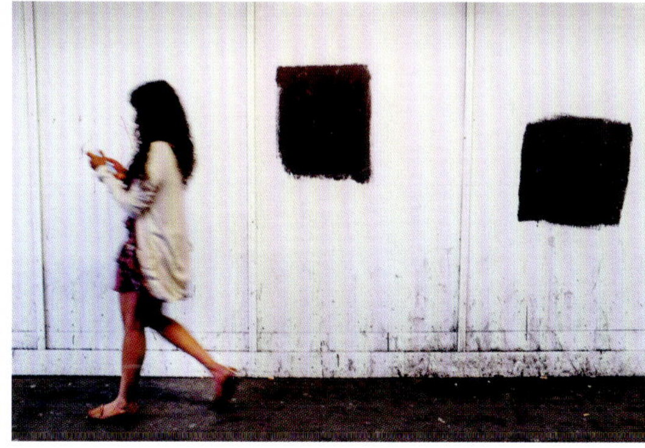

UNTITLED
SOHO, LONDON, UK

Camera: Fujifilm X100S
Lens/Focal length: 23mm f/2 (35mm equivalent: 35mm)
Aperture: f/5.6
Shutter speed: 1/40 sec.
ISO: 1250

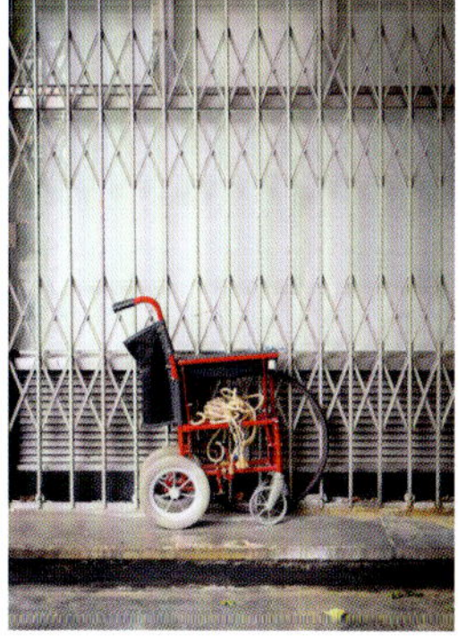

UNTITLED
BLOOMSBURY, LONDON, UK

Camera: Fujifilm X10
Lens/Focal length: 7.1-28.4mm f/2-2.8 at 14.2mm (35mm equivalent: 56mm)
Aperture: f/2.5
Shutter speed: 1/200 sec.
ISO: 250

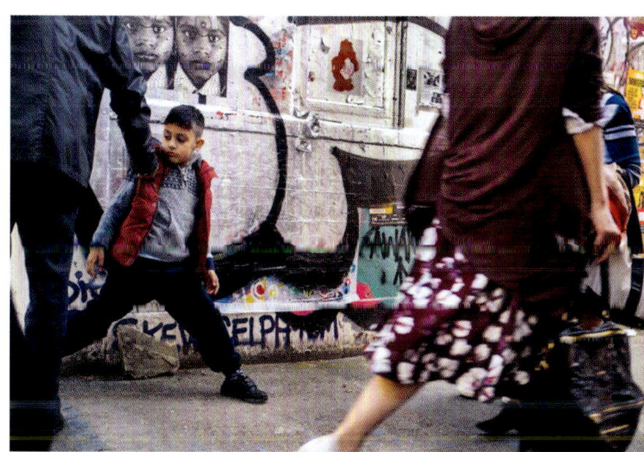

UNTITLED
BRICK LANE, LONDON, UK

Camera: Fujifilm X100S
Lens/Focal length: 23mm f/2 (35mm equivalent: 35mm)
Aperture: f/2
Shutter speed: 1/125 sec.
ISO: 250

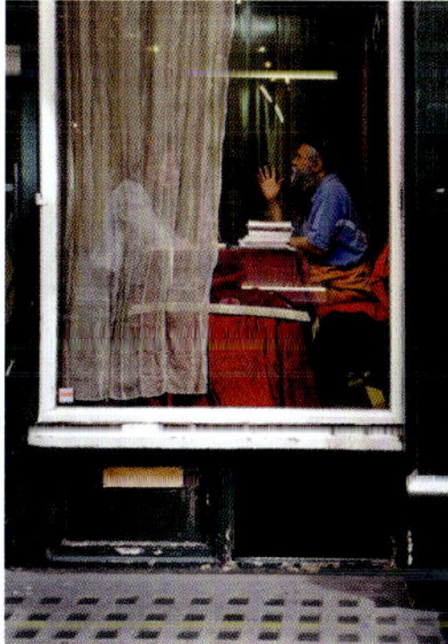

UNTITLED
SOHO, LONDON, UK

Camera: Fujifilm X100S
Lens/Focal length: 23mm f/2 (35mm equivalent: 35mm)
Aperture: f/2.8
Shutter speed: 1/640 sec.
ISO: 500

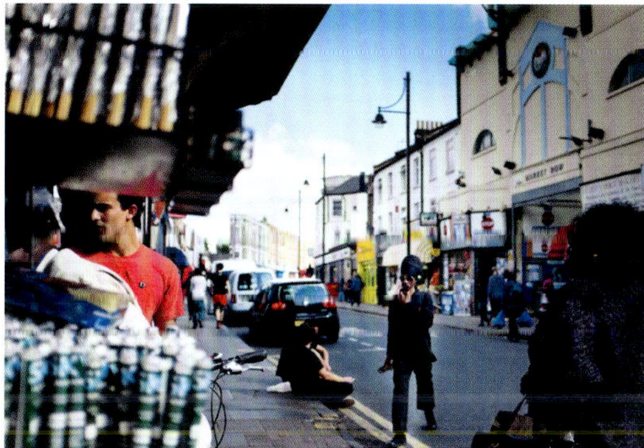

UNTITLED
BRIXTON, LONDON, UK

Camera: Fujifilm X100S
Lens/Focal length: 23mm f/2 (35mm equivalent: 35mm)
Aperture: f/2
Shutter speed: 1/280 sec.
ISO: 200

MASTER OF URBAN LANDSCAPE
SALLY DAVIES

Sally Davies moved from Canada to Manhattan's East Village in New York in 1983, where she still lives and photographs. Following a full-time career as a painter, Sally took a break to focus on photography in 2000, and has been shooting ever since. Her earliest influencers were both women: Diane Arbus and Helen Levitt, for different reasons. "The moment I saw the drama of Arbus's Sword Swallower, and the ordinary grace of Levitt's Girl/Green Car," she recalls, "I knew my life was about to change."

Sally loves to shoot at night more than anything. "Something magical happens as the daytime funk and grime fade away. The Avenue starts to sparkle as moonlight settles on the garbage bags. There is a boozy quality to night photography and the story feels different. There is a feeling that anything can happen at night. My work cuts a wide swath, and its appeal isn't limited to any particular financial bracket, gender, or age group. In those ways, I feel my work succeeds."

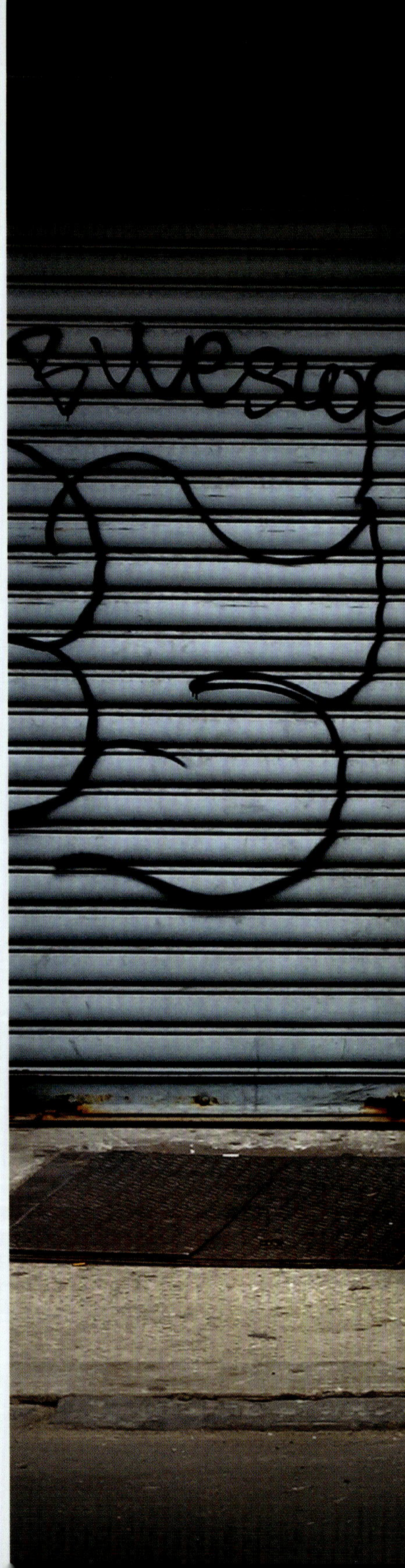

AVENUE B LIBERTY
This section of storefronts is right around the corner from where I live, and I walk this street several times a day. This graffiti is done by a well-known local named Chico, who has been tagging the neighborhood for as long as I can remember. This particular afternoon, I was walking on the other side of the street, when I spotted the woman approaching the graffiti. I waited for her to hit the mark, and fired the shutter. If you carry your camera with you all the time, luck will find you.

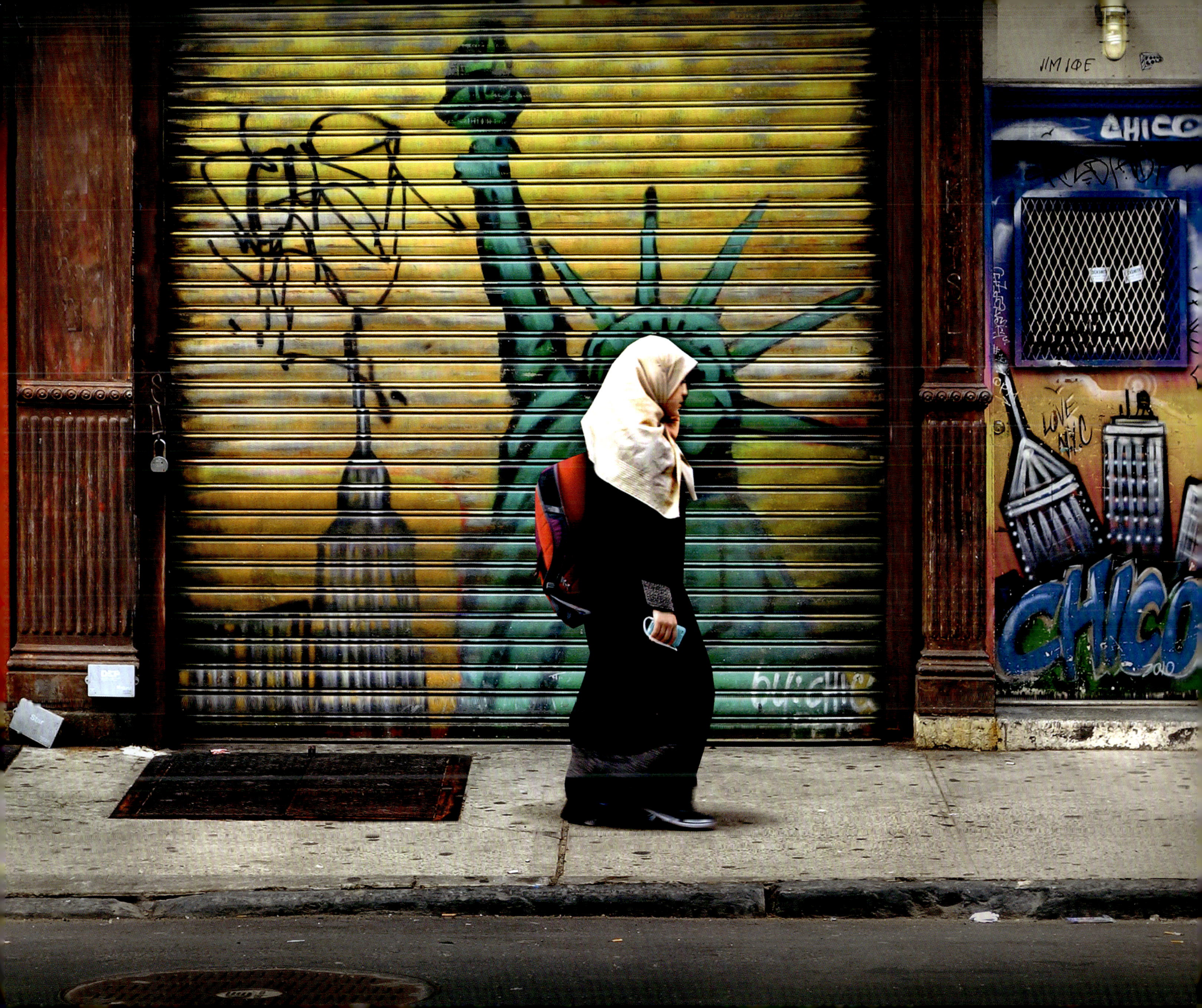

JIM IФE
CHICO
LOVE NYC
CHICO
2010
ou:CHIC

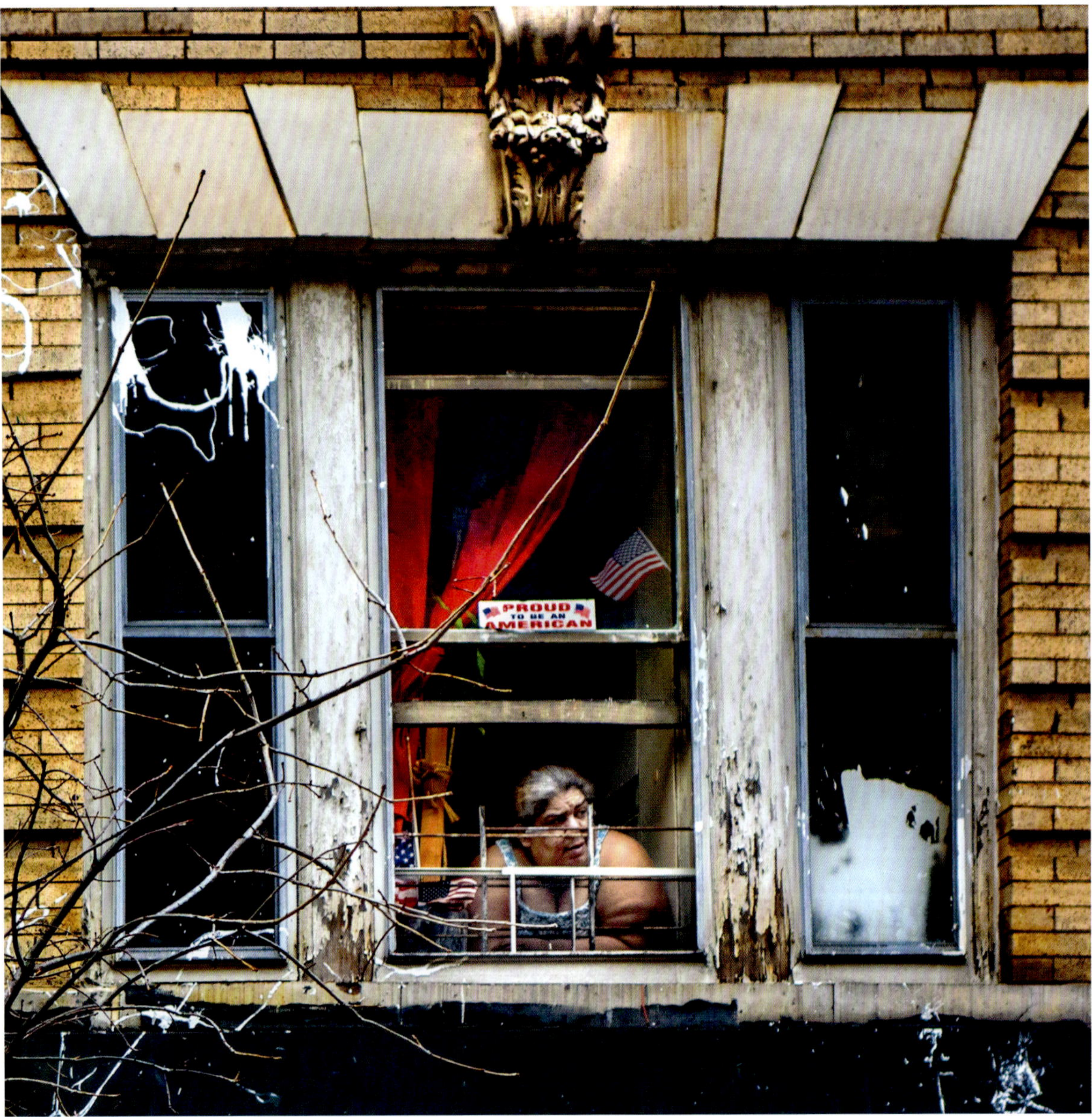

PROUD TO BE AN AMERICAN (WOMAN IN WINDOW)

This woman works at the laundromat underneath her window. She sits at that window in the warm weather, and surveys her corner of the block. As the area gentrifies, and working class people can no longer find jobs and can't afford the rent, this type of image is getting harder and harder to find. As these people die or move away in search of a sustainable life, we lose our witnesses. In the end, all we will have to tell the stories will be our photographs.

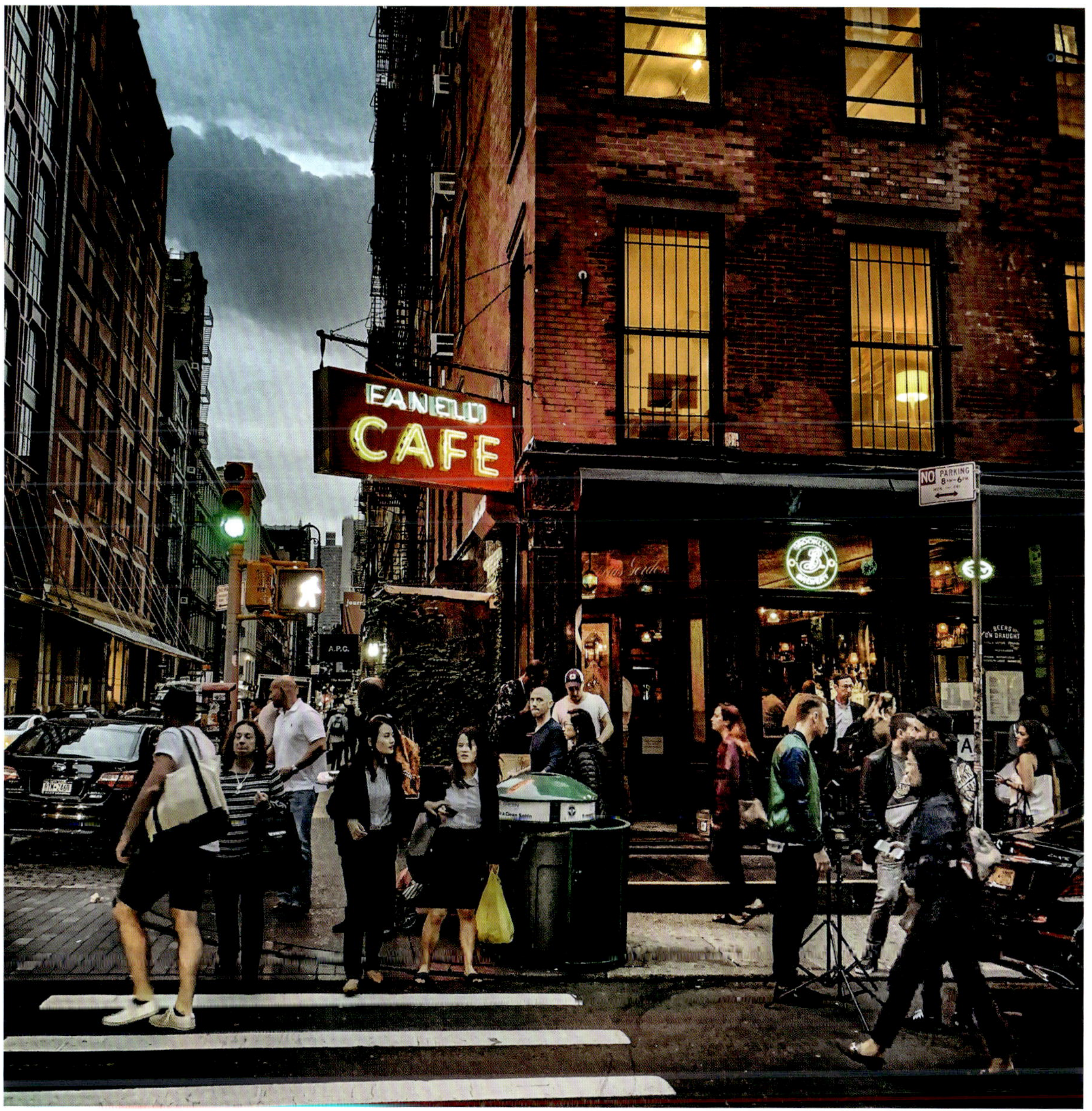

FANELLI CAFE

I bike past Fanelli's several times a week, sometimes a few times in one day. It's one of the few remaining watering holes in Soho. Back in the day, it was mostly a hangout for local artists when Soho was all art galleries and giant artist's lofts. Depending on the time of day, there can be a single person in the upstairs window or a mob scene on the street, but there's almost always a good photo to be had. I love the sign at dusk when the neon starts to glow.

Q

+

A

How has your background as a painter affected your approach to street photography?

I graduated from college with a painting major and a photography minor. Painting taught me how to problem-solve on a finite 2D space. I studied light, and then learned how to communicate darkness and light on that same flat piece of canvas. I struggled with all this, and so much more, before I even began to find my emotional voice. The same challenges are inherent with photography. Painting and photography are two very different ways to explain yourself, yet there are surprising similarities, most importantly with "the square." Whether it's vertical or horizontal, we only have a finite space to say what's on our mind. By the time I put down my brushes and picked up my camera full time, I had already spent 25 years learning how to explain myself inside a rectangle. At this point, I "see" in terms of that rectangle crop. Five college years of rigorous color theory never left me, adding yet another context to all my visual decision-making. I do shoot in black and white sometimes, but ultimately I will favor the image in color. For me, everything I learned about painting applies in equal measure to taking photographs.

How do you go from observing and recording with a camera, to developing a "voice" or style?

These days we stand on the river bank as a tsunami of images races past us all day long. Styles are copied and repeated by millions of photographers. The search for authentic style and a visual voice that is compelling should be the frame of reference for our artistic undertakings. That said, there is absolutely a time and place in our learning curve to copy heroes. We must understand and value who came before us, otherwise our work will be thin and likely short-lived. So we analyze. We copy. We try to emulate. Eventually we learn how they gave us the work we love, and we practice. We learn to shoot as they shot. Then we must move on and continue the search for our own voice. If you are paying attention, you will hear it when it speaks. We shoot every day, all the time; we accept offers to shoot weird things, weird people, or strange events. We go for walks wherever we live, and shoot, shoot, shoot. We aspire to honesty, to staying as close to our emotional truth as possible when we are out there pounding the pavement. As Oscar Wilde once said, "Be yourself, everyone else is taken."

What intrigues you about the scenes you shoot, and makes you trigger the shutter?

Years of shooting and printing have taught me a few things. Just because something is cool and makes you stop walking to take a second look, doesn't necessarily mean it will be a great final image that I would let loose on the world. There is a mental checklist that I carry around in my head. At this point, it's almost unconscious, but it's there: interesting light, check; interesting person in the scene, check; some nice texture on a building, check; if no people, then some tell-tale sign that someone was there, check; maybe something nutty or out of context, check. It's important to have an emotional response to what I'm photographing, but hopefully it also tells some sort of story, or implies some narrative that will strike a chord with the viewer. Maybe it's shooting someone through their apartment window having a cigarette or making breakfast, or perhaps it's an open window with no-one there, but I am arriving right in the middle of something, of someone's story. I always look up. So much life is happening on the upper floors here. As high-rises usurp the old, small, family-owned buildings, it's getting harder and harder to stumble upon these little vignettes. But when I do, that's it. I've got my shot.

You recently moved from photographing in New York to shooting in California— what was behind the change?

I have lived in the East Village for 36 years. Three years ago, I lost a very good friend to suicide, and shortly after that my dog passed away at 18½ years old. I was inconsolable and needed to see the world somewhere else. My good friends in LA had been inviting me for years, and I finally took them up on it. I wanted to get lost. I wanted to smell the ocean and photograph palm trees. It was a difficult transition at first, but it was exactly what I needed. I had to give up what worked here in NYC and start again from scratch. So much of Los Angeles has been over-shot, and the resulting photos can be so cliché. The challenge was to continue telling my story in the context of all this new visual, which was easier said than done. Ultimately I stopped thinking for a few months and just shot, everywhere I went. I have a thing for vintage cars, and I hit pay-dirt—I felt like I had died and gone to automotive heaven. You never know what you're going to discover about yourself if you keep moving.

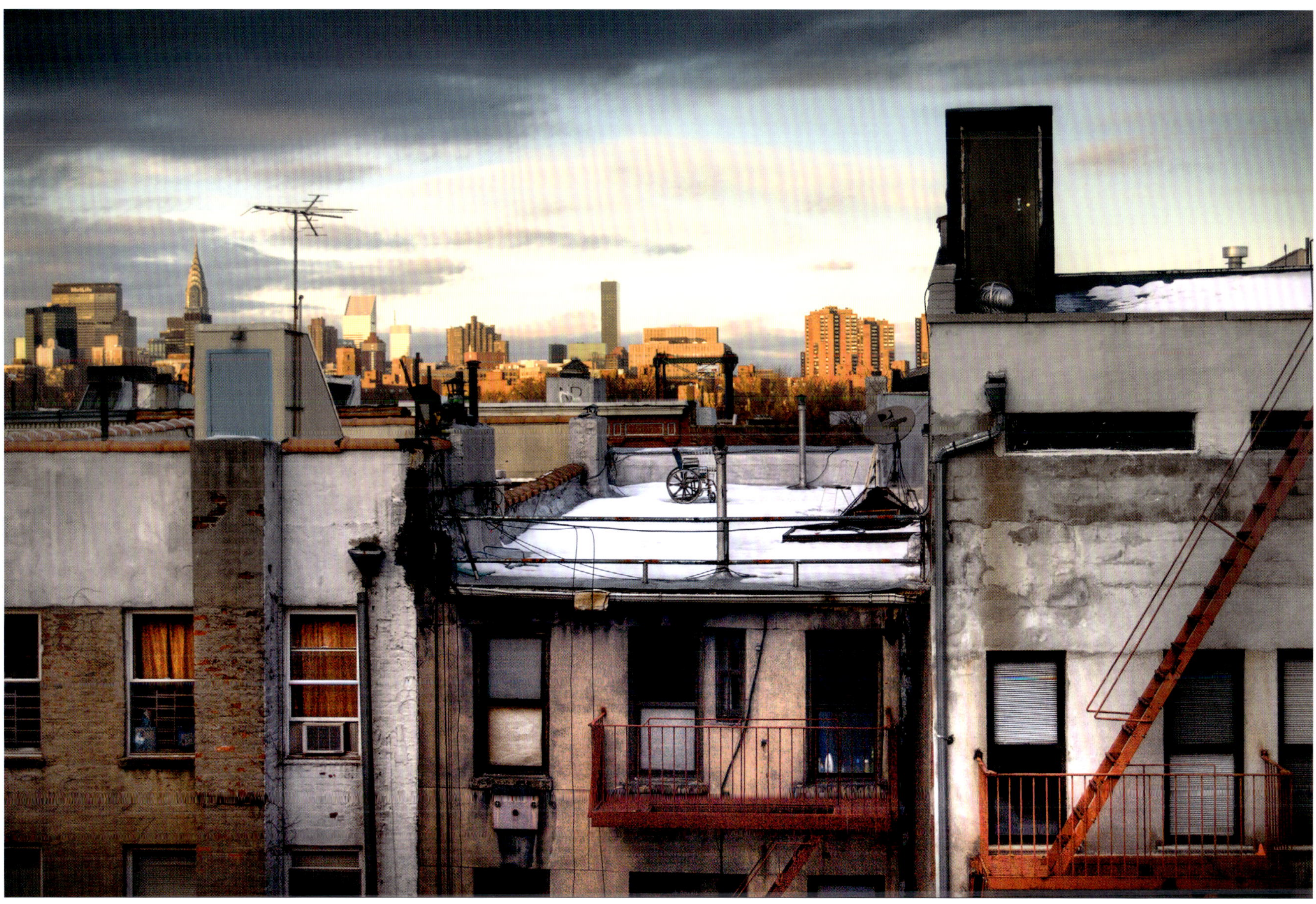

REARVIEW (WHEELCHAIR ON ROOF)

This is the view from my living room window. One summer night in 2010, there was a wild party on this roof.
Even though the police were called several times, the celebration went on until the early hours. When I woke
up the next morning, there was no sign of the previous night's debauchery, but this wheelchair was there.
That building doesn't have an elevator, so god only knows how it got up seven flights of stairs to the party.
The wheelchair stayed there for a couple of years, and then, one morning, it was gone.

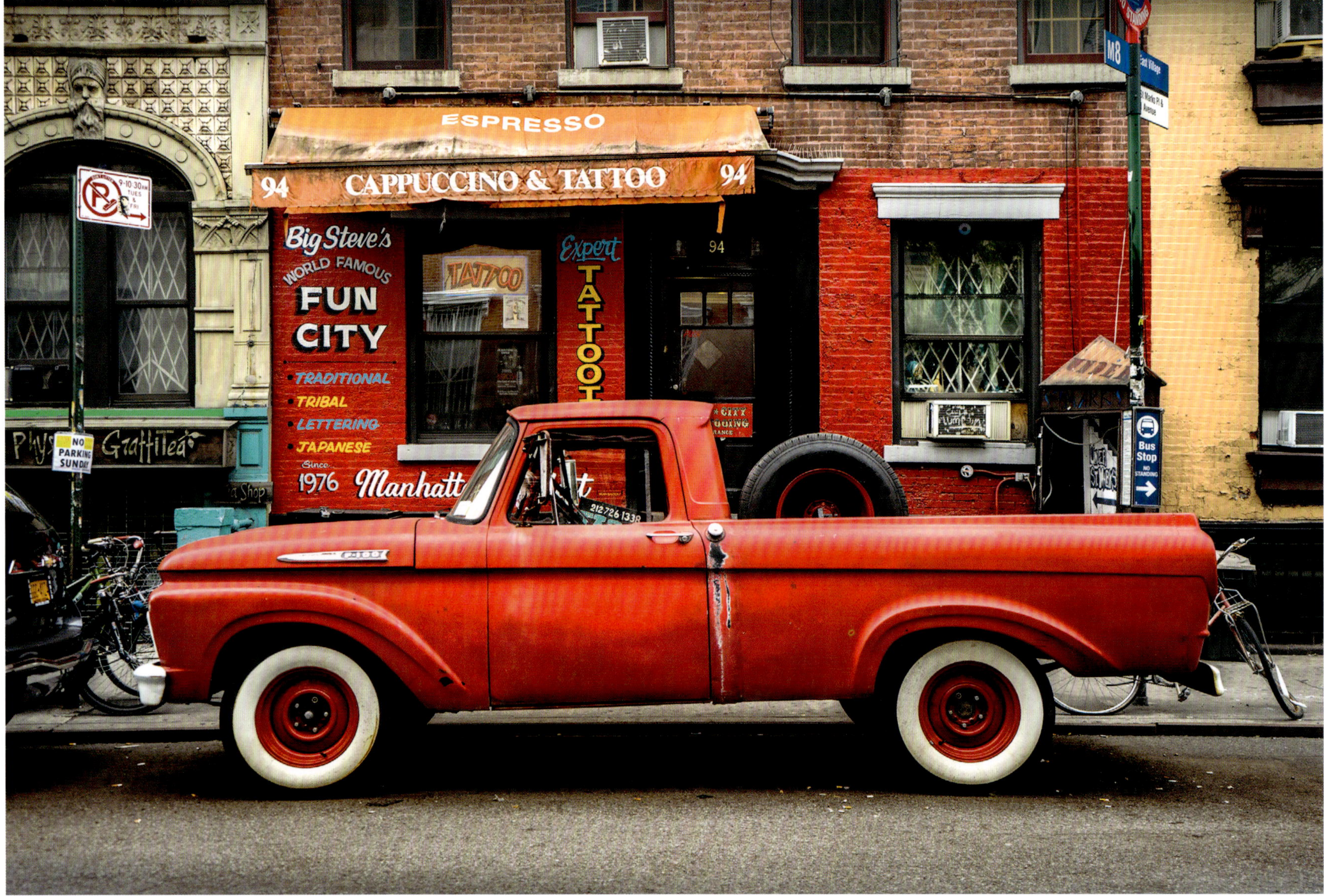

RED TRUCK

Tattoos are as common around here as a cup of coffee, but that was not always the case. Tattooing was marginalized by society and was actually banned in New York from 1961 until 1997. This shop claims to be the oldest tattoo establishment in Manhattan. Now named "Big Steve's," it has changed hands since the old days. Back in '89, it was owned by Jonathan Shaw, son of famous jazz artist Artie Shaw. Dozens of humdrum modern cars are usually parked in front of this shop, making a good photo impossible, but every now and then—if my timing is right—something remarkable appears.

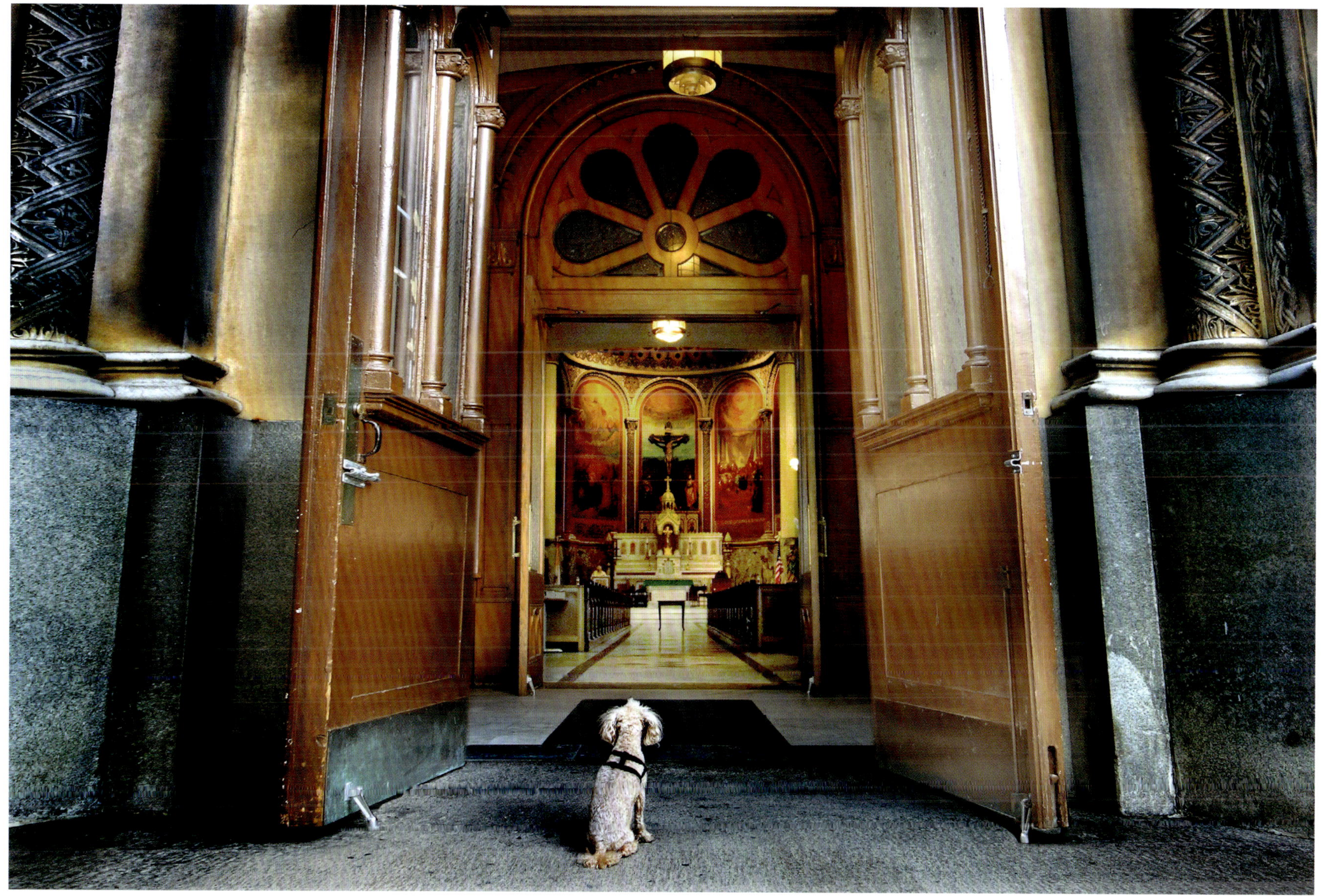

CHARLIE AT CHURCH

Early weekday mornings, you can often find this local church empty, with its doors propped open as the cleaning people go about their business. My dog Charlie was fascinated with the goings on in there, always looking intently inside as we walked past. One day, he just ran up into the doorway and sat down. I think he sat there for 20 minutes. Charlie died a few months later, and this has always felt like his memorial photograph.

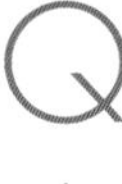

Some of your photographs could be seen as voyeuristic—do you think privacy is more of an issue in street photography now?

Yes, I agree, 100 per cent. It is the ultimate voyeuristic moment. Is there something wrong with that? I don't think so. It is impossible to live in a jam-packed urban environment and not be a voyeur. Most of my photos are taken from the street looking up or in, and you will rarely see a person's face clearly in my work. I don't think that's the point. We don't need to know who is in the frame, we just need the suggestion of a person doing something privately. There was a recent legal case here where a photographer was charged with photographing people in their apartments, through high-rise glass windows. The photographer won the case, as he should have. They were beautifully constructed images, almost like Mondrian compositions. No-one in the shot was recognizable. It is still legal here in the USA to photograph a person in a public space. A small camera or an iPhone can get you a wonderful shot, hopefully avoiding a confrontation with a camera-shy pedestrian. Other countries are not so accommodating. I was in Paris a few years ago and it is illegal now to photograph people anywhere without their permission. I imagine that has changed French street photography, as you can't publish any images of people who did not agree to having you shoot them. It makes me sad; the French have been key players in the history of street photography.

What would you say are the key elements that make a street photograph "work?"

I try to avoid overused visuals. There are too many photos of umbrellas and people walking past billboards. I, too, have been guilty of the above, but we learn as we go. Times change and we must change also. Judging a few photography contests showed me what not to do. As amazing as an umbrella shot can be, or a person with a long shadow on a cobblestone alley, there are too many of them in the world. And yes, that is the question that I ask myself every time I press the shutter: "Does the world need this photo?" Sometimes the answer is no, which pushes me to look harder.

What post-processing do you typically undertake?

If I'm shooting with a digital camera I always shoot Raw, but my post-processing work is pretty minimal. I used to do more, but now I might spend one minute on an image at most. I only use Photoshop. I learned Photoshop 20 years ago and at this point it's the fastest and most efficient means to an end for me. I also have Photoshop on my iPhone. I normally darken the entire image, and adjust the contrast a bit. The combination of those two things usually gets my image where I want it to be. Lately, I find myself desaturating and adding a small Gaussian Blur. Digital cameras sharpen to a fault. I am no longer interested in seeing the color of someone's eyes half a block away.

What inspires you to go out again and again to take photographs?

That is an existential question. I envy people who are not visually driven, but one can't "un-be" an artist. It's like wanting to be a different nationality. It is who I am and I suspect it's in my DNA. When I was five, I was building chandeliers out of plastic flowers I found in the garbage; at six, I was re-arranging my bedroom furniture trying to solve the "spatial dilemma." Artists are challenged by life, in ways other people are not. Andy Warhol once gave me this advice: decide what you want to do, and spend every day getting really, really good at it. Don't give up when the world is focused on something else. Eventually what you are mastering will be in vogue, and by then you will be the best at it. I never forgot that and I think it's true, at least as true as any advice can be. I have no Plan B, so this is what I do every day.

"Andy Warhol once gave me this advice: decide what you want to do, and spend every day getting really, really good at it. Don't give up when the world is focused on something else."

TECHNICAL INFORMATION

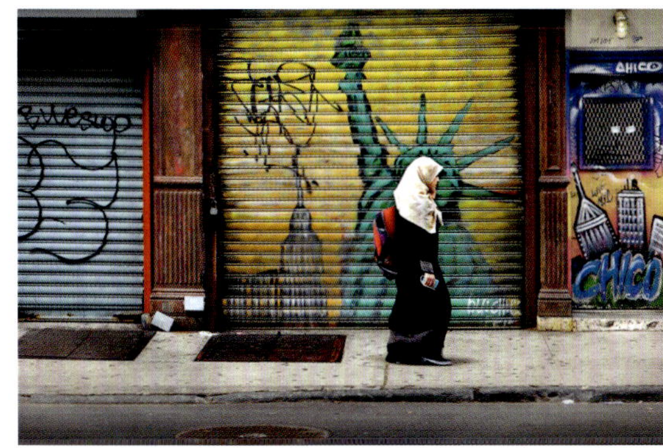

AVENUE B LIBERTY
AVENUE B, EAST VILLAGE,
NEW YORK,
USA

Camera: Sony RX100
Lens/Focal length: Zeiss 10.4–37.1mm f/1.8 at 23mm (35mm equivalent: 62mm)
Aperture: f/5
Shutter speed: 1/100 sec.
ISO: 125

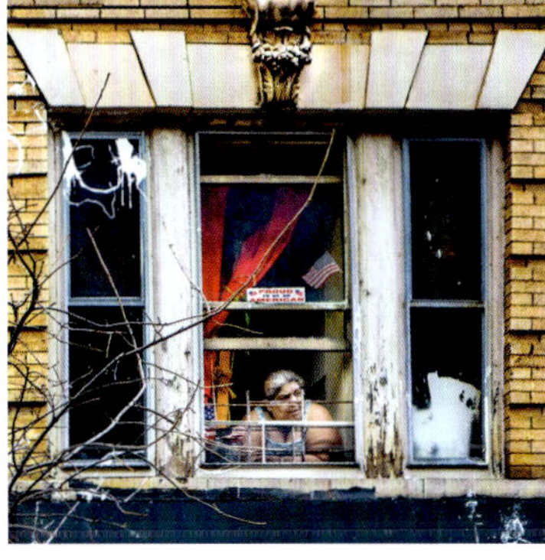

PROUD TO BE AN AMERICAN
(WOMAN IN WINDOW)
EAST 10TH STREET, EAST VILLAGE,
NEW YORK, USA

Camera: Sony RX100
Lens/Focal length: Zeiss 10.4–37.1mm f/1.8 at 25mm (35mm equivalent: 67mm)
Aperture: f/4
Shutter speed: 1/160 sec.
ISO: 320

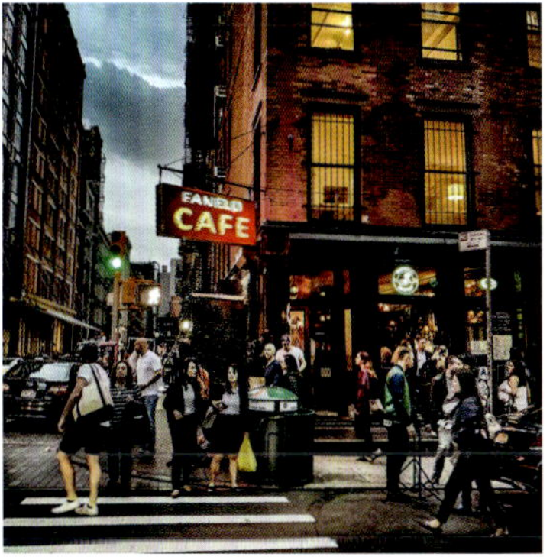

FANELLI CAFE
PRINCE STREET, SOHO,
NEW YORK,
USA

Camera: iPhone X
Lens/Focal length: iPhone 8+ 3.99mm f/1.8 (35mm equivalent: 28mm)
Aperture: f/4
Shutter speed: 1/160 sec.
ISO: 320

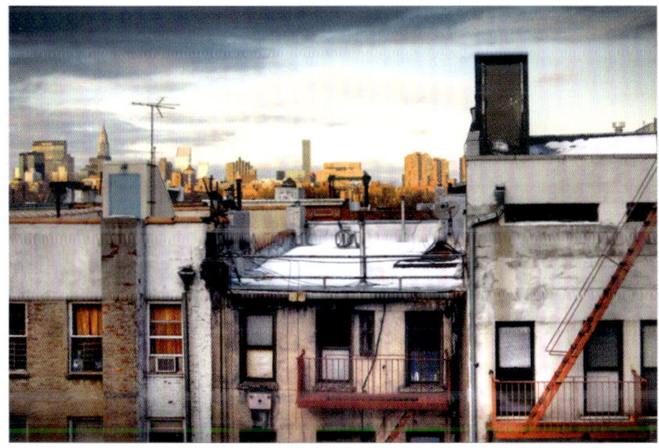

REARVIEW (WHEELCHAIR ON ROOF)
EAST VILLAGE,
NEW YORK, USA

Camera: Canon EOS 5D
Lens/Focal length: Canon EF 100mm f/2.8
Aperture: f/5
Shutter speed: 5.7 sec.
ISO: 100

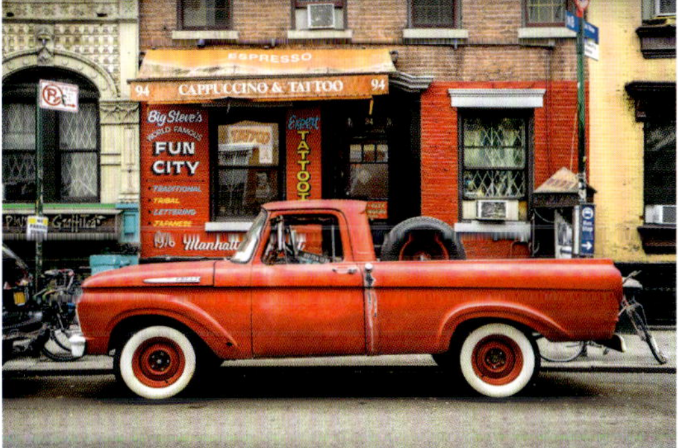

RED TRUCK
ST MARKS PLACE, EAST VILLAGE,
NEW YORK, USA

Camera: Sony a7R
Lens/Focal length: 28–70mm f/3.5–5.6 at 35mm
Aperture: f/4.5
Shutter speed: 1/160 sec.
ISO: 100

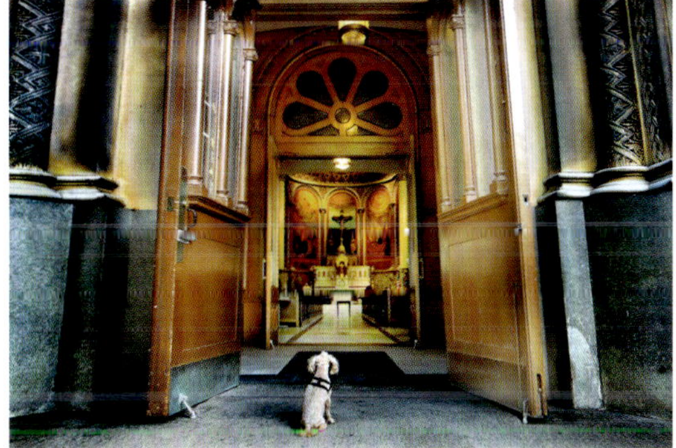

CHARLES AT CHURCH
MOST HOLY REDEEMER CHURCH, EAST 3RD
STREET, EAST VILLAGE, NEW YORK, USA

Camera: Sony RX100
Lens/Focal length: Zeiss 10.4–37.1mm f/1.8 at 23mm (35mm equivalent: 62mm)
Aperture: f/1.8
Shutter speed: 1/50 sec.
ISO: 125

GEORGE GEORGIOU

George Georgiou was born in London in 1961. He received a BA Honours in photography, film, and video arts from the Polytechnic of Central London (University of Westminster) in 1987. In 1999 he joined Panos Pictures in London and began to work exclusively on his own long-term projects. George has photographed extensively in the Balkans, Eastern Europe, and Turkey, having lived and worked in Serbia, Greece, and Istanbul from 1999 to 2009. His work from this period has been published in most of the world's major magazines and exhibited in many countries. Awards include *The British Journal of Photography* project prize 2010, two World Press Photo prizes in 2003 and 2005, and Pictures of the Year International first prize for Istanbul Bombs in 2004.

In 2010, George's book *Fault Lines/Turkey/East/West* was released and exhibited internationally. This work was included in the prestigious New Photography 2011 exhibition at the Museum of Modern Art (MoMA), in New York, USA. His book *Last Stop* was self-published in 2015. George's work is collected by several institutions and private collectors, including MoMA and the Elton John collection.

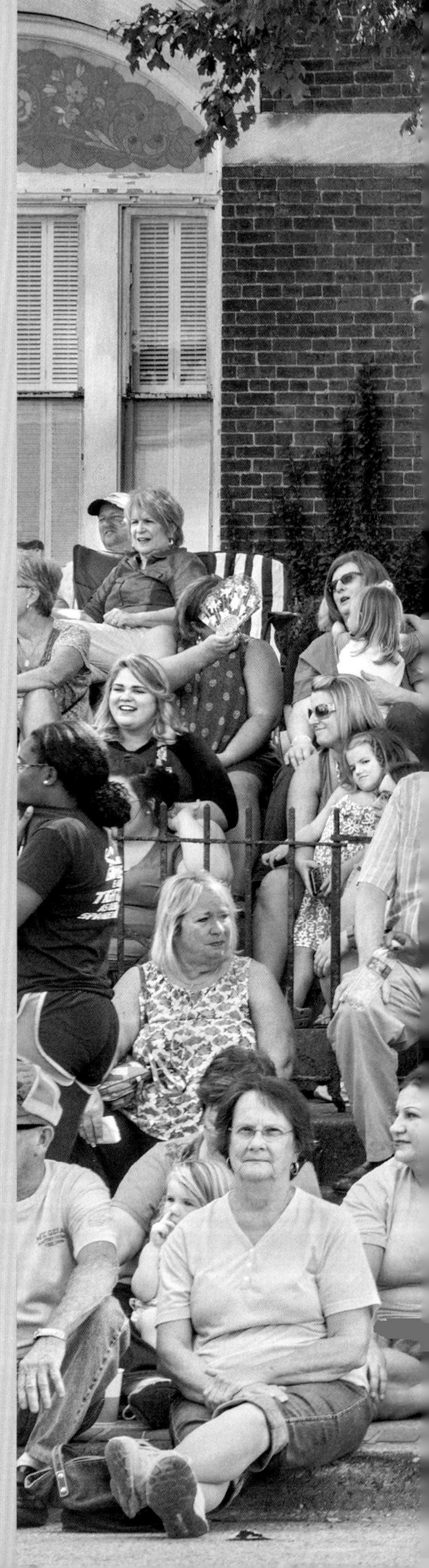

PIGASUS PARADE, LEBANON, KENTUCKY, 2016, FROM THE SERIES *AMERICANS PARADE*
This was at the Marion County Country Ham Days Pigasus Parade, in Lebanon, Kentucky. I was attracted to this event as I was curious about a parade that celebrates ham, but, more importantly, there is also a fairly big African American minority population. It was one of the most ethnically mixed parades outside New York City, and people mixed freely together.

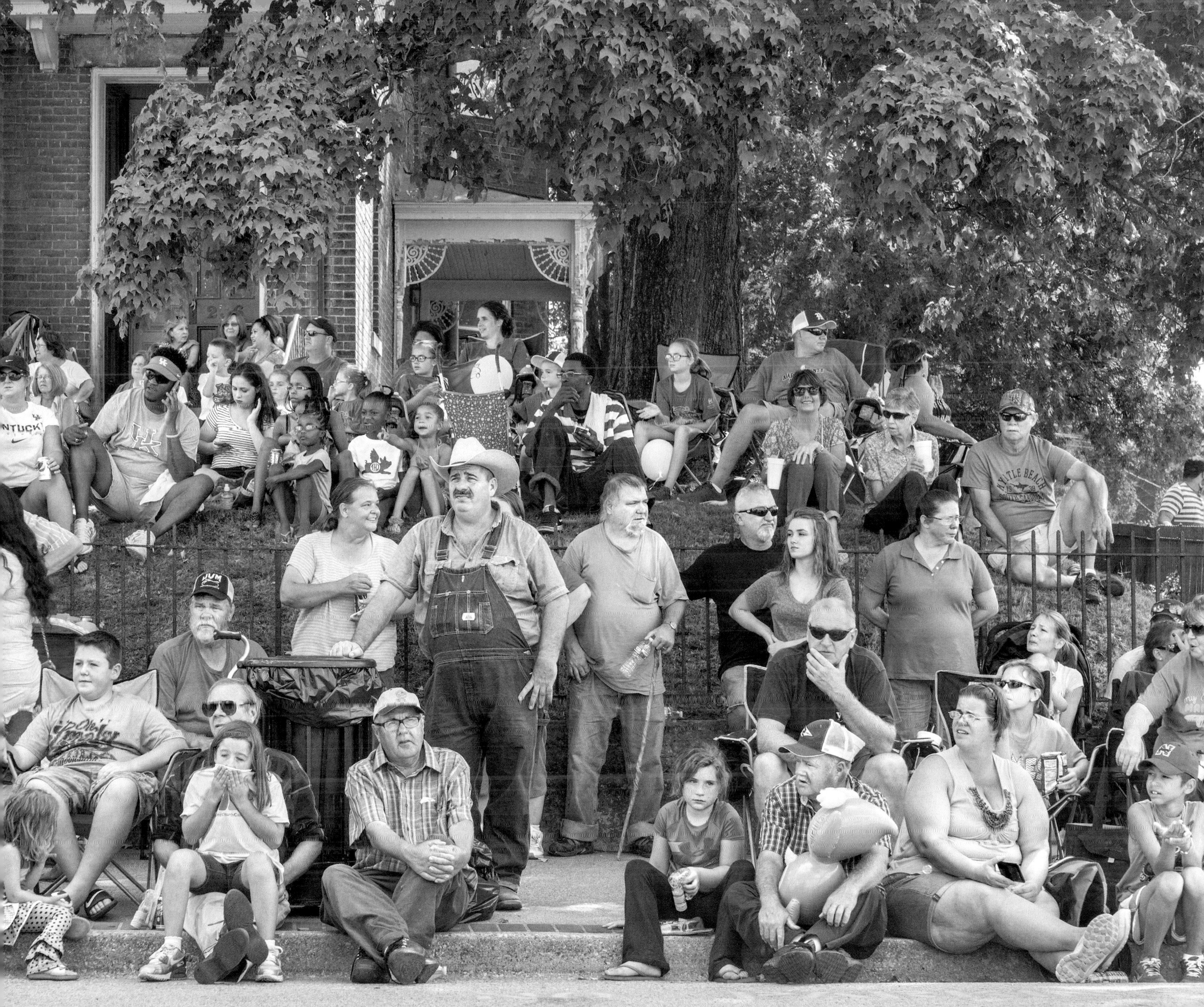

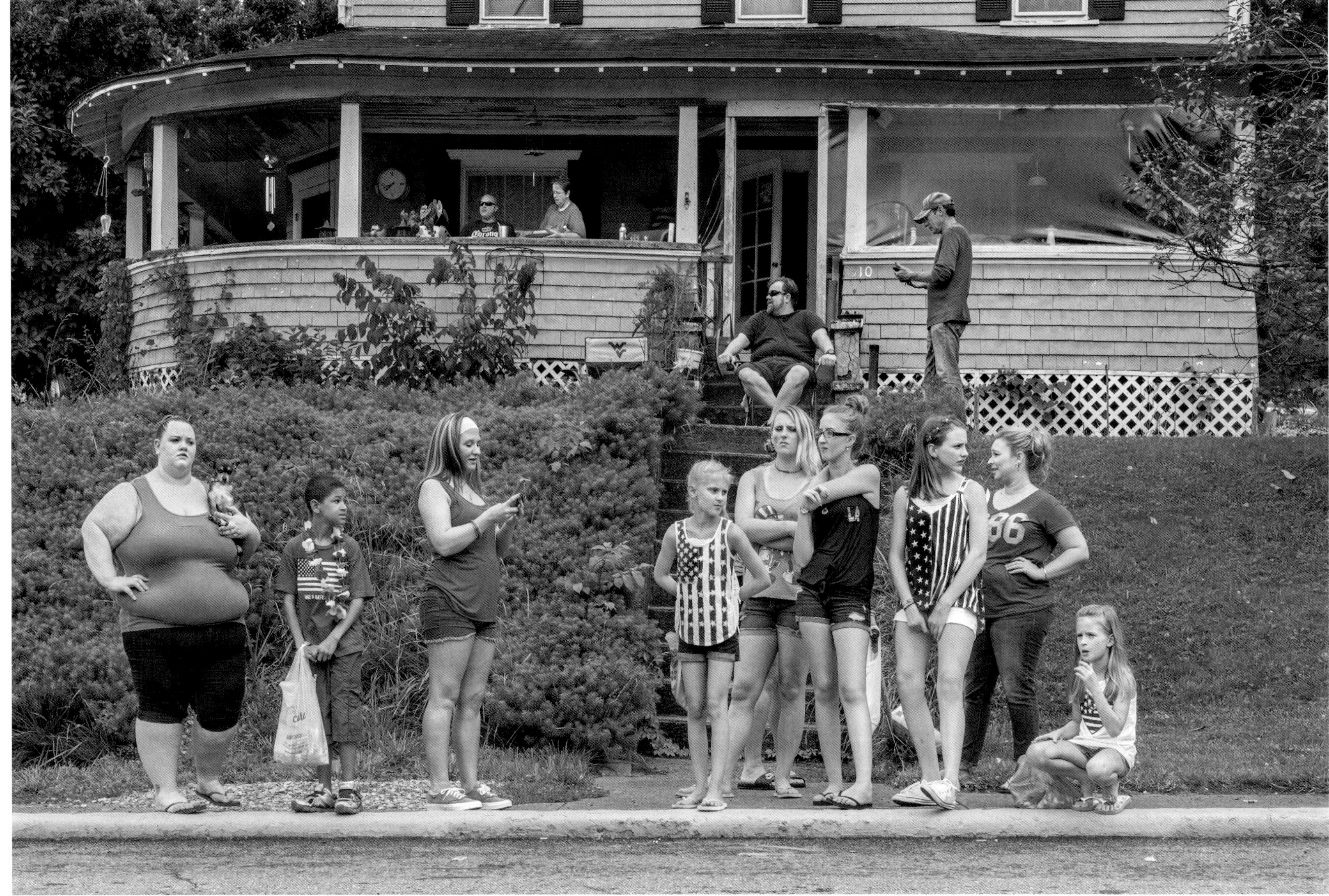

JULY 4TH PARADE, RIPLEY, WEST VIRGINIA, 2016, FROM THE SERIES *AMERICANS PARADE*

I chose Ripley in West Virginia as it prided itself as the biggest small town July 4 parade in the world, and I also wanted to represent the white working-class population from Appalachia. Appalachia is a large mountain region in the US that stretches across a number of states. This particular region has been associated with poverty over the years and the population there live in small, rural mountain towns and villages. The day before I arrived, there had been a number of flash floods in the region. All the parades in the other villages had been canceled apart from the one in Ripley.

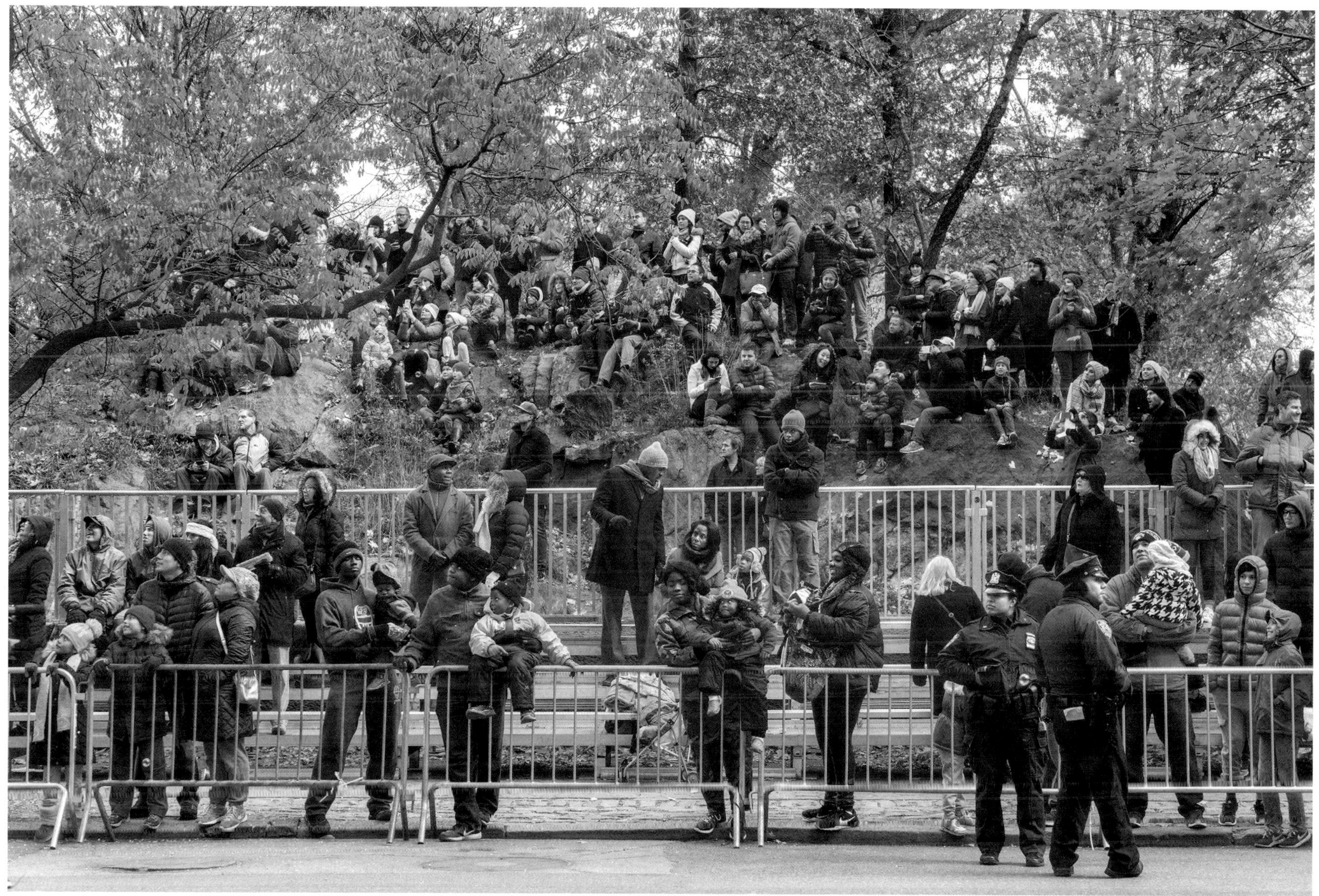

MACY'S THANKSGIVING DAY PARADE, NEW YORK CITY, NEW YORK, 2016, FROM THE
SERIES *AMERICANS PARADE*

Macy's Thanksgiving Day Parade in New York City was a wonderful parade, running alongside Central Park and
down 6th Avenue. New York is the most ethnically diverse city in the USA, with people from all social and ethnic
groups coming out for the parade. What caught my attention here was the element of self-segregation that has
taken place. Behind the first barrier, people can stand wherever they want.

**Q
+
A**

How has your style developed over the years?

After living in Serbia and Kosovo just after the NATO bombings—which had been a very intense time—I felt I couldn't continue with the reportage style I'd developed. So, when I moved to Turkey I began to question what I was saying with my images. Was I really looking at the place, or imposing my own interests and style on it? I felt that I needed to find the right graphic language. When I was shooting the book *Faultlines*, a contemporary commentary on Turkey, the country had started a new housing program, and they were building tower blocks in these amazing pastel pinks and blues, often in quite barren landscapes. I liked the idea of looking at the color in relation to the landscape. It acted as a metaphor about the conflicts and changes in Turkey, so I adapted my style of photography to help convey these issues.

How do you set about choosing a theme for one of your series?

I don't really like working in single images—I find it better to convey my take on a society using a group of images. For me, it's vital to have an idea or concept behind a body of work. My projects usually grow from previous ideas and knowledge. A lot of the time, my search for a theme is fairly organic, and it shifts and changes—the more I learn about a place or a people, the more I start to consider the important questions I want to examine in that place. And I often find that the earlier ideas I had don't really hold true any more—I begin to realize there's another story that's more important. In the case of the US parades series, I'd actually spent at least 10 months prior to that traveling around the US with my wife. All the time, I was looking—trying to understand the country. I started thinking about the role of the road in the US—how it's shaped the society, what it does to community, how it segregates economic and racial groups, how it separates shopping districts from residential areas, and so on. Sometimes in the US, you see so few people wandering the streets, so you only really know a place by reputation. One day, we were in Louisiana in Lafayette, and there was a parade on—all of a sudden, the whole community had come out, and society became visible. There were these family groups coming out and enjoying themselves. And I knew exactly how I wanted to portray the themes.

Why did you choose the style of shot for your series In the Company of Strangers, *including reverting to black and white?*

I'm a big fan of old photography—I've collected some old group photographs from the 1900s, and I was wondering how you make a modern-day group portrait, showing a whole community. There was a time when it was easier to get everybody in a town or village out to stand together, but now it's kind of impossible. I saw the parade images as modern group portraits— this is how we are today, we might all be standing together in that image, but everyone's in their own world, all reacting as individuals, with different animations. I knew instinctively how I wanted to shoot the parades—frontal, in landscape format—and I knew I wanted to do it in black and white, like old family or group portraits. I also knew I was going to include a lot of the faces and gestures of people, which was the most important part. Color would have distracted from these details.

What techniques did you use to photograph the parades?

Quite often, I would walk along the route of the procession, following the parade all the way to the end, then I would walk to the back, and then all the way back to the front again. This was quite an interesting technique, because I would often capture the same groups of people two or three times—from the start to the end of the parade, three hours later—and the groupings and gestures would change during that time. Almost all of the images in the project were shot using 50mm and 70mm lenses—I was standing back, almost across the road from the subjects. In some places, because the roads were quite wide, I had to go a bit closer, but I tried to keep a certain distance from people, to help frame the sort of group portraits I was interested in. I did take a lot of pictures at closer range, but I never used them because they changed the dynamic of what I was trying to do.

MARTIN LUTHER KING DAY PARADE, LOS ANGELES, CALIFORNIA, 2016, FROM THE SERIES *AMERICANS PARADE*

This is where the whole project started—a Martin Luther King Day parade in Los Angeles. The parade takes place in an African American neighborhood in South LA. The vast majority of people who came out were African Americans, along with a few Hispanic people who live in the area. I was again surprised how few white people attended—I don't think I saw more than 30 white faces the whole time. I particularly like this image as the trees firmly place this in LA. The landscape was of great importance for me in this work.

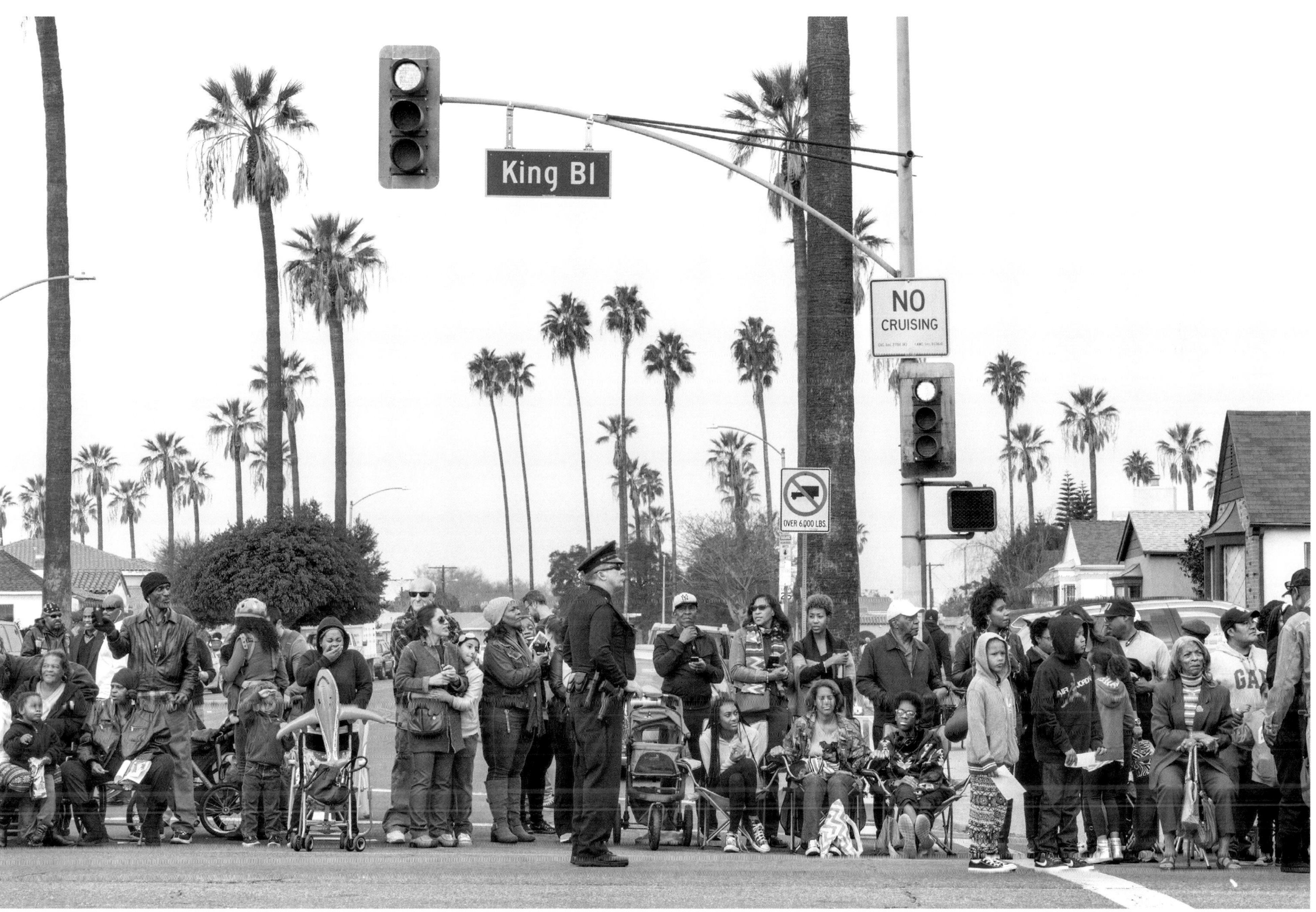
King Bl
NO
CRUISING
OVER 6,000 LBS

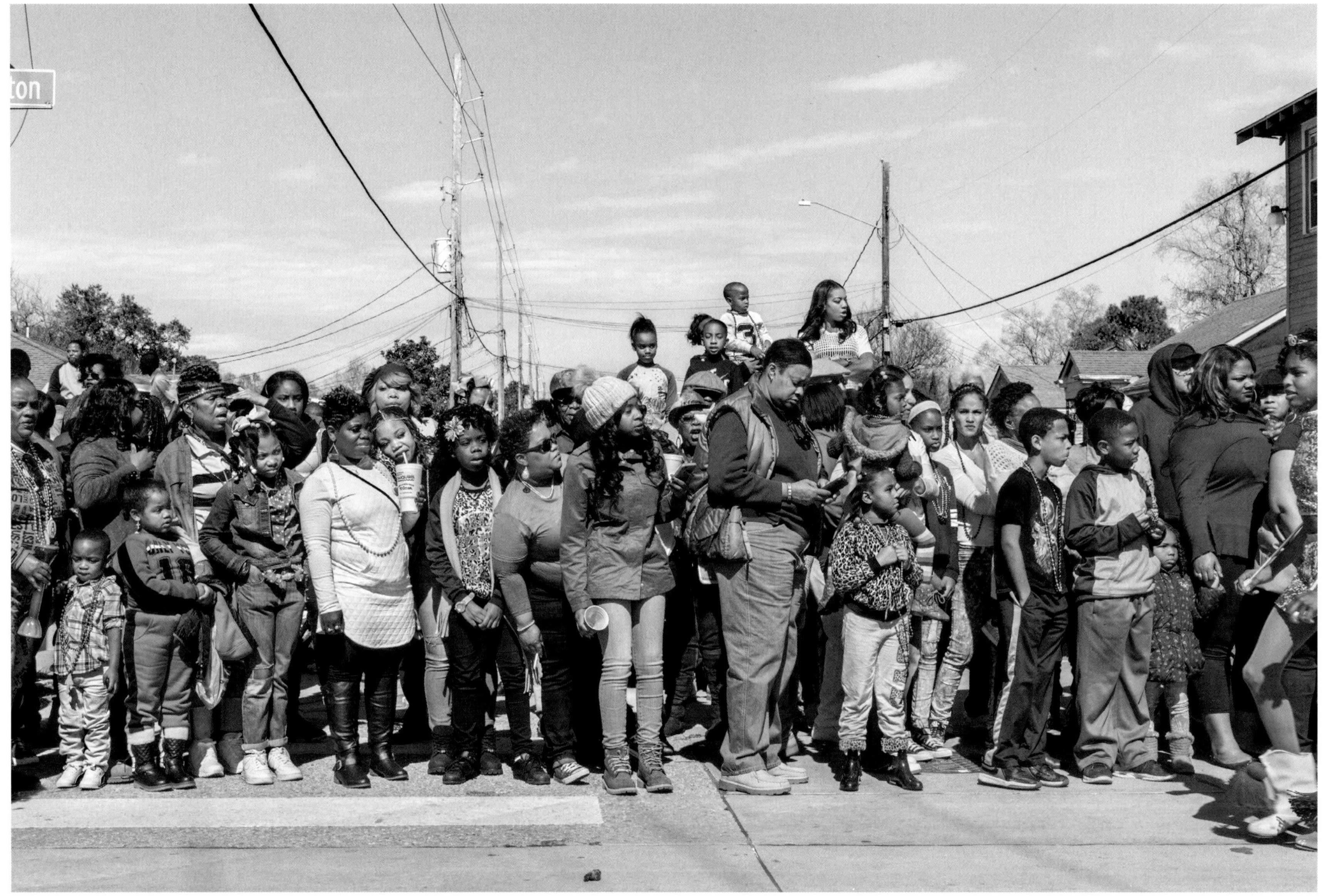

MARDI GRAS PARADE, NEW ORLEANS, LOUISIANA, 2016, FROM THE SERIES *AMERICANS PARADE*

This photograph was taken in the morning in Algiers, an African American neighborhood of New Orleans that is known as the birthplace of jazz. It is the only neighborhood on the west bank of the river, and has a high poverty rate. The parade consists of African American Krewes who dress up for Mardi Gras in suits influenced by Native American ceremonial clothes. It's a famous parade, but I was surprised by the lack of white faces in the crowd.

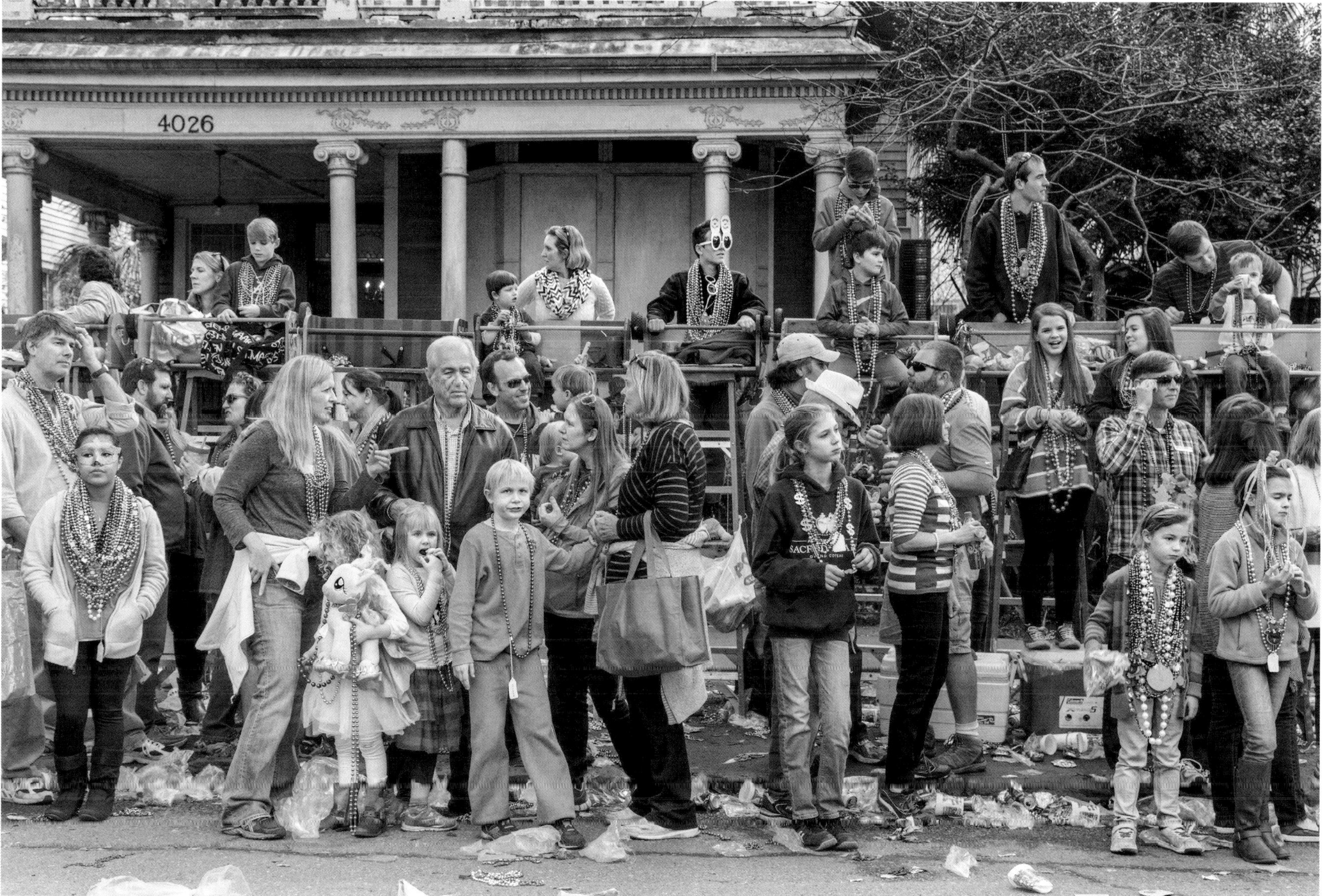

MARDI GRAS PARADE, NEW ORLEANS, LOUISIANA, 2016, FROM THE SERIES *AMERICANS PARADE*

Taken on the same day as the photograph from Algiers, this is a middle class white neighborhood in New Orleans. Many people set up stepladders with a seat on the top and leave them out for the duration of Mardi Gras. During the parade, thousands of beads are thrown from the floats.

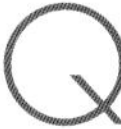

Q + A

Is it important that your photography conveys a message or meaning?

I've always had a very strong interest in social questions. When I was working in reportage, I started to find that method of working was a little bit limiting, because you're maybe honing in too much, and making a judgment on something. You also need to dramatize the scene in your images, because that's the way news works. I now prefer to use my images to raise issues and questions that I find interesting. For instance, when I was considering the parades project, it was the beginning of the Trump run for presidency, and the commentary I was hearing in the media focused on the demographics—on how African-Americans would vote for Hillary Clinton, white working-class men would vote for Trump, and so on. So, there was this narrative of dividing the nation into groups, and you can see this when you travel across America. You see these ethnically or economically separate subgroups, and this became one of the themes that I found interesting and wanted to explore.

How has your style of photography influenced your choice of camera and technique?

I travel very light. For at least 15 years now, I've been using the LCD screens on digital cameras—I don't lift the camera to my eye. I like the rotating screens because they allow me to see more, to survey the whole scene more easily. This method is also very non-aggressive—if you're not pointing the camera directly at people, they take less notice of you, so it's not quite as intrusive. I can shoot from the waist, and I hold the camera above my head quite often, the height also helping to provide perspective. Even this technique is not so intrusive. Also, it's very useful if I don't want the subject looking directly at the camera—I can make eye contact with them, and shoot them from a different angle.

Do you consider street photography intrusive, and do you ever feel you are invading your subjects' privacy?

I don't think street photography is an invasion of privacy—people give away their privacy all the time now. But if someone doesn't want me to photograph them, then that's fine, I won't—to me there are so many other pictures out there that I can take. I'm quite happy to "miss" photographs to focus on the content—such as the interactions between people—that I want to capture. I often focus on shooting within a narrow frame—as I did during my London bus project—knowing that there would be great images just out of my reach. But I never find that frustrating because I know there will always be something that comes up.

What tips would you give to those who wish to master street photography?

You have to be comfortable with the idea of photographing people in the street—I've come across a lot of people who want to do it, but feel they're intruding. If you feel that, then it's not for you. For me, the street is a social platform for ideas—I like the social and political aspects, so I work to portray those themes. I'm not so interested in clever compositions and visual puns, which is probably the biggest trend in popular street photography today. Wherever I go, I start randomly taking street pictures, to try to understand the limits of the people—how they'll react to me. That gives me the confidence in what I can do straight away, and that helps me to find my comfort zone. Another way to approach things, to get yourself started, is to pick a subject, and follow that, and that gives you confidence gradually, and you can then build on that. I observe when I'm out on the street—I look at how people move, or stand together—I find there are clues to society in everything on the street. And when you start collecting your images together, suddenly you find you have a story.

"For me, the street is a social platform for ideas—I like the social and political aspects, so I work to portray those themes."

TECHNICAL INFORMATION

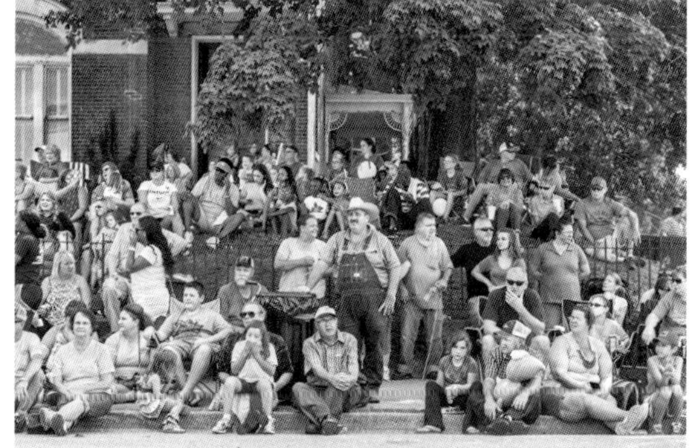

PIGASUS PARADE, 2016, FROM
THE SERIES *AMERICANS PARADE*
LEBANON, KENTUCKY, USA

Camera: Sony a7R
Lens/Focal length: Carl Zeiss 24–70mm f/4 at 70mm
Aperture: f/9
Shutter speed: 1/250 sec.
ISO: 320

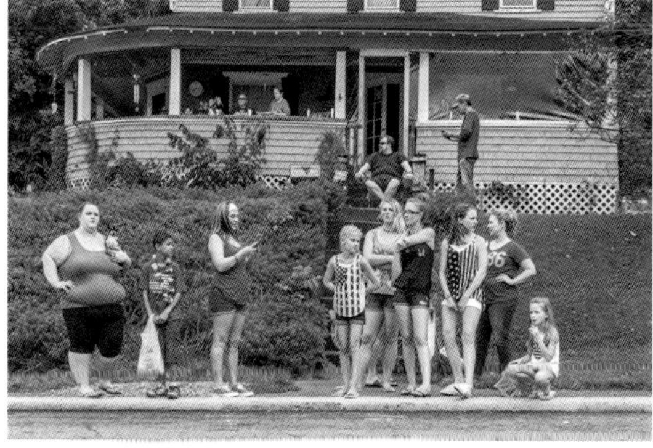

JULY 4TH PARADE, 2016, FROM
THE SERIES *AMERICANS PARADE*
RIPLEY, WEST VIRGINIA, USA

Camera: Sony a7R
Lens/Focal length: Carl Zeiss 24–70mm f/4 at 63mm
Aperture: f/11
Shutter speed: 1/320 sec.
ISO: 400

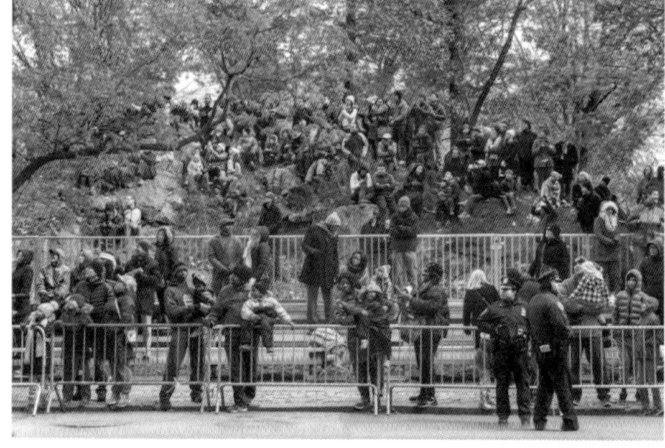

MACY'S THANKSGIVING DAY PARADE, 2016,
FROM THE SERIES *AMERICANS PARADE*
NEW YORK CITY, NEW YORK, USA

Camera: Sony a7R
Lens/Focal length: Carl Zeiss 24–70mm f/4 at 70mm
Aperture: f/6.3
Shutter speed: 1/200 sec.
ISO: 640

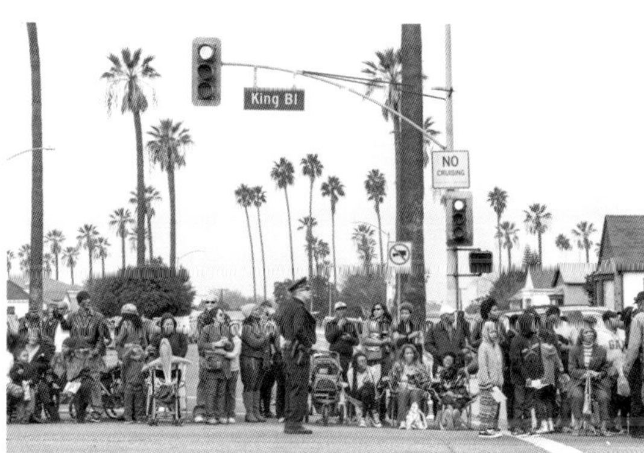

MARTIN LUTHER KING DAY PARADE, 2016,
FROM THE SERIES *AMERICANS PARADE*
LOS ANGELES, CALIFORNIA, USA

Camera: Sony a7R
Lens/Focal length: Carl Zeiss 24–70mm f/4 at 68mm
Aperture: f/13
Shutter speed: 1/320 sec.
ISO: 500

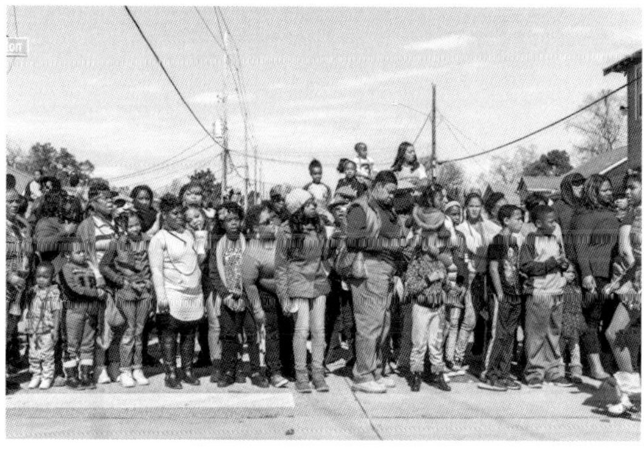

MARDI GRAS PARADE, 2016, FROM
THE SERIES *AMERICANS PARADE*
NEW ORLEANS, LOUISIANA, USA

Camera: Sony a7R
Lens/Focal length: Carl Zeiss 24–70mm f/4 at 49mm
Aperture: f/16
Shutter speed: 1/320 sec.
ISO: 250

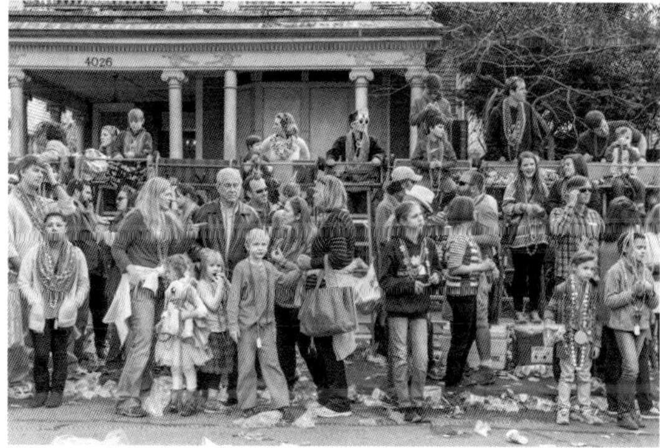

MARDI GRAS PARADE, 2016, FROM
THE SERIES *AMERICANS PARADE*
NEW ORLEANS, LOUISIANA, USA

Camera: Sony a7R
Lens/Focal length: Carl Zeiss 24–70mm f/4 at 44mm
Aperture: f/5.6
Shutter speed: 1/200 sec.
ISO: 400

ASH SHINYA KAWAOTO

Ash Shinya Kawaoto was born in 1980 in Kanagawa, Japan. He is a self-taught photographer, who started out taking portraits but soon discovered the art of street photography when he was taking pictures in the street for relaxation one day. Ever since then, Ash has been drawn to the accidental nature of street photography, and particularly to the expressions of the people he meets. Today, he specializes in shooting images of passersby on the streets of Tokyo, Japan, capturing the essence of the life of the city through the faces of the people who live and work there.

Ash is a member of the street collective VoidTokyo, which consists of 11 leading Tokyo-based photographers. The *VoidTokyo* magazine sells to 40 countries around the world. Ash's work featured in the private exhibition Scrap and Build in Tokyo, 2018. His many awards include being a finalist in the Lensculture Magnum Photography Awards 2017, and being shortlisted for the Sony World Photography Awards the same year.

UNTITLED

The elderly are as important a part of street life in Shibuya as the young people, and, for me, this image expresses this. I watched this old woman walking, but she wasn't in a place that had good light. So I waited, predicting her movement, and prepared to shoot when she entered the light. Light is very important in street photography—I always wait until my chosen subject is in the best light available before firing the shutter.

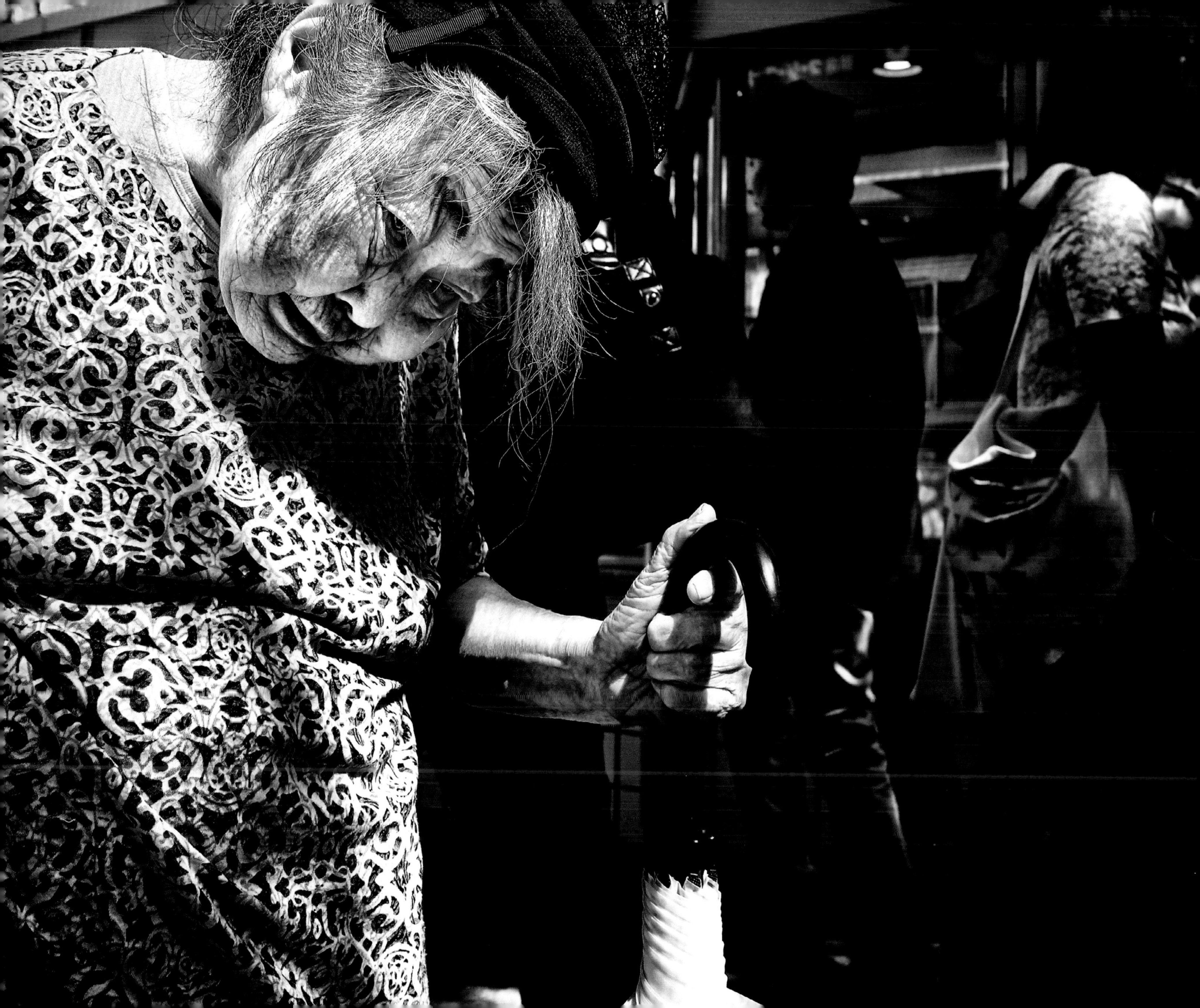

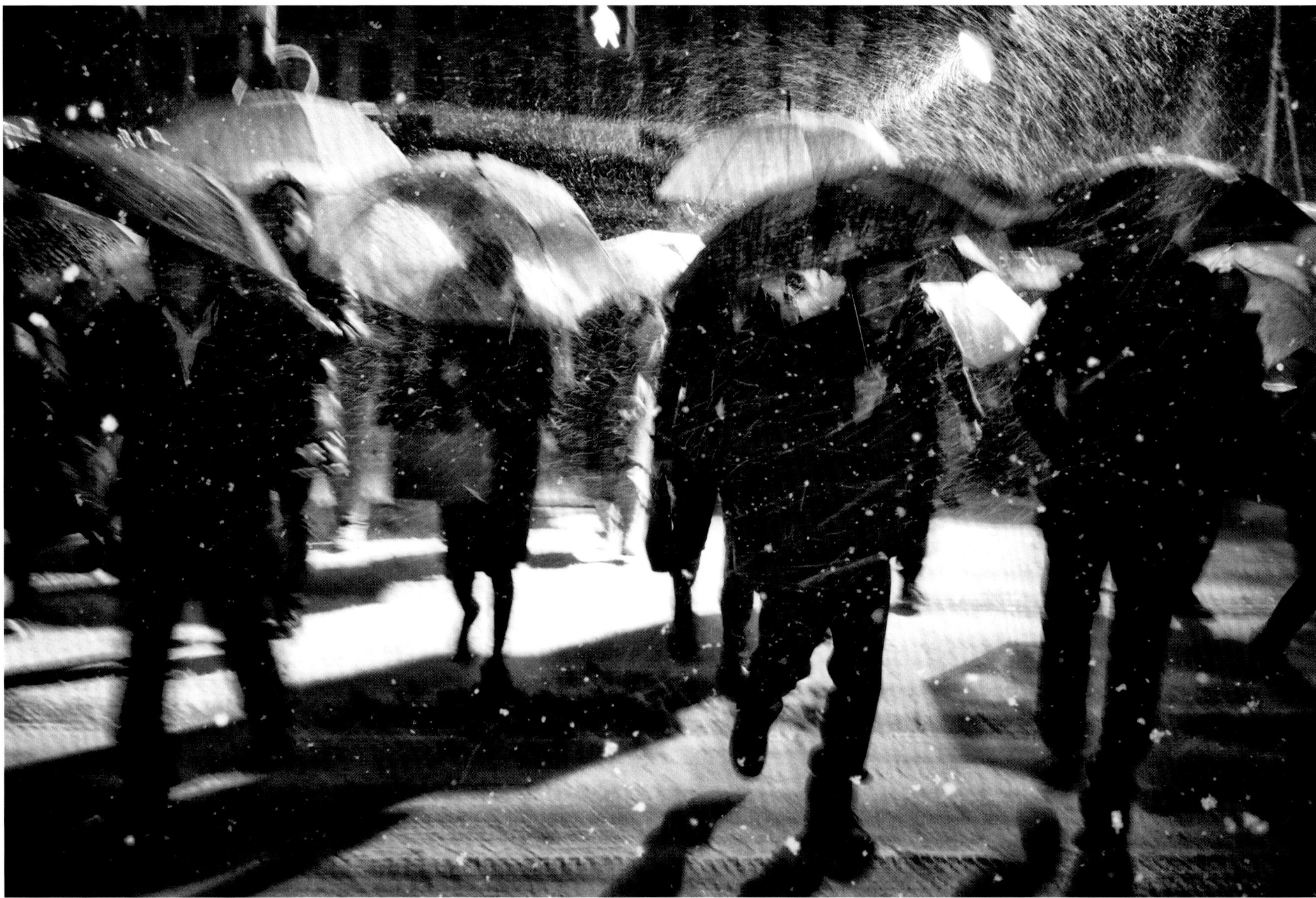

UNTITLED

I took this photograph in the evening. There was a record snowfall in Tokyo on that day, which meant
the transportation network was paralyzed. This made it hard for people to get their train home, so they
began to appear in the streets. I shot this image with a slow shutter speed using flash, enabling me to
capture the movement of the people as well as the falling snow.

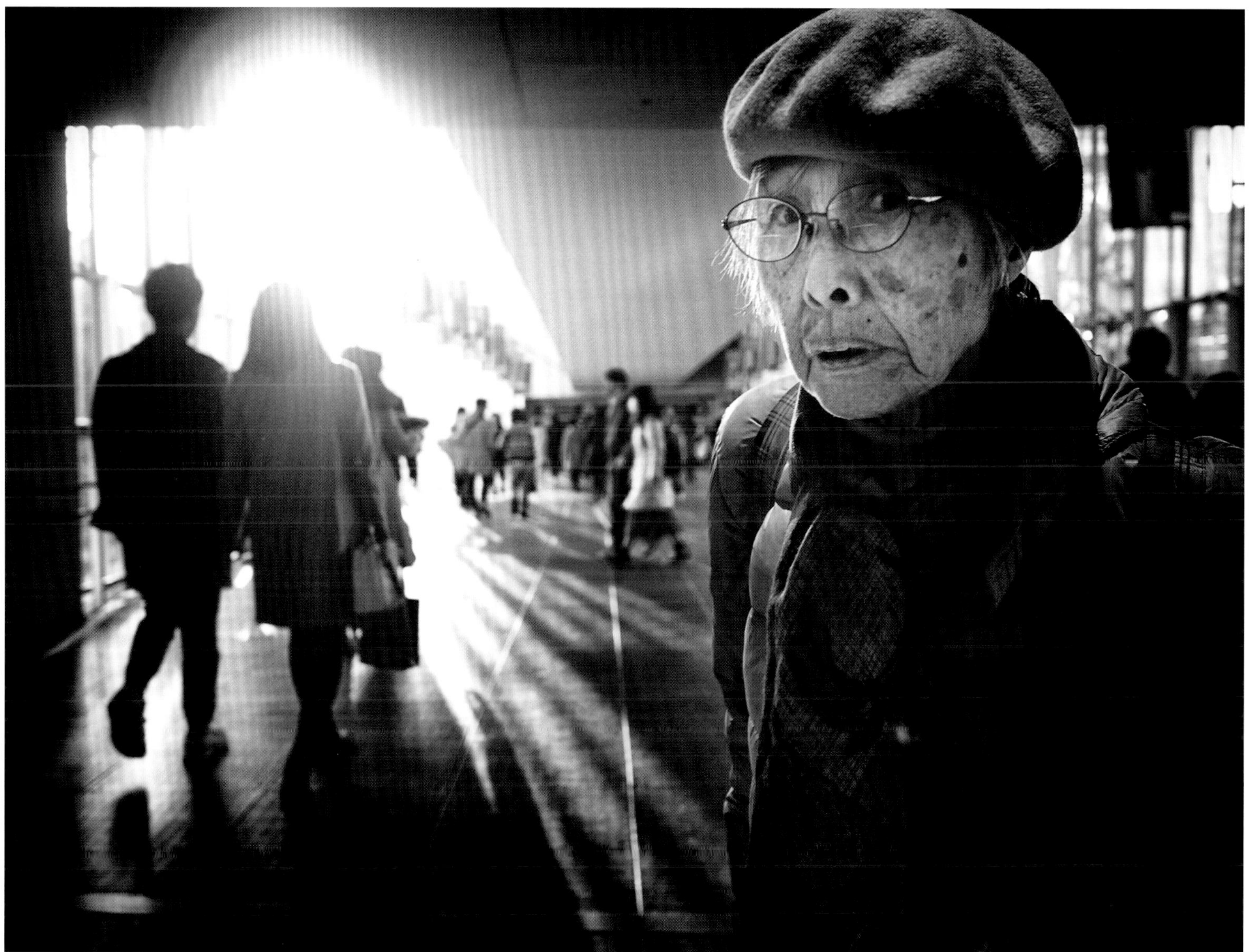

UNTITLED

It was slightly dark when I took this shot, so I chose an aperture of f/2.8 to expose correctly for the face of the subject and manually set the focus to around 0.7m (2¼ft); when the woman got close to this distance I pressed the shutter. I often photograph people moving, so tend to use a shutter speed of 1/500 sec. to prevent camera shake or too much motion blur.

Q

+

A

How did you get started in street photography, and what inspires you?

I began photography as a way of relaxing after work about six years ago—and I used to mainly shoot portraits in those days. I only took up street photography about three years ago, but I still like to capture people's expressions very much. I'm particularly interested in capturing a sense of tension or discomfort on the faces of my subjects. People's expressions change a lot depending on their environment—they are very different when they're comfortable in their own home compared to when they're in a public place. The public space—the street—is where a person comes into contact with society, and that's where I'm able to capture these expressions of tension that appeal to me so much.

Who or what has influenced your work the most?

I love William Klein's photographs, and I've learned a lot from him. I have also been heavily influenced by the portrait photographs of Diane Arbus. Her style is unique; she doesn't glorify her subjects, rather she uncovers the truth that a subject wants to cover up, removing the superficial and expressing the personal emotions of the subject using the visual beauty of her photography. I think studying Arbus's photographs has taught me what to look for when shooting street portraits. There's a great deal of chance in street photography, but I set out with the aim of expressing the personality of the street in the personality of my subjects. I want to try to capture the essence of a city in the portrait of a person.

What do you love most about shooting in the street?

You can find such a wide variety of people in the street—a foreign tourist, a businessman, a student, a youth, an elderly person, a homeless person, or a street performer, and in every one, their facial expressions betray their inner life. The street is the best place to capture the portraits of so many different kinds of people.

How does shooting in Tokyo affect your street photography?

Although I focus on capturing people's expressions, the cityscape as a background is extremely important, and it has its own character. Tokyo is a city of great change. Shooting in London is different to shooting in Tokyo—many of London's beautiful buildings are old, but they have been preserved and are still used. However, in Tokyo, historic buildings are often considered to be unimportant, and are demolished and built on—Tokyo's cityscape is always changing at a very high speed. This is even more true now, with Tokyo being the home city for the 2020 Olympics; new buildings are being constructed everywhere. This means Tokyo is changing even more quickly, maturing into a huge creature. An important part of my street photography is to capture this evolution, and the city's character, through the people who live there.

"I'm particularly interested in capturing a sense of tension or discomfort on the faces of my subjects. People's expressions change a lot depending on their environment—they are very different when they're comfortable in their own home compared to when they're in a public place."

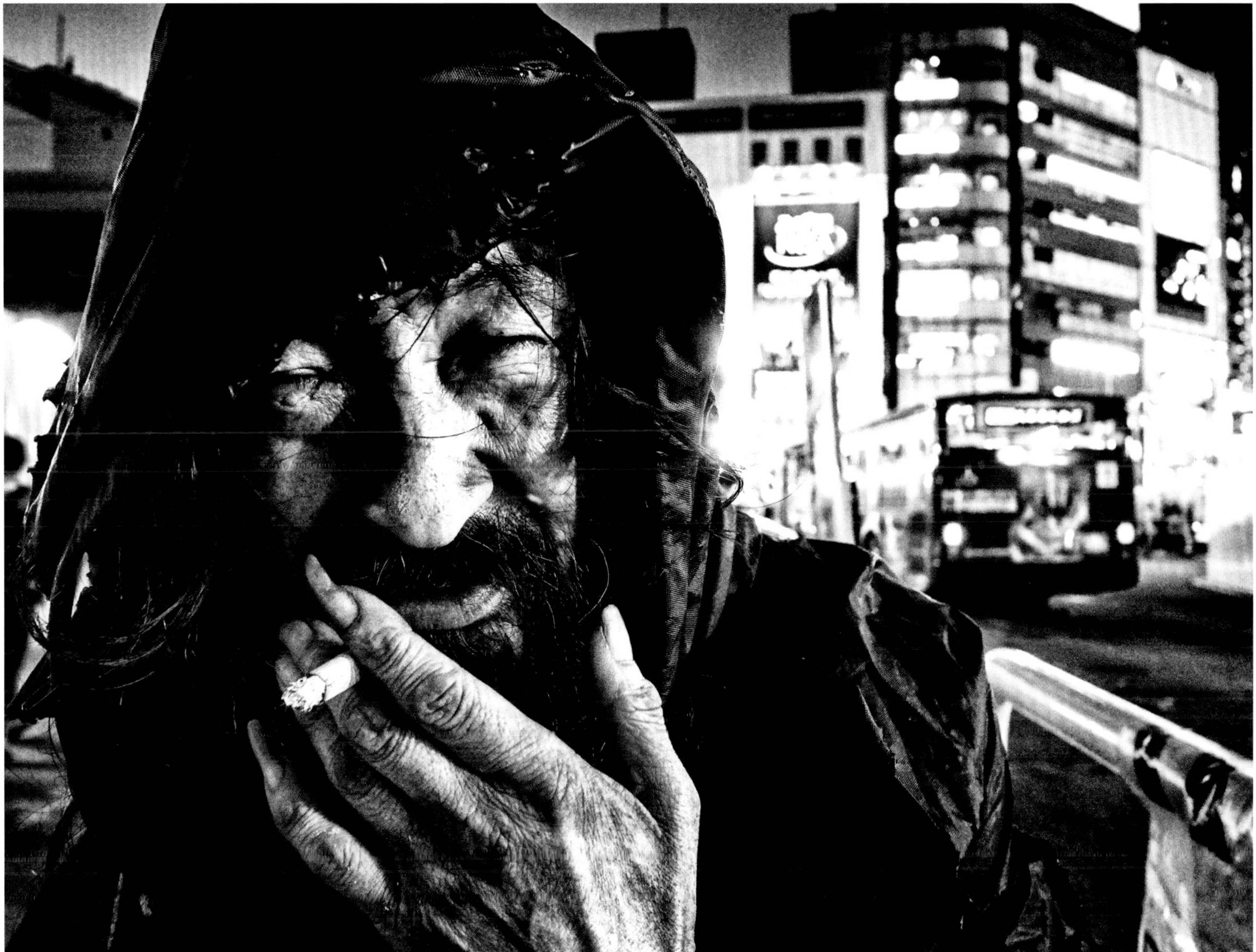

UNTITLED

This man is homeless. He used to work in sales and as a truck driver—but he lost his job, the money disappeared, and he lost his home. We had a good talk and I was able to build a relationship of mutual trust with him, winning his confidence and understanding him better. I took this photograph quickly—without warning him or asking his permission— when he started to smoke. I was able to do this because of the relationship I had built beforehand.

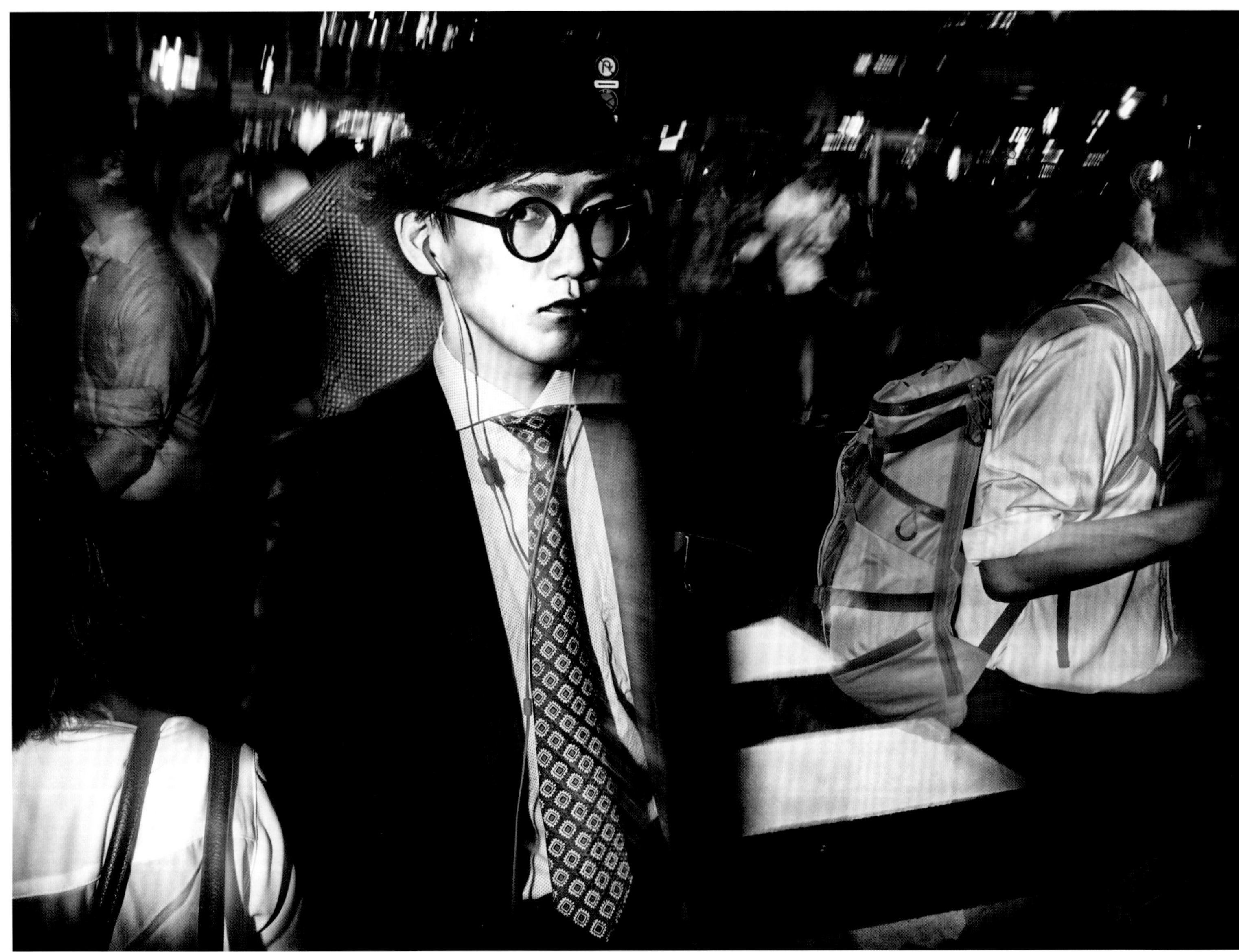

UNTITLED

For this shot, I used a remote flash in my left hand while holding the camera in my right. I angled the flash, so the light fell on the subject from the top left, creating the slight diagonal shadow. This makes the image more dramatic, and lifts the subject from the background. I do not use autofocus very often, instead setting the aperture to allow for zone focusing. Here, I manually set the focus distance to roughly 1m (3ft) beforehand, and released the shutter just as the subject came close to this distance.

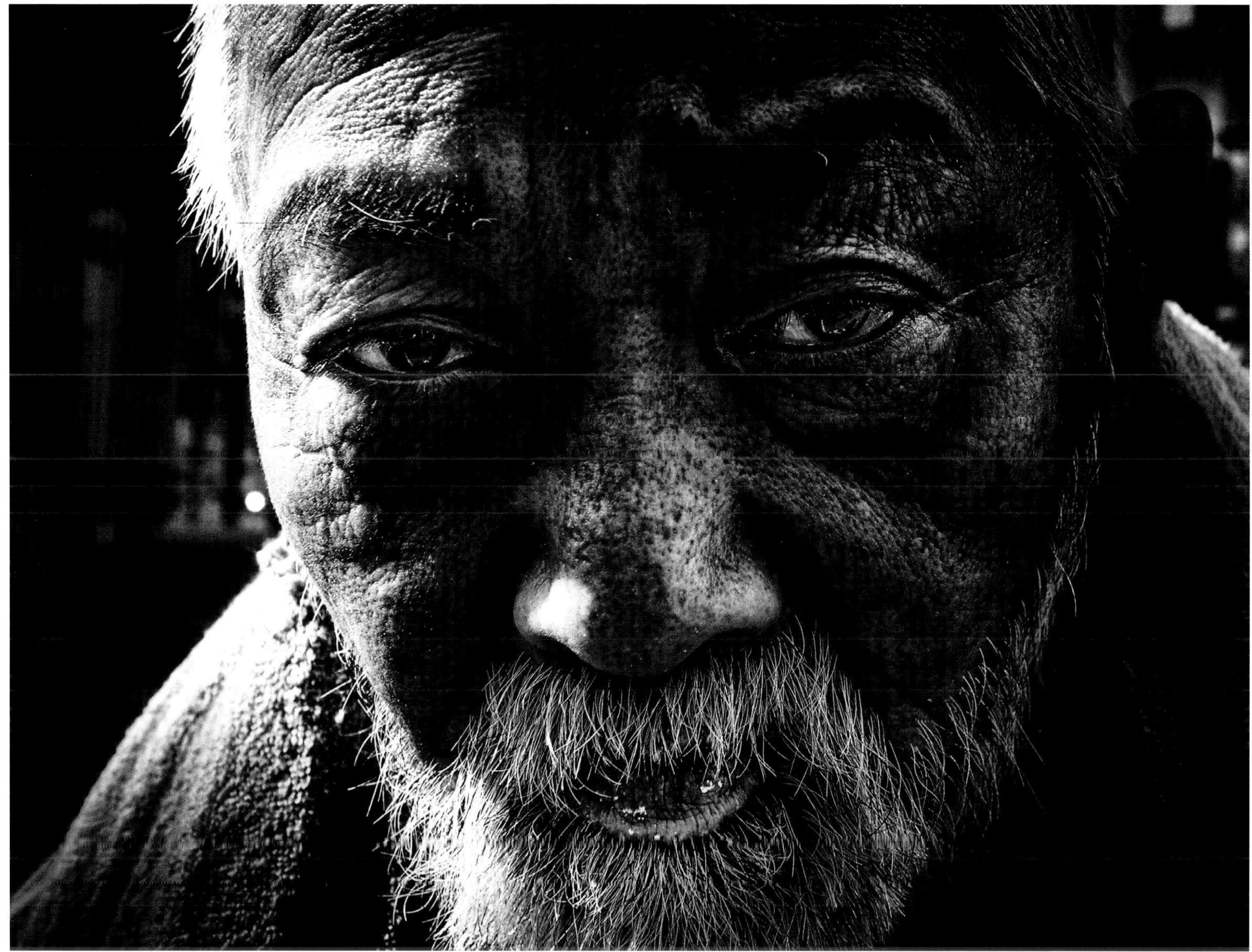

UNTITLED

This is another homeless man, although I didn't recognize him, so know he had only recently arrived in Shibuya. This time, I didn't try to engage with him, as I wanted to capture the strain on his face; talking to him would have changed this, probably making him look friendlier. I think this image captures the feeling of a homeless person who is uncertain and unfamiliar with their surroundings.

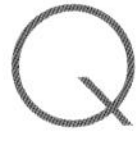

Q + A

What adjustments do you usually make to your images during post-processing?

The main software I use is Capture One, Photoshop, and the Nik collection. To start with, I fine-tune the exposure in Capture One and Photoshop, then I increase the contrast slightly using Nik software. I often set a high ISO when shooting, to create more noise in the image, and I may even increase it further using the Nik software. Adding noise gives an image texture and helps it to appear more three-dimensional. This shows even more when an image is printed.

What is the most challenging aspect of street photography?

I think being ready to capture whatever occurs when you're walking around is one of the most difficult skills to master. You need to be able to react quickly and not miss that chance. To that end, you should set out to research the best photography spots in the city by exploring every day. This means walking around a lot, looking for the best light, and then remembering where to go at each time of the day, and at each time of the year. For example, I memorize the best spots where the light is good for a particular crossing on an April morning. That means that I can plan to be there, and give myself a better chance of capturing the right subject at the right moment.

Many of your portraits are taken close to your subject—does this create any problems?

Yes, it often causes problems, but I think it is important not to be afraid of getting close. The subject's expression is the most crucial part of my photography, and to capture their expression properly I need to get really close—I deliberately invade someone's personal space. This always puts them on their guard, and creates or enhances that feeling of tension I'm looking for—and this shows on their face. I once photographed a homeless man at such a tense moment and he ran after me in anger—I often experience anger from my subjects in the street. In these cases, I always tell them that I'm a photographer, and explain carefully why I took their photograph. It is always important to remember why you are doing this, and to respect the people you are photographing.

What tips would you give to those who wish to master street photography?

I think it is important to understand your city, and that means exploring and taking lots of photographs. Always have your camera ready in your hands, so you can shoot at a moment's notice when you see something interesting—it will pass in an instant. I also recommend that you learn to shoot using manual focus—by using zone focusing you give yourself a much better chance of capturing that moment than you would using autofocus. Never be afraid to aim your camera at a stranger, but always think about why you are taking their photograph, so you can carefully explain to them why they're so important to you. Finally, always respect your subjects.

"Never be afraid to aim your camera at a stranger, but always think about why you are taking their photograph."

TECHNICAL INFORMATION

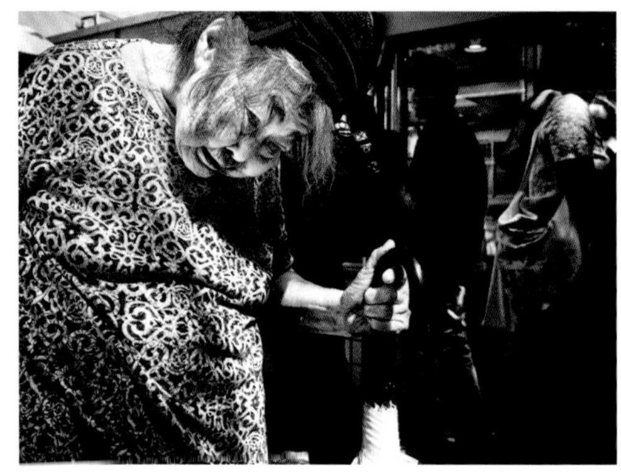

UNTITLED
SHIBUYA, TOKYO, JAPAN

Camera: Olympus PEN-F
Lens/Focal length: M.ZUIKO DIGITAL 17mm f/1.8 (35mm equivalent: 34mm)
Aperture: f/4
Shutter speed: 1/1000 sec.
ISO: 400

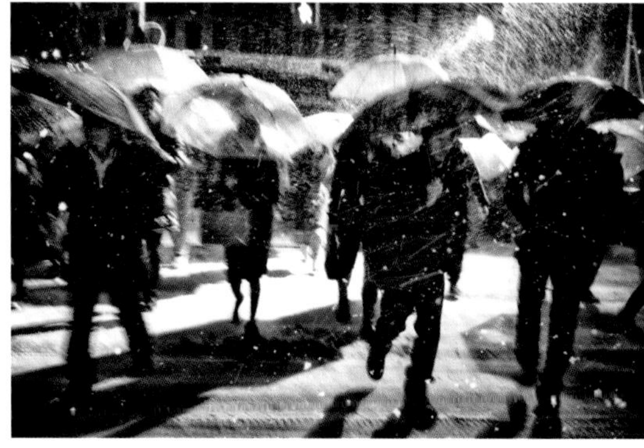

UNTITLED
SHIBUYA, TOKYO, JAPAN

Camera: Sony a9
Lens/Focal length: Zeiss Sonnar T* FE 35mm f/2.8
Aperture: f/22
Shutter speed: 1/20 sec.
ISO: 6400

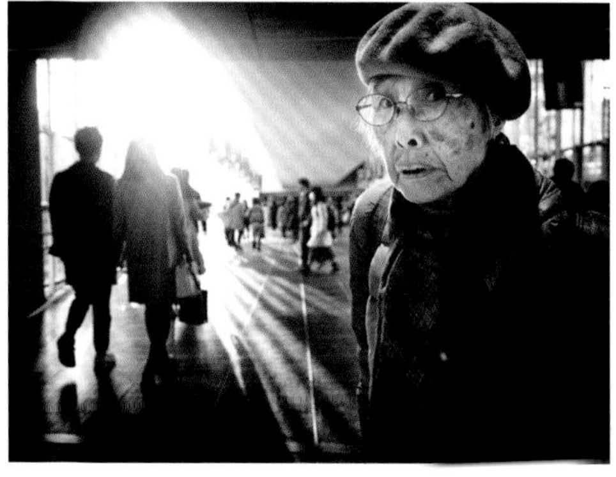

UNTITLED
SHIBUYA, TOKYO, JAPAN

Camera: Olympus PEN-F
Lens/Focal length: M.ZUIKO DIGITAL 17mm f/1.8 (35mm equivalent: 34mm)
Aperture: f/2.8
Shutter speed: 1/500 sec.
ISO: 800

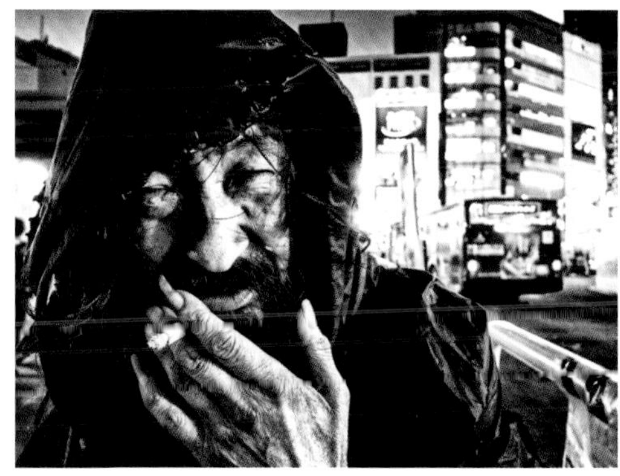

UNTITLED
SHIBUYA, TOKYO, JAPAN

Camera: Olympus PEN-F
Lens/Focal length: M.ZUIKO DIGITAL 17mm f/1.8 (35mm equivalent: 34mm)
Aperture: f/5.6
Shutter speed: 1/30 sec.
ISO: 3200

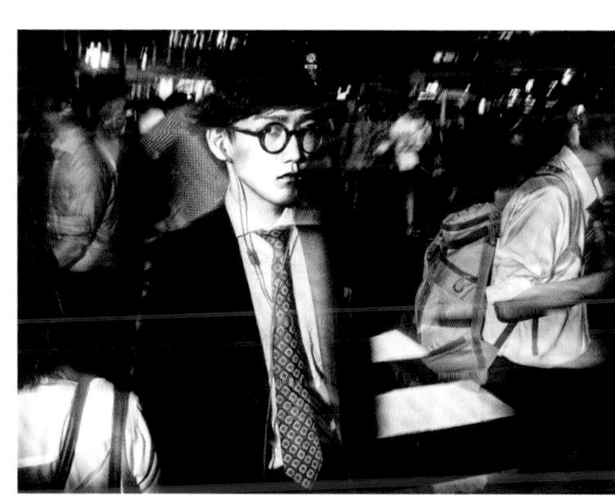

UNTITLED
SHIBUYA, TOKYO, JAPAN

Camera: Olympus PEN-F
Lens/Focal length: M.ZUIKO DIGITAL 17mm f/1.8 (35mm equivalent: 34mm)
Aperture: f/11
Shutter speed: 1/10 sec.
ISO: 1250

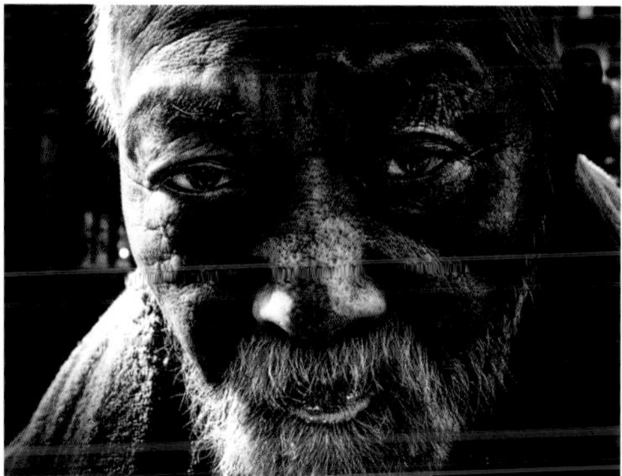

UNTITLED
SHIBUYA, TOKYO, JAPAN

Camera: Olympus PEN-F
Lens/Focal length: M.ZUIKO DIGITAL 17mm f/1.8 (35mm equivalent: 34mm)
Aperture: f/5.6
Shutter speed: 1/200 sec.
ISO: 160

JAY MAISEL

Jay Maisel studied Graphic Design with Leon Friend at Abraham Lincoln High School in Brooklyn, New York, then studied painting with Joseph Hirsch, and attended Cooper Union. He received his Bachelor of Fine Arts degree at Yale, where he studied color with Josef Albers.

While his portfolio features the likes of Marilyn Monroe and Miles Davis, Jay is perhaps best known for capturing the light, color, and gesture found in everyday life. Some of his commercial accomplishments include five *Sports Illustrated* swimsuit covers, the first two covers of *New York* magazine, the cover of Miles Davis's *Kind of Blue* (the best-selling jazz album of all time), 12 years of advertising with United Technologies, and awards from such organizations as the ICP, ASMP, ADC, PPA, and Cooper Union.

Since he stopped taking on commercial work in 1995, Jay has continued to focus on his personal work. He has developed a reputation as a giving and inspiring teacher as a result of extensive lecturing and photography workshops throughout the USA, as well as at his residence at the Germania Bank in New York City, from 2008–2015. He continues to sell prints, which can be found in numerous collections.

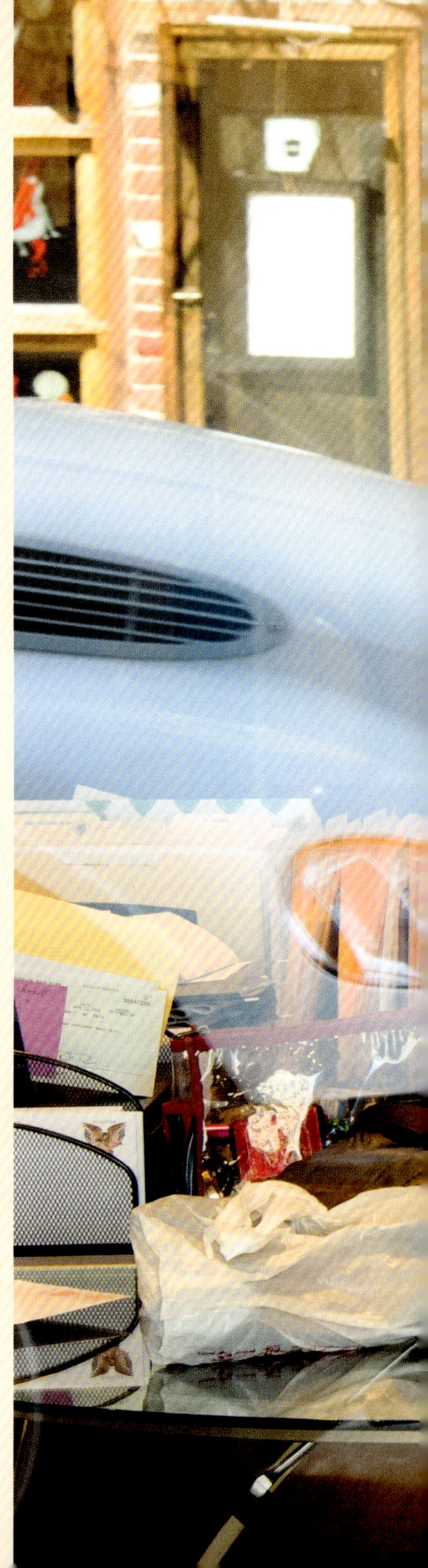

SELF PORTRAIT (2014)

Shooting a girl in a window.

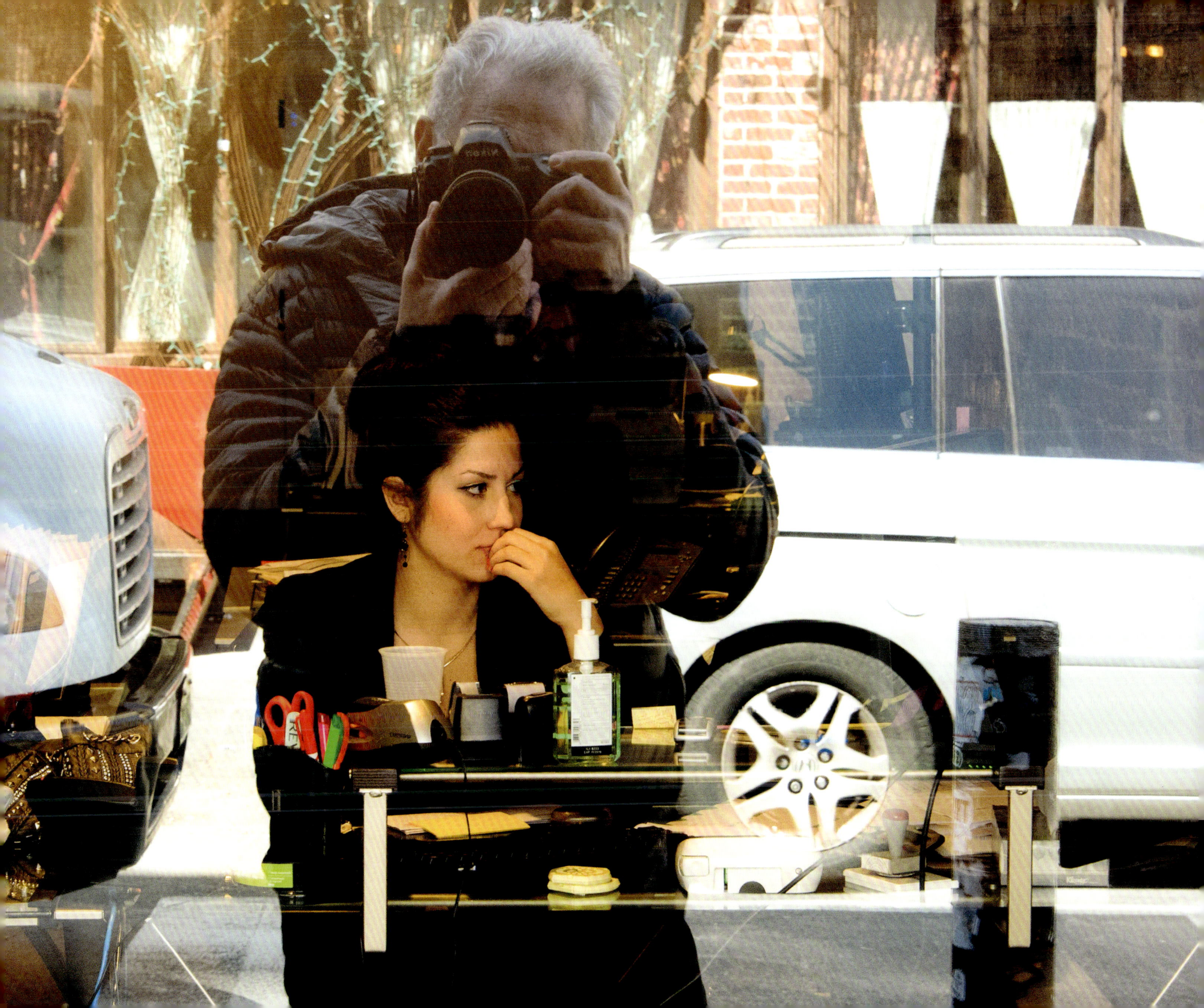

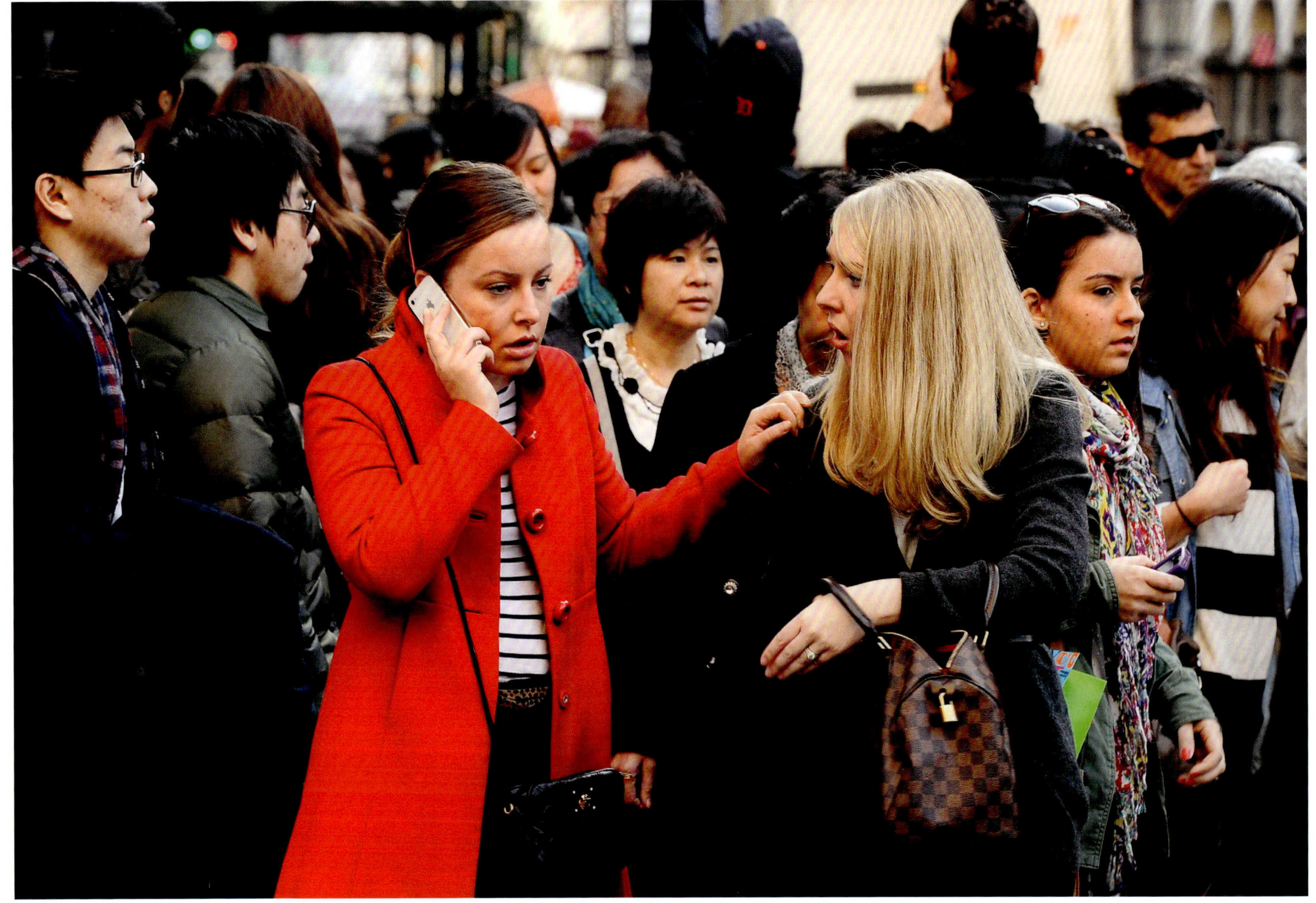

THE PHONE CALL

Pure luck. I was scanning the crowd when this happened. There was no plan.

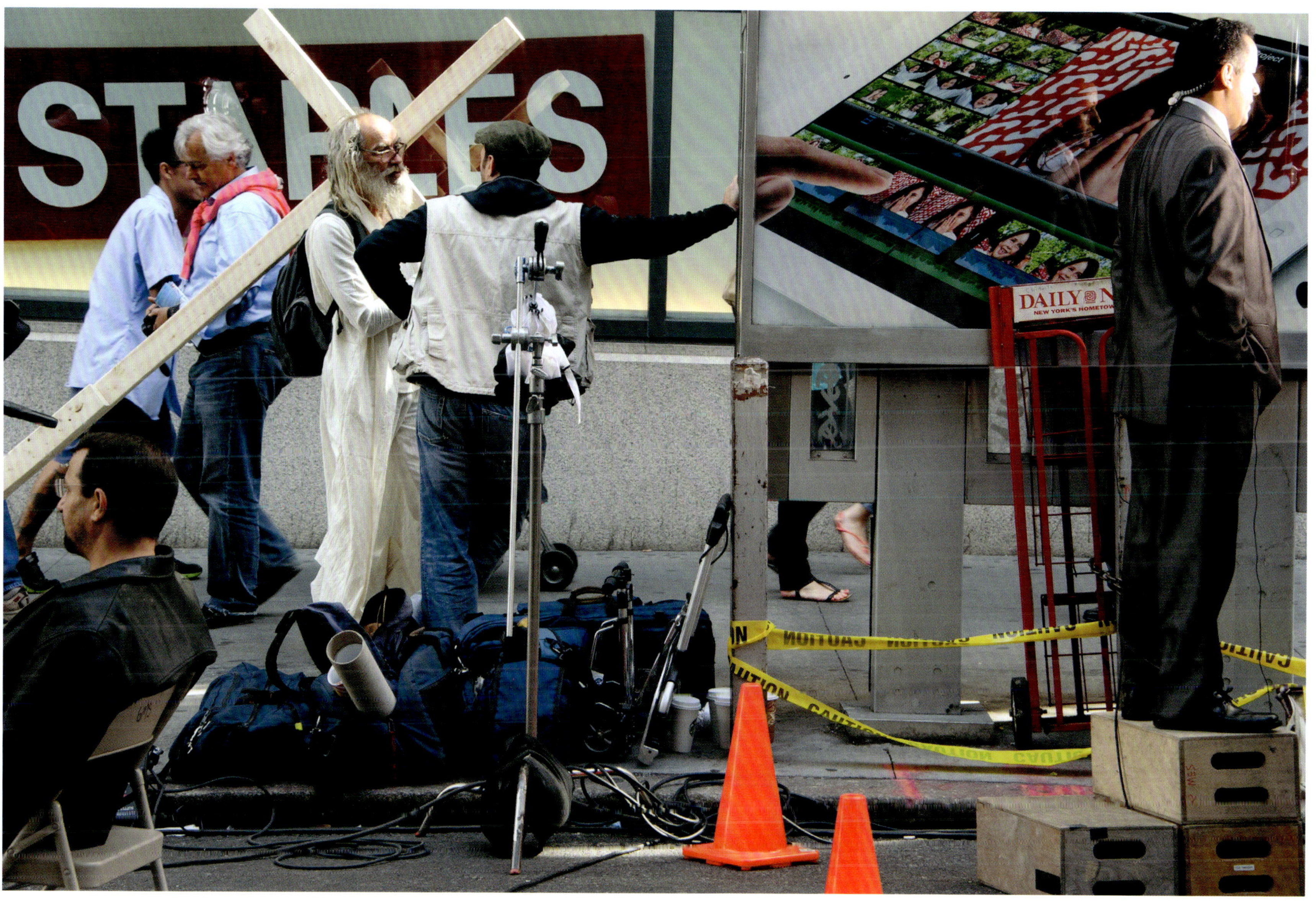

CRUCIFIX

I walked around all afternoon shooting but didn't get much. Then I saw
this and was blown away by the busyness and surrealistic quality.

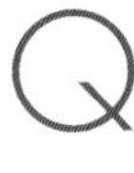

Q + A

Do you have favorite light, time of day, or weather for taking photographs?

Of course, the golden time and wonderful light can be a great addition to any image in graphic terms. However, I'm looking for wonderful moments—interactions between people. When these moments occur, you can't legislate what the light will be. Therefore when I go out to shoot, light is certainly a consideration, but not my main imperative.

Humor crops up frequently in your work—does this reflect your feelings about the world you live in?

Humor is the savior in a horribly conflicted world. You can choose to shoot the horror or be attracted to those moments when we are kindest to each other. These moments are so rare and so beautiful that I am often choked up, and sometimes close to tears. The horrible aspect of our behavior puts me into a blind rage and stymies any desire to delve into it photographically. When we're having fun, being eccentric, or just in general displaying the potentials of relationships, that's when the creative juices start flowing for me. We all shoot what we are. Your nature shows in your work. I like to have a good time. I love to laugh. I'm not a "funny" photographer like Elliot Erwitt (who I think is a total genius), but if I see positive stuff, it's going to get way more play from me than something depressing.

You say that you never intrude upon or change a situation—does that mean that you tend to shoot without people knowing? Do you feel more comfortable working this way?

I should probably learn never to say "never." I don't want to be intrusive, I don't choose to be intrusive, I don't try to be intrusive, but let's not kid ourselves—you're there, your subject may very well be aware of you, and if they are it changes everything. What happens then is up to you. It's a new ball game. You can fight it or go with it. The nature of street photography is that you have no control over it. I would love to be a fly on the wall, but confrontations can be very productive and they can be negative, unpredictable, and at worst violent. You will have to figure out ways to defuse these moments—with humor, deference, diplomacy, whatever you can muster.

You say that New York has long attracted street photographers, but why do you think that is?

Density. Eccentricity. History.

"Humor is the savior in a horribly conflicted world. You can choose to shoot the horror or be attracted to those moments when we are kindest to each other. These moments are so rare and so beautiful that I am often choked up."

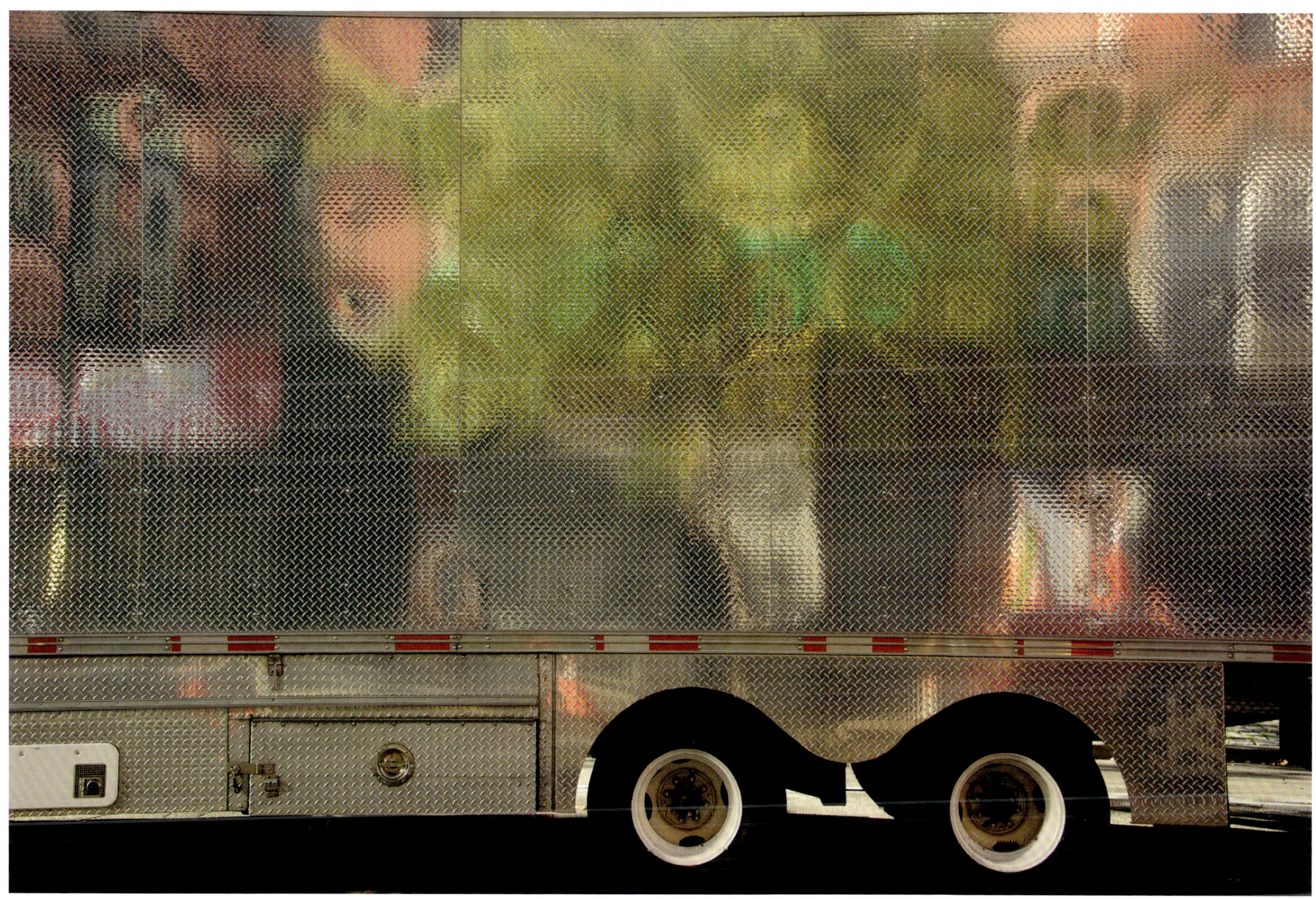

TRUCK WITH REFLECTION

This is a moment that doesn't last: as soon as the truck moves the picture's gone.

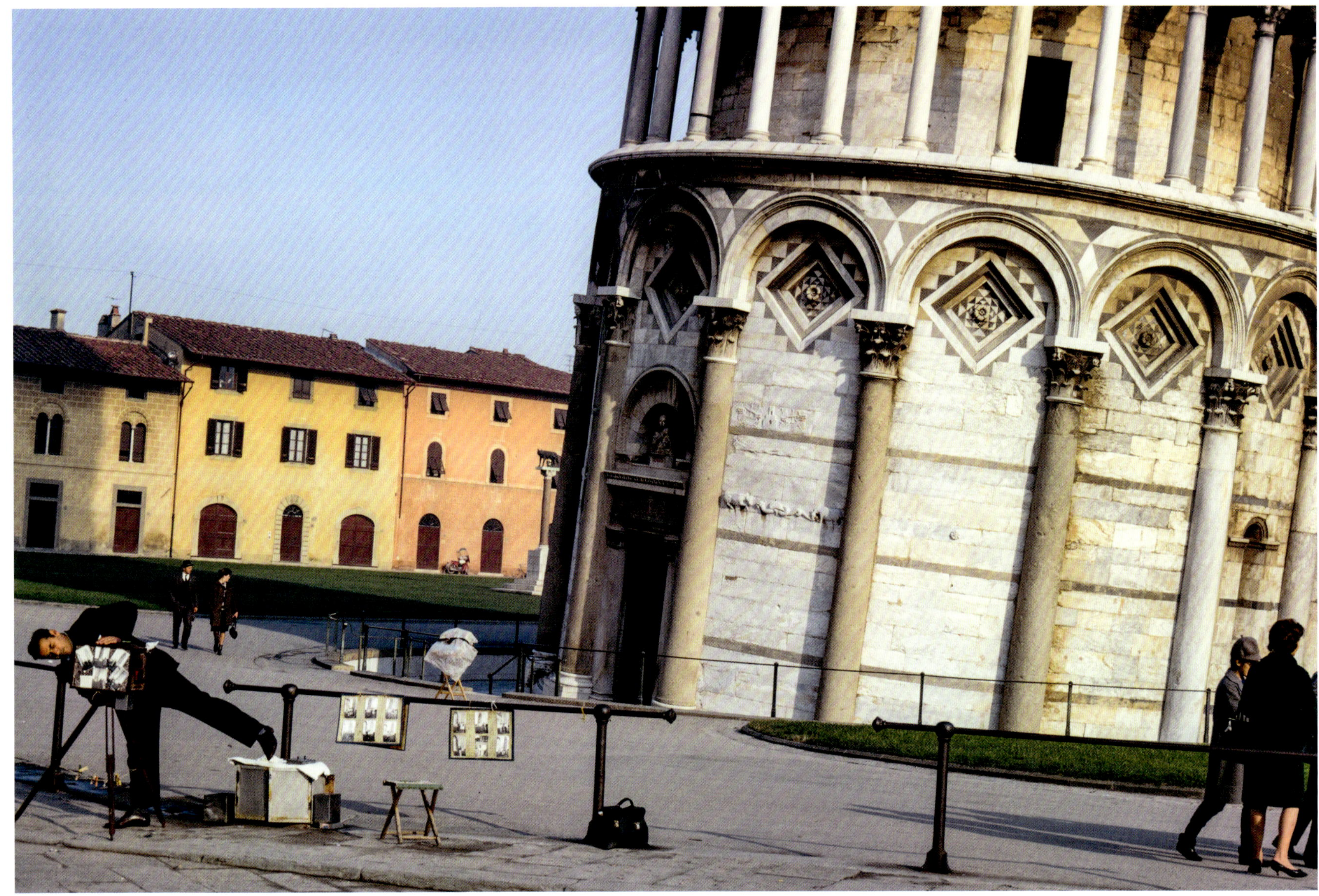

LEANING PHOTOGRAPHER OF PISA

I was shooting the Tower of Pisa and saw this. I had only one or two seconds before it was gone.

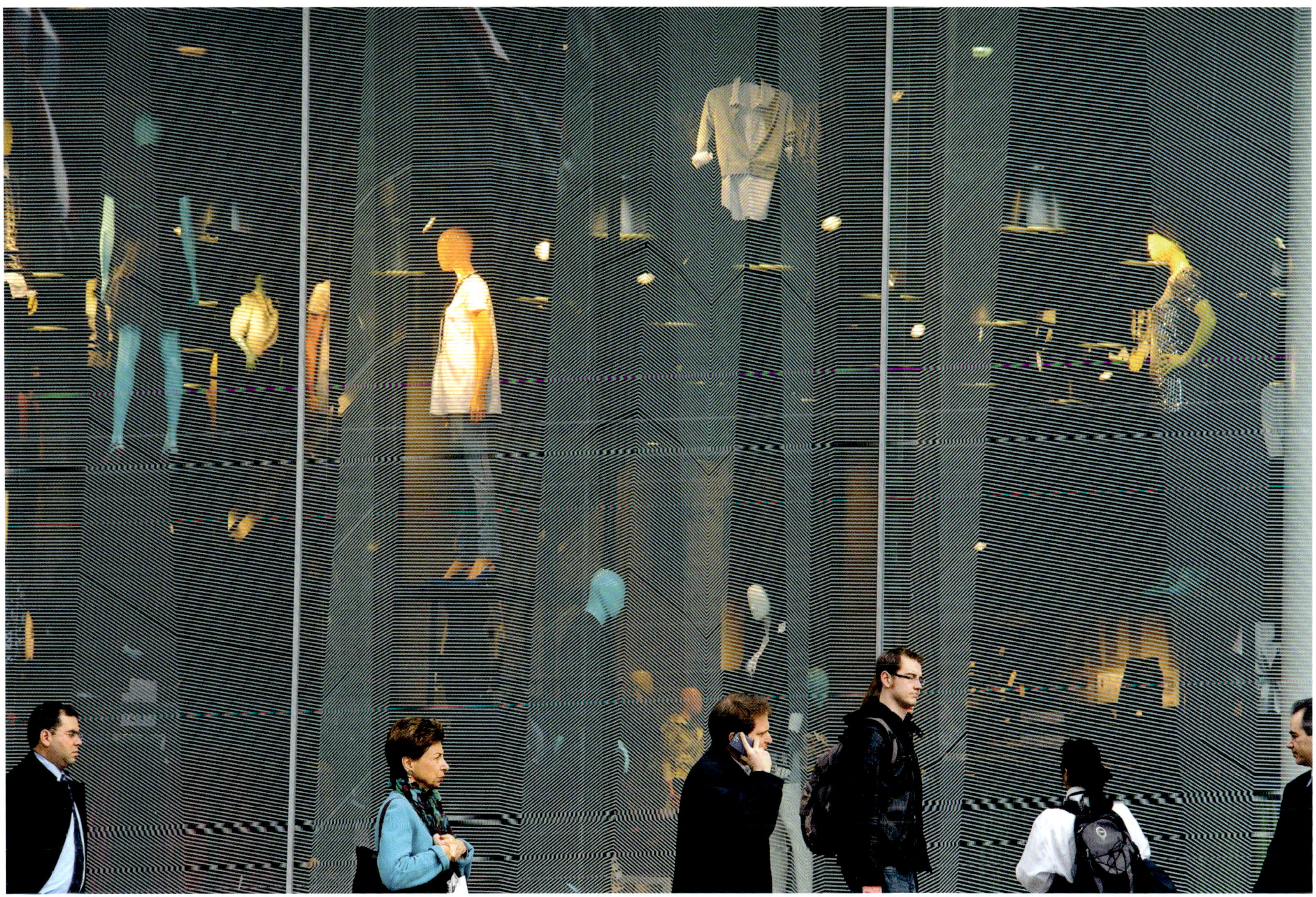

PEOPLE ON STREET WITH STORE MANNEQUINS

I shoot in Midtown Manhattan a lot because density equals opportunity.
This is a store window near 5th Avenue and 42nd Street.

Q
+
A

How important to your work was your background in painting?

It was of major importance to me, making me aware of aesthetic considerations that change the way you look at life and your work. It made me aware of our history, from prehistoric time to now, of making marks on surfaces. It made me keenly sensitive to so many things that we don't necessarily keep at the ready when we look at the world. It can, however, be a two-edged sword. You can get too wrapped up in the formal aspects—the play of light, the subtleties of color, all kinds of details that are critically important in your work but can keep you from making the statement you want to make in terms of content, because you're so hooked on the form.

What makes a great photograph, and what do you look for in a scene that makes you fire the shutter?

If I knew what made a great picture I wouldn't take so many bad ones. When I'm out shooting, the impulse to shoot, if I'm hot, it is visceral—from the gut, the heart—it's not intellectual. I've read many quotes from people I admire, and they all boil down to this: you can't analyze too much (that's the job of critics and writers). The work gets done as a result of perception, delight, fascination, and finally possibility.

Do you ever feel you are invading a person's privacy, and does that matter to you?

I often do feel intrusive and in my head I start playing these defensive mind games and rationalizations. I'm not ever trying to make fun of anyone or trying to make them feel bad. I'm not peeking into their private lives. They're out in public and have no expectation of privacy. I don't hide my camera, and I'm always respectful and sensitive to others, and with all that rattling around in my brain, if anybody gets upset with me in any way it's a really bad and depressing day for me.

What is your favorite choice of camera and lens, and why?

Before going into this, a little background. When I was doing commercial work, I felt I owed it to the client to have every lens possible with me at all times, up to a 1000mm. When I quit doing commercial work in 1995 to work on my own stuff, I wanted to carry as little as possible. When I taught classes, I would always make a point of explaining that the more equipment you take, the less images you take. Ever since Nikon introduced its first single lens reflex camera in 1959, I've only used Nikon cameras and lenses. For some years, I used a 70–300mm and a 24–70mm lens, with a small belly-bag to hold the lens I wasn't using. Since the 24–70mm fit the bag better (and I'm partial to longer lenses), I shot very little with the 24–70mm. However, when Nikon came out with the 28–300mm, I was delighted, even though I thought they were overreaching. I was wrong: the lens is terrific. So, for the last five years, all I ever carried was a D3S, then a D4S, always with the 28–300mm lens, and I shot a lot more wideangle stuff, as it was in my hands all the time.

"When I'm out shooting, the impulse to shoot, if I'm hot, it is visceral—from the gut, the heart—it's not intellectual."

TECHNICAL INFORMATION

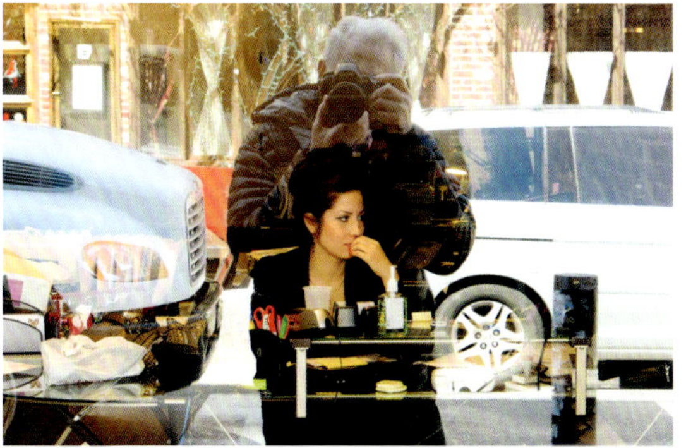

SELF PORTRAIT (2014)
NEW YORK CITY, NEW YORK, USA

Camera: Nikon D3S
Lens/Focal length: Nikkor 28-300mm f/3.5-5.6 at 92mm
Aperture: f/11
Shutter speed: 1/125 sec.
ISO: 6400

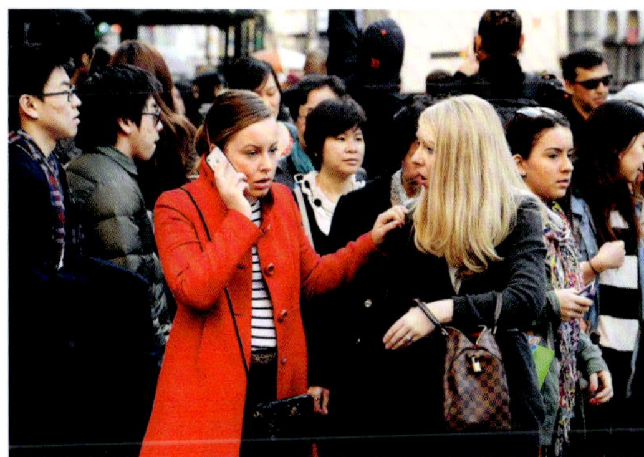

THE PHONE CALL
NEW YORK CITY, NEW YORK, USA

Camera: Nikon D3S
Lens/Focal length: Nikkor 28-300mm f/3.5-5.6 at 108mm
Aperture: f/8
Shutter speed: 1/200 sec.
ISO: 1600

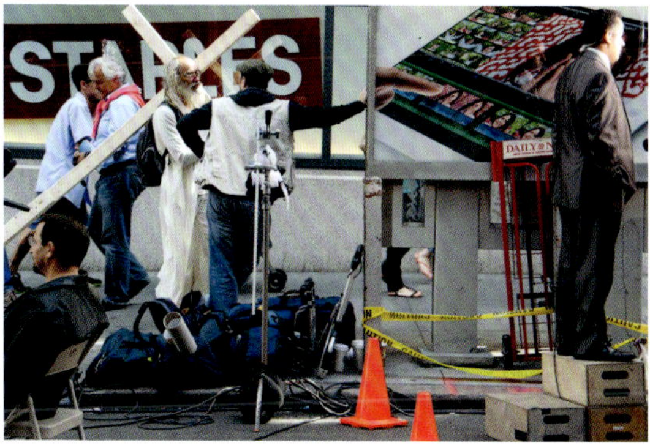

CRUCIFIX
NEW YORK CITY, NEW YORK, USA

Camera: Nikon D3S
Lens/Focal length: Nikkor 28-300mm f/3.5-5.6 at 100mm
Aperture: f/10
Shutter speed: 1/125 sec.
ISO: 1600

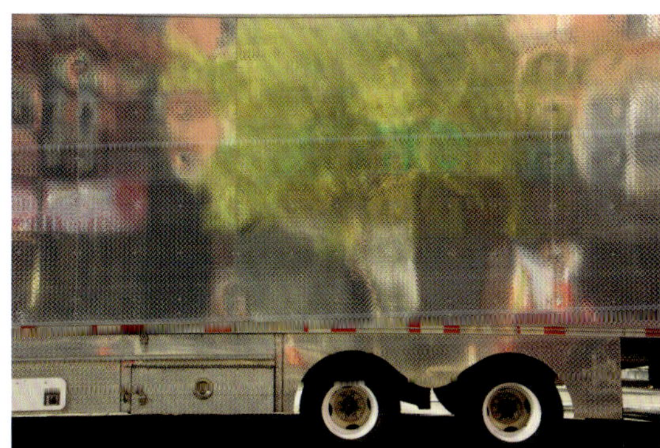

TRUCK WITH REFLECTION
NEW YORK CITY, NEW YORK, USA

Camera: Nikon D3S
Lens/Focal length: Nikkor 28-300mm f/3.5-5.6 at 48mm
Aperture: f/5.6
Shutter speed: 1/1250 sec.
ISO: 1600

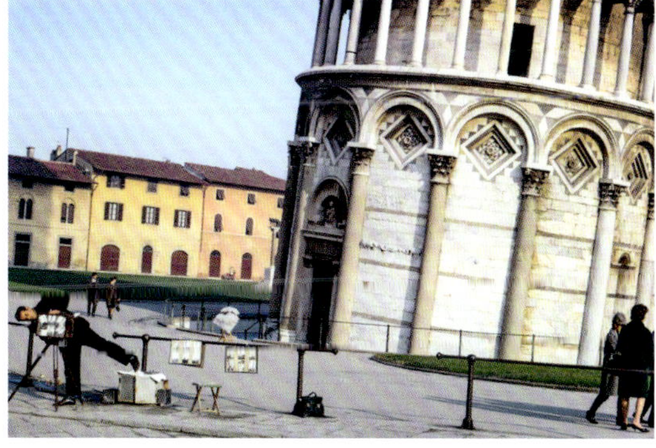

LEANING PHOTOGRAPHER OF PISA
PISA, ITALY

Camera: Nikon F
Lens/Focal length: Unrecorded
Aperture: Unrecorded
Shutter speed: Unrecorded
Film: Kodachrome 64

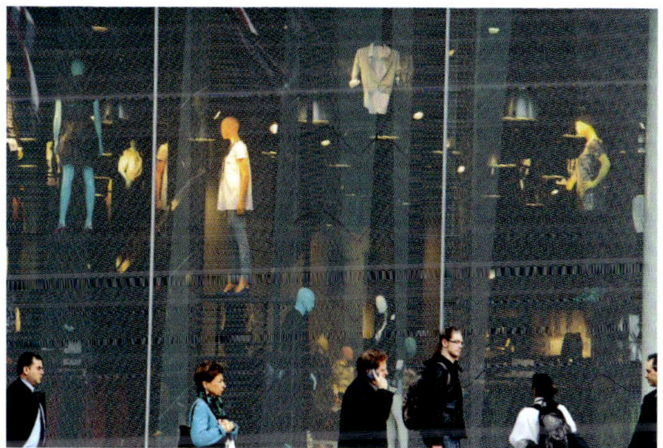

PEOPLE ON STREET WITH STORE MANNEQUINS
NEW YORK CITY, NEW YORK, USA

Camera: Nikon D3
Lens/Focal length: Unrecorded
Aperture: Unrecorded
Shutter speed: 1/500 sec.
ISO: 1600

JESSE MARLOW

Jesse Marlow is based in Melbourne, Australia. Over the last 20 years he has worked as a photographer for a range of local and international editorial and commercial clients. His photographs are held in public and private collections across Australia and the world, including the National Gallery of Victoria and the Australian Parliament House Art Collection.

In 2003, Jesse's first book of photographs, *Centre Bounce: Football from Australia's Heart*, was published, followed in 2005 by a collection of street photographs titled *Wounded.* In 2006, Jesse was selected to participate in the World Press Photo Joop Swart Masterclass in Amsterdam. In 2010, he was one of 45 street photographers from around the world profiled in the book *Street Photography Now*, and in 2014 his third monograph, *Don't Just Tell Them, Show Them*, was published.

Jesse has won many awards for his work. In 2011, he was the inaugural winner of the International Street Photography Prize, and in 2012 he won the MGA Bowness Prize. In 2018, he collaborated with Leica Australia when they produced the Limited Edition Leica Q—Australian Edition. The camera was limited to 30 units and was accompanied by a limited-edition book of his work. Jesse is a member of the international street photographer's collective iN-PUBLiC.

WOODSMEN (2007)

Midday is normally a time when many photographers pack their camera away. I've never been one of those who subscribes to that theory—I've always felt that, no matter the time of day, there's always a photo to be taken. The workers with their fluorescent clothing and timber boards proved to be a visually interesting combination.

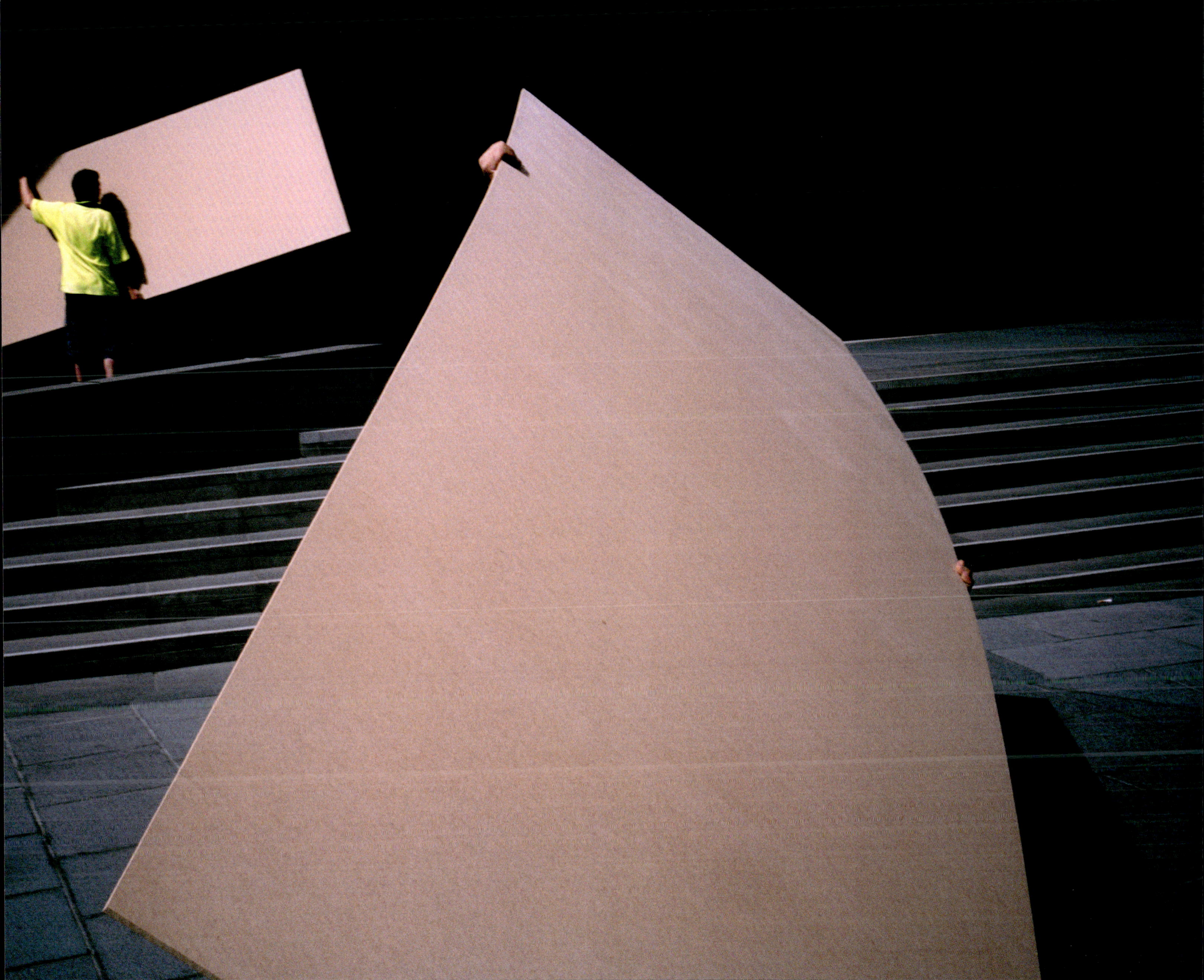

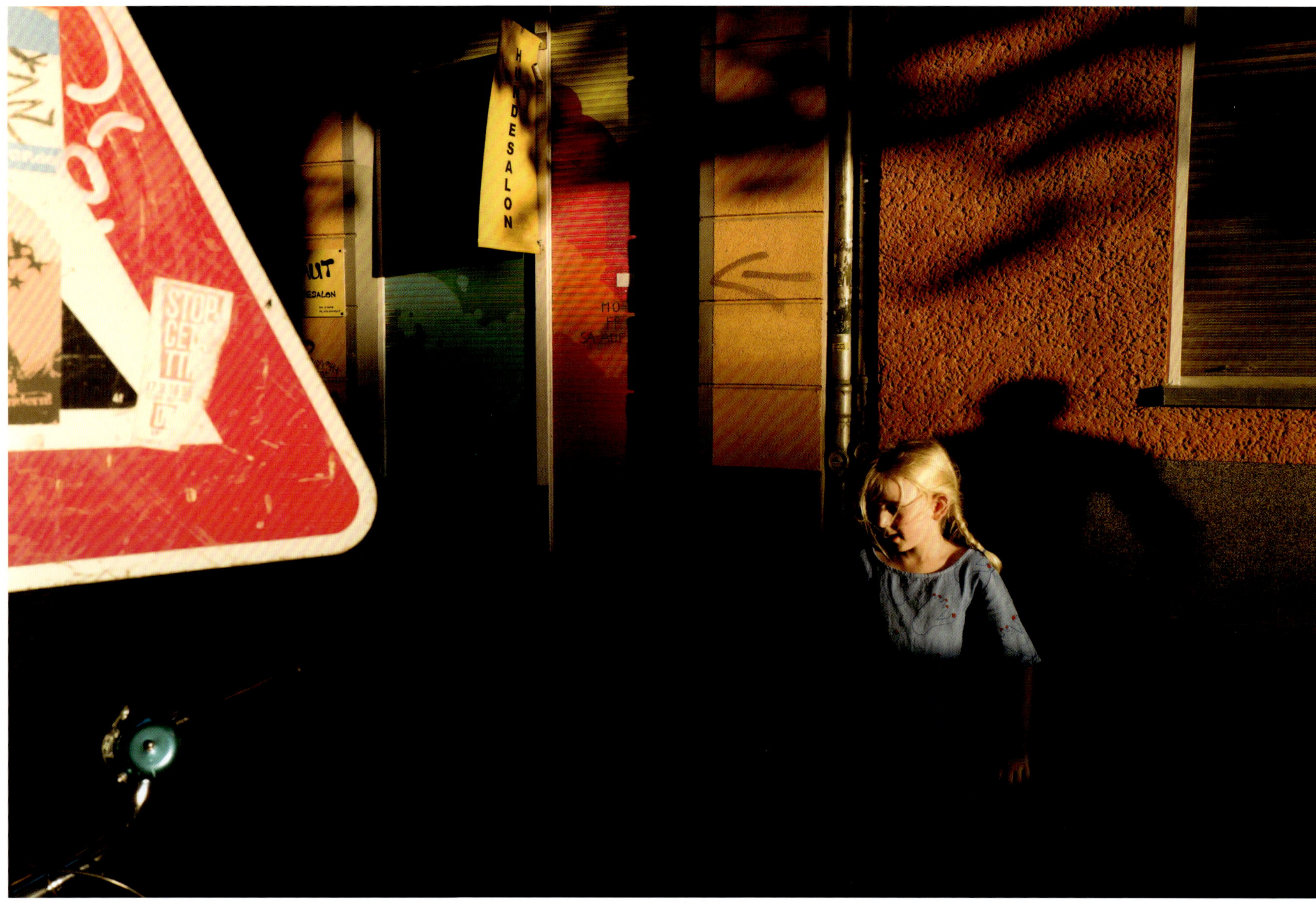

BERLIN (2018)

I was out walking with my daughter in Berlin on our way to pick up some take-away food. The evening light, striking color, graphic elements, and my daughter skipping along without a care in the world combine well to make this pleasing composition.

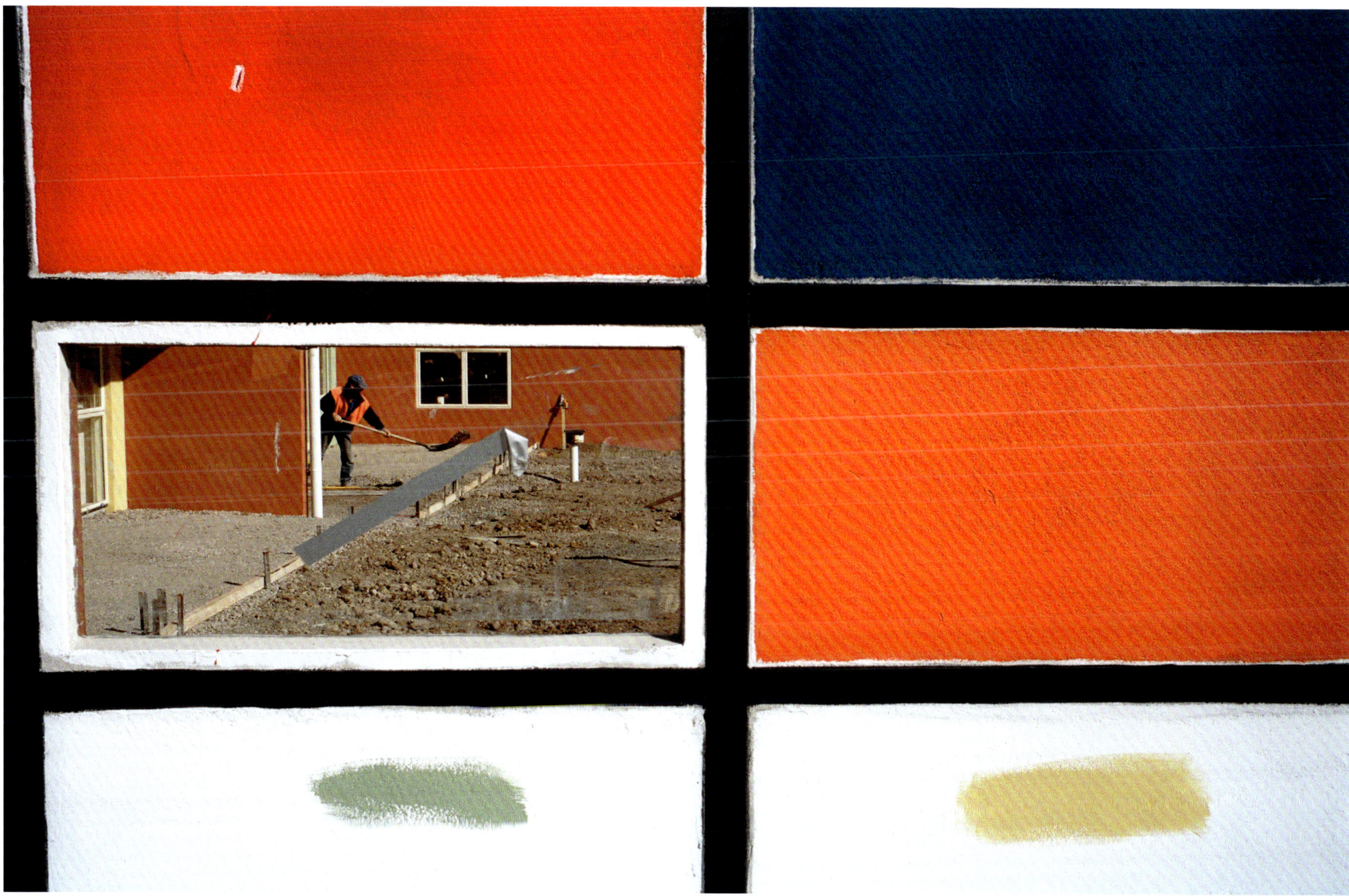

SIX PANELS (2009)

Over the last 10 years or so, one of my visual triggers has been "workers," particularly when I see them in their high-visibility workwear. I'm drawn to their photographic potential and the quirky situations I sometimes find them in. I love it when color, graphic compositions, and a human presence all come together in one frame.

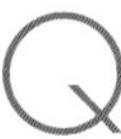
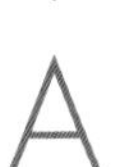

Q + A

How did you get hooked on street photography?

In the mid-1980s, my uncle gave me a book called *Subway Art* and it triggered something in me. As a young boy, I began taking photos of the brightly colored graffiti walls that had started to appear around Melbourne. I continued to do this through my teenage years, and after high school I studied photography for a couple of years. I was lucky enough to have an inspiring lecturer who encouraged us to go out and shoot the real world around us as opposed to studio work, and this is what I've been doing ever since. What continues to drive and excite me is the element of surprise and unknown that comes with shooting random candid photos. If I knew what I was going to shoot when I left the house in the morning, I'd lose interest pretty quickly.

What attracts you to the strong color you use in your work?

My fascination with interesting and unique color stems back to my interest in graphics—as a teenager, I had hoped this would end up being my profession. My mother is a fashion designer who has always repurposed interesting vintage fabrics in her designs. Being exposed to these amazing, colorful, and patterned fabrics as a child and teenager has definitely played a part in shaping my aesthetic and my search for color when out on the street. When shooting color, the particular scenes I approach and come across are completely different to when I've shot in black and white. I'm drawn to shooting in strong lighting situations where color is accentuated and deep shadows are cast.

How do you set about composing your images?

I've always searched for photographs depicting colorful, graphic, and sometimes playful situations that in turn challenge the viewer to question the composition. For me, photos that raise questions more than give answers are central to my practice as a photographer. Often, I'm drawn to the subtle moments in back streets away from the crowds, where color, form, and shape quietly collide, creating an ambiguity that lies just below the surface. I do have a couple of recurring themes and visual triggers that I'll always explore photographically when I chance upon them. Other than that, I try to keep a really open mind when out shooting. I always feel there's a photo around the next corner. I have a couple of different working styles. When I come across a simple, quieter, static graphic scene, I'll experiment and really work the compositional possibilities. My other working approach stems from having worked as a press photographer for a number of years—essentially, work fast and don't leave until you have the photo.

Which photographers or artists inspire you and why?

Henri Cartier-Bresson, Lee Friedlander, Joel Meyerowitz, Garry Winogrand, and Alex Webb all inspired me in my early years. As I developed as a photographer, I began finding inspiration through painters such as the Australian artists Jeffrey Smart and Howard Arkley. Jeffrey Smart's use of color and his unique depiction of the urban environment particularly inspired me when I began shooting color.

LASER VISION, 2011

When I'm out and about in my car, I often take note of interesting walls or backdrops with the intention of returning when the light might be better or I may have more time to shoot. One day, while stuck in traffic, I noticed the reflection of the zebra crossing and distressed painted diagonal lines on the window of this fish and chip shop. What I love about street photography is the element of surprise. The woman with her headscarf walking through my scene was that little bonus that we street photographers are occasionally rewarded with.

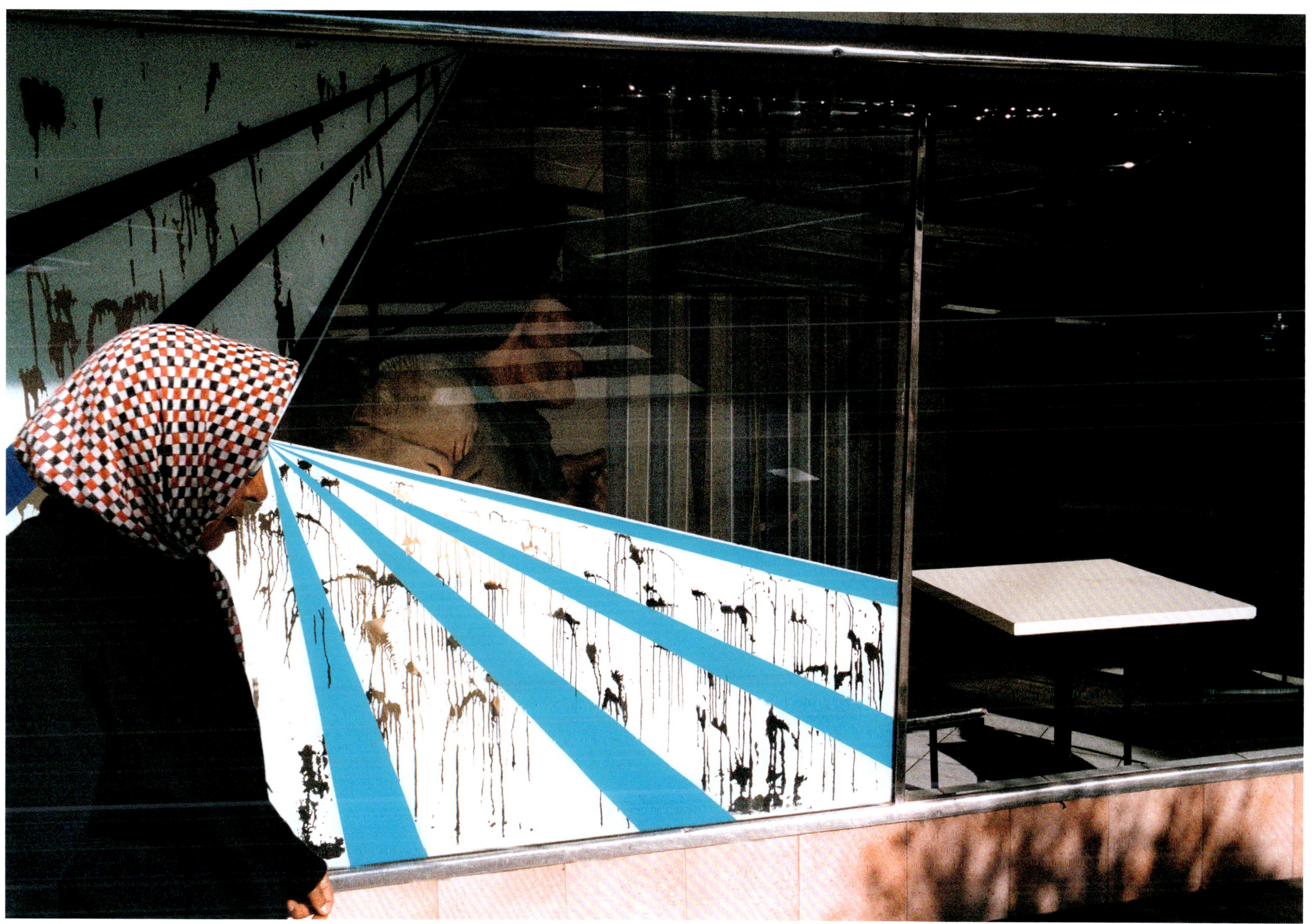

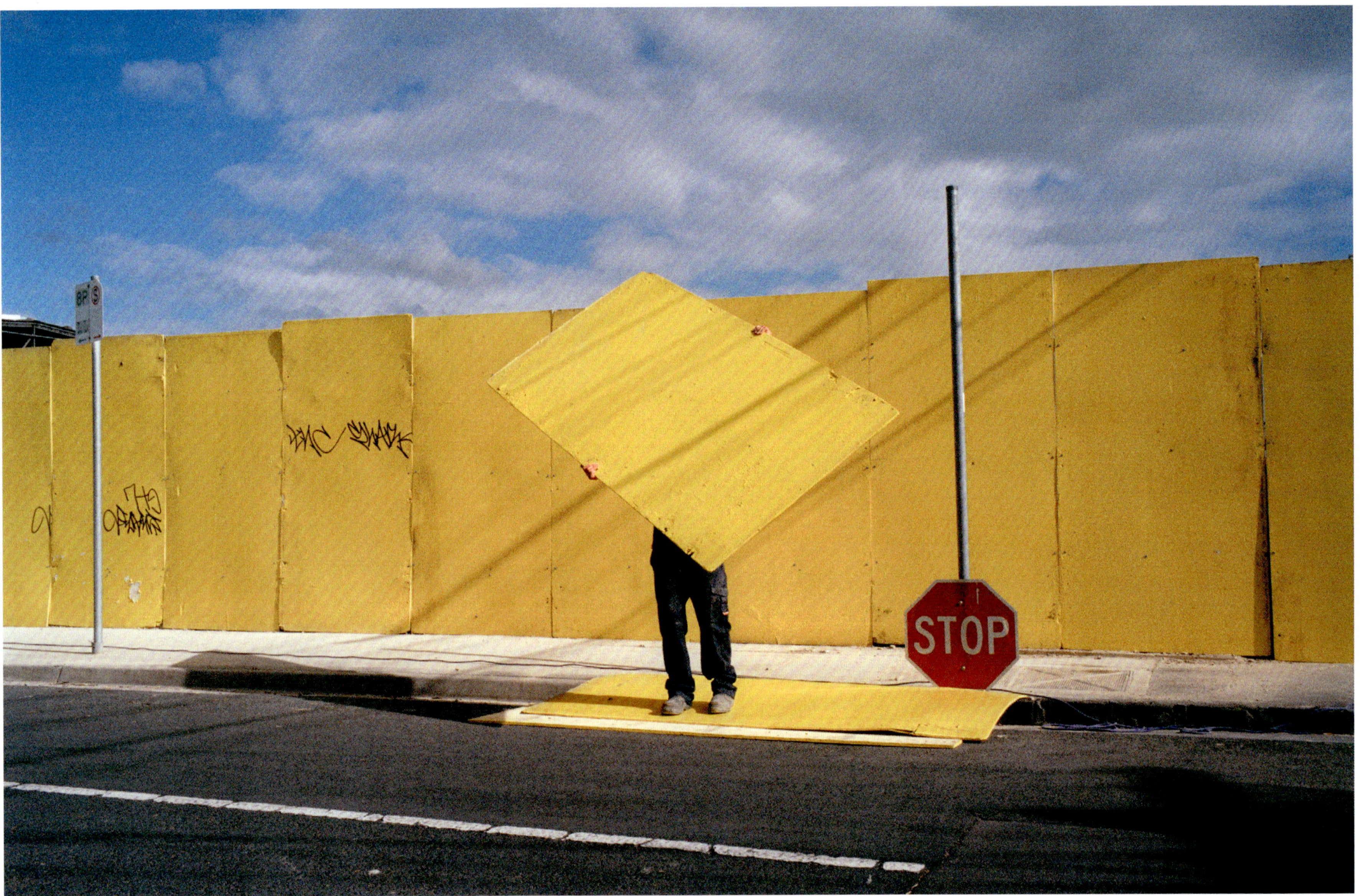

STOP (2011)

I had driven past this brightly colored wall several times, as it was very close to
home. One afternoon, things looked slightly different. The stop sign had fallen
and the workers happened to be dismantling part of the hoarding. Naturally,
I stopped the car to see if I could turn the situation into a picture, and proceeded
to stand there capturing the bizarre scene as it unfolded.

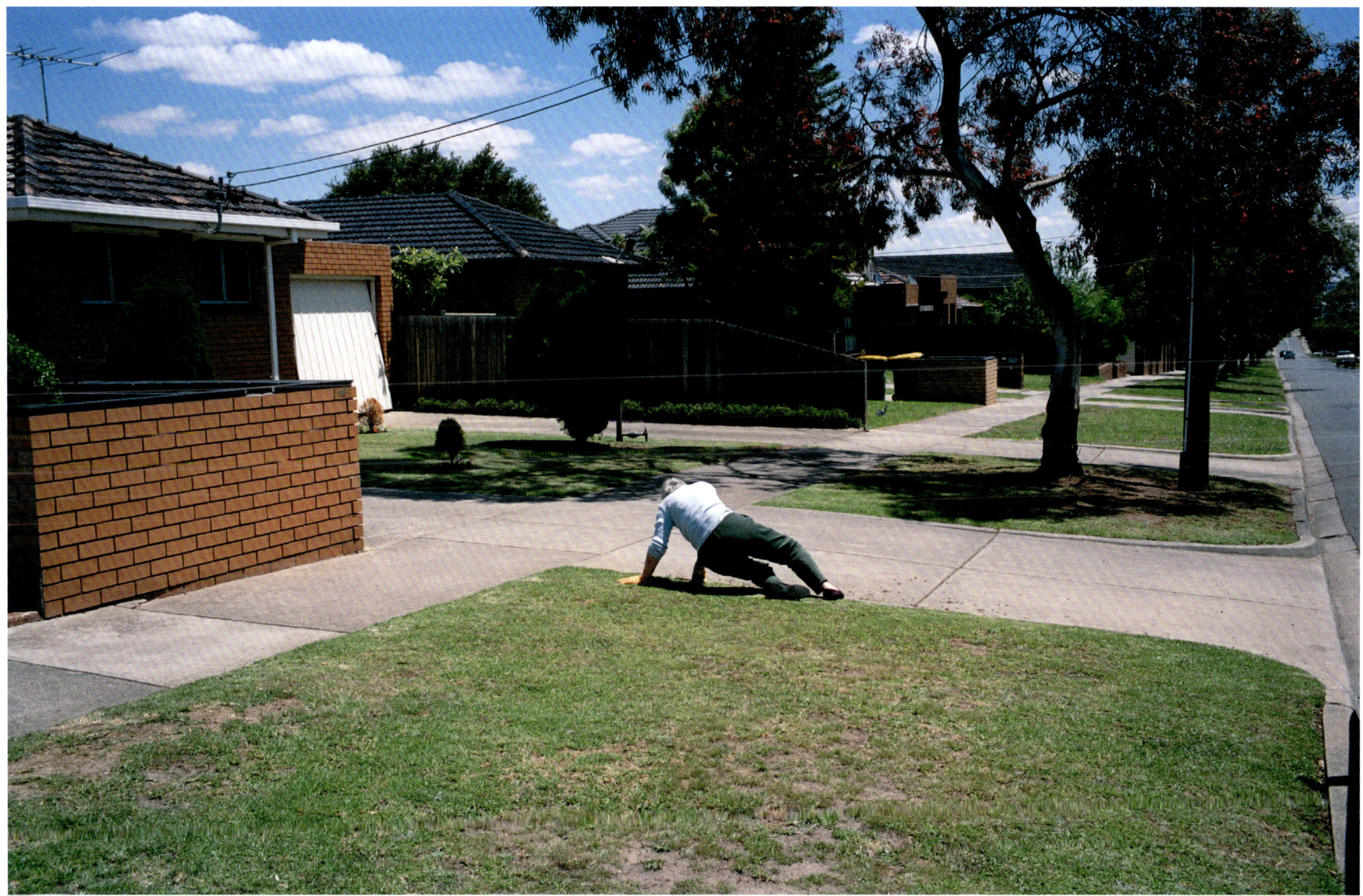

SUNDAY MORNING (2009)

I went through a period back in 2009 when I'd become bored of walking around the city center of Melbourne looking for pictures. I felt the urge to explore another side of my home city and began driving around the outer suburbs of Melbourne looking for different types of photos—those that were quieter and had a sense of mystery. The wide strips of grass are a very common feature of suburban Australia.

Q
+
A

What inspires you to keep taking your camera out to shoot?

When I'm out on the streets, I never start the day with any preconceived ideas about what I'm going to photograph. I love the creative freedom of just being out there with an open mind, my camera, and a healthy sense of optimism. I've found this approach works best for me. Some days I'll come home with nothing, and others I'll capture a moment that will be with me forever. It's the uncertainty and challenge of this style of photography that continues to excite and inspire me.

You're a member of iN-PUBLiC photography collective—what are the advantages of being part of such a group?

At times, living in Australia can feel quite isolated from the wider photographic community, so being a part of iN-PUBLiC has always been something I've cherished. When I first joined the group in 2001, I was 23 years old and my knowledge and skill were in their infancy. To be taken in by a group of photographers who I had admired and to have them critique my work on a daily basis via our (then) private discussion board was immeasurable for my development as a street photographer. Eighteen years later, the group has grown and evolved, and so the greatest strengths of the group, for me, are the friendships with like-minded and spirited photographers that I've made around the world.

Do you ever feel you are invading a person's privacy—does that matter?

I'm always respectful of people and their situation, and there are definitely certain things I won't shoot. In a lot of my more recent work, the people I shoot are often a smaller part of the image, or their faces may not be visible. That's not to say I don't shoot photos with faces, it's just that my style has evolved over the years and sometimes there's a more interesting or ambiguous photo to be taken by not including a face. One of the recurring themes in my work has been "workers," and on a number of occasions I've been mistaken for a building inspector or insurance claims officer, which is quite amusing when it happens.

What tips would you give to those who wish to master street photography?

I'm a really strong believer that if a scene allows you to shoot multiple pictures, you should. Often it's the second or third composition of a particular scene where other elements begin appearing and the strength of the picture reveals itself. It's sometimes these extra little elements that elevate a picture beyond others. Street photography can at times be really unrewarding. I think it's important to understand that there are days when you will come home empty-handed, and accepting this is important for your development as a street photographer. This is what also makes it so exciting for me. Often, it's good to have a few themes running through your work that can give you purpose on the days when you may not be feeling inspired.

"*Often it's the second or third composition of a particular scene where other elements begin appearing, and the strength of the picture reveals itself.*"

TECHNICAL INFORMATION

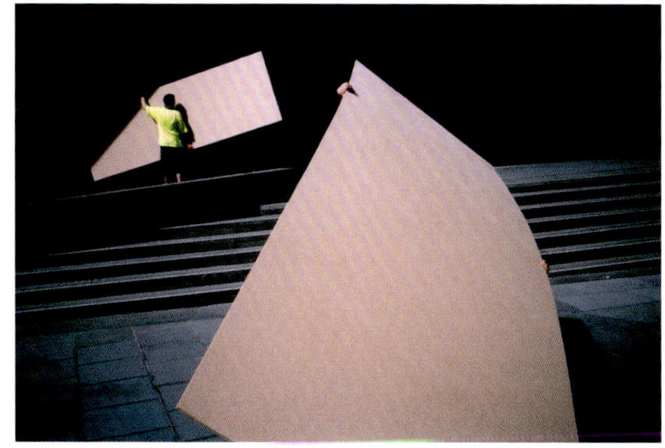

WOODSMEN (2007)
MELBOURNE, AUSTRALIA

Camera: Leica M6
Lens/Focal length: 35mm Summicron
Aperture: f/11
Shutter Speed: 1/250 sec.
ISO: 400
Film: Fuji 400 Superia

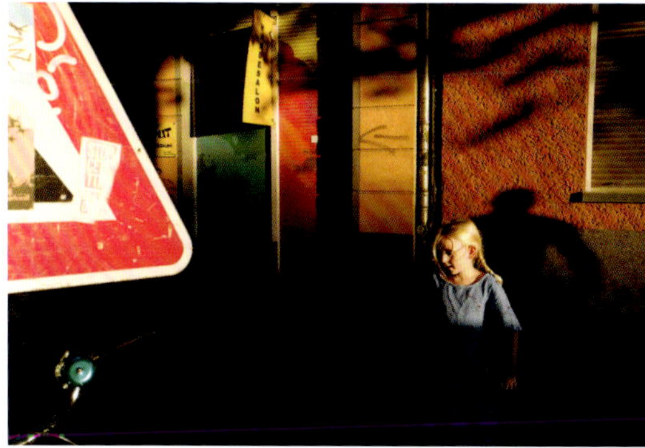

BERLIN (2018)
BERLIN, GERMANY

Camera: Leica Q
Lens/Focal length: 35mm Summicron
Aperture: f/8
Shutter Speed: 1/500 sec.
ISO: 400

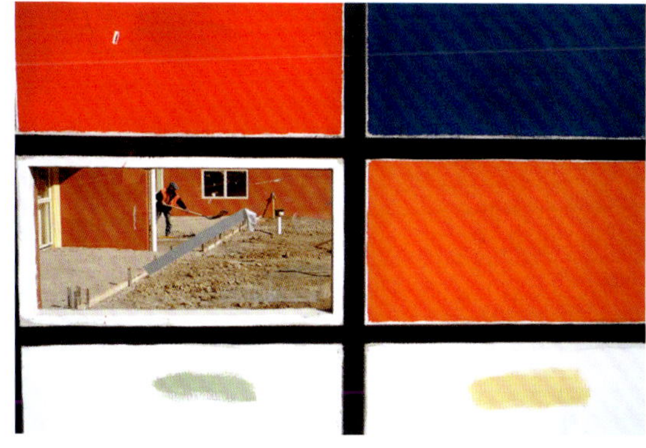

SIX PANELS (2009)
MELBOURNE, AUSTRALIA

Camera: Leica M6
Lens/Focal length: 35mm Summicron
Aperture: f/11
Shutter Speed: 1/500 sec.
ISO: 400
Film: Fuji 400 Superia

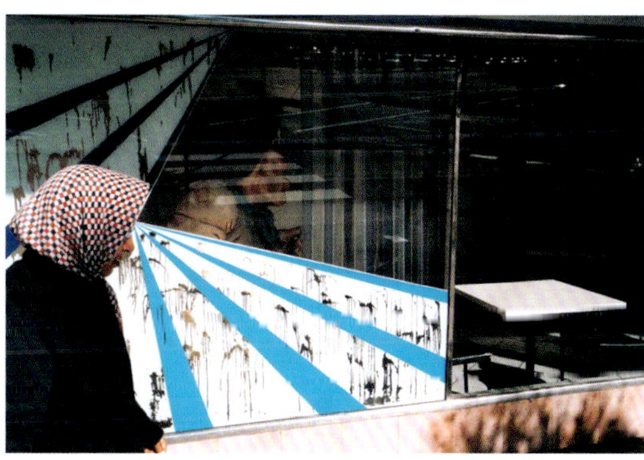

LASER VISION (2011)
MELBOURNE, AUSTRALIA

Camera: Leica M6
Lens/Focal length: 35mm Summicron
Aperture: f/8
Shutter Speed: 1/500 sec.
ISO: 400
Film: Fuji 400 Superia

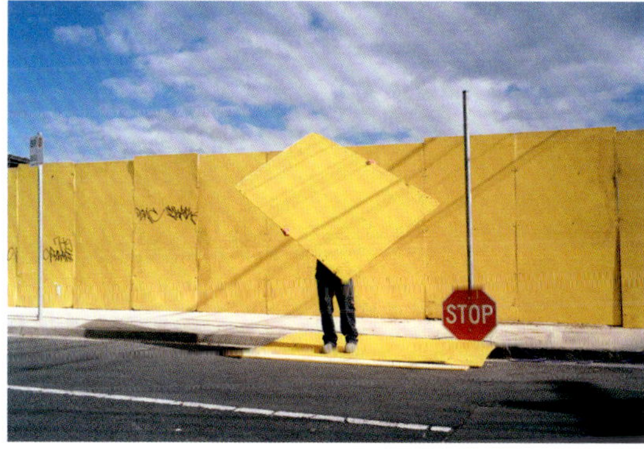

STOP (2011)
MELBOURNE, AUSTRALIA

Camera: Leica M6
Lens/Focal length: 35mm Summicron
Aperture: f/8
Shutter Speed: 1/500 sec.
ISO: 400
Film: Fuji 400 Superia

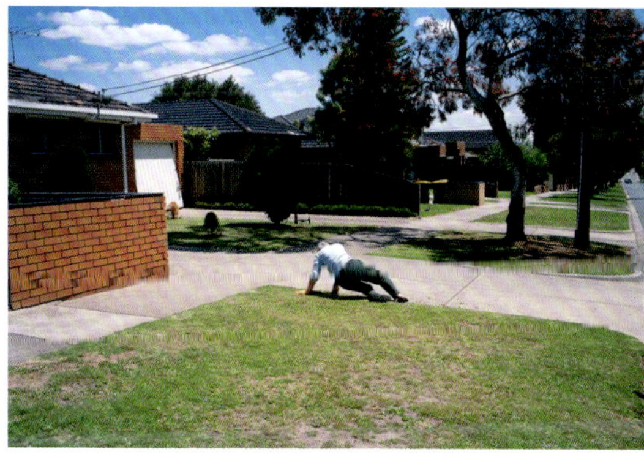

SUNDAY MORNING (2009)
MELBOURNE, AUSTRALIA

Camera: Leica M6
Lens/Focal length: 35mm Summicron
Aperture: f/11
Shutter Speed: 1/500 sec.
ISO: 400
Film: Fuji 400 Superia

DIMITRI MELLOS

Dimitri Mellos was born in Athens, Greece, but since 2005 he has called New York City home. Dimitri studied philosophy and psychology, and is a largely self-taught photographer. As a child, he used to walk around with an old Kodak Instamatic camera (with no film loaded), pretending to take pictures. He rediscovered his passion for photography many years later, this time making sure there was film (or an SD card) in the camera. He works mainly on long-term, self-initiated projects.

Dimitri's work has been exhibited internationally in group and solo shows, and has garnered several prestigious awards and accolades, including Finalist for the Visura Grant and the Magnum Expression Award, and a Juror's Pick at the Lensculture Magnum Photography Awards. His key influences include Garry Winogrand, Ray Metzker, Raghubir Singh, Alex Webb, William Klein, Saul Leiter, Harry Gruyaert, and Jens Olof Lasthein. He prefers spending time walking and photographing than on social media.

CHURCH STREET, NYC (2014)

I like this photo as it combines quite beautiful light with an emotionally charged moment. I noticed the patch of light against this otherwise dark wall and lingered a little, hoping for an interesting person or situation to materialize. I see a lot of photos these days trying to utilize light and shadow, but I feel it's not enough to just put a dark silhouette against a bright background (or vice-versa) to make an interesting photo; it just turns into empty formalism unless there is something emotionally resonant going on, such as this guy's ecstatic expression in the sunlight.

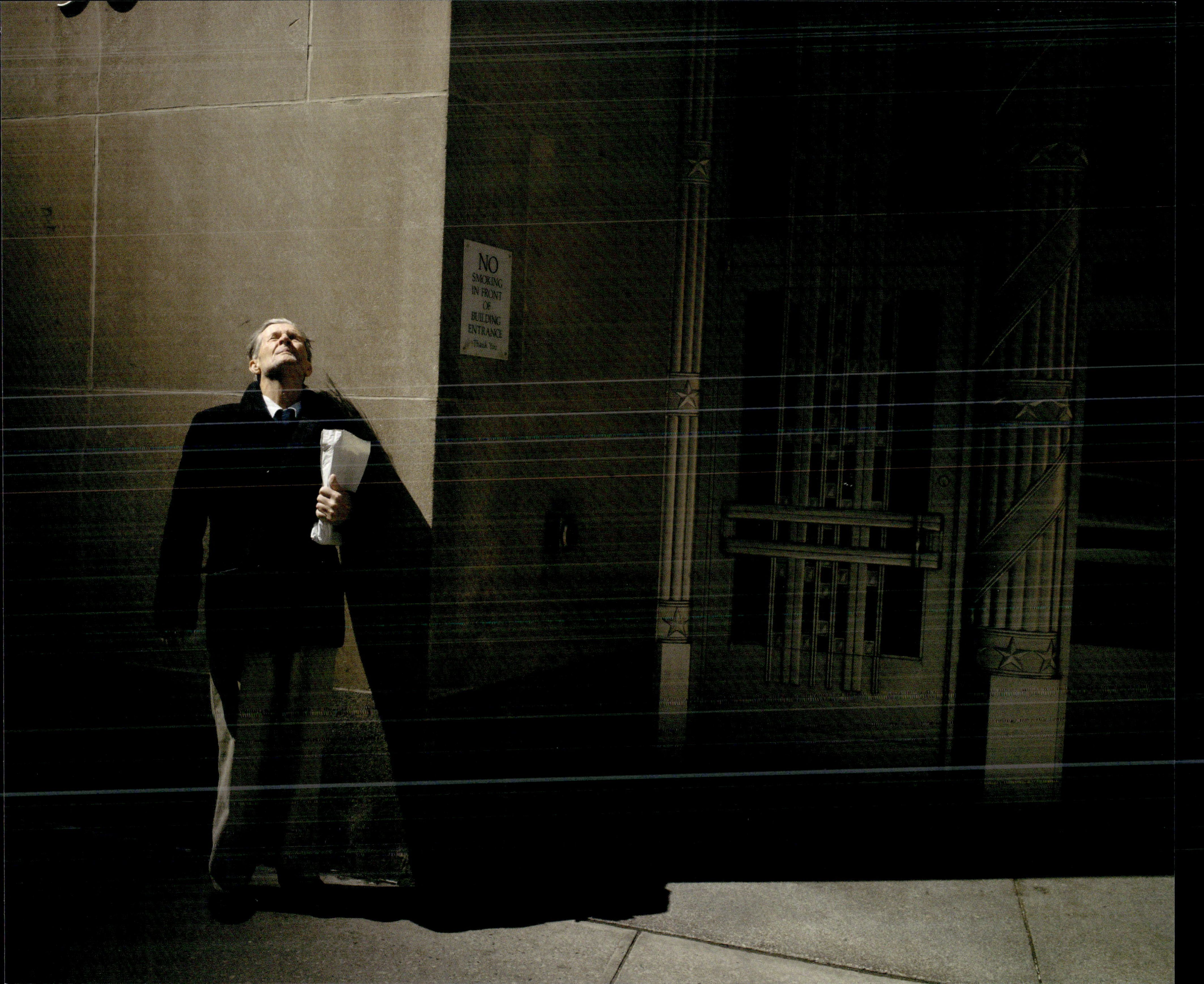

NO
SMOKING
IN FRONT
OF
BUILDING
ENTRANCE
Thank You

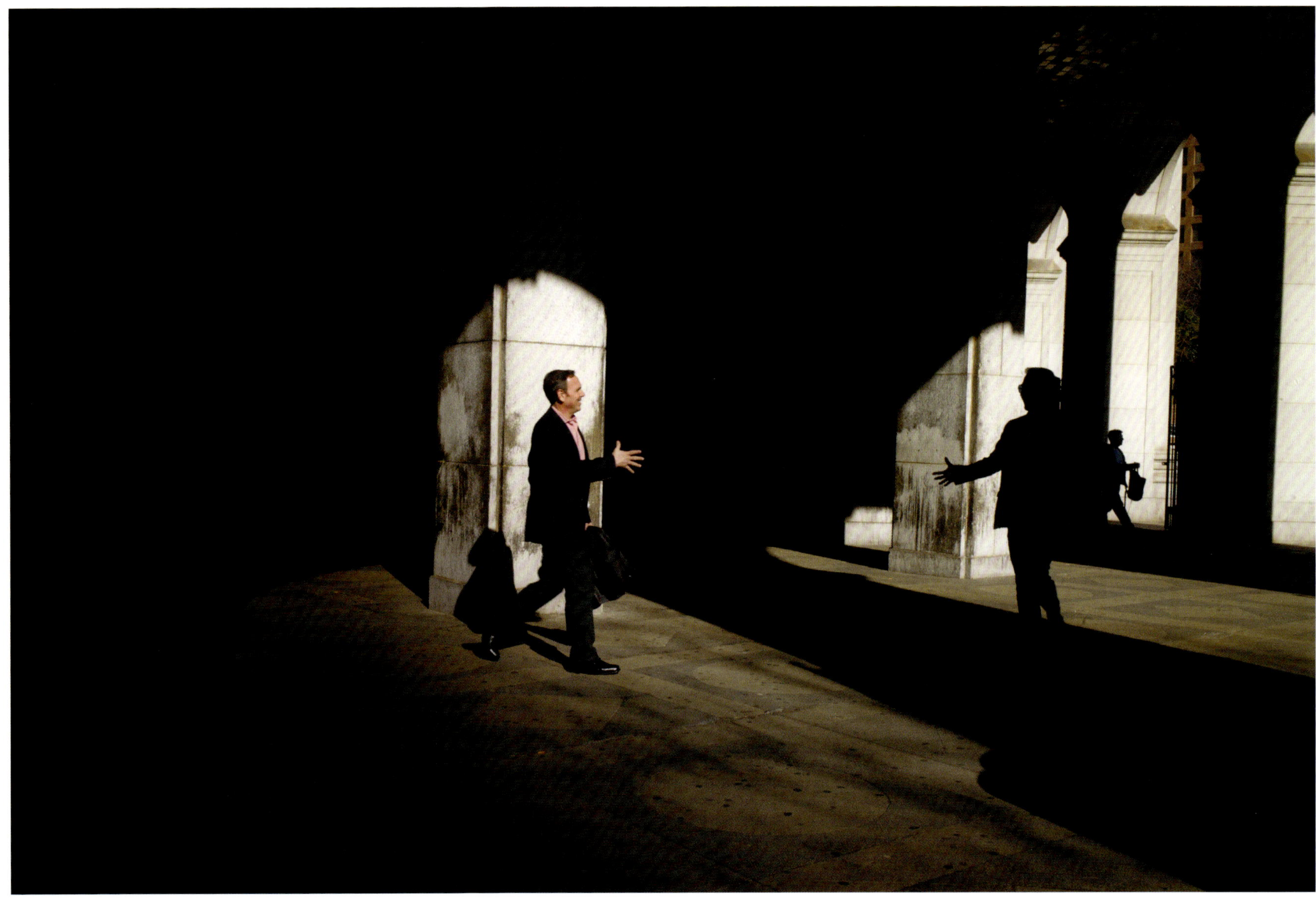

CITY HALL, NYC (2016)

When you're paying attention, sometimes life and serendipity offer you amazing, unexpected gifts. This is how I feel about this photo, taken in the arcades underneath New York's City Hall. Normally, I never pass by that spot, and this is the only time that I've photographed there. By lucky accident, I happened to be passing by at the exact right time of day, when the slanting sunlight was briefly reaching beneath the ceiling of the arcade. I lingered for about 10 minutes, and did not shoot more than 15 frames. This was almost the last one. As I was getting ready to leave, this incredible coincidence occurred—two acquaintances happened to bump into each other, and the light and shadow created this uncanny mirroring between their extended hands, one catching the light and one silhouetted in darkness.

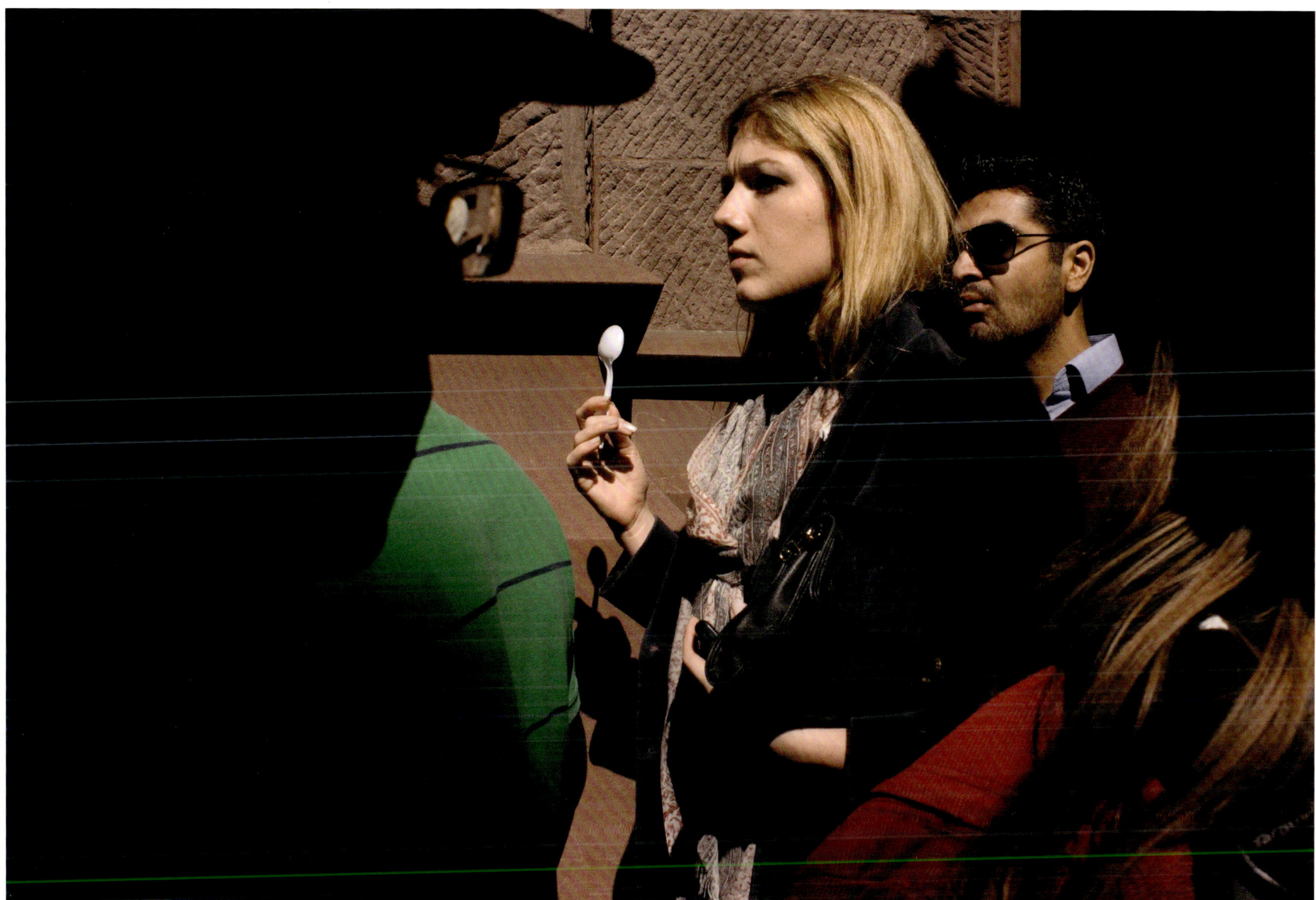

W 55TH ST, NYC (2010)

This photo demonstrates the importance of serendipity, but also how serendipity in itself may amount to nothing unless the photographer can think and react instantaneously to take advantage of it. I noticed the woman holding the little plastic spoon in this almost mysterious way, but the street was very crowded. As I was preparing to take the picture, I saw the silhouetted guy approach fast from the left. For a split second I thought he would ruin the shot, but then I realized that if I timed it right his silhouette would make for a more interesting composition.

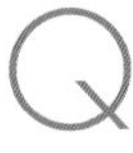

Q + A

How did you learn street photography, and what were the most important lessons?

I didn't go to school to study photography—I'm largely self-taught. Having said that, I first dabbled with photography for a brief period in my early twenties in Greece, and at that time I took a year-long photography class that was focused on the history of the medium rather than the technical nitty-gritty. In a sense that provided me with a terrific foundation, because by looking at the work of the great photographers, I realized what the medium was capable of—my eyes were opened to its possibilities. As Winogrand said, the main thing is to learn how to see—you can always learn the technical stuff later. I then abandoned photography for several years, but then re-engaged with it about 12 years ago and started photographing consistently. I have essentially been working on my own, mainly learning by doing, by engaging in the practice. The most important lesson (and the reason street photography is my favorite genre), is the realization that almost everything can become interesting and aesthetically significant when seen photographically. The photograph can be transcendent even if what it depicts is completely mundane and ordinary. Good street photography is art made out of nothing.

What drew—and still draws— you to photographing city life?

I live and spend most of my time in a city, so partly I photograph in that context out of necessity. I have a need to photograph as much as I need to breathe, so I make the time to photograph wherever I happen to be. I wish I could travel more, but I am mostly tethered to New York City for work, so I try to make the best of it photographically. New York is, of course, a very inspiring habitat for a street photographer, not least because of its deep connections to the history of the genre, but all cities are fascinating. The ability of the photographic gaze to provide a momentary (and likely illusory) antidote to the impersonality and indifference of the city creates an interesting dynamic that really resonates with me. The city provides a wonderful backdrop; a stage within which myriad small, everyday human dramas and comedies unfold, most of which go unnoticed. I feel a compulsion as a photographer to notice life around me, to pay attention, to preserve something from oblivion. That being said, if I've learned one thing as a photographer it is that any place, not just a city, is rife with photographic opportunity.

How do you set about capturing the characters and emotions of complete strangers—what do you look for in people and situations?

I'm not looking for something in particular—I don't have an agenda set in advance. Part of the joy of street photography is the opportunity to learn to embrace the unexpected, surprise, and serendipity. But, in general, a photograph resonates with me only when it achieves a kind of dynamic equilibrium between form and content. Formal aesthetic parameters are important, but even the most formally and technically stunning photograph strikes me as empty and pointless unless it also hits a nerve on an emotional register. Of course, I'm not talking of maudlin, one-dimensional sentimentality here. A photograph should be emotionally complicated, both in terms of the emotions of the people depicted in it and the emotions it evokes in the viewer. So, I am more interested in images that pose questions which remain suspended, rather than ones that provide simplistic, straightforward messages. In my work, I'm interested in the interplay between public space and people's inner private space, and in capturing something of the often infinitesimal outward signs of people's inner emotional life. One thing I abhor is crude visual puns and simplistic jokey images—such photos are not only emotionally shallow, but in fact insulting to the intelligence and sensitivity of the viewer.

What are your favorite techniques for finding suitable situations?

Walking and paying attention.

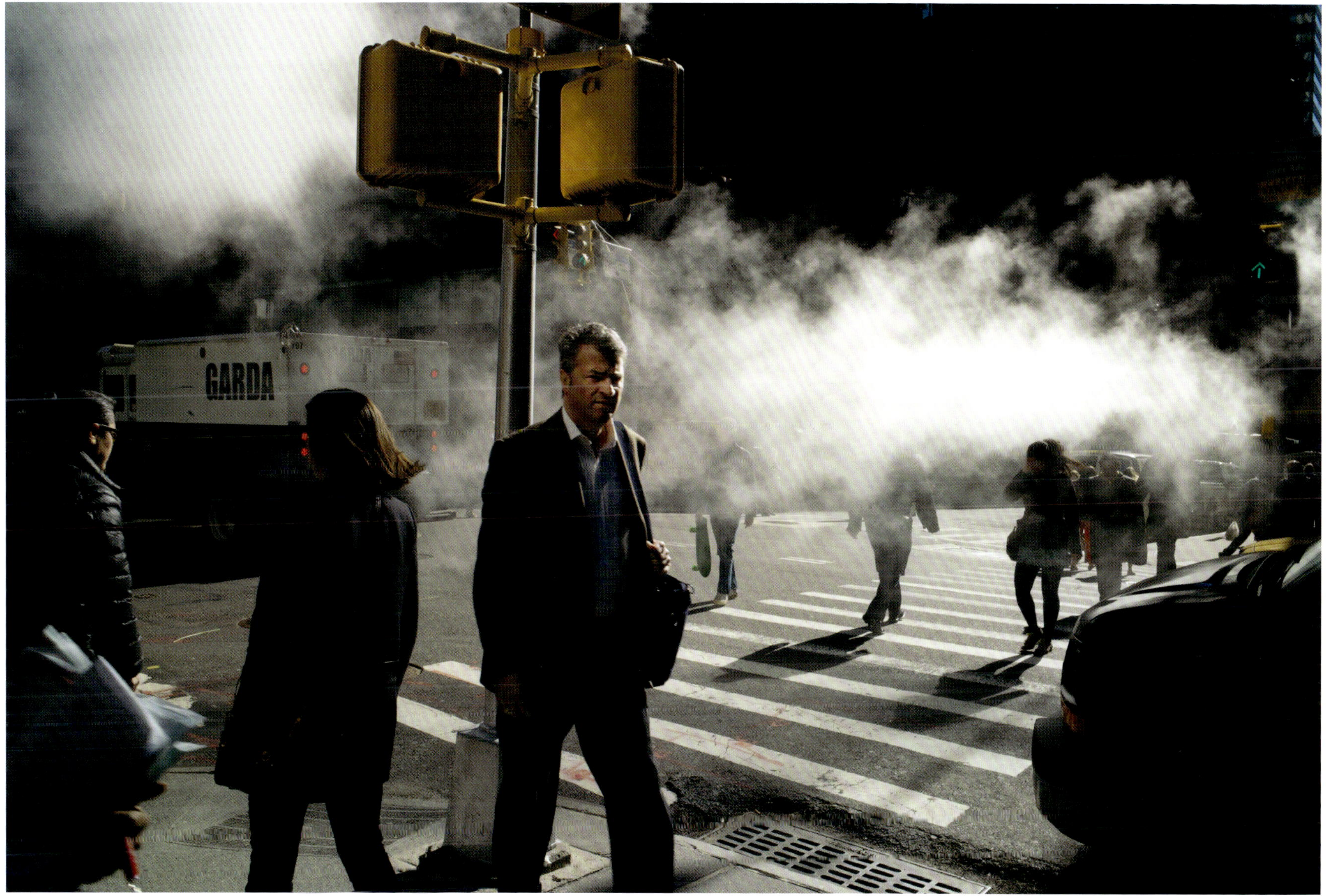

MADISON AVENUE, NYC (2014)

This is just an image of everyday life in the city. It is a very mundane scene, but there is beauty in moments like this. You don't need supposedly "funny" moments or unusual situations to make for an interesting photo. This image resonates with me especially because it quite literally depicts the ephemerality of life: the luminous, evanescent clouds of steam will be gone instantly, never to recur in quite the same configuration. And yet, there is beauty in the sadness of transience—the Japanese have the concept of *mono no aware* to express this complicated, bittersweet emotion.

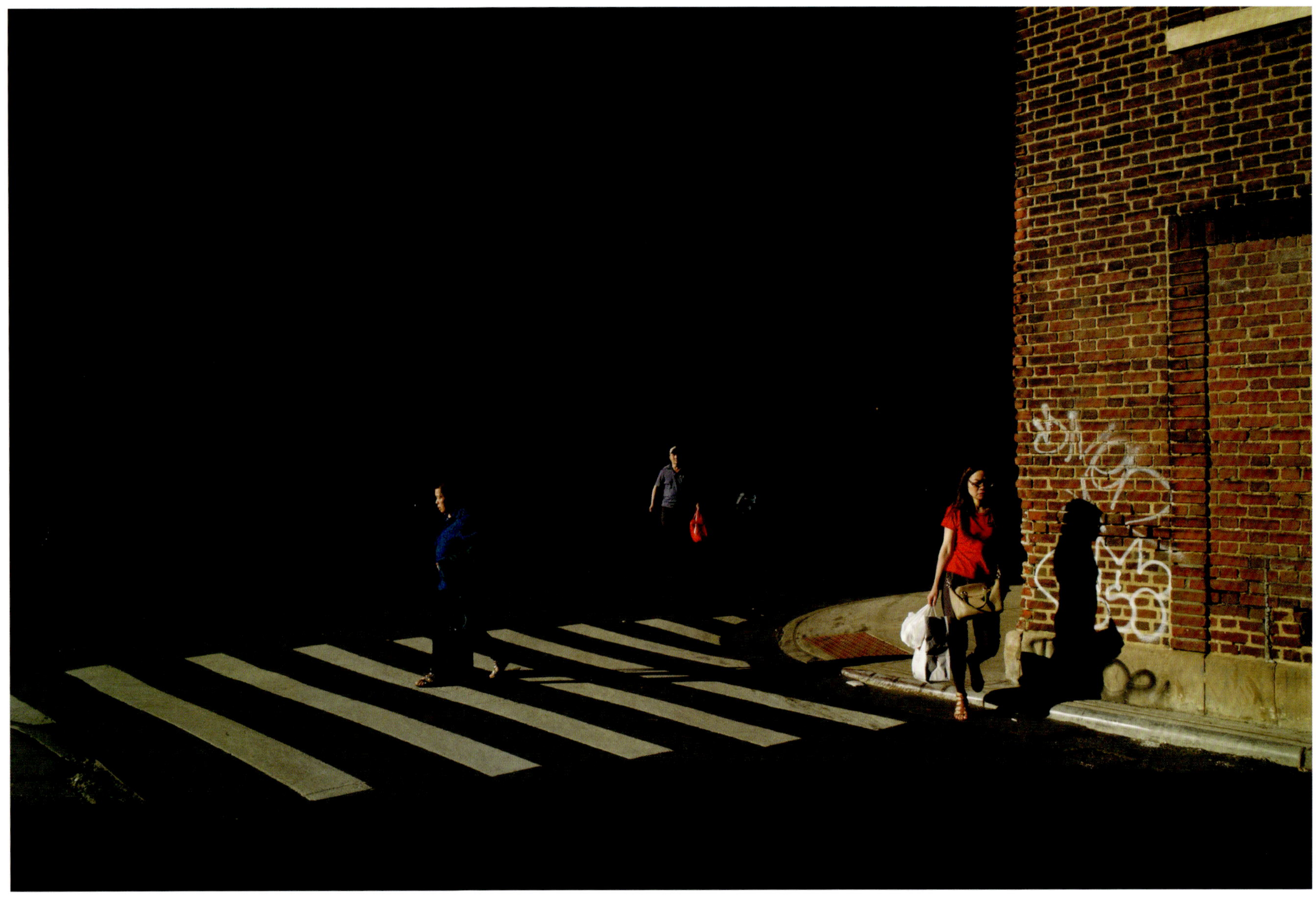

MECHANICS ALLEY, CHINATOWN, NYC (2017)

I have been photographing extensively in Chinatown for years, and one of the reasons I love the neighborhood is the fact that its bustling, small streets retain something of the atmosphere of a bygone, less gentrified New York. This photo was taken early on a summer evening, as the beautiful, slanting, golden light attests. Again, serendipity lent a helping hand, as I could not have wished for a better choreography among these pedestrians with their grocery bags. When I posted this photo on Instagram, I was very amused by an unfriendly comment from a self-described cinematographer. He asserted, in a smugly knowing tone, that the scene must have been artificially lit, because he thought the lighting was too good to be just available, natural light.

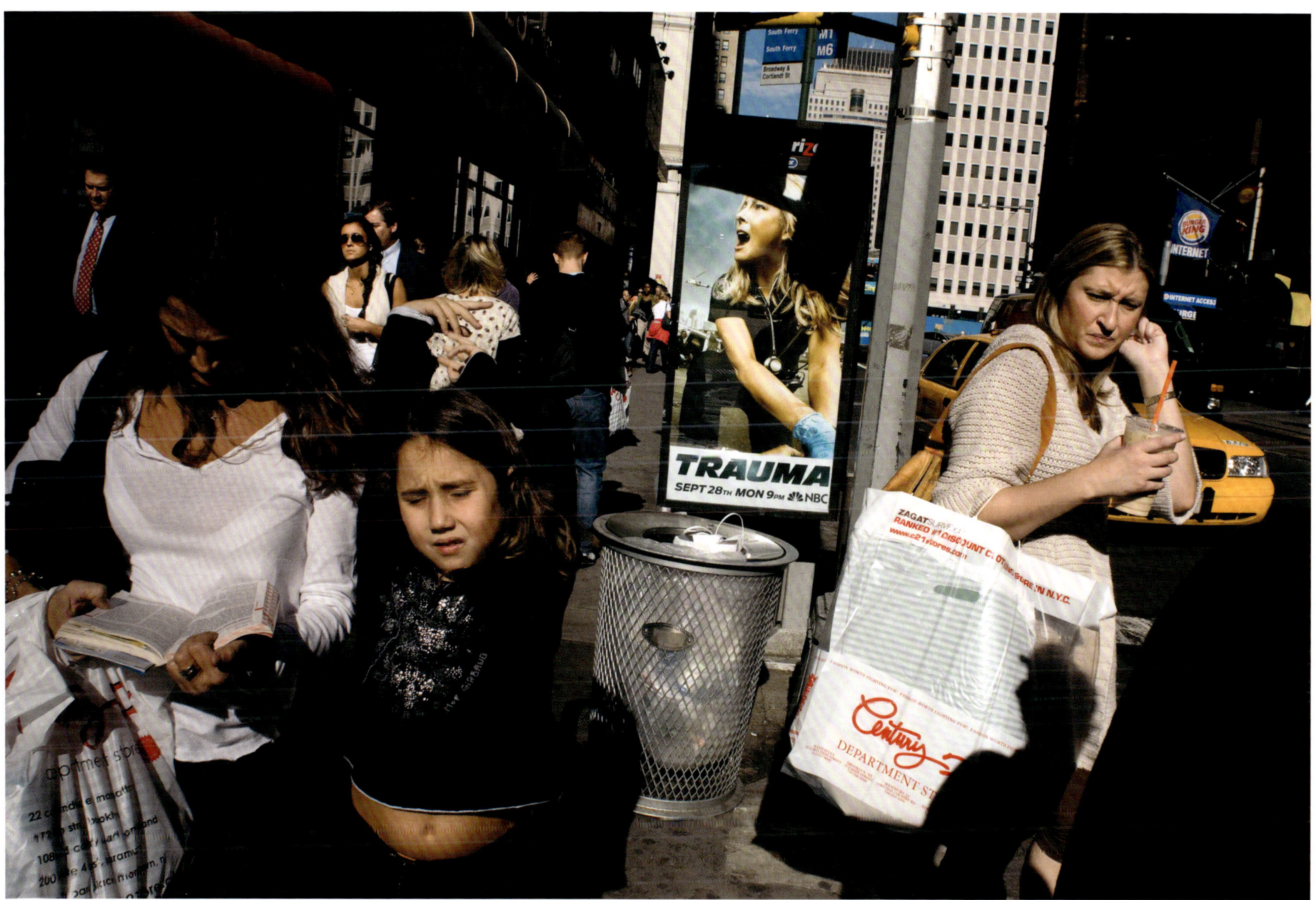

LOWER BROADWAY, NYC (2009)

This image epitomizes the fact that the street photographer has to think on his or her feet, and that the difference between a good photo and a failure may come down to no more than a few milliseconds. I was waiting for the green light to cross the street and I happened to turn around and look behind me, and saw this fleeting, uncanny parallel, or mirroring, between the little girl's expression and that of the woman on the right. I had to react instantly. Often, street photography is more of an intuitive process than a fully conscious one.

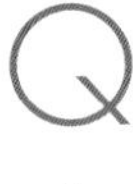

Q + A

For many people, photographing strangers, especially if obviously emotional, is very difficult—do you feel you're being intrusive at all?

I agree that it's not easy crossing that mental barrier, even when you know that, technically speaking, you're not intruding into someone's private space—there is no presumption of privacy on the street, especially these days when our likeness and movements are captured countless times a day on security cameras. In my own case, overcoming this emotional inhibition has been the greatest challenge and obstacle to my work. It gets a little easier with time, but it's really a constantly renewed struggle—it is not something achieved once and for all. I still often censor myself and avoid taking photos, especially when it feels like I would be intruding in a gratuitously voyeuristic or exploitative way, or when I fear that I would make the other person feel uncomfortable. I know that some other street photographers would likely be able to take some great photos in the same situation, but sometimes I just cannot overcome my inhibition. However, for the most part, I feel that taking photos of strangers—when done discreetly and with kindness—is akin to paying a compliment; it is a celebration and affirmation of the lives of others. But although I know this on an intellectual level, it's still a difficult process emotionally.

Many of your photographs use strong contrast—what challenges does this create, and how do you overcome them?

Rather than thinking of this as a challenge, I've come to appreciate it as an opportunity. The fact that in a photograph you cannot expose correctly for all areas of such a scene attests to the crudeness of our photographic equipment compared to our eyes: our eyes can see gradation and detail across the board, but with a camera you have to either expose for the light areas or for the shadows. Initially, I thought of this as a limitation and a defect, but then I recognized the esthetic possibilities it opens up. There is something moving and uncanny about an image in which people's faces seem to be emerging from a black void, for example. In general, I think it is liberating to work within the constraints of a specific medium and bend them to creative purposes rather than try to bypass them. Of course, there are also some risks and challenges inherent in the use of a pronounced formal device such as this. More than anything, one should always be on guard against the danger of devolving into an empty mannerism; form should follow content.

How do you focus quickly on your chosen subject?

For the last few years I have mostly been using a Leica M9, which, even though capable of producing exceptional images, is quite primitive compared to modern, fully automated digital SLR cameras, as it is essentially a manual camera with no autofocus. Because I need to work very quickly—and also because I actually like images with a wide depth of field—I use zone focusing whenever there is adequate light. But even when I'm using a DSLR with autofocus, I try to set the aperture at f/11 or smaller, because I like things to be sharp throughout the image. I always avoid shooting in bursts. I sometimes see people shooting at 10 frames per second, or whatever, but unless you're shooting sports that kind of approach makes no sense to me. I may shoot lots of frames if I see something interesting, but some thought goes into each and every one of those frames. Shooting in automatic bursts is just random luck-of-the-draw photography—it's a lazy approach, and I believe you will never learn how to really see if you indulge in that.

What tips would you give to those who wish to master street photography?

I would suggest delving into the history of the genre. Look at photography books and not just social media. I have a feeling that many young aspiring street photographers don't have much knowledge of, or exposure to, what came before the early years of this century. As a result, I get the sense that many people who are not informed enough end up equating street photography to a particular type of image—mainly images of eccentric or funny-looking people or obvious and crude visual puns—just because such images have somewhat dominated the contemporary street photography scene, at least on social media. That is a shame, because there is a lot of amazing contemporary street photography that is much better than that. The genre contains infinite possibilities. So, it is important to train one's eyes by looking at the work of the great street photographers of the past, as well as contemporary ones. Other than that, my only advice is this: have open eyes and an open heart. Be interested in the world, not in yourself.

TECHNICAL INFORMATION

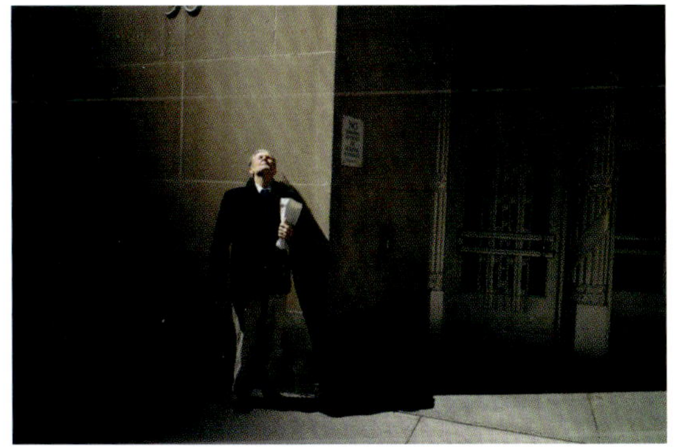

CHURCH STREET, NYC (2014)
NEW YORK CITY, NEW YORK, USA

Camera: Leica M9
Lens/Focal length: Elmarit 28mm f/2.8
Aperture: f/19
Shutter speed: 1/250 sec.
ISO: 400

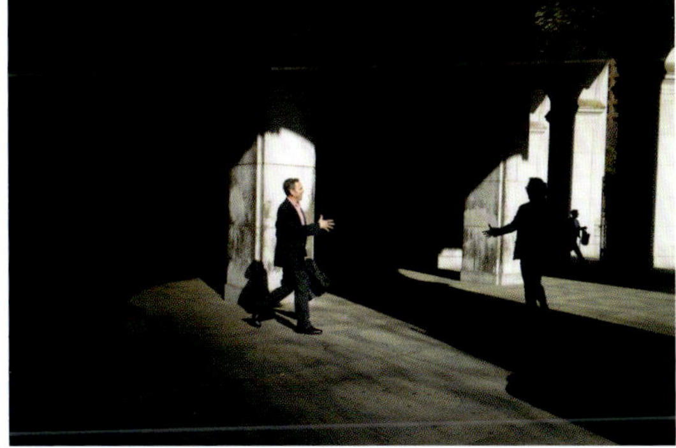

CITY HALL, NYC (2016)
NEW YORK CITY, NEW YORK, USA

Camera: Leica M9
Lens/Focal length: Elmarit 28mm f/2.8
Aperture: f/23
Shutter speed: 1/180 sec.
ISO: 400

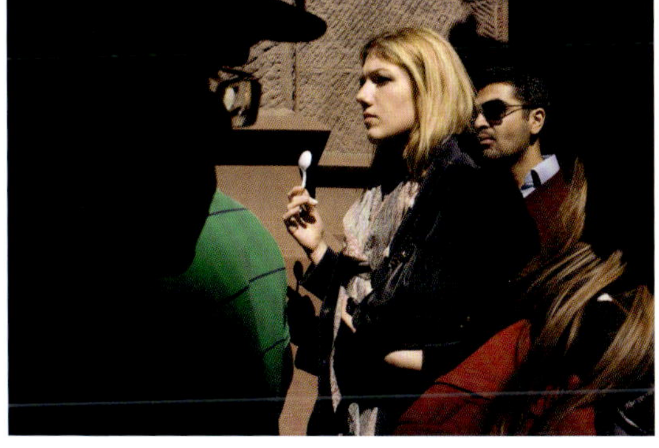

W 55TH ST, NYC (2010)
NEW YORK CITY, NEW YORK, USA

Camera: Nikon D80
Lens/Focal length: Nikor 20mm (35mm equivalent: 30mm)
Aperture: f/13
Shutter speed: 1/640 sec.
ISO: 320

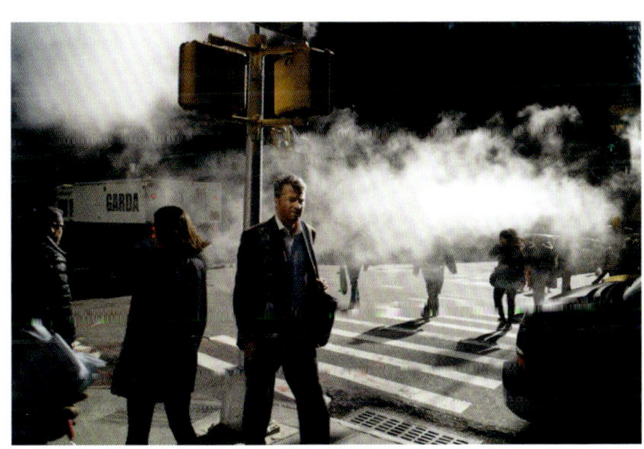

MADISON AVENUE, NYC (2014)
NEW YORK CITY, NEW YORK, USA

Camera: Leica M9
Lens/Focal length: Elmarit 28mm f/2.8
Aperture: f/9.5
Shutter speed: 1/250 sec.
ISO: 400

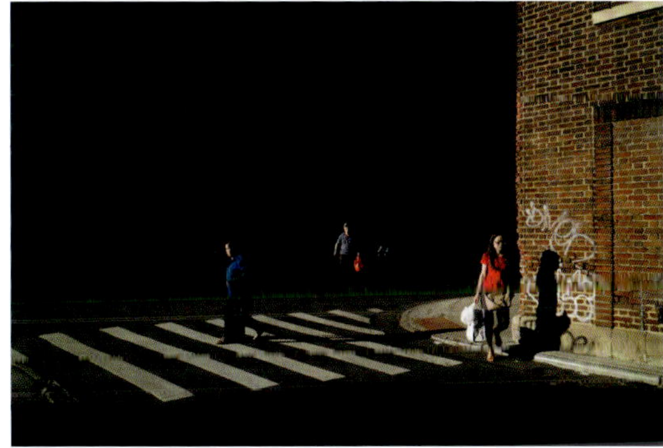

MECHANICS ALLEY, CHINATOWN, NYC (2017)
NEW YORK CITY, NEW YORK, USA

Camera: Leica M9
Lens/Focal length: Elmarit 28mm f/2.8
Aperture: f/16
Shutter speed: 1/350 sec.
ISO: 500

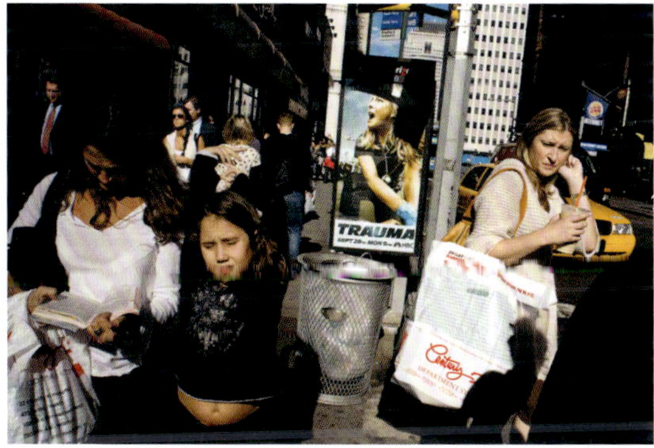

LOWER BROADWAY, NYC (2009)
NEW YORK CITY, NEW YORK, USA

Camera: Nikon D80
Lens/Focal length: Nikor 20mm (35mm equivalent: 30mm)
Aperture: f/13
Shutter speed: 1/250 sec.
ISO: 200

RUI PALHA

Rui Palha was born in Portugal, in 1953, and is based in Lisbon. Photography has been his hobby (with many interruptions) since he was 14 years old. In 2001, he began to devote almost all of his time to street photography. Rui says: "Photography is a very important part of my space… it is to discover, it is to capture, giving flow to what the heart feels and sees in a certain moment, it is being in the street, experiencing, understanding, learning and, essentially, practicing the freedom of being, of living, of thinking…"

Rui sees himself as a storyteller, walking around Lisbon capturing the everyday lives and emotions of the many people he encounters, and the beauty of them and their normal, real lives. Rui is a proud amateur photographer, relishing the freedom from constraints this gives him, and believing that it is the only way that he can photograph what he wants, how he wants.

UNTITLED

House of Music, Porto, Portugal.

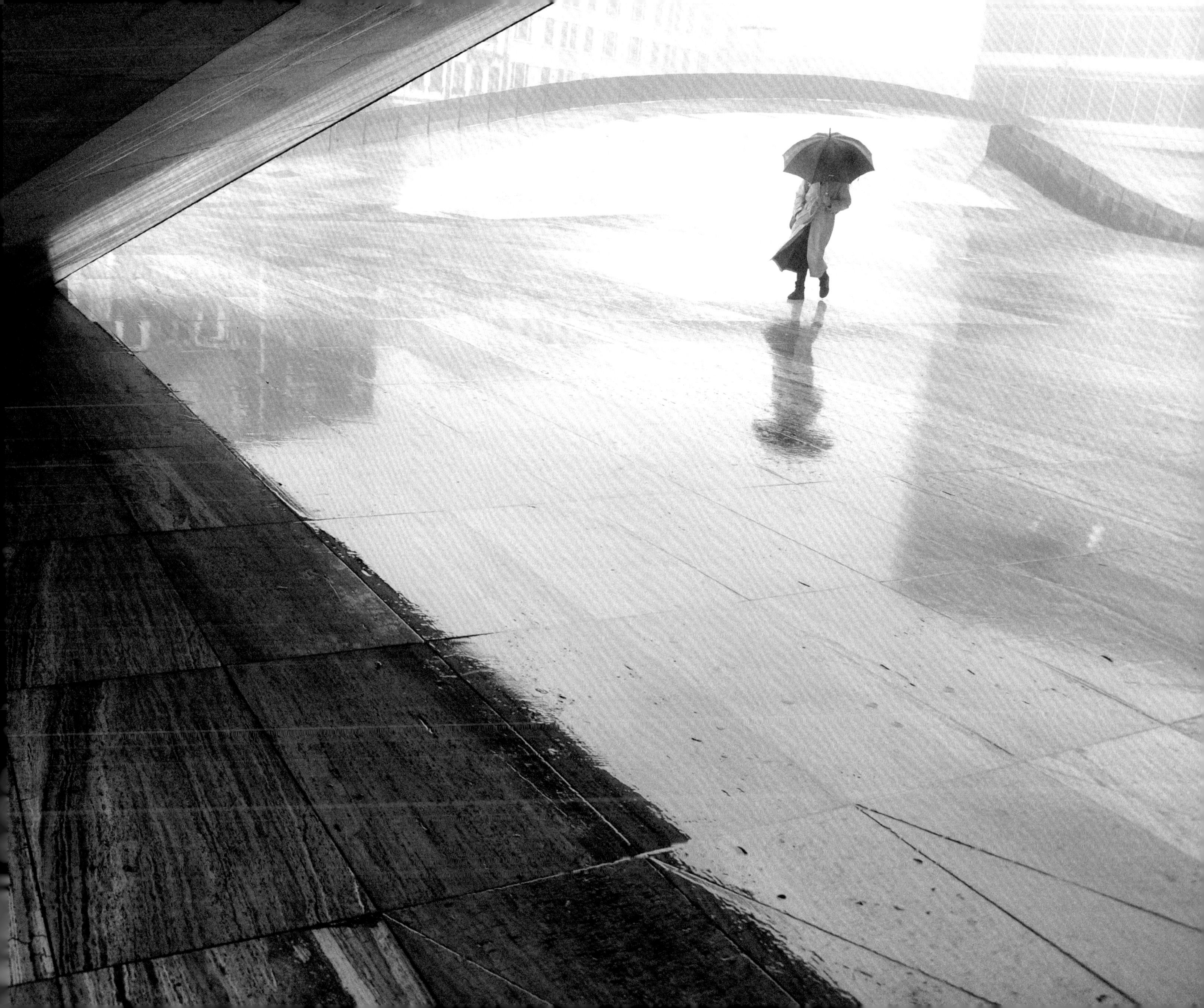

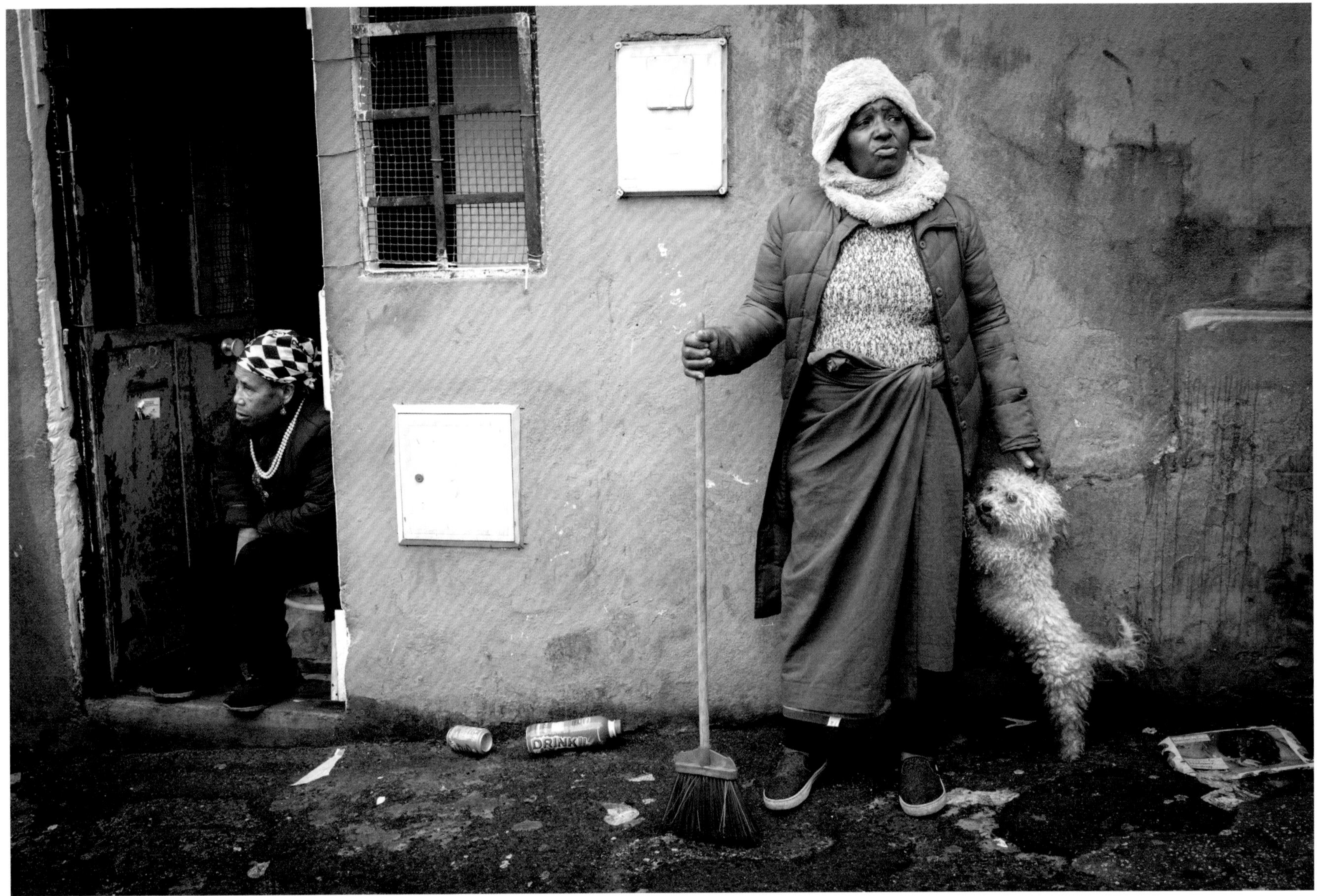

UNTITLED

Cova da Moura Community, Damaia, Portugal.

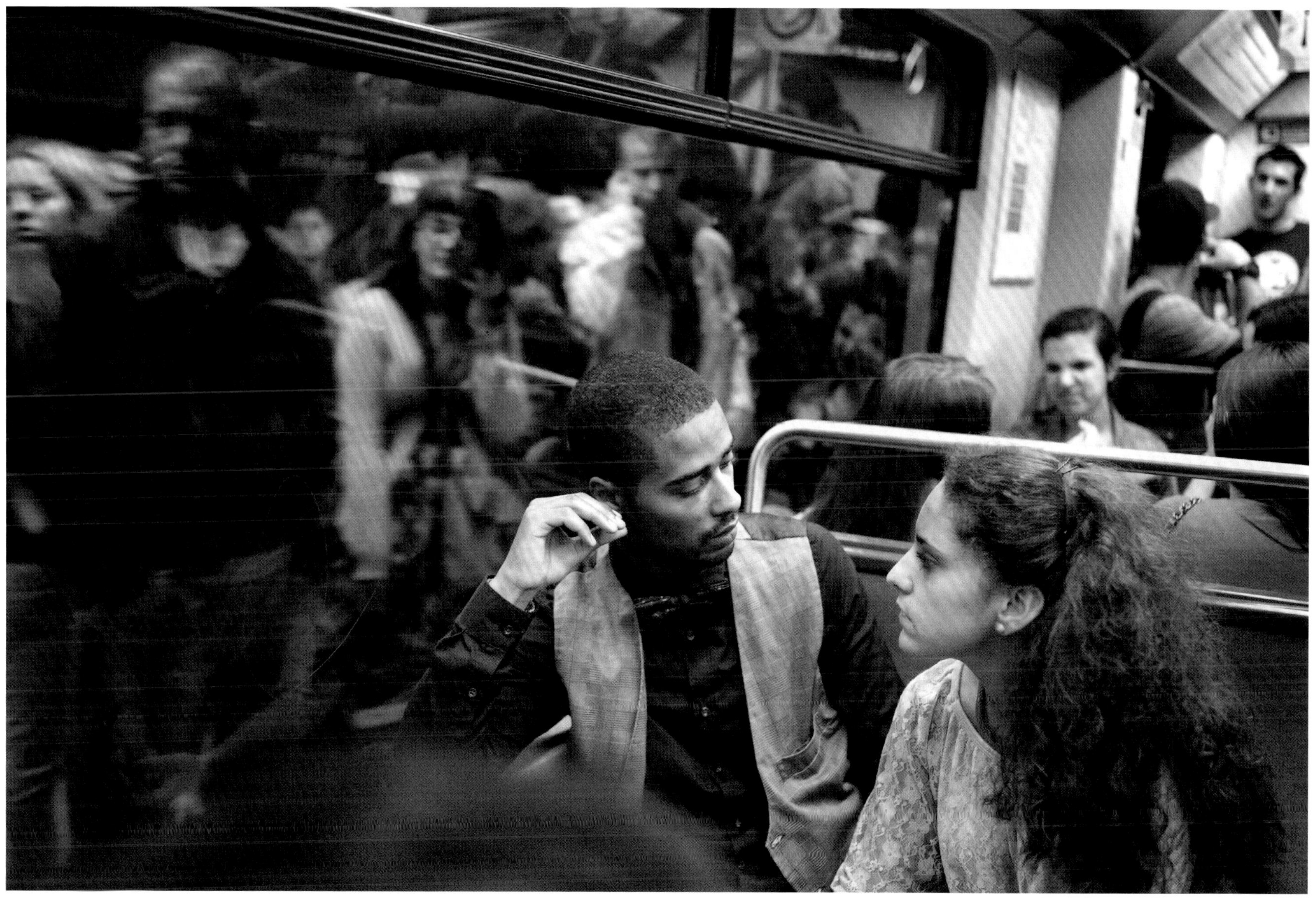

UNTITLED

Metro, Lisbon, Portugal

Q + A

What drew you to photography, and especially street photography?

Photography has been a hobby for me since I was 14 years of age. I even had my own darkroom, but, to be honest, I've only ever enjoyed "pressing the shutter" on the streets. Stopping a moment in time is an amazing feeling and I always leave home excited because I never can imagine what or who I will find, see, or meet during the day. I can repeat the same routes thousands of times and still feel that there is something different to photograph. I'm often hypnotized by the movement of people, and by their expressions and their reactions. It's a fantastic challenge to try to capture all the bustle of everyday life, and you learn a lot about the world. There are so many appealing elements to street photography—capturing a moment as well as possible, the lighting, the graphic forms that people create while they are moving. In these scenes of everyday life, there is always a beauty to unknown people—my "street models"—that is independent of color, religion, and politics. Over the years I've learned that you need to see through the camera, not only with your eyes, but with your heart too, and to try to capture some of the poetry in the surrounding world.

What sort of challenges do you have to overcome in street photography?

Street photography is not an easy way to make photographs—you have to be brave and astute, and be able to anticipate the moment before it happens. Another challenge is creating something new. I always set out to create different images in some of the most visited and photographed spots—creativity is obligatory in street photography. I actually like dangerous places—they're challenging for me. I'm not afraid of anything, because I know I am not doing anything wrong. Sometimes I have had problems with very aggressive people, but after talking to them we often become friends, and I lose any fear I had in that location. I have had lots of memorable experiences while shooting—the street is a school, so a big part of me is what I learned on the streets. I've learned to respect people a lot, so if people don't want to be photographed then I respect that—I never publish a photo of someone who's objected to that photo being taken.

How do you approach looking for images in the street?

One of the things I love about street photography is the creative possibilities. I can "play" with everything—lines, shapes, the positions of people, balance, details, and textures—and draw on a wide range of "tools" to help me compose images. I'll call on the rule of thirds, symmetry, asymmetry, leading lines, patterns, positions of people, and so on, but by far the best way to approach composition is to experiment: be creative and mad!

You seem drawn to rain—why is that? Are you ever tempted to use flash?

Rainy days are special for me, for all kinds of reasons. The lighting is great, because the Portuguese pavement helps to reflect the light. The lighting is also uniform, so it's very easy to measure. I've never used flash, and never will. In my country, people don't enjoy being the target of a flash—they never react well and often become very aggressive. They assume there is a big lack of respect and don't tolerate it. One of the rules I always follow is to respect people—they are the main component of my photographs, so I have to respect them. I also believe that flash "kills" natural shadows, or produces artificial shadows where they didn't exist. I prefer the magic of the available light that exists on the streets, and also in dark places, such as in the underground, or churches, for example. You can produce wonderful and very artistic images by learning how to use available light.

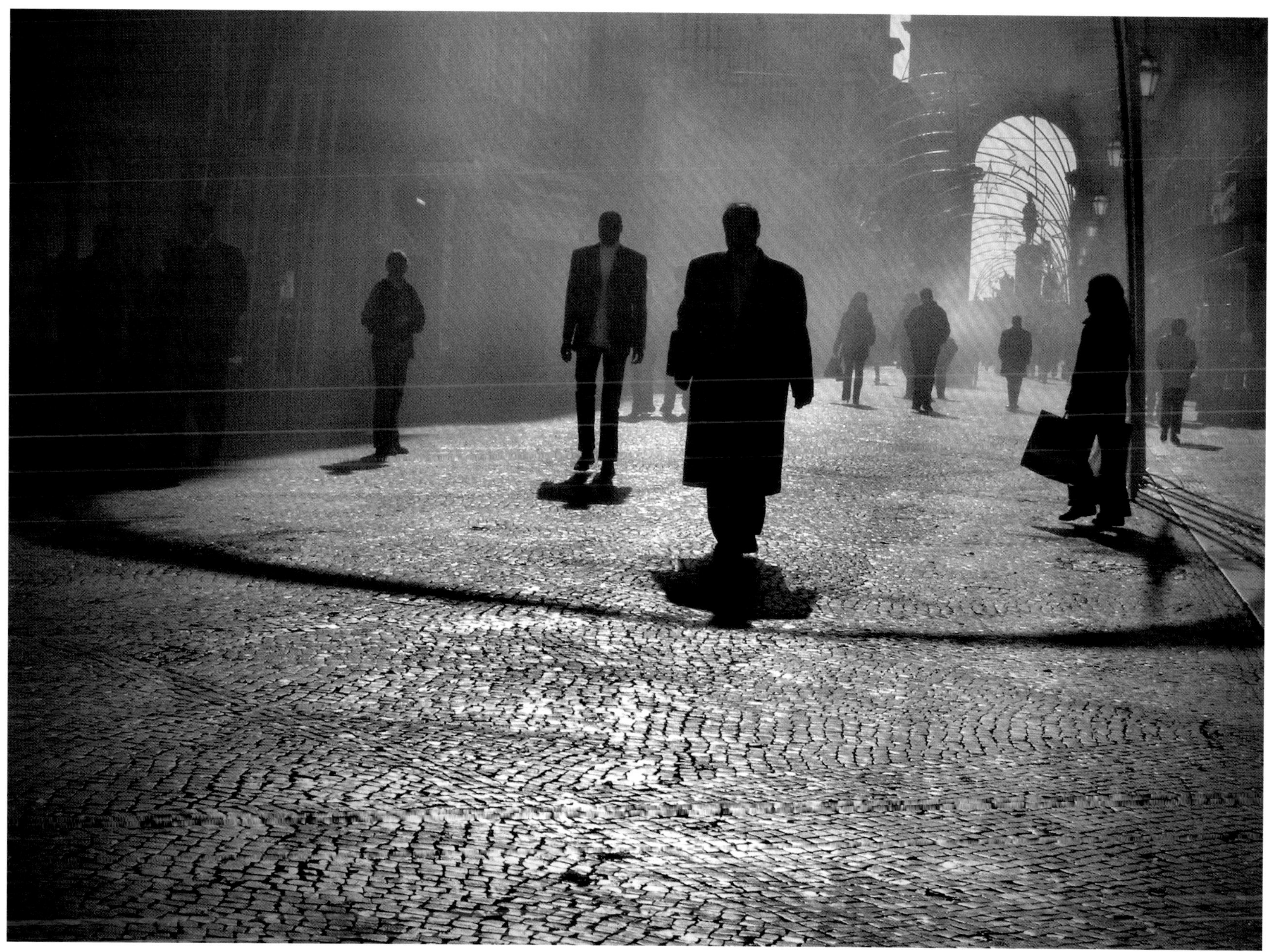

UNTITLED

Rua Augusta, Old Town, Lisbon, Portugal.

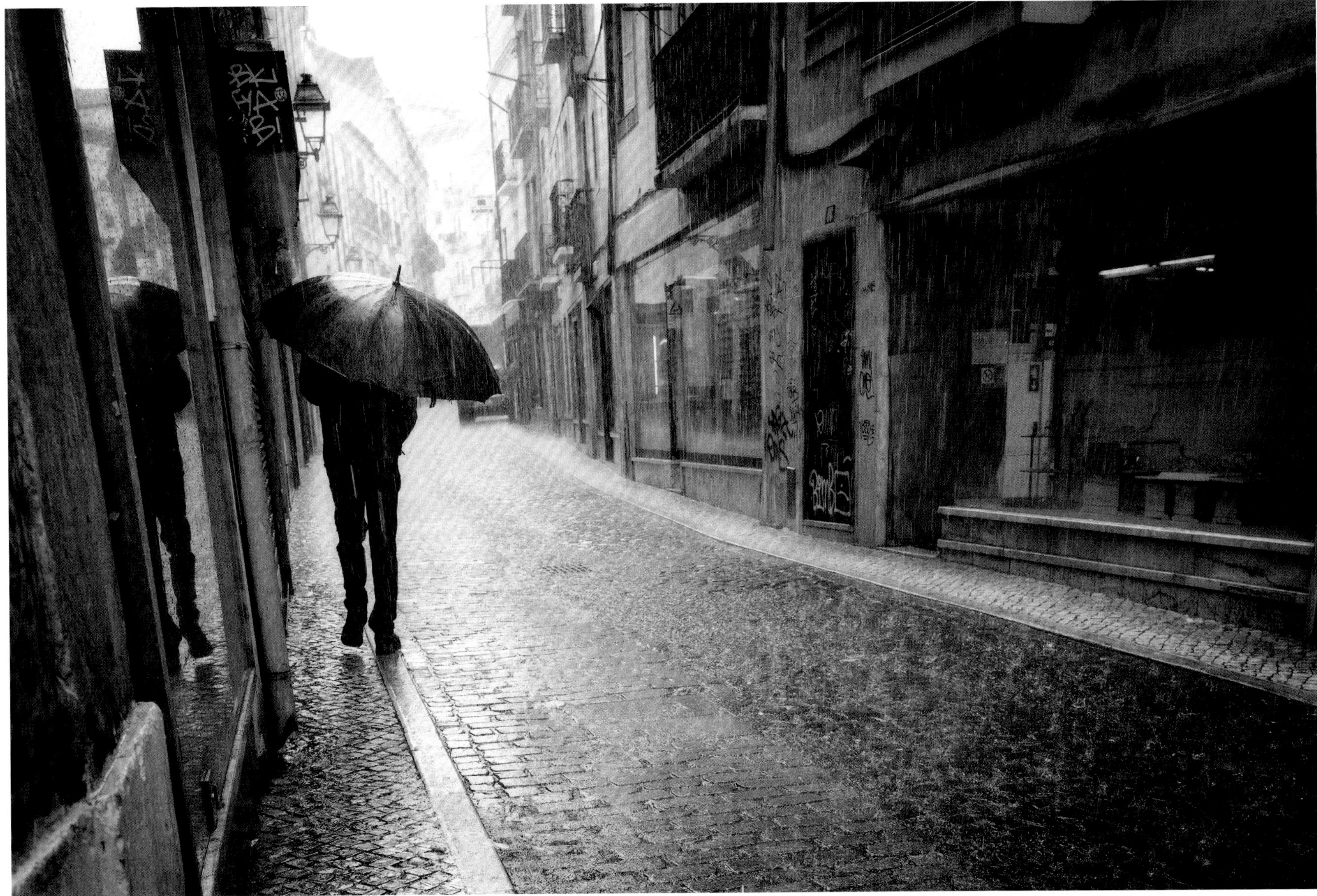

UNTITLED

Old Town, Lisbon, Portugal.

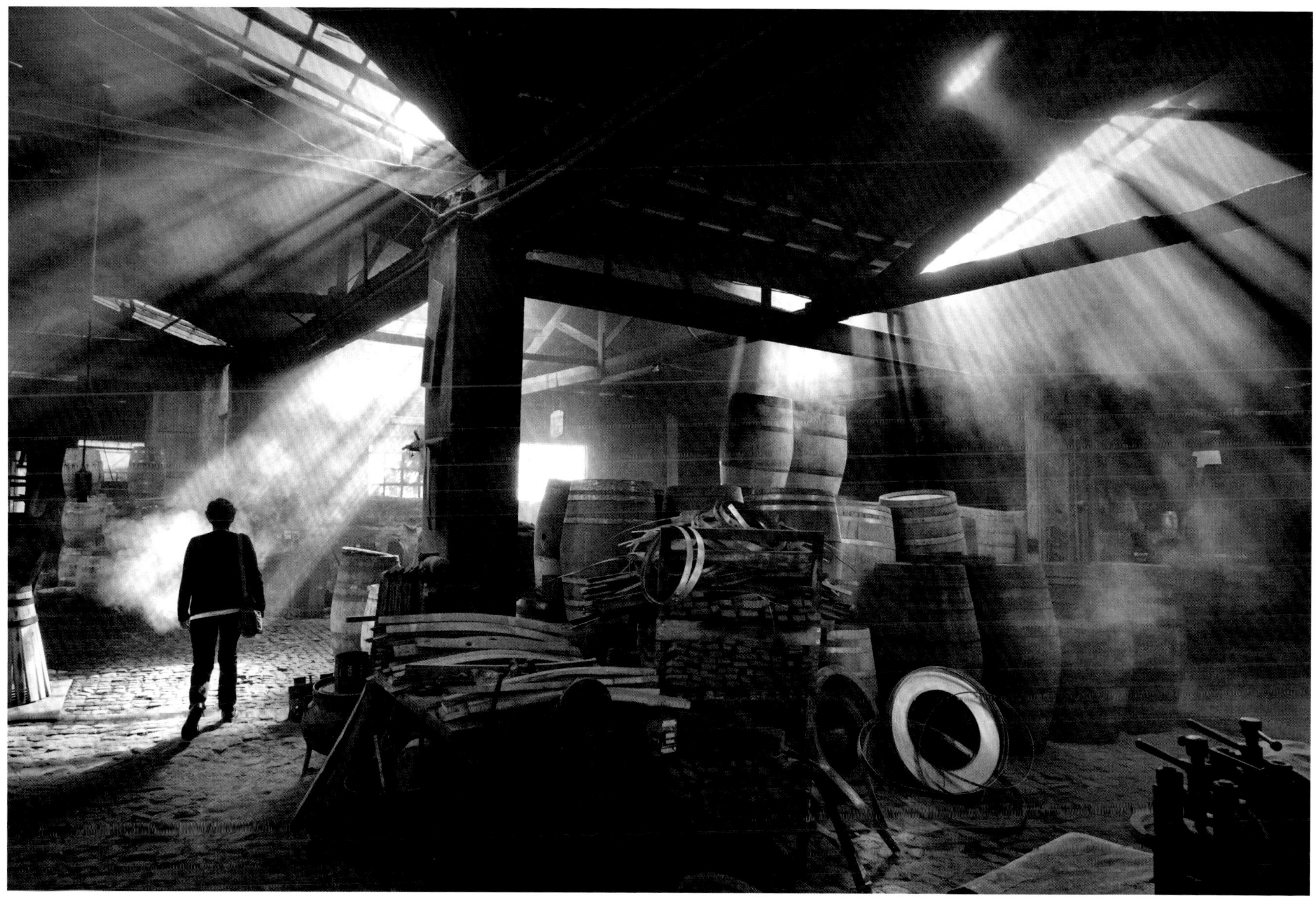

UNTITLED

Cooperage, Esmoriz, Portugal

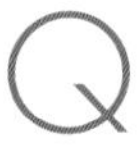

What appeals to you about working in black and white? And how do you create your monochrome images?

I've tried to shoot in color in the past, but I've always loved and preferred black-and-white images. There are people who say "no color, no lie" and, in a way, I agree with this. If you look at a black-and-white photograph, and you like it a lot, the photograph is telling you something without artifice. Sometimes a color photo is appealing just because of the beautiful combinations of colors. This doesn't mean that I don't like color photos—there are great photojournalists working in color. But I only use black and white, nowadays. I agree with Ted Grant, who wrote: "When you photograph people in color, you photograph their clothes. But when you photograph people in black and white, you photograph their souls!" If I use my Leica M Monochrom or shoot Tri-X film, I don't need to convert files to black and white; but if I use a color digital camera, I use a plug-in called B/W Styler, which emulates the traditional darkroom.

Like many street photographers, you wish to keep the interpretation of your photographs open, leaving it to the viewer to draw their own conclusions—why is that?

I sometimes give my photographs titles, but only if I think of it at the moment I take the picture—if I don't, the image will be untitled. I certainly don't agree with providing an explanation for a photograph—the image itself must tell a story, without needing words. An image is worth more than a thousand words, so if words are needed to "explain" a photograph, the photograph isn't good enough. The image, by itself, must attract the viewer, and it's fundamental they have the freedom to interpret it the way they want, never directed by words next to the picture.

What is your favorite camera and lens, and why?

I now have two favorite cameras: a Leica Q with a fixed 28mm lens, and a Leica M Monochrom that I use with either a 21mm or 35mm lens (35mm is my favorite focal length). The Leica Q is my daily camera, while the Leica M Monochrom is my second camera, although I will take both on some occasions. For political meetings, street events, and festivals, I like to use the 21mm lens with the Leica M Monochrom because it allows me to be among people, and to get very close to them. However, I don't think the gear is that important—I can use any camera, really. The most important thing is to feel comfortable with your equipment, and to be able to find your "eye" with whatever camera you use.

What tips would you give to someone who wants to master street photography?

Firstly, love and respect people. Try to understand them, their thoughts, their movement, their feelings, their soul. Always listen to people, as they will truly teach you everything about life. Also, be brave and courageous. Try to be as close as possible to the people you photograph. This way you will know and feel their soul, and vice versa. Always be happy with your own street work before sharing it everywhere—it is important to be very critical and demanding with yourself. Make sure you enjoy people, enjoy life, and enjoy your street photography. This way you are enjoying the entire world, which helps you to grow as a person. Finally, always try to be creative and different from other photographers, even if you are visiting the same places.

"I agree with Ted Grant, who wrote: 'When you photograph people in color, you photograph their clothes. But when you photograph people in black and white, you photograph their souls!'"

TECHNICAL INFORMATION

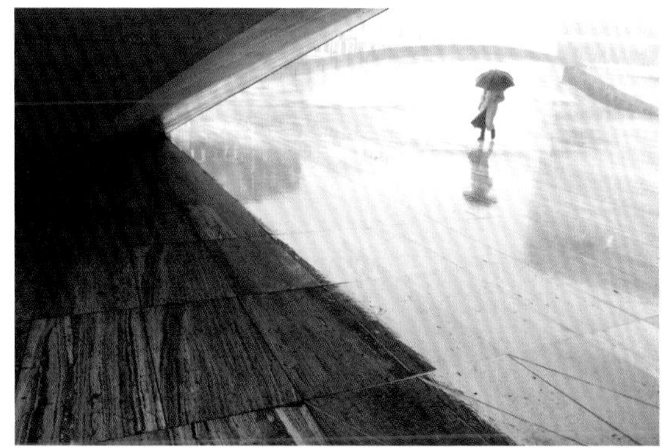

UNTITLED
HOUSE OF MUSIC, PORTO,
PORTUGAL

Camera: Nikon D700
Lens/Focal length: 28mm f/3.5
Aperture: f/6.3
Shutter speed: 1/160 sec.
ISO: 1000

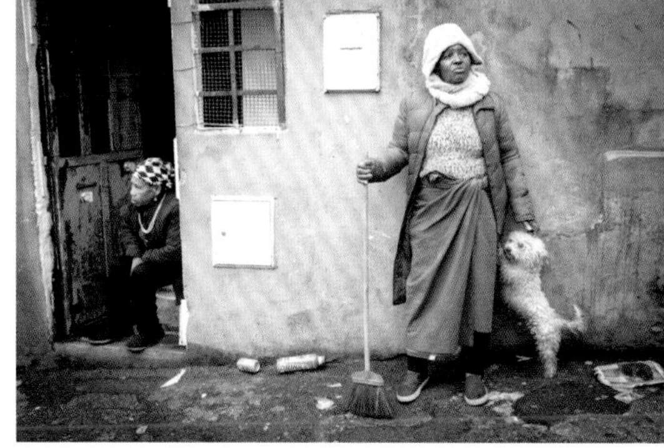

UNTITLED
COVA DA MOURA COMMUNITY,
DAMAIA, PORTUGAL

Camera: Leica M Monochrom
Lens/Focal length: Leica Summilux 35mm f/1.4
Aperture: f/9.5
Shutter speed: 1/250 sec.
ISO: 4000

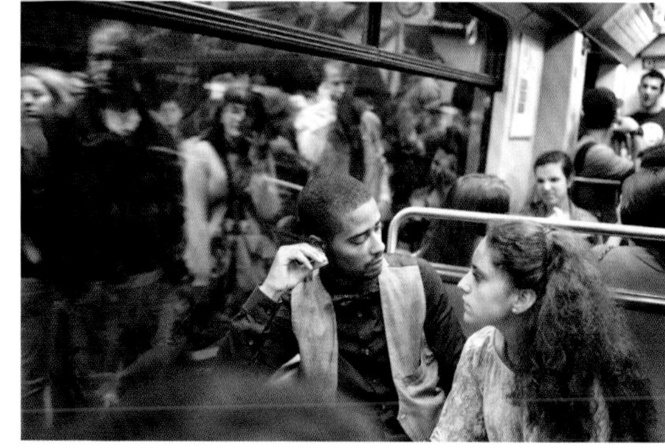

UNTITLED
METRO, LISBON,
PORTUGAL

Camera: Sony RX1
Lens/Focal length: Fixed 35mm f/2
Aperture: f/2
Shutter speed: 1/200 sec.
ISO: 2500

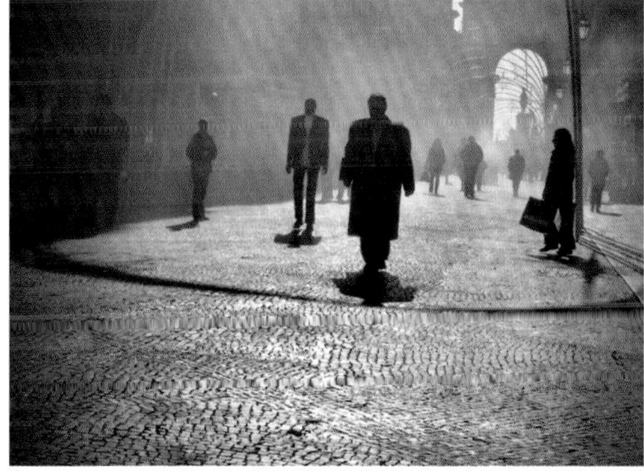

UNTITLED
RUA AUGUSTA, OLD TOWN, LISBON,
PORTUGAL

Camera: Olympus C 7070
Lens/Focal length: 5.7-22.9mm f/2.8-4.8 at 17mm (35mm equivalent: 82mm)
Aperture: f/11
Shutter speed: 1/640 sec.
ISO: 100

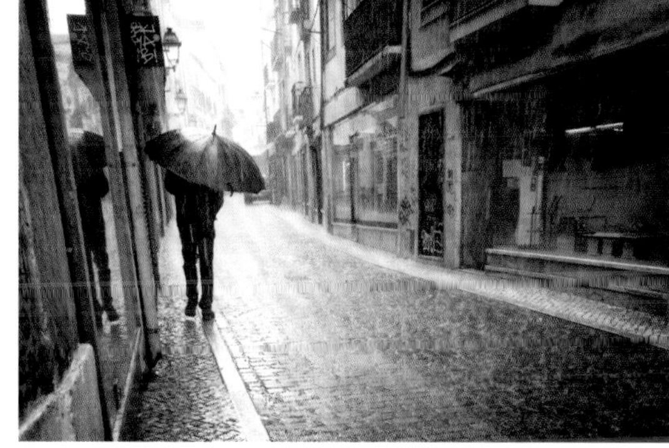

UNTITLED
OLD TOWN, LISBON,
PORTUGAL

Camera: Leica Q
Lens/Focal length: 28mm f/1.7
Aperture: f/6.3
Shutter speed: 1/250 sec.
ISO: 1000

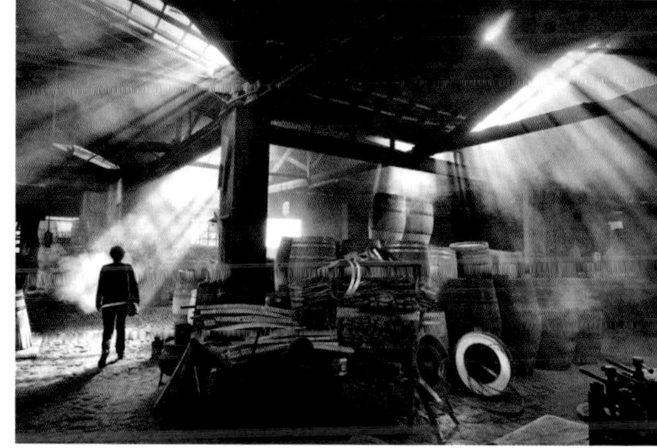

UNTITLED
COOPERAGE, ESMORIZ,
PORTUGAL

Camera: Sony a7
Lens/Focal length: 24mm f/4
Aperture: f/9
Shutter speed: 1/160 sec.
ISO: 2500

MASTER OF COMPLEXITY
ED PETERS

Ed Peters didn't begin life wanting to become a photographer. He has an early memory of being given a camera by his mother to photograph a primary school outing, but he can't remember using a camera for anything else until he was almost 30 years old. Then, a professional photographer showed him the work of some well-known photographers, and introduced him to the fundamentals of using a camera and a darkroom. Soon Ed was doing freelance jobs for local newspapers, and shortly afterward he was given a staff position. Later, he joined a photo agency and started to shoot topical news stories, including the plight of Burmese refugees, war in the Balkans, and famine in Somalia.

As time passed, Ed became more enamored with street photography. Inspired by the work of a number of artists in various disciplines, he began to work on long-term projects in locations in the United States, India, and Mexico. Today, Ed regularly exhibits his photographs around the world and is a member of the photography collective, Vivo.

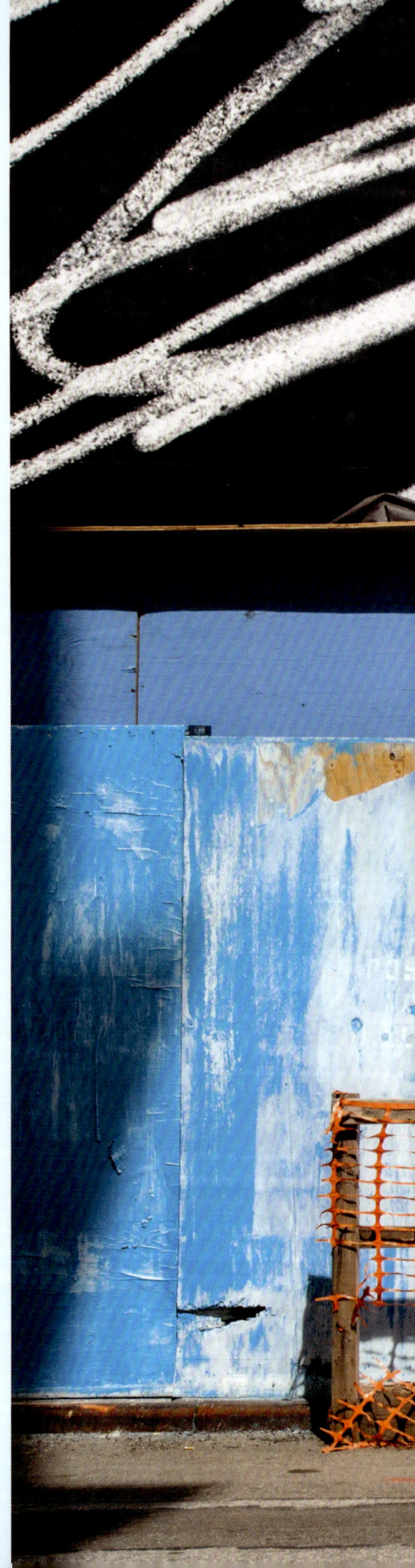

UNTITLED

This photograph was taken near a construction site in Lower Manhattan. I remember that it was the gestural black-and-white painting that first caught my eye. It seemed to me as if a giant artist had chosen to use the side of the building as a personal sketchpad. When I looked more closely at the scene, I was also intrigued by the relationship of the construction site's blue barrier to the building. After positioning myself at what I considered to be the best spot, I took several photos while people passed along the busy street. I thought that several of the pictures were good, but decided that the one of the man in the red hat was the best.

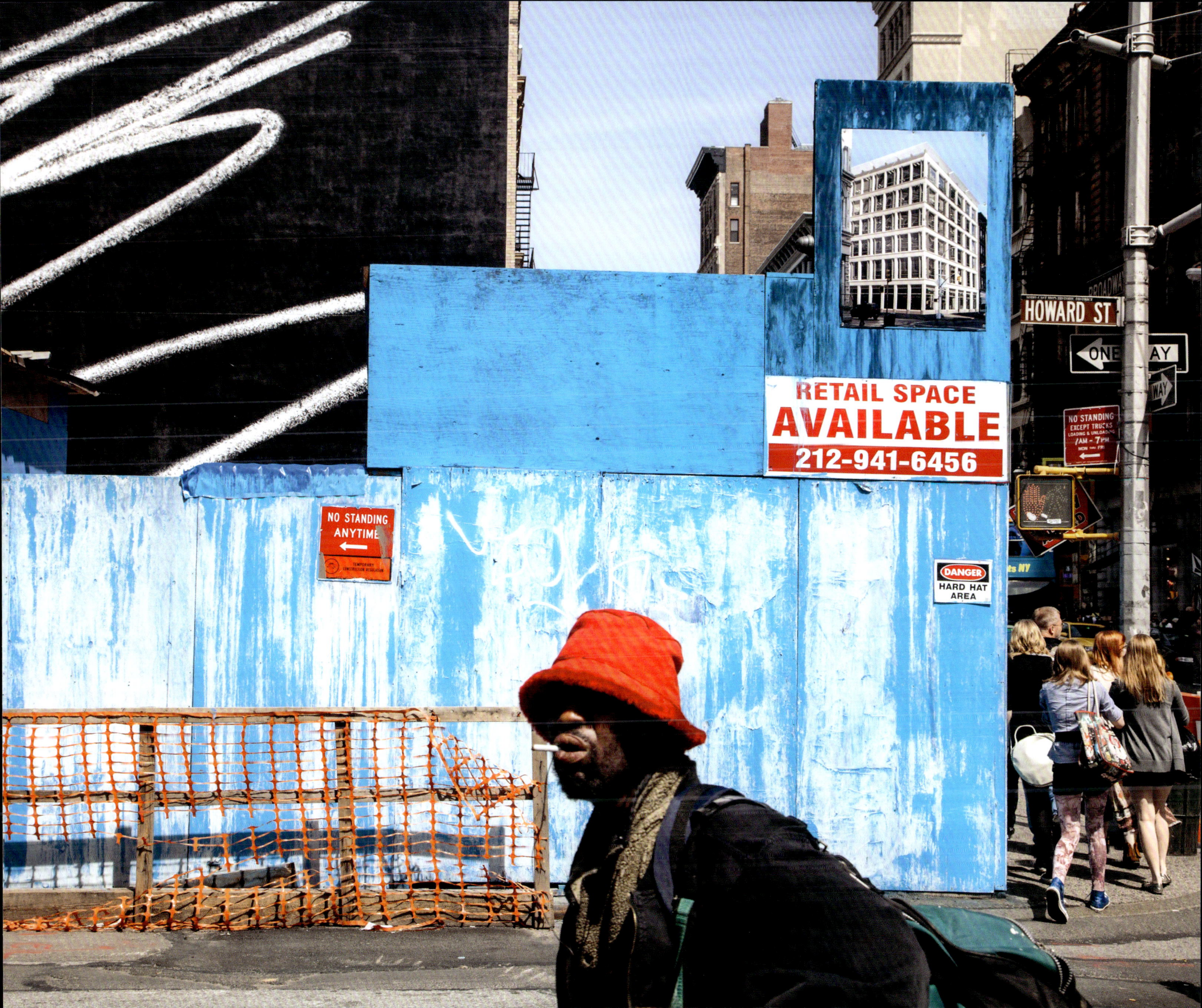

HOWARD ST
ONE WAY
WAY
RETAIL SPACE
AVAILABLE
212-941-6456
NO STANDING
ANYTIME
NO STANDING
EXCEPT TRUCKS
LOADING & UNLOADING
7AM - 7PM
MON - FRI
DANGER
HARD HAT
AREA
BROADWAY

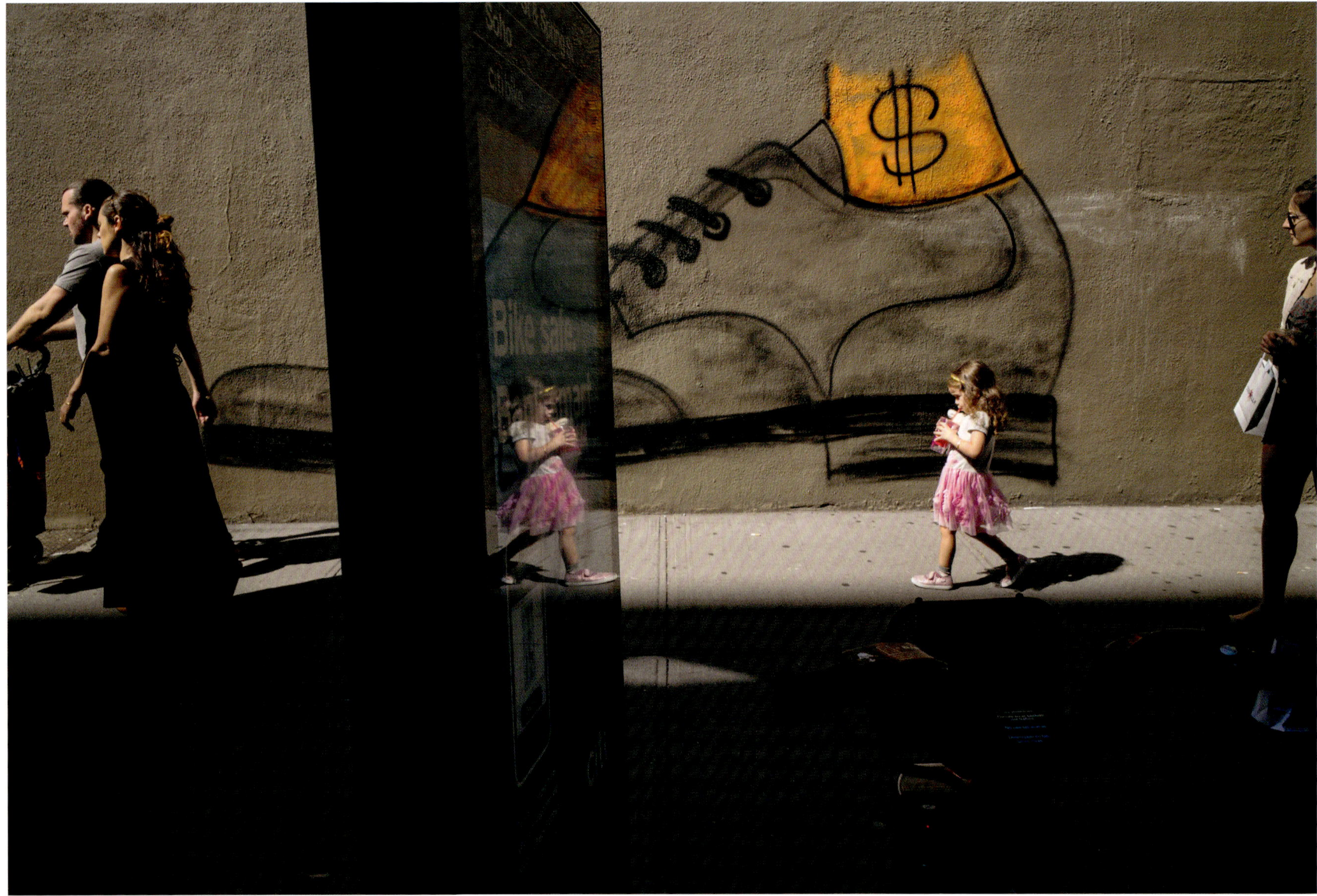

UNTITLED

First, I noticed the quality of the light, then I saw the shoe, and I knew that I had to take a picture.
There were a good number of people walking by, but the little girl with a big drink really stood out.
I also appreciated the way that the adults in the picture played on the edges of the frame—they
remind me that photographs aren't transparent copies of the real world, but constructed abstractions.
Inside their frames life seems frozen, but outside of a picture's edges, time inevitably moves on.

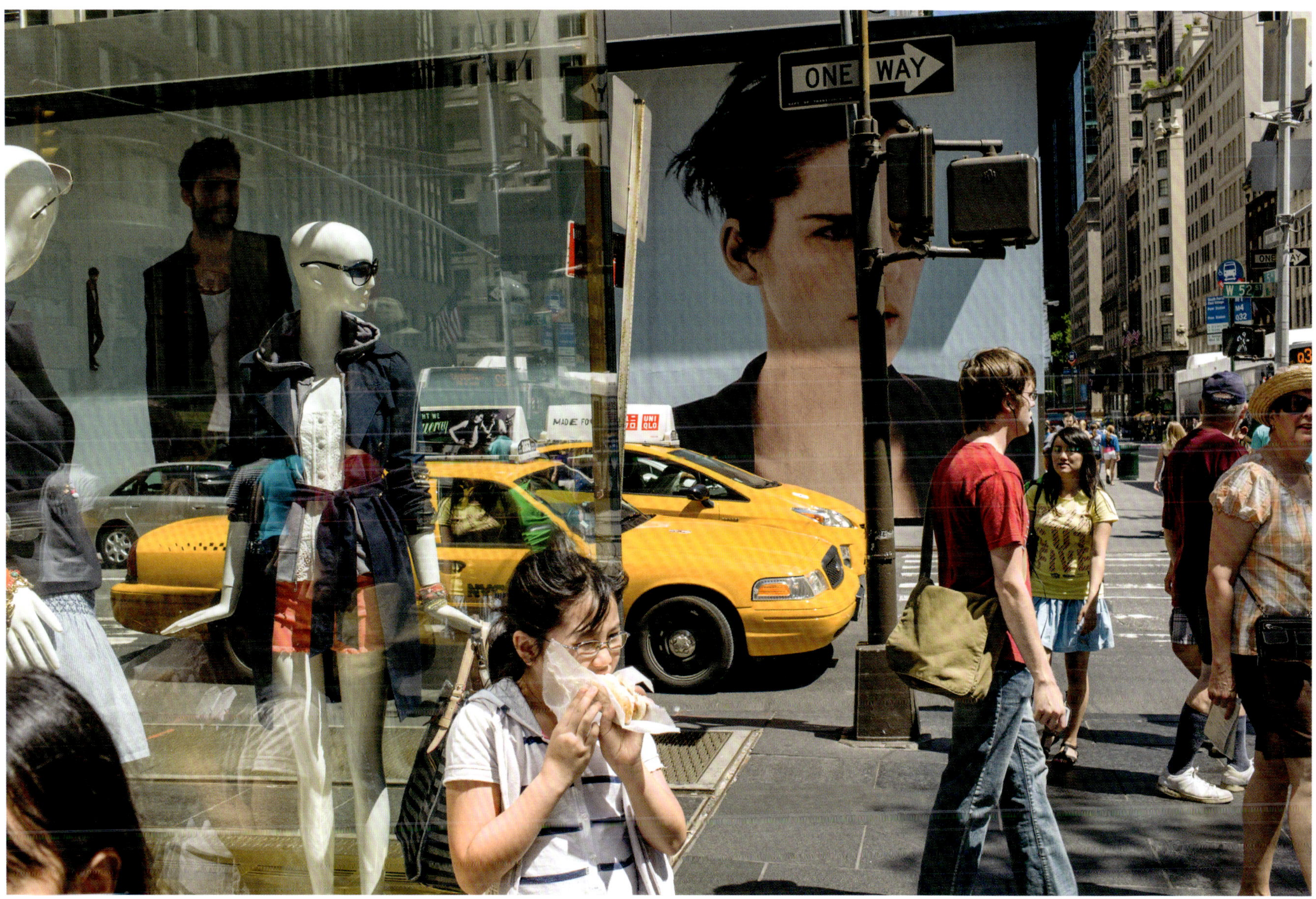

UNTITLED

Fifth Avenue can be a crowded place. On this day it was particularly packed with people, and I wanted to convey the crazy kind of chaos that can go on in that kind of urban environment. At the same time, I wanted to take a photograph that imposed a brief and precarious order on that chaos. I really like the way that all the elements in this complicated picture came together, especially the girl eating a hot dog. She anchors the composition and ties the whole thing together.

Q + A

Has your photojournalism background shaped your approach to street photography?

When I first started in photography, I generally found that I wasn't attracted to the work of photographers who relied on preconceived, arranged sets to create their images, at least not as much as I was attracted to the work of photographers who attempted to relate to their surroundings in a more directly analytical fashion. But I don't think photojournalism has had a great influence on the way that I see. Due to the nature of mass media, the bulk of the photographs might sometimes be informative, but they usually engage viewers on a one-dimensional level. I was intrigued by photographers like Gilles Peress and Alex Webb. Their photographs had a very distinct, personal quality, and I think they pushed back against some rigid notions of what photojournalism could be. All things considered, I'd have to say that photographers like André Kertész, Henri Cartier-Bresson, Walker Evans, Robert Frank, and Lee Friedlander have probably shaped my work more than any traditional photojournalist has.

How much do you plan your day's shoot?

I meander quite a bit. I'm not a great planner, so I tend to walk and let my interactions with the street take me to where I hope I'll take a successful photograph. I feel that my projects are more about communicating a process of discovery than they are about making definitive visual statements. When I'm in the street I try to be open and relaxed, and to allow my eye to take me to unique new experiences. Although they're sometimes loosely conceived, I typically photograph with the notion that my individual pictures will ultimately be part of a larger project. Through an extended body of work, I try to create personal visual commentaries about my encounters with specific places. My wish is that these pictures will collectively convey, at least in some small sense, the texture of life as I find it. When I'm out of town, the pattern of my daily practice is similar to what it is at home, but more intense. That's because I know that I have a limited amount of time to "get the job done."

Many of your photographs are composed of lots of strong graphic elements, colors, and layers—how do you create such images?

We all use cameras in unique ways. The choice of subject matter, and how to photograph it, is the result of a complex set of influences that have come together to define each of us as individuals. Sometimes, we're conscious of these influences, but just as often they are likely fated to remain unconscious forever. With that in mind, I'll stick to some of the influences that I'm consciously aware of. I've always been influenced by other art forms, such as literature, motion pictures, and painting. During the last century, art movements such as Dadaism, Surrealism, and Pop appropriated the everyday objects that surround us to comment on the modern world. I've always been drawn to these movements, and I recognize kindred spirits in the complex work of artists like Stuart Davis, Kurt Schwitters, Robert Rauschenberg, Jasper Johns, Claes Oldenberg, and Elizabeth Murray. Although I realize that I've been affected by a lifetime of cultural influences, street photography has largely been, for me, an intuitive process. Frequently, an opportunity appears suddenly, and I'm able to quickly take a photograph that pleases me. On other occasions, however, I look at a street like it's a vacant stage, and I wait for the actors to enter, perform their roles, and then exit.

You seem to use wide-angle lenses and a large depth of field a lot—is this a conscious technique to include multiple elements?

The trick for me is to use equipment that allows me to create order out of inherently chaotic situations. Right now, I'm mostly using 28mm and 35mm lenses, and they're good choices for juggling multiple elements into a composition. Since many of my pictures are about the relationship of people to urban environments, they are also useful tools for depicting the integration of people into those kinds of street scenes. I also mostly use rangefinder cameras, as they're very useful for working on the streets. Unlike a single lens reflex camera, I can pre-focus the lens, stop it down, and have a pretty good idea of what will be in focus. In addition, when I look through the viewfinder, everything is clear and sharp. That makes it easier to rapidly compose complicated compositions across the picture frame. But photographic equipment is just a means to an end, and there isn't any one type of camera that's a perfect choice for every task.

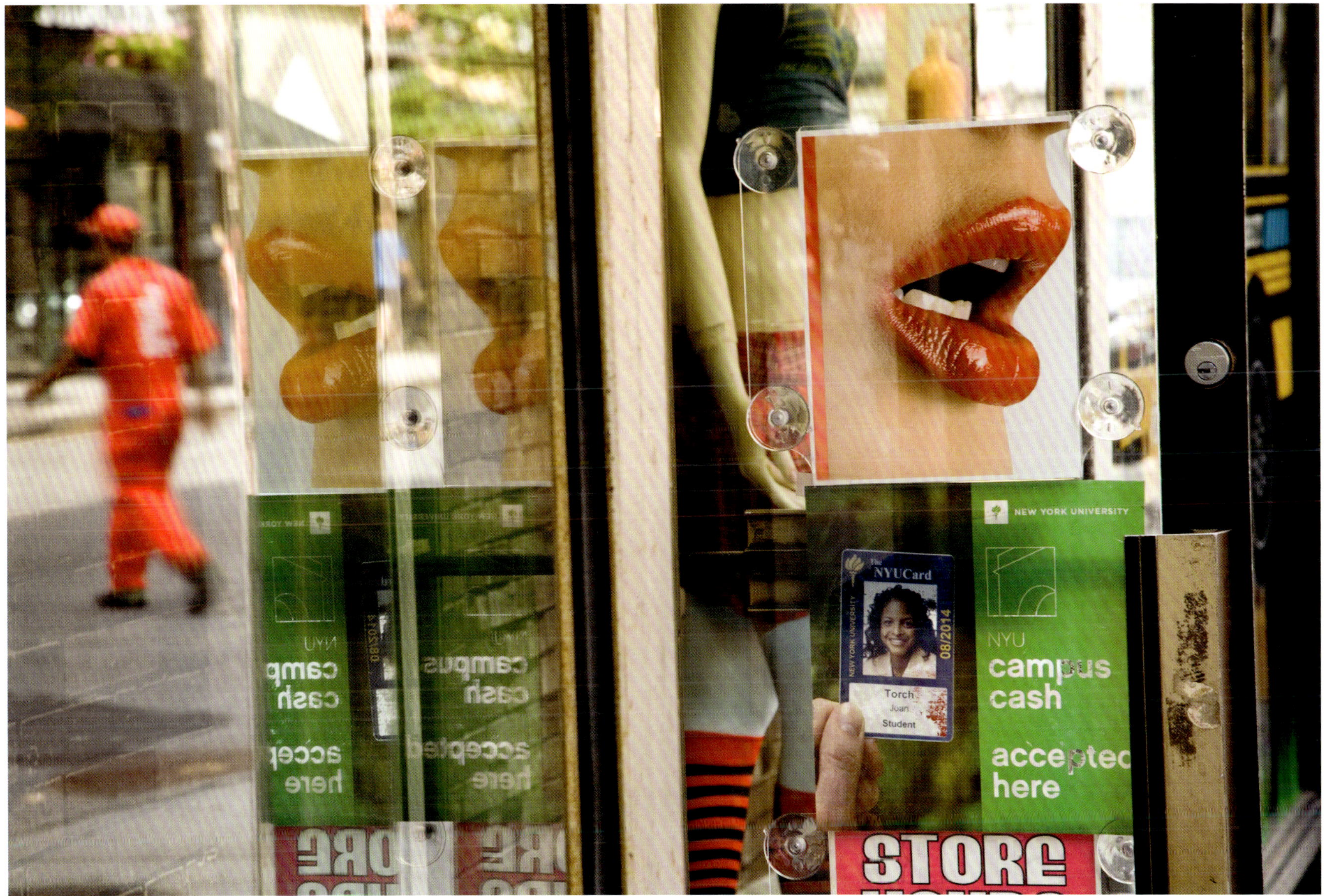

UNTITLED

This photograph shows a somewhat bizarre collection of objects in the doorway of a store in Greenwich Village. It is formally much more tightly framed than most of my pictures; I used a zoom lens to get in close. On some level I believe that the picture can almost be thought of as a kind of surreal still life, and those red lips have always puzzled me: I've looked at the picture multiple times since I took it, but I can't figure out exactly what product those lips were supposed to be promoting. I'll probably never know.

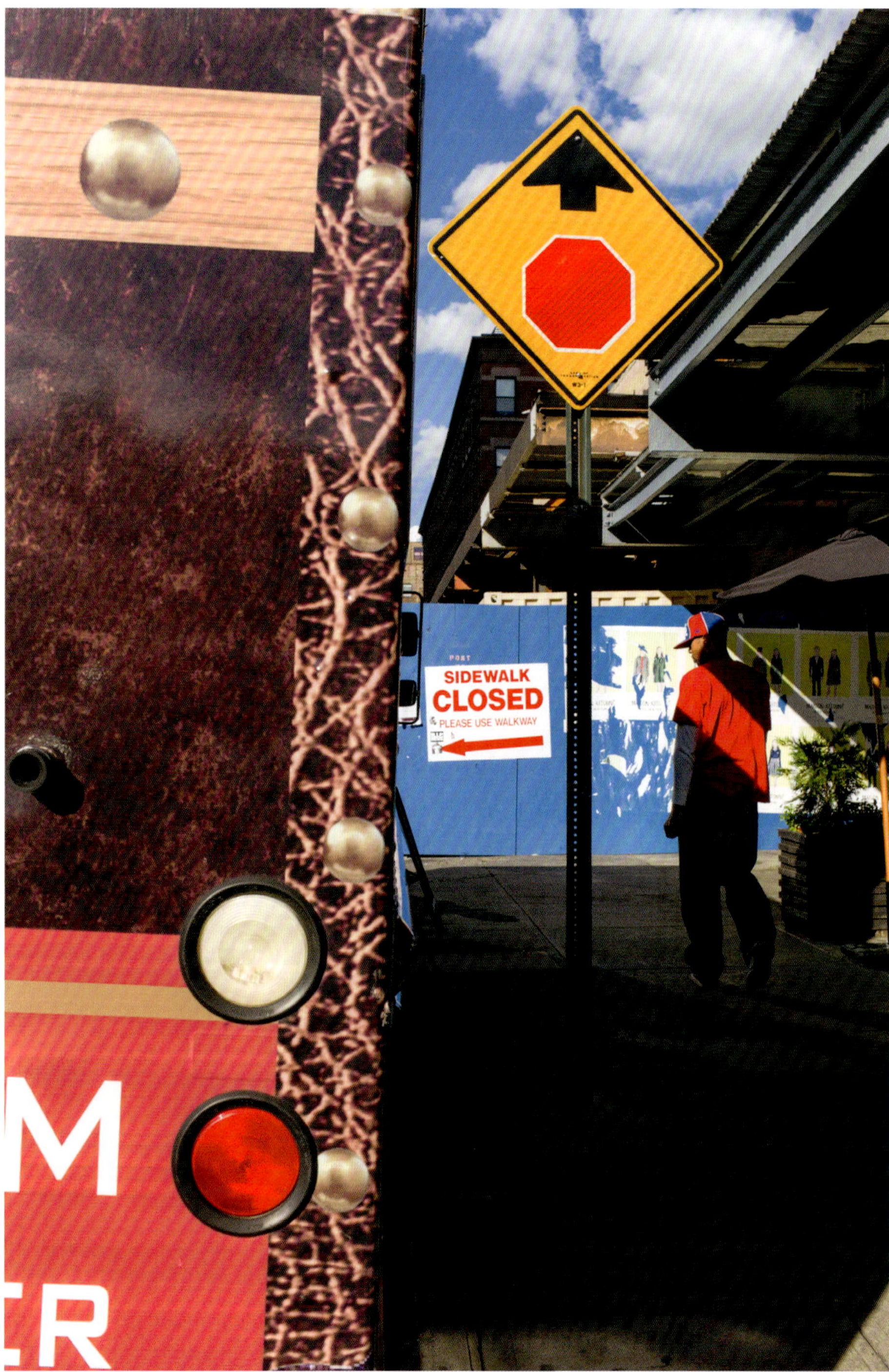

UNTITLED

I remember that this was the last photograph that I took after an especially productive day of photographing in Manhattan. I was feeling pretty good, the light had become very nice, and I was lucky enough to see the potential for a successful photograph in a place where there initially didn't seem to be much happening. I had noticed, however, the way that the rear of a parked van lined up with its surroundings. After waiting for a little while, a young man walked into the frame, and everything fell into place. Sometimes, things work out just right.

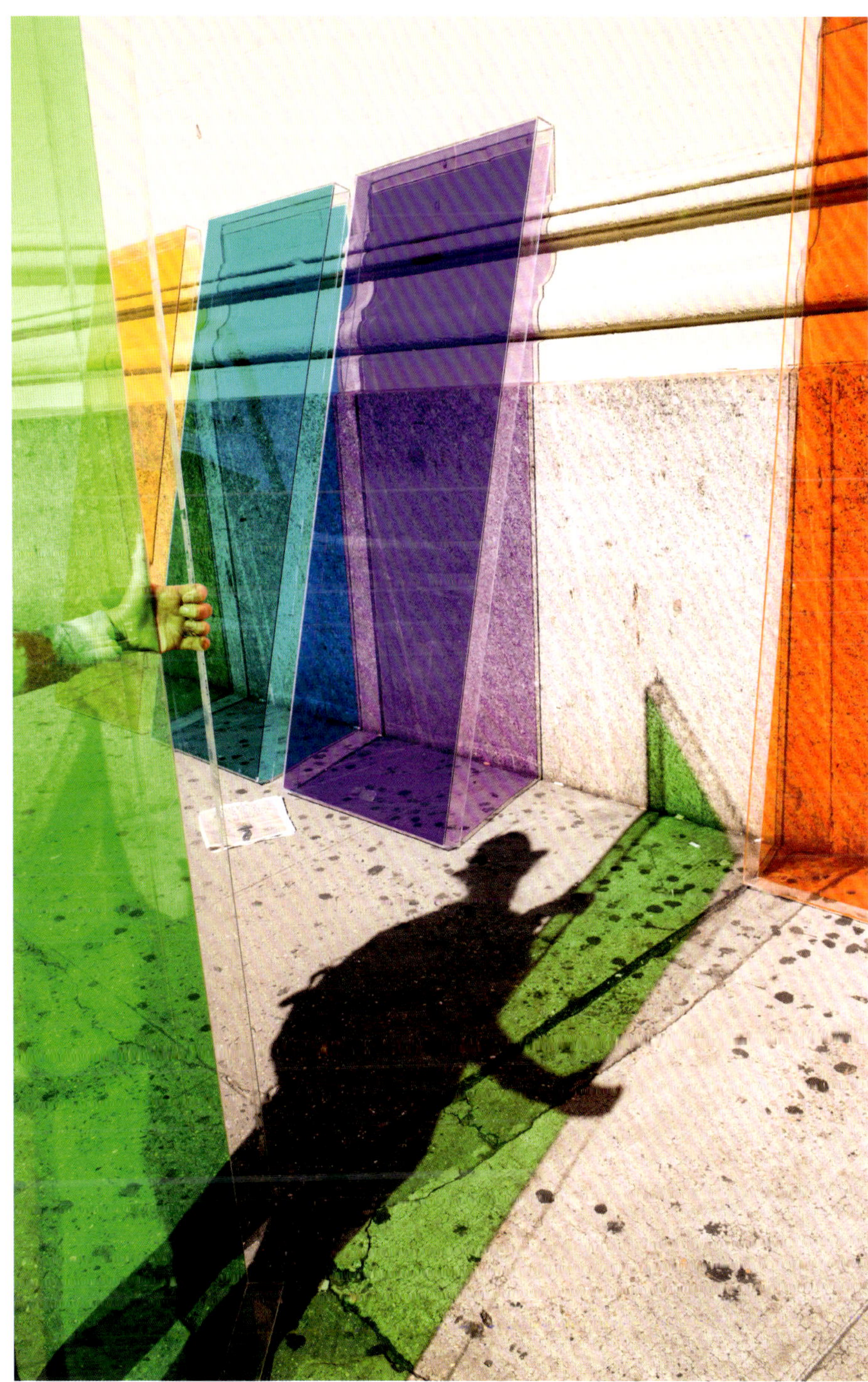

UNTITLED

This photograph might be somewhat difficult for a viewer to read. It's actually a performance by an artist that I came across by chance. With the assistance of collaborators, the artist was continually moving colored panes of glass into different positions. As the glass panes moved, I also moved and tried my best to keep up with both the panes and the performer's shadows. This is the kind of street encounter that I love to come across—it's just too bad that I forgot to write down the artist's name!

Q + A

What draws you to these complex, multi-layered images?

First of all, the world is a complicated place. Like most people, I try to make sense of it the best I can, so I guess on some level you can interpret my work as a metaphoric attempt to pose questions about the confusing situations that we all find ourselves in. On another level, however, I think that my pictures can be appreciated on more formal terms. For me, the arrangement of a picture's subject matter, in an elegant composition, offers its own inherent rewards. Although street photography can sometimes be frustrating when things aren't going well, there's also the joyful experience to look forward to when things do go well. I suspect that most street photographers love the process of creation almost as much as the finished results. The fact is, I enjoy pounding the pavement in anticipation of my next good picture—and I'm excited when I find it.

What is it that makes an image that satisfies you?

There really isn't a set of rigid criteria that can describe a satisfying photograph. Photographers have historically used a wide range of tools to make their pictures, and sometimes they're successful in their pursuits, and sometimes they aren't. Although I think that it's pointless to impose any overarching set of rules on anyone, including myself, it's also fair to say that when I'm working on a project I do think about how a series of images will work together in a satisfying way. A good example of what I'm talking about involves the use of color. I've seen photographers successfully use both black and white and color in the same series, but up until now that hasn't worked for me. Wherever I've photographed, color has always been an essential ingredient to help me relate to the culture of the street. Soon I'm going to be finishing a project on Las Vegas, and I knew from its inception that color would be the language that I used to describe the gaudy glitz of that city.

What is your favorite choice of camera and lens?

Over the years, I've used a variety of different camera and lens combinations. Sometimes, this required me to use equipment that was quite large and heavy, but I've always preferred smaller cameras. My first digital camera was a Canon EOS 5D with a 24–105mm lens, and I later picked up a Canon EOS 5D MkII. They were good cameras, and I've always found that a zoom lens can be a very flexible tool, but since Leica started producing digital M rangefinders, they've become my primary cameras. I've used a few different versions, and currently have the M10, which is a great camera for street photography. When it comes to a lens, my choices are either a 35mm or a 28mm. I really appreciate the clear viewfinder of a Leica, and I also like the ability to pre-focus, using the scales on the lens. These features allow me to respond quickly to surprises unfolding in the streets. Lately, I've been considering adding a mirrorless camera to my kit—they're small, don't take up too much room when traveling, and the quality of some of the newer cameras is supposed to be very good.

What tip would you give to those who wish to master street photography?

I know that some very fine photographers have said that they only take a few pictures in any given situation, and then they move on down the street. Often that's fine, and everybody works differently, but when I look back on my own experience, I frequently remember waiting for a long time for the right moment to present itself. Often, it seems that a scene needs an extra something to transform it into a good photograph. When that happens, it really becomes necessary to be patient and wait. Most of our photographs are failures. The sun always seems to go behind a cloud when you don't want it to, or some kid will inevitably turn their back to the camera at the wrong moment. So, I'm suggesting that it's sometimes a good idea to exercise a little patience, and pray that the fickle god of chance chooses to smile on you.

"Often, it seems that a scene needs an extra something to transform it into a good photograph. When that happens, it really becomes necessary to be patient and wait."

TECHNICAL INFORMATION

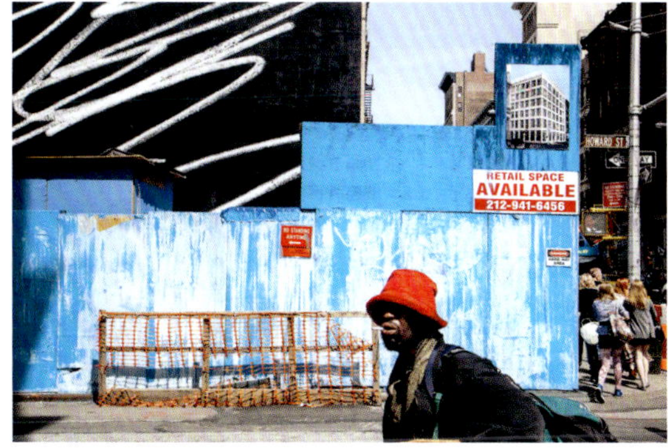

UNTITLED
MANHATTAN, NEW YORK, USA

Camera: Canon EOS 5D MkII
Lens/Focal length: 24–105mm f/4 at 40mm
Aperture: f/11
Shutter speed: 1/500 sec.
ISO: 200

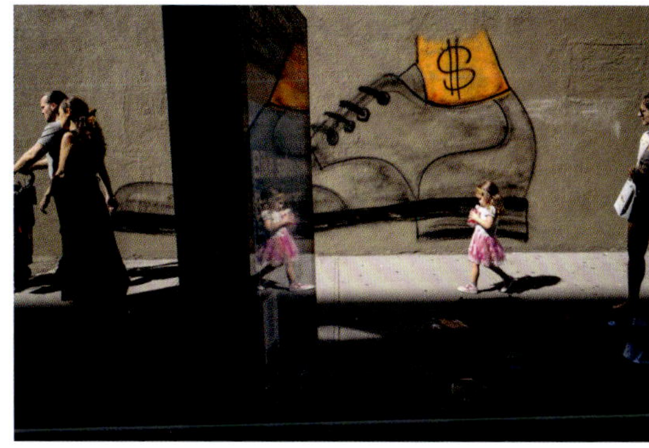

UNTITLED
MANHATTAN, NEW YORK, USA

Camera: Leica M (Typ 240)
Lens/Focal length: Leica Elmarit-M 28mm f/2.8 ASPH
Aperture: f/11
Shutter speed: 1/250 sec.
ISO: 320

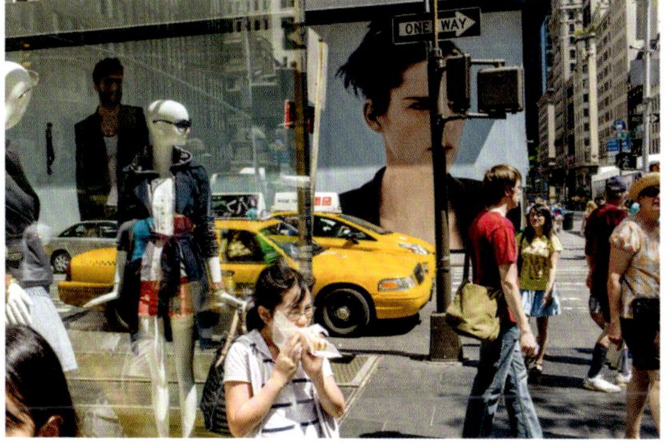

UNTITLED
MANHATTAN, NEW YORK, USA

Camera: Leica M9
Lens/Focal length: Leica Summarit-M 35mm f/2.5
Aperture: f/13
Shutter speed: 1/350 sec.
ISO: 350

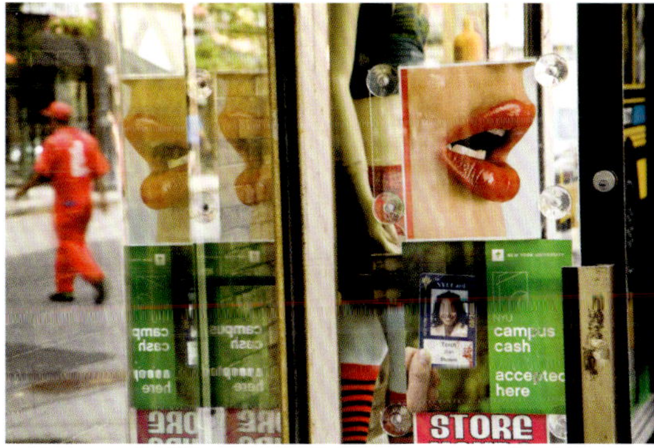

UNTITLED
MANHATTAN, NEW YORK, USA

Camera: Canon EOS 5D
Lens/Focal length: 24–105mm f/4 at 105mm
Aperture: f/9
Shutter speed: 1/13 sec.
ISO: 100

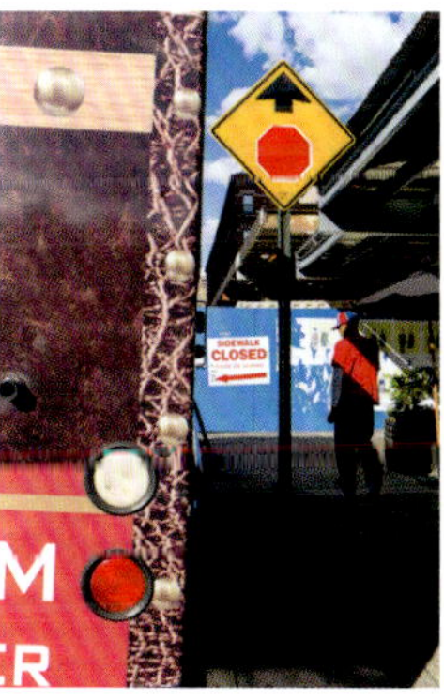

UNTITLED
MANHATTAN, NEW YORK, USA

Camera: Leica M9
Lens/Focal length: Leica Summarit-M 35mm f/2.5
Aperture: f/13
Shutter speed: 1/500 sec.
ISO: 250

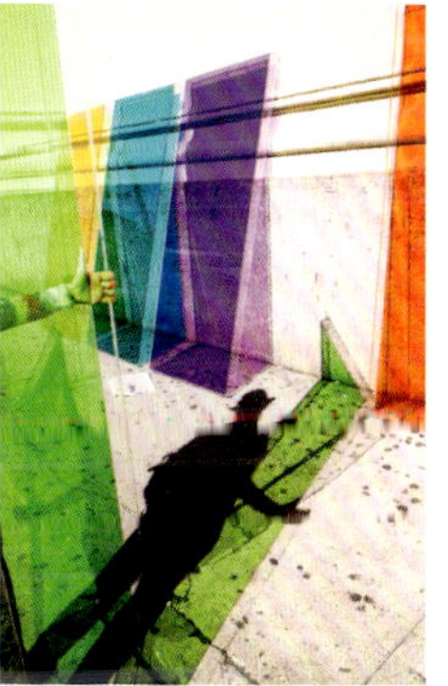

UNTITLED
MANHATTAN, NEW YORK, USA

Camera: Leica M (Typ 240)
Lens/Focal length: Leica Elmarit-M 28mm f/2.8 ASPH
Aperture: f/11
Shutter speed: 1/500 sec.
ISO: 500

ALAN SCHALLER

Alan Schaller is a London-based photographer who specializes in black-and-white photography. His work is often abstract and incorporates surrealism, geometry, high contrast, and the realities and diversities of human life. UK-based publications that have featured his images include the *Guardian*, the *Financial Times, Time Out*, and *The Independent*. His work has also been internationally published online and in print. Alan has exhibited at spaces including the Leica Gallery in London, The Saatchi Gallery, and Edit Space in Milan, and has also worked with many leading brands, such as Apple, Philips, Huawei Mobile, Kew Gardens, and London Fashion Week. He is a brand ambassador for Leica Cameras.

In 2015, Alan co-founded Street Photography International (SPi), to promote the best work in the genre and to give a platform to talented yet unrepresented photographers. Today, the SPi Instagram account is the most viewed dedicated street photography platform in the world.

Apart from photography, Alan has written articles for *The Independent* focusing on humanitarian issues, and he is also a multi-instrumentalist with a background in music production, a field he worked in before photography.

UNTITLED

This photograph should never have happened. I was meeting a friend at Liverpool Street station in London at 6pm one night. I got there and called him. He'd had a few drinks and told me he had forgotten about our meeting, apologizing profusely. He said if I didn't mind heading to Old Street to meet him, we could hang out. I was a bit annoyed, but said alright and got back on the Underground. This image was taken at Old Street station; I was walking to the exit when I spotted this girl, and quickly took the shot.

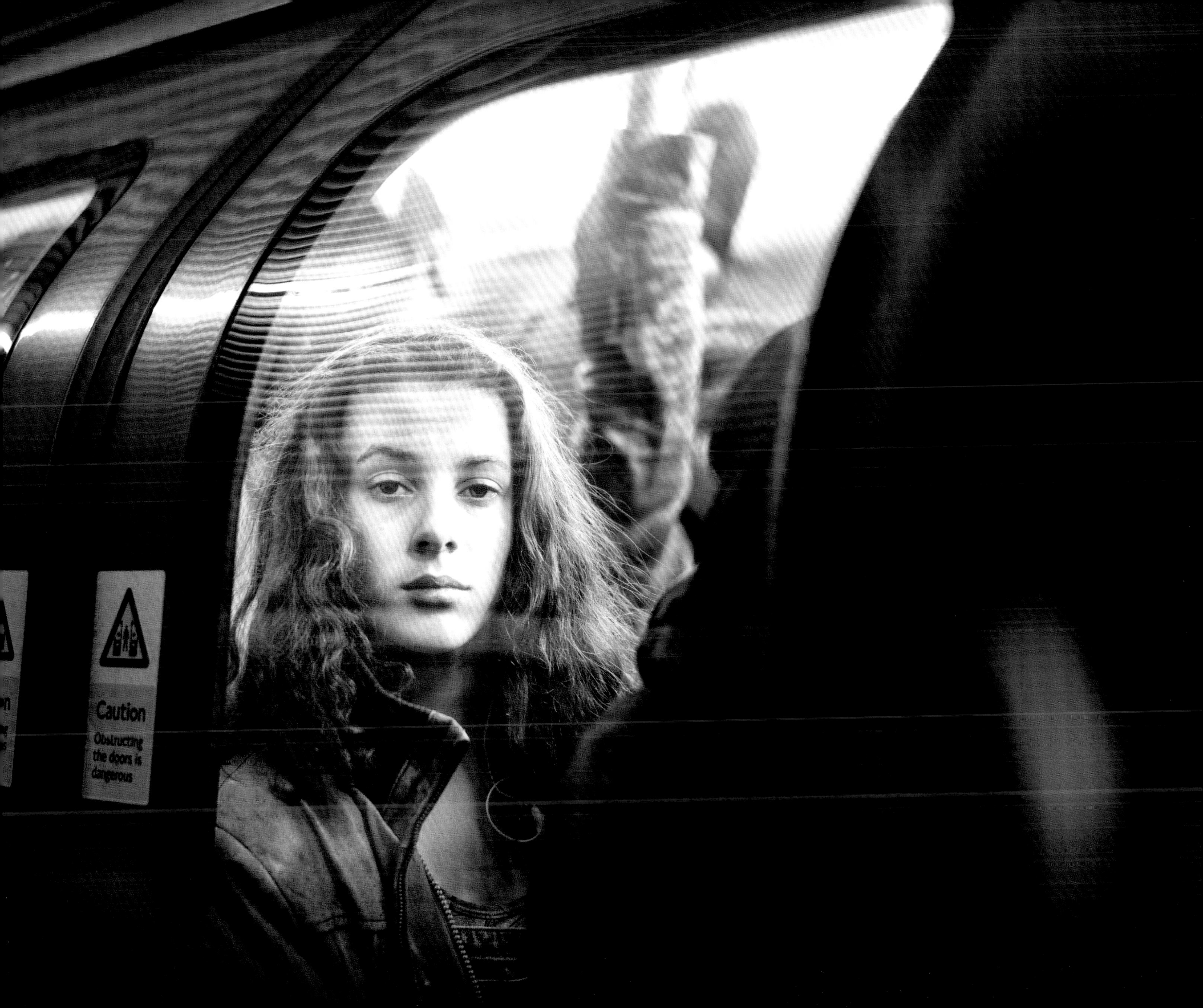

Caution
Obstructing
the doors is
dangerous

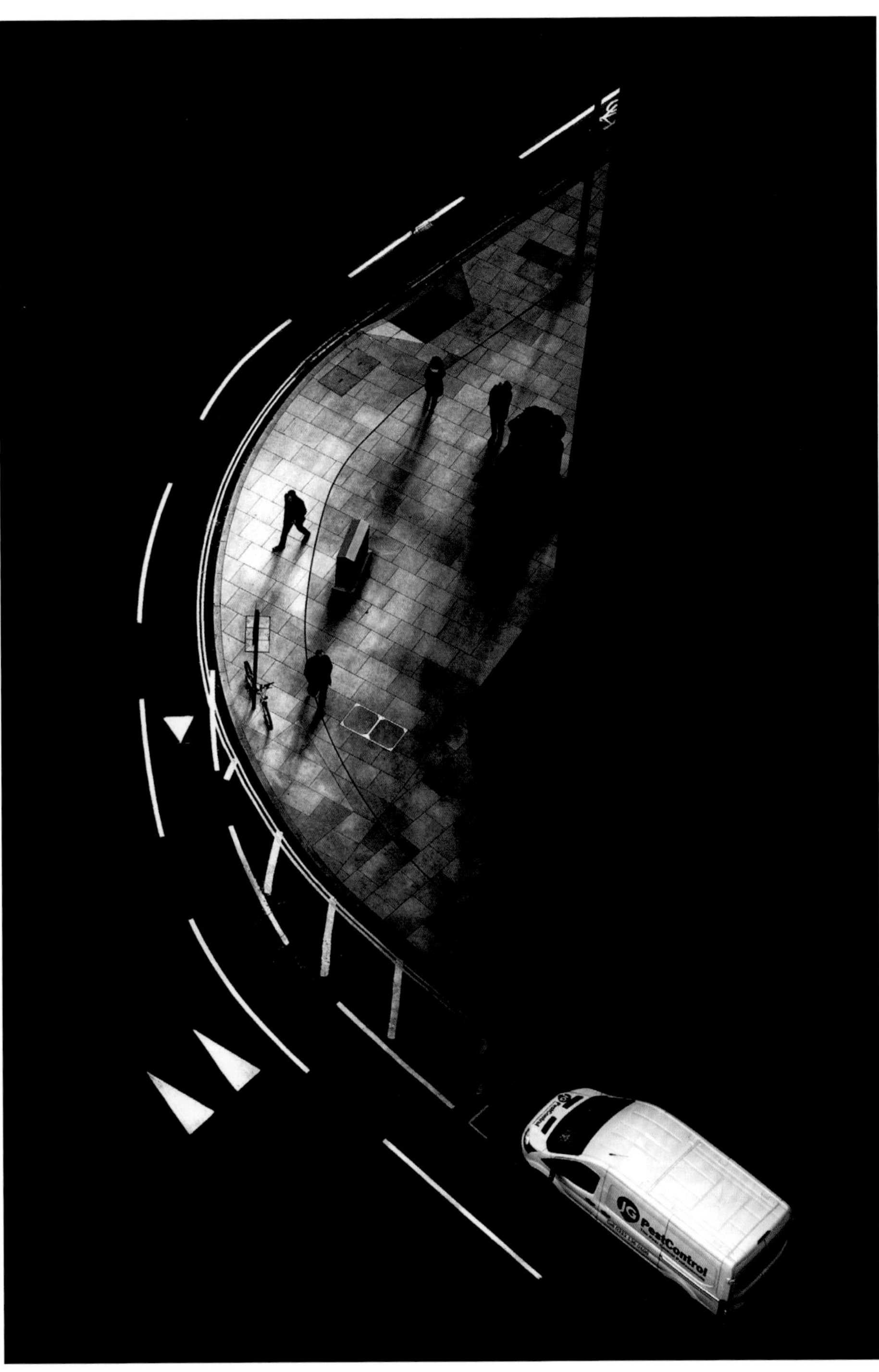

UNTITLED

I spotted the shape of the road markers and took this from the 10th floor of the Tate Modern in London; the light was very high contrast, which helped achieve much of the negative space. It was the very first photo I attempted in a new kind of direction, splicing street photography and graphic art. I enjoy this approach, as it adds variety to my work and allows me to explore a new way of seeing.

UNTITLED

This type of photograph is only possible when the sun is low in the sky. It was taken outside the British Museum in London, where I spotted these people chatting and smoking, with the light hitting them at just the right angle to create this rim light. I have tried to capture similar images since, but the conditions have never aligned in quite the same way, be it the angle of the light, the environment, or the subjects.

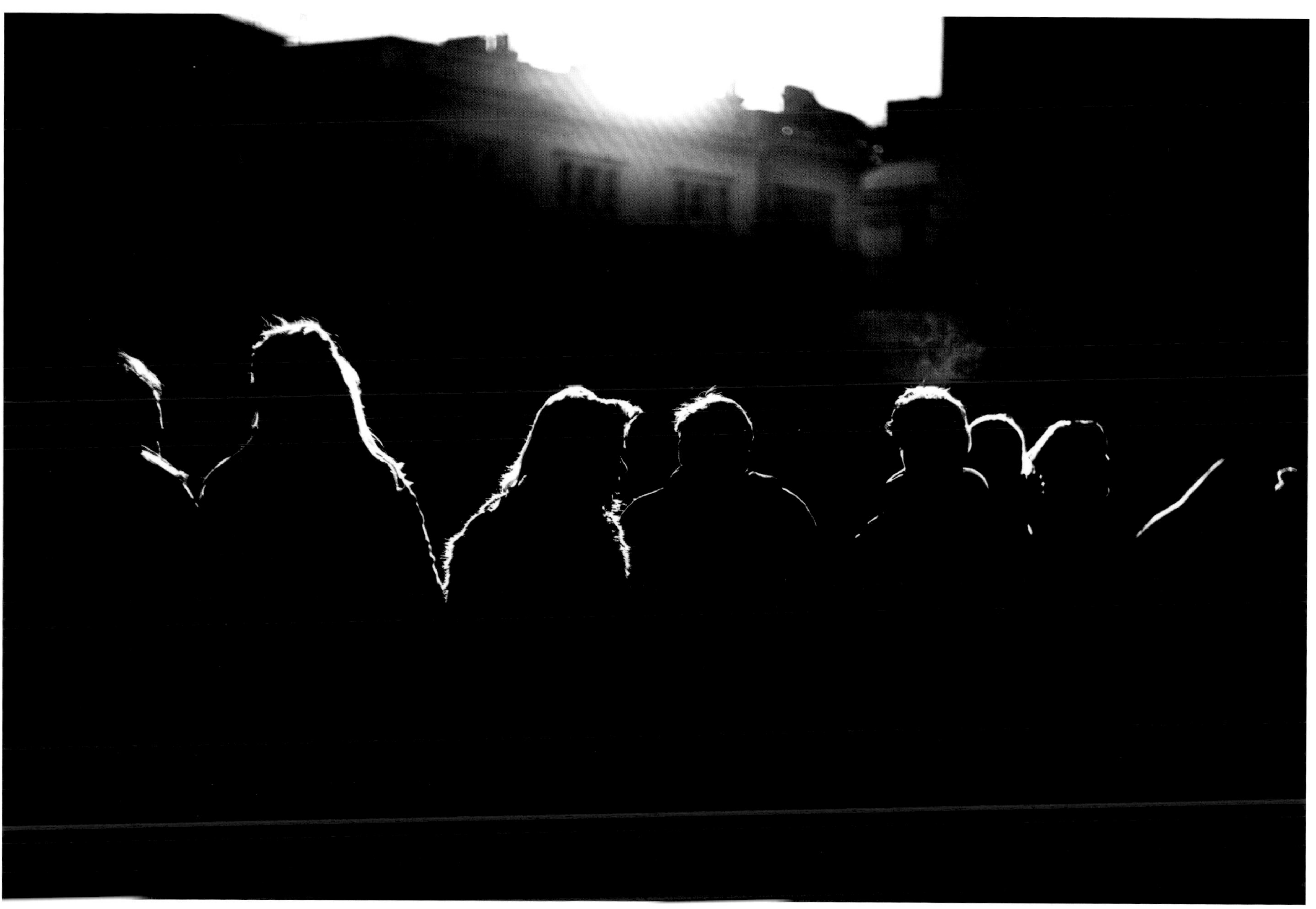

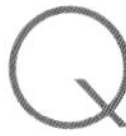

Q + A

What drew you to street photography?

I began my creative career as a musician. I studied music and I wrote music for TV and films, and I did that for about five or six years. It's quite a tough industry to keep going in, and hard to impose your own style of creativity on the briefs you're given by clients, so I started thinking I needed a new creative outlet, and that's what led me towards photography. That—combined with a girlfriend who was a street photographer—got me into street photography. I bought a camera to impress her—that's honestly the truth! It's a much faster process than creating music—you go out and make your creation immediately, which is exciting for me, compared to what I'd been doing, and so I really fell in love with it. I was freelancing in music before, so I started taking time off to shoot and build my portfolio. I was just doing it for the love of it—I didn't really have any particular goal in mind—I thought of it as an opportunity to do what I wanted to do, and not be told how to work. I've learned quite a lot of lessons from my music career, because now I do quite a lot of commissions, and I really enjoy working with brands as well, because I'm able to stick to my own style. I've now fully transitioned to photography as my career.

What do you like about black-and-white photography in particular?

I bought a few photography books at the beginning—they're all from the Magnum era, old-school black-and-white photography—and I just loved the style, so I gravitated toward it, it's what I enjoyed. A lot of people use black and white for the sake of it, but I wanted to study what makes a really good black-and-white picture. There are certain things that can be enhanced in black and white, such as shape, structure, line, and even human expression can really hit home. I made it my mission to do something fresh—a modern twist on black-and-white photography. That was where I wanted to go, and I didn't really know how to do that, so I started off emulating others, but then went off in my own direction once I'd got the skills. I find it quite amusing now that I shoot in black and white as a choice, and some of the agencies I work for tell me that's really "out there." It's funny how it's come around again—you had no choice once, but now you're seen as brave to use it.

Your photography features very strong, graphic lines and shapes—how did you develop your style?

I used to photograph human emotion—the main subject of the image would be a person and their expression, and I explored that quite a lot. But I found that there were other ways to evoke human emotion, where people weren't the main focal point of the image, but were part of something bigger. Isolation and separation have been studied by artists for many decades. It's part of how the world's changing; you can feel somewhat dwarfed by the world, and that was the initial inspiration for trying to pick out these moments in our cities that are hugely overcrowded. I used to shoot reactively and capture moments quickly, but now I prefer to research places, identify scenes, then go to them and wait, almost like a fisherman, rather than a hunter. It's a different process, a different way of thinking. It's become quite a trendy thing to do now, but when I started putting out images like this, it seemed really different, and people could tell it was my work, because of the style.

How important is it to develop your own style?

I think it depends what you want out of your photography. If you're a hobbyist, and you just enjoy shooting, you can experiment and do what you like. But if you want to be represented, to do exhibitions, and to get commissions, then the only way is to separate yourself from everyone else by having your own "thing." Many photographers start off doing a bit of everything—landscape, portraiture, food photography—but it's better to have a niche, and to be well known in your niche, rather than floating in a sea of ambiguity. Think about who you are, and why someone should commission you, or even follow you on Instagram. For instance, if someone finds something they like of yours on Instagram, and they go to your page to see more of it, but you have lots of different kinds of shots, then they'll just switch off and go away. So, it's good to have a signature—not just in photography, but in the arts in general. It's important to find your voice, and play to your strengths, and develop that style to see where it goes.

"Now I prefer to research scenes, then go to them and wait, almost like a fisherman, rather than a hunter."

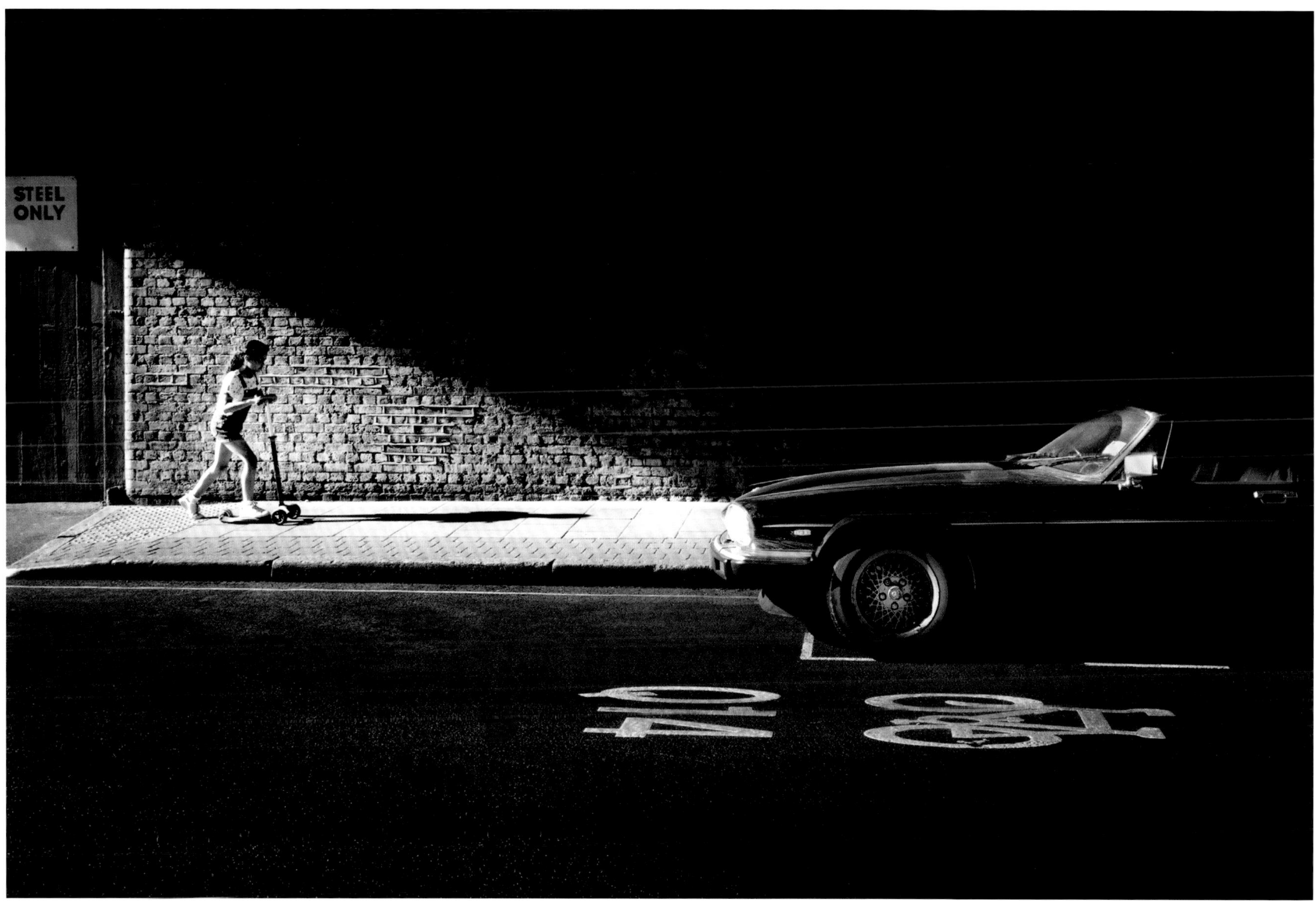

UNTITLED

I quite enjoy playing with perspective and incorporating a touch of surrealism to my images where possible. I was walking around Southwark in London when I spotted this light under a bridge. I lined up the camera so it appeared almost as if the light was being emitted from the car at the right of the frame, and waited for the right subject. The light comes from the sun coming in from the left, and the car is in fact parked and unoccupied. It is a bit of a trick of the eye, and has confused some viewers, who have asked me how it is possible that the shadow of the girl on the scooter is going the "wrong way." Goal achieved!

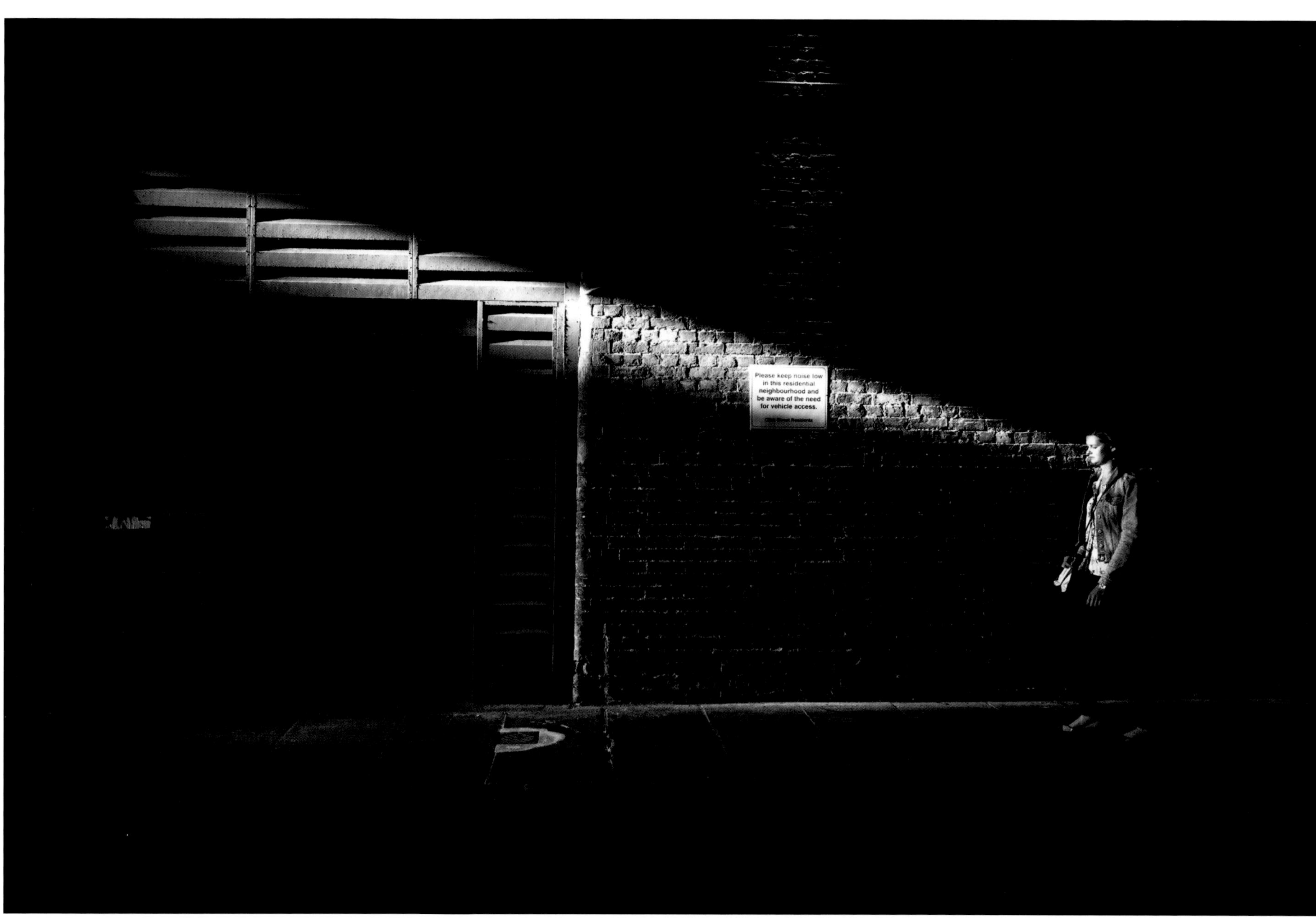
Please keep noise low
in this residential
neighbourhood and
be aware of the need
for vehicle access.

UNTITLED

This was taken near the South Bank in London. It was a case of spotting the triangular light on the wall and imagining what I could do with it. I decided it could be amusing to make it look like the finest point was beaming out of someone's eyes. The sun was setting, and the shape was changing by the minute. I had to be patient and wait for somebody who was the right height to line up with the shape. Fortunately this happened quite quickly, with nobody else present in the frame to distract the eye.

UNTITLED

This was taken near Bank station in London. I love the area for its architecture and rather serious-looking Londoners walking to and fro, about their business. At night, this particular archway is bestowed with a fine shadow line originating from the street lamp above. The combination of nice light, shape, as well as an interesting subject is something that does not happen very often, so for me these opportunities have to be taken when they can.

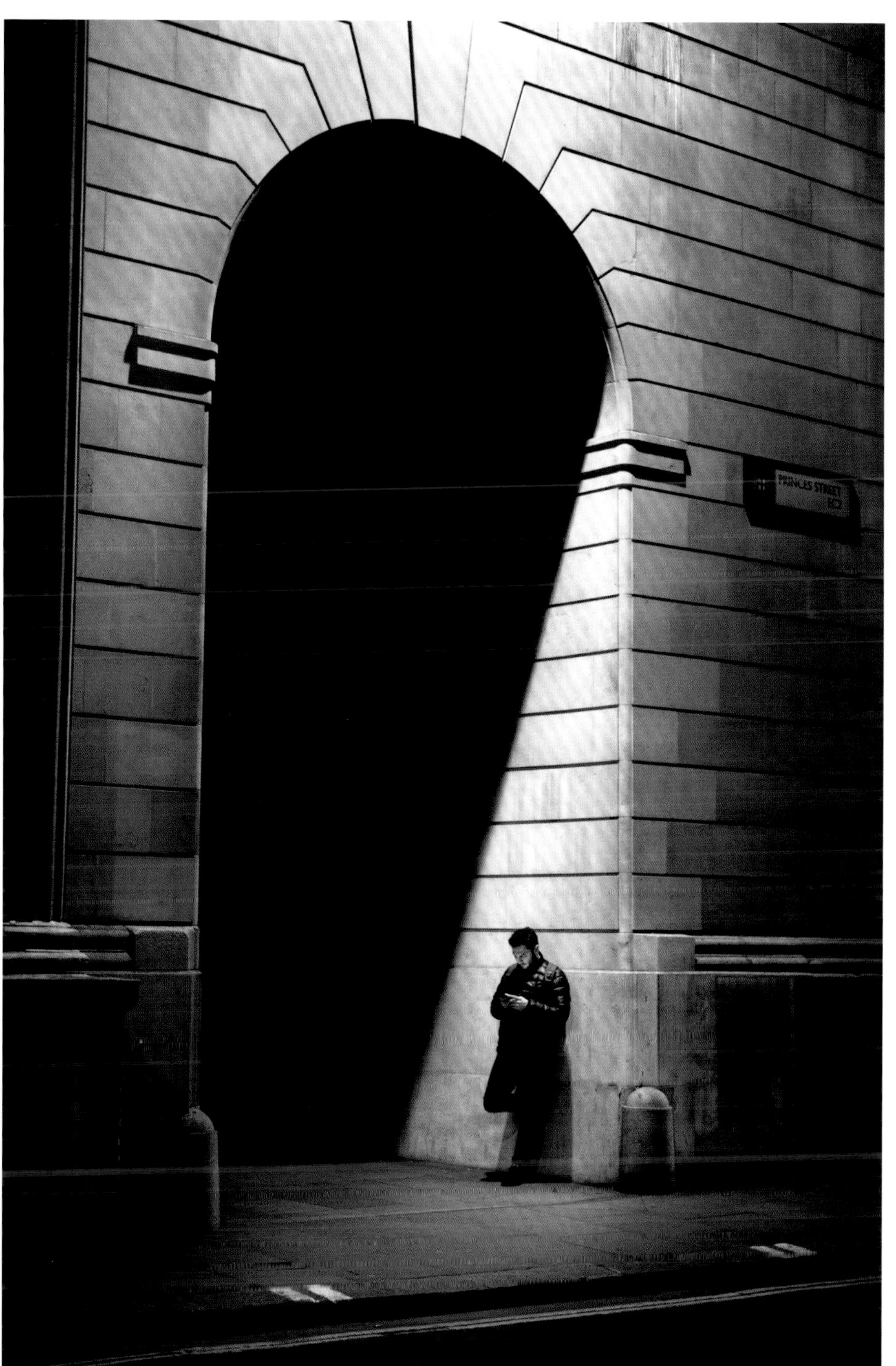

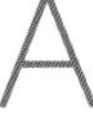

What techniques do you use in capturing or post-processing your high-contrast images?

Those negative-space images that have a lot of black around them are only possible in areas of naturally occurring high contrast. You meter from the brightest point and use exposure compensation to pull it down two stops, and then you get that black look in-camera. I tend to try to get it as right as I can when shooting. But the mood is something you can't change in a picture, and I try to get the composition as close to perfect as possible. I'm quite ruthless at the editing stage. If a picture just isn't right, I won't force it, which is a good philosophy, because it forces you to be better in the moment. This means that it has to be the right kind of conditions, and I look out for those all the time—I'm generally looking for backlit scenes. It's something you can't really teach: the right moment when to press the shutter, a sensitivity to what's going on around you, or who is a good subject. All this is instinctive, it's intuition, but the instinct comes from hard work as well.

What techniques do you use for shooting candid portraits?

I'm not a big fan of standing back from people—I like to get up close and engage with them. I tend to take pictures by shooting from the hip when I'm close, and my Leica cameras are very discreet, so I very rarely encounter any problems; people hardly notice you're taking pictures if you're doing it properly. There are lots of techniques, such as not staring people in the face when you're taking the picture, using your peripheral vision, and not overshooting. Don't take 10 pictures of someone: wait for the one that's going to be good. But I seldom get approached by anyone. I think it's the only way to take candid photographs—if you put the camera to your eye, everyone knows what that means, but not if you're shooting from your waist or lap. Because I use Leica equipment, it's all manual, so I'm able to pre-focus, and then all I have to do is walk up to them. Having shot tens of thousands of pictures using a 24mm lens I know instinctively what the camera is seeing, so don't need to raise it to my eye. Shooting like this means you can get away with a lot of shots that would be impossible otherwise.

What was the idea behind the Street Photography International (SPi) collective you co-founded?

I set up the SPi with my friends Craig and Walter to create a platform that didn't really exist elsewhere. A lot of collectives just put out their members' work—and we still do that with our own images—but we wanted other people to submit their work as well, and to create this place where we could champion unsung photographers who didn't have big agencies backing them. We wanted to promote work of a high quality—that was the only requirement, not how deep your portfolio is, or where you're from—and, in two years, it's gone from zero followers to gaining more than 1,000 a day. It's now the biggest street photography resource in the world, with 14 or 15 million views per month, which shows how popular the genre is. It gives people inspiration and ideas. Social media is a way of building a community and getting people to events we're running as well.

What tips would you give to those who wish to master street photography?

I think it's important to be inspired by other photographers, but to think for yourself. Carry a camera with you everywhere—if it's too big and you're not going to take it out with you, get a smaller camera. Also, shoot something in your home town. It's amazing how many great photographers built up their first series just where they lived. Being a visitor is an important perspective as a photographer, but you have the authority to say something special about where you've grown up.

"I'm quite ruthless at the editing stage. If a picture just isn't right, I won't force it, which is a good philosophy, because it forces you to be better in the moment."

TECHNICAL INFORMATION

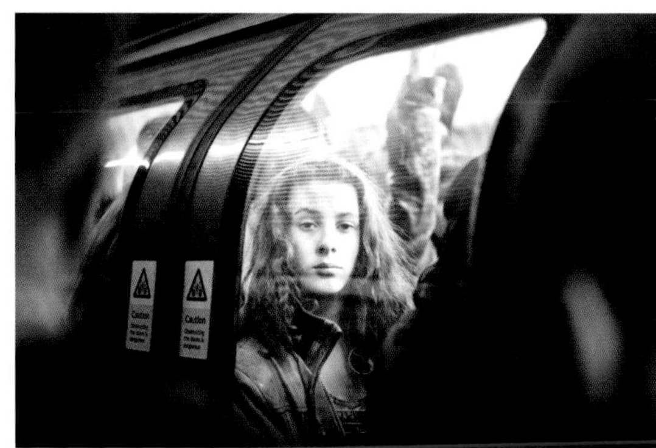

UNTITLED
LONDON, UNITED KINGDOM

Camera: Leica Monochrom M (Typ 246)
Lens/Focal length: Leica Summilux ASPH 50mm f/1.4
Aperture: f/1.4
Shutter speed: 1/250 sec.
ISO: 320

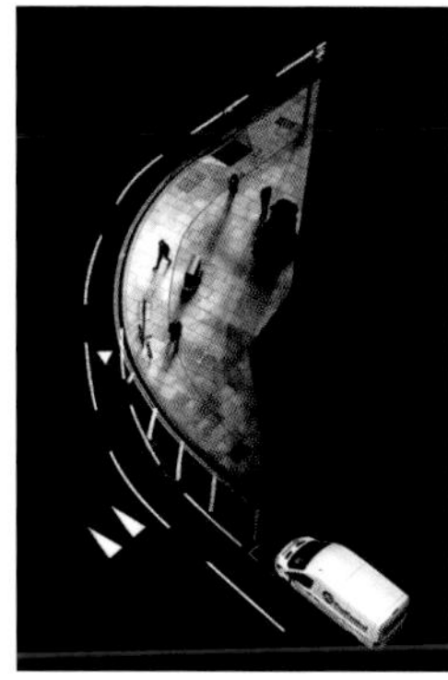

UNTITLED
LONDON, UNITED KINGDOM

Camera: Leica Monochrom M (Typ 246)
Lens/Focal length: Leica Summilux ASPH 50mm f/1.4
Aperture: f/1.7
Shutter speed: 1/3000 sec.
ISO: 320

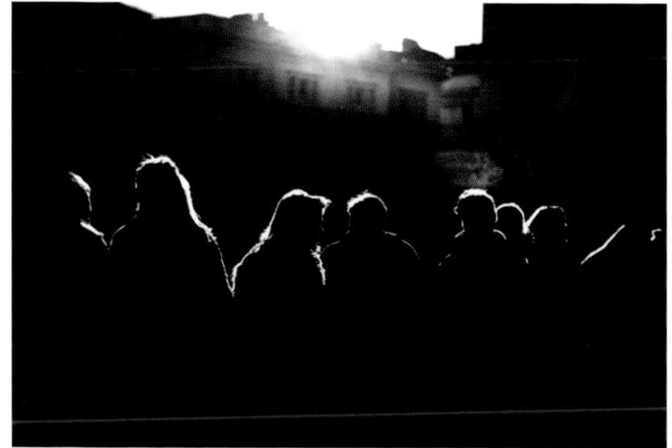

UNTITLED
LONDON, UNITED KINGDOM

Camera: Leica Monochrom M (Typ 246)
Lens/Focal length: Leica Summilux ASPH 50mm f/1.4
Aperture: f/9.5
Shutter speed: 1/4000 sec.
ISO: 320

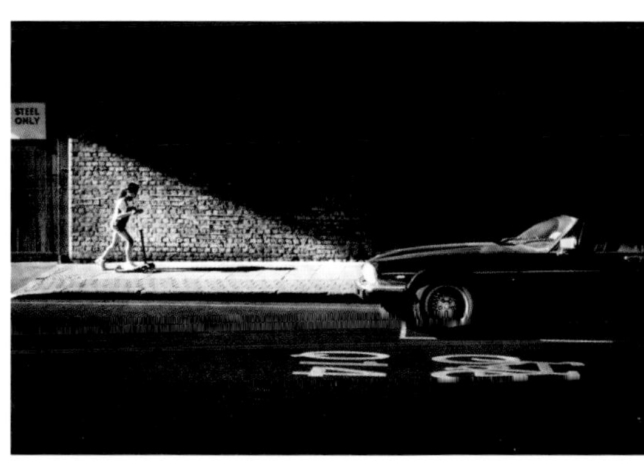

UNTITLED
LONDON, UNITED KINGDOM

Camera: Leica Monochrom M (Typ 246)
Lens/Focal length: Leica Summilux ASPH 50mm f/1.4
Aperture: f/13
Shutter speed: 1/350 sec.
ISO: 640

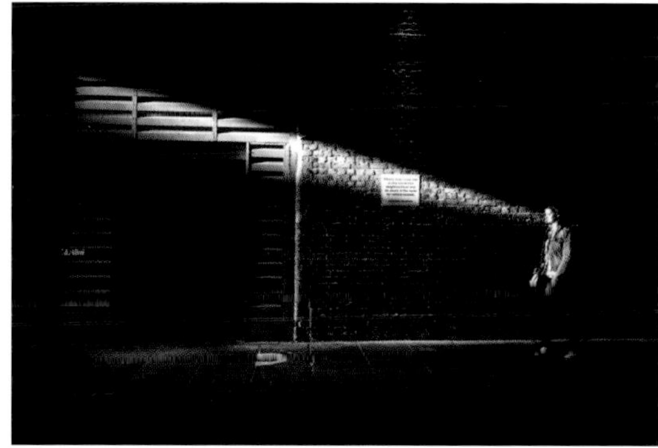

UNTITLED
LONDON, UNITED KINGDOM

Camera: Leica Monochrom M (Typ 246)
Lens/Focal length: Leica Summilux ASPH 50mm f/1.4
Aperture: f/4
Shutter speed: 1/1000 sec.
ISO: 320

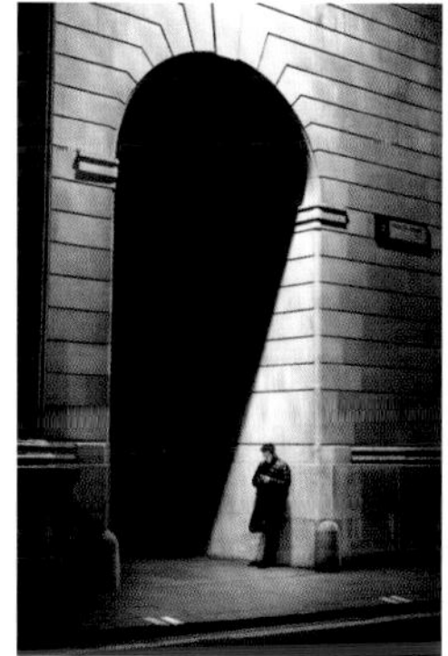

UNTITLED
LONDON, UNITED KINGDOM

Camera: Leica Monochrom M (Typ 246)
Lens/Focal length: Leica Summilux ASPH 50mm f/1.4
Aperture: f/2.8
Shutter speed: 1/180 sec.
ISO: 2000

MARINA SERSALE

Marina Sersale is a self-taught photographer who lives and works in Rome, Italy. By profession she is a creator of fragrances, but she started taking photographs when she purchased her first iPhone in December 2012 and began posting on Instagram. Marina joined the Hikari Creative collective in 2014, and in November 2015 her work was shown for the first time in the Hikari Creative exhibition, Chance Encounters, in Tehran, Iran.

In March 2016, Marina's first solo exhibition, Unexpected Stories, opened at the Ilex Gallery in Rome, and in May of the same year the exhibition moved to Photo London. Subsequently, in 2017, a selection from her on-going project, Dreaming the Sea, was presented at Photo London and at the Hikari Creative collective exhibition in the mObgrafia Cultura Visual Festival in Sao Paulo, Brazil, and the Hyderabad Photography Festival in India.

UNTITLED

This was taken on a work trip to Australia to launch a new fragrance brand. It was a short trip and jet-lag pursued me throughout—by the time I got over it I was on the plane back home. In Sydney we had a few hours off from a pretty grueling schedule and went to have lunch at Bondi Beach. Afterward, we took a short stroll on the beach and I started shooting. Whenever I'm on work trips, taking photos always happens on borrowed time—there's inevitably somebody waiting for me to hurry up and finish so we can move on. In this case it was my husband Sebastian and a charming woman who was taking us to our next appointment.

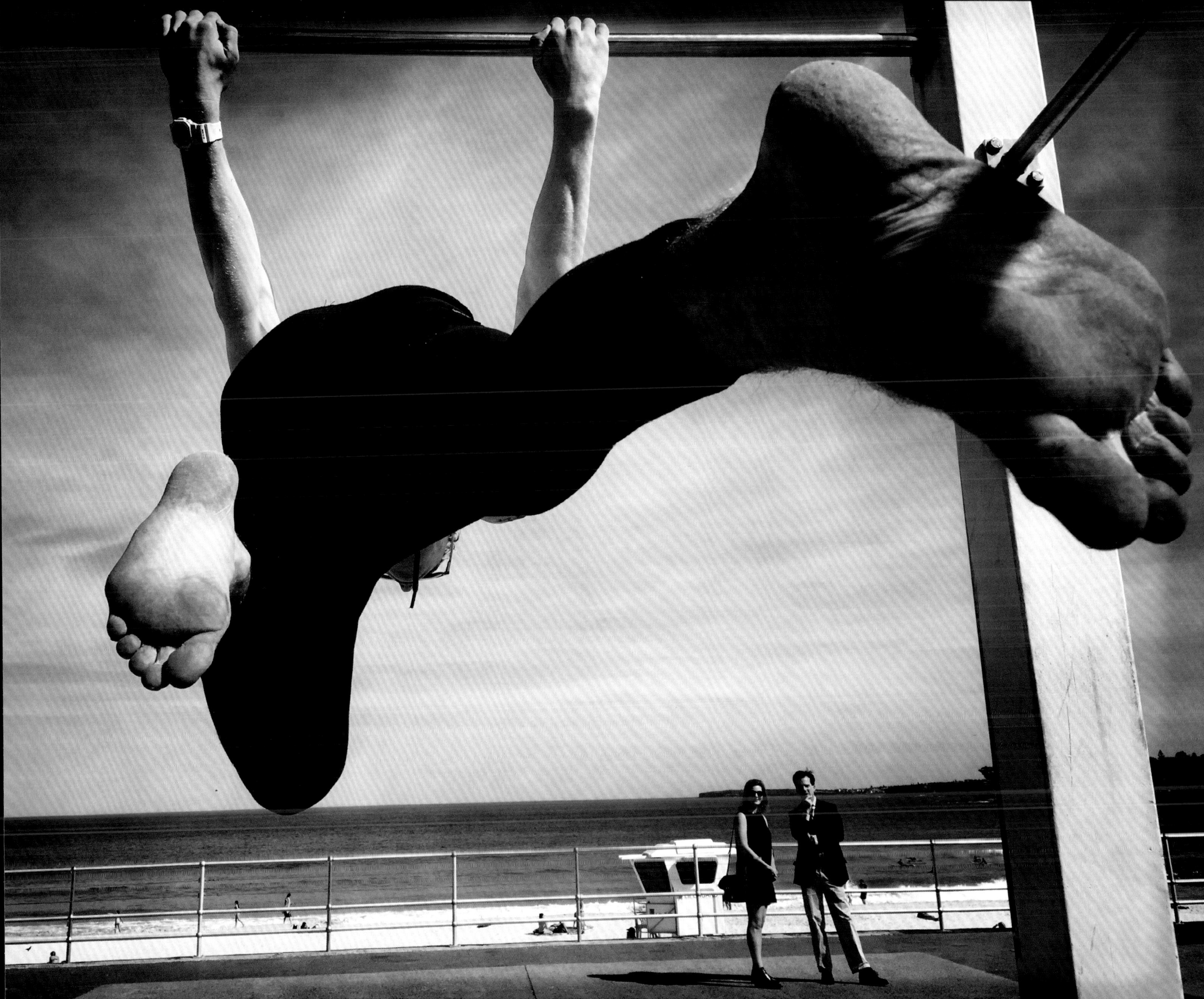

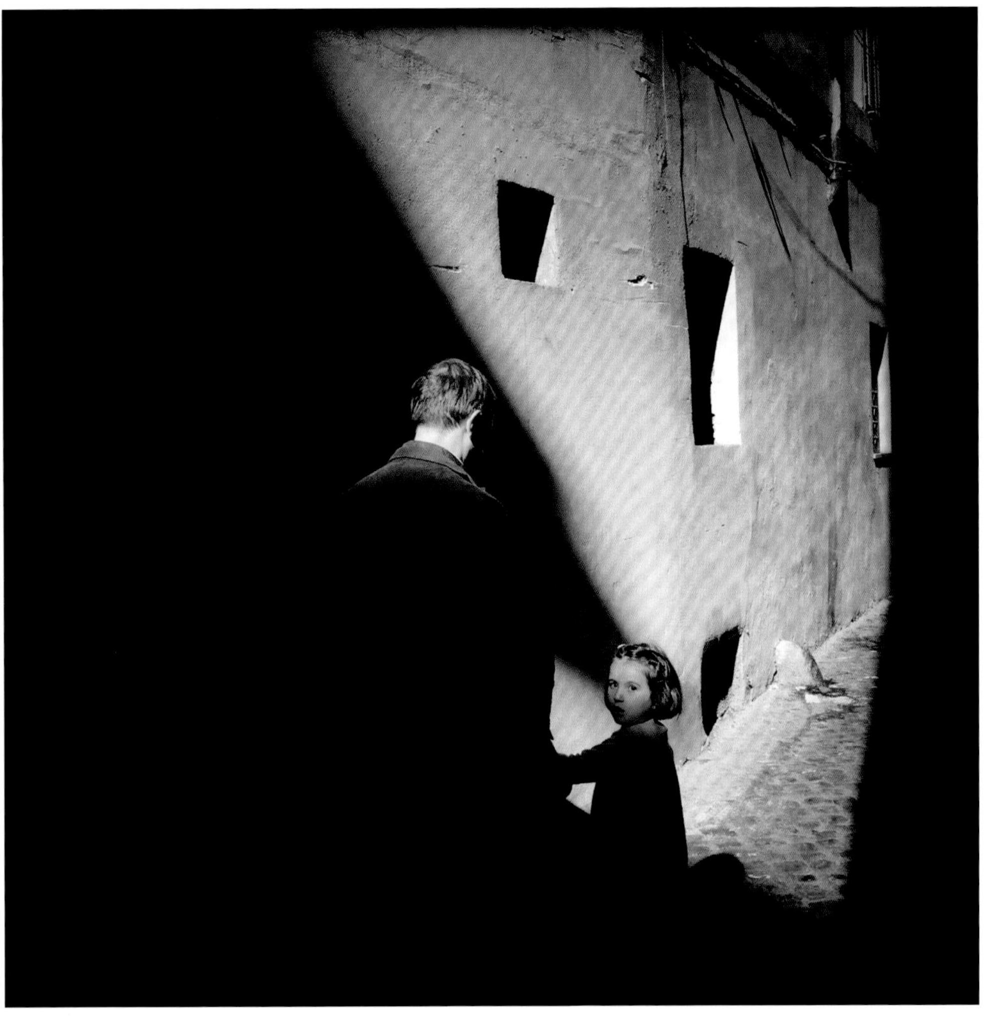

LOOKING BACK

I think this is my favorite photo, although I'm not sure why. Maybe it's because the little girl realized I was waiting for her and her father to walk past me into the shadows so I could capture them exactly where I wanted them. She knew I was doing something unusual and felt rightly doubtful as to what exactly I was doing. It was midday, right below where I live in Rome, which I suppose goes to prove that you don't need to travel far to find inspiration.

A COLD MORNING

I shot this on a very cold and foggy January morning in Venice. The trip was meant to be a 50th birthday present from my husband, except that my husband and I had been too busy to do it earlier, and the trip was about four years late.

Venice was practically empty, which is what I'd hoped—I'm not keen on crowds, and much prefer wandering around in semi-empty places. This image was shot on a Sunday morning in an empty boatyard on the island of La Giudecca.

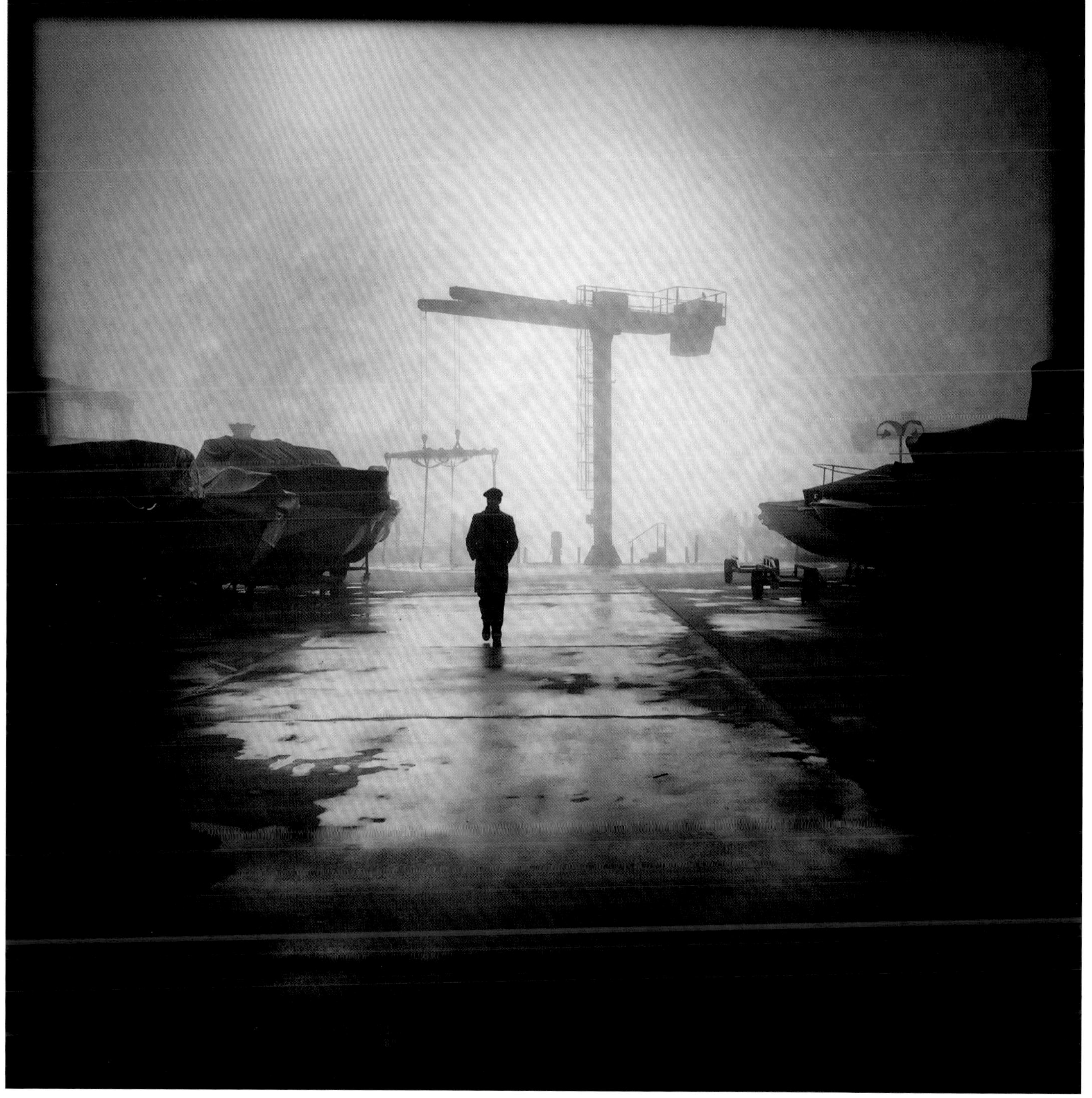

Q + A

How has your background influenced your photography?

Images and the visual arts have always interested me. I grew up in the center of Rome, in Italy, where aesthetic beauty is the norm and permeates everything and every place. I think that must have been one of the reasons why, in my twenties, I wanted to become a photojournalist. My life took a different path and I eventually became a documentary film-maker, then my life took another twist and I ended up creating fragrances, but my love for images—photography in particular—stayed with me. In late 2012, I took up photography again when I purchased my first iPhone and a friend got me on Instagram, where I discovered a brilliant community of very interesting photographers that I found enormously inspiring.

Why use an iPhone over a conventional digital camera?

I use an iPhone because I find it very easy to use and I like its immediacy. It's a point-and-shoot par excellence, and I love that people don't find it threatening or take it seriously. Occasionally, somebody asks me what I'm doing, but normally I'm invisible and nobody pays me any attention. The phone is with me all the time—because it's a phone—and if I find myself in an interesting situation and I have the time, I can just stop and photograph. It's less of a statement than a camera, both to myself and to others, and that's what I like about it. Also, the quality of images produced with phones is incredibly good these days, and getting better all the time.

What are the strengths of black and white versus color photography?

I just love black and white, I always have. I understand it better than color, and I know how to use it better than color. For some reason, for me, black and white is photography, maybe because it focuses my attention in a way that color photography doesn't. My love for photography started in black and white, and the work of photographers that inspired me is in black and white. But that may change, nothing is written in stone, and I love learning new tricks. Maybe at some stage I'll fall in love with color and find myself choosing subjects based on that—who knows? I'd like it if that happened.

Is experimentation important in your work, and how do you stay creative?

I don't think of myself as a particularly creative photographer, or as someone who experiments with photography, I just do what comes to me and what I find interesting. I also prefer not to analyze how I shoot because I feel that if I look at it too closely I'll discover all kinds of inconsistencies and get confused. The less I know and think about my creative process, the happier I am. As far as staying creative is concerned, I don't have an answer for that one, although I think the fact I'm not feeling the pressure to deliver helps to keep it a natural process, so it's something that just happens when I feel like it. Sometimes it hasn't been like that and I've taken on commissions, but that doesn't make me happy and I think I work less well when I have to deliver.

> *"For some reason, for me, black and white is photography, maybe because it focuses my attention in a way that color photography doesn't."*

LITTLE STEPS

I was on my way to the gym, in the old part of Rome close to where I live, when I saw these gorgeous shadows forming on the building. I waited a bit till they grew longer and more enticing, and then a baby girl appeared—her slightly wobbly steps taking her fast downhill as her mother hurried to catch her before she fell on the cobblestones. I missed my workout, but it was for a good cause.

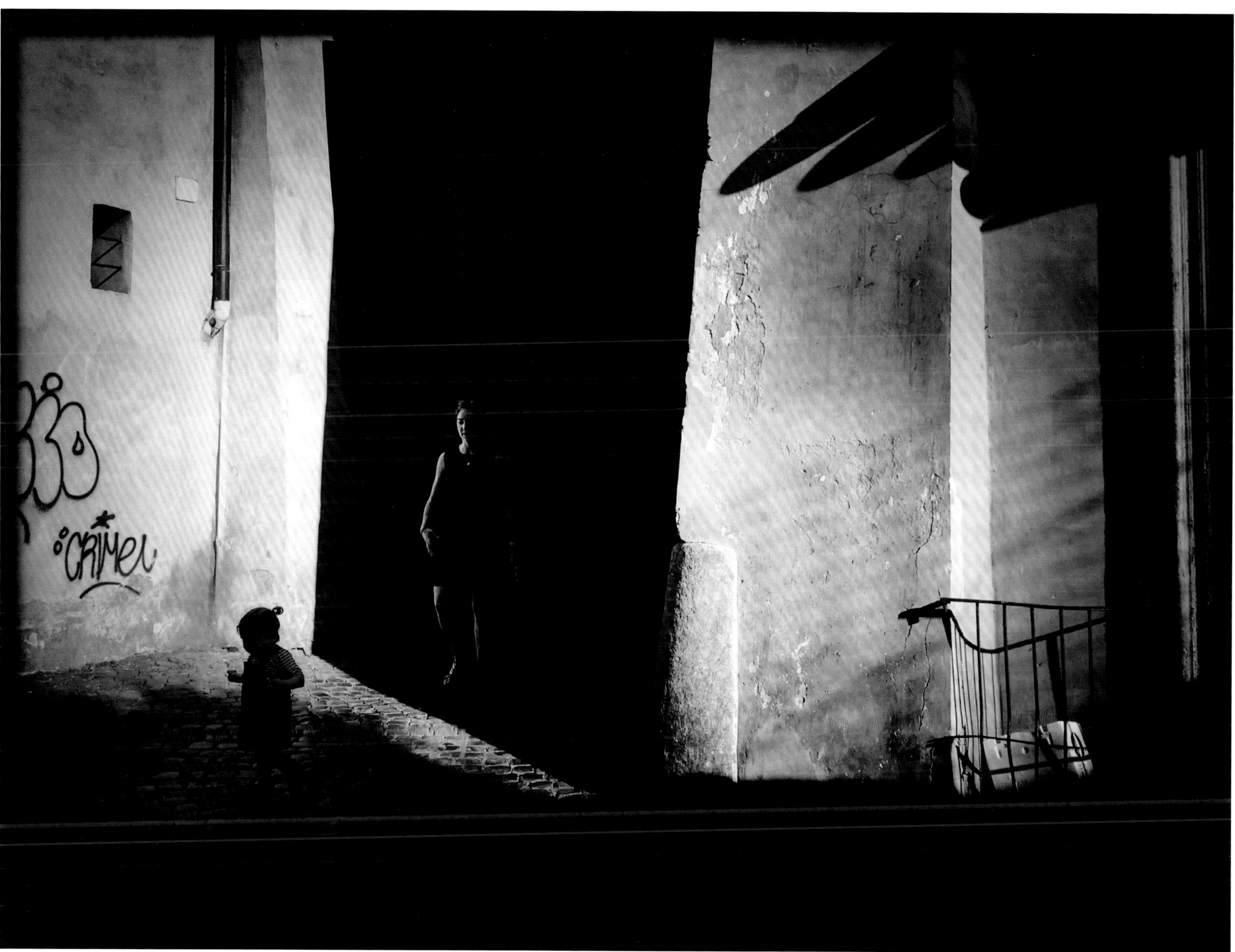

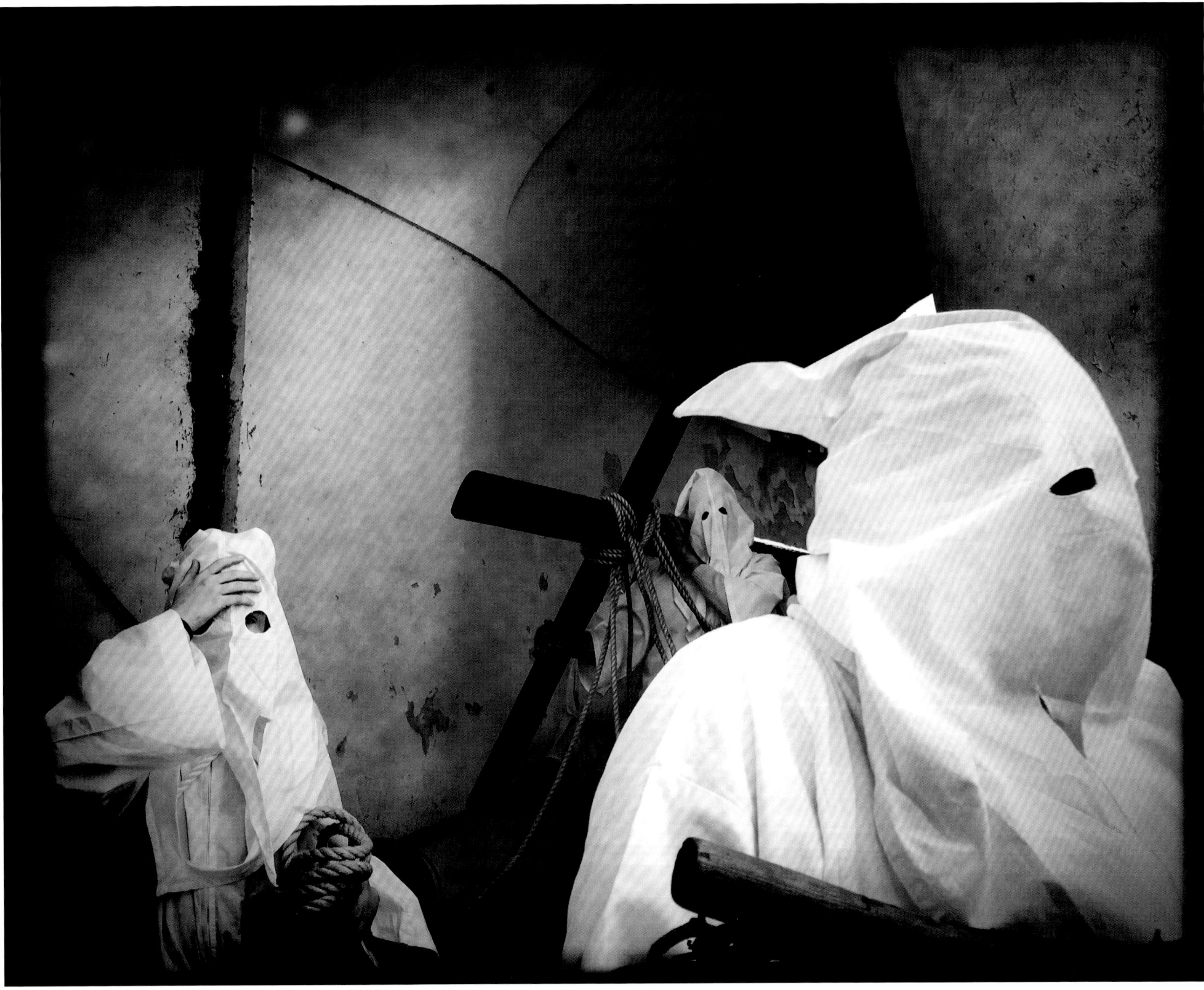

GOOD FRIDAY

Although I've been going to Positano on the Amalfi Coast since I was a baby, I rarely happened to be there over Easter—at least not since I'd started taking pictures—so this time, in March 2016, I grabbed my iPhone 6 and off I went. Traditionally, in all Catholic countries, the Good Friday celebrations are the most interesting, and Positano was no exception. I shot a lot that day, but in the end my favorite photo was this one, as the cross emerged in slight disarray from a tunnel on its way down to the beach, and the kid adjusted his costume to be able to see the stairs.

DELUGE

I was in New York for the launch of a fragrance and we had a pretty full schedule of deckside appointments with beauty editors from various magazines. It was pouring with rain, and we were stuck in traffic somewhere in Lower Manhattan, on our way down to the World Trade Center. I was depressed because it never stopped raining and I'd had no time—and, above all, not one dry day—to go out and shoot. So, I shot whatever I could from inside whichever vehicle I happened to be in. In this case it was a taxi, and a kind cyclist decided to pass by and give me my picture.

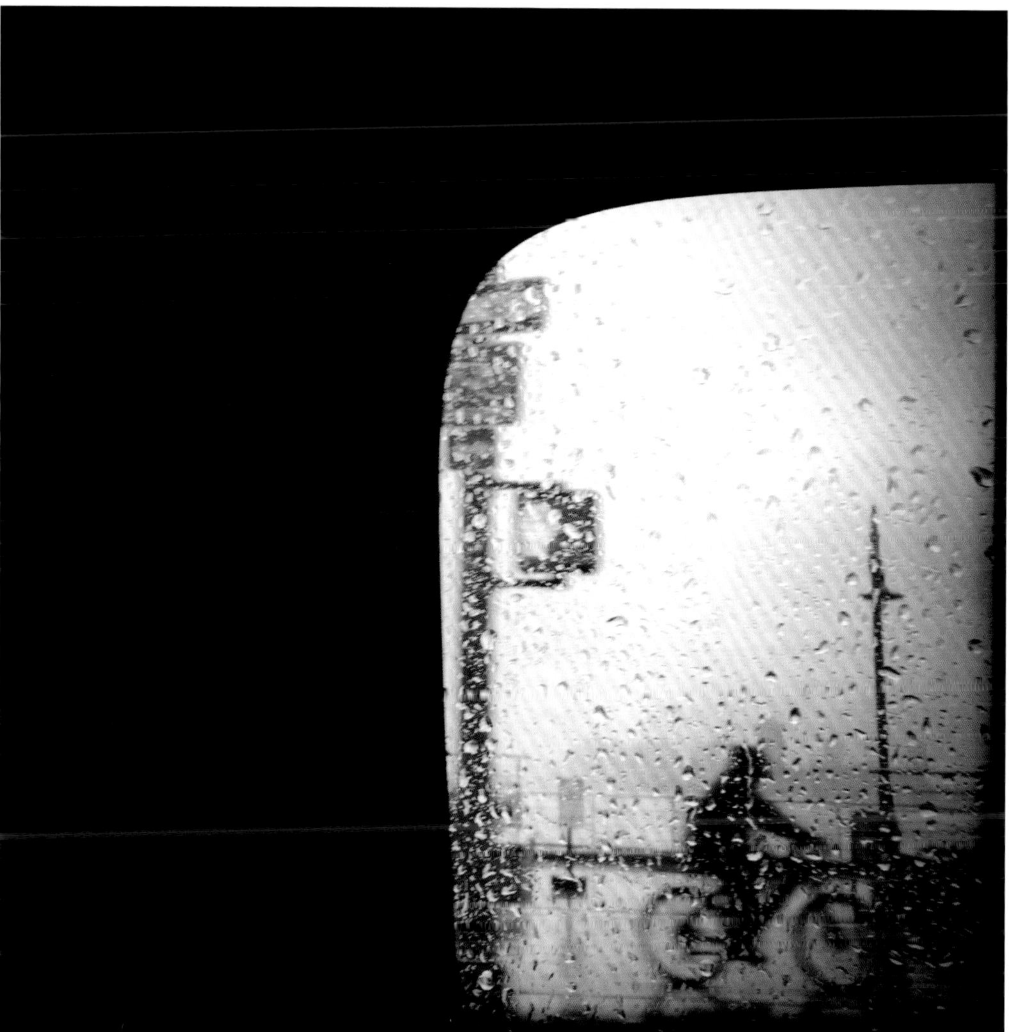

Q + A

What special techniques do you use when using a smartphone for photography?

When I'm using a phone I don't really use any particular technique, except maybe to adjust the exposure using the phone's metering system. I just basically point and shoot. I do a bit of post-processing using the phone apps Snapseed and Hipstamatic, but I use the phone's settings when shooting. I then use Hipstamatic to convert the photos into black and white, and Snapseed to do a bit of fine tuning. When I started, I was keen on trying out apps, but now I concentrate more on the photo itself: the less I need to retouch it, the happier I am.

What attracted you to Instagram?

A friend got me on it and the original idea was that I was supposed to shoot and post images of our fragrance brands, but early on I discovered I didn't enjoy that and—more importantly—that I wasn't particularly good at it. In the meantime, I'd discovered the iPhone camera and enjoyed using it, so I started taking pictures just for myself and posting the ones that I liked. Then I discovered there were lots of brilliant photographers—amateurs and professionals—on Instagram, and that's when it became a source of inspiration. For me, Instagram has become more than just an inspiration: it's brought me an audience, exhibitions, work opportunities, and, last but not least, some very good friends.

Street photography can be intrusive— do you ever feel you are invading a person's privacy, and does that matter to you?

I agree it can be intrusive, and it is definitely something that matters to me, but at the same time I find what goes on in the street very interesting and very inspiring. I realize that when I photograph people in the street I'm doing it without their permission and most of the time without them even knowing. Some people may think this isn't right, but for me the limit is not to photograph people in distress—I'm not a photojournalist and I'm not paid to do that. Apart from that, I don't see why I shouldn't photograph people on the streets.

What tips would you give to those who wish to master street photography?

I have two main suggestions. The first is to be patient and keep your fingers crossed: if you wait long enough something interesting is bound to happen. The second is to prepare yourself: be ready with your camera or phone when you go out on the street; and when you're at home, do your homework. Study the work of other photographers who inspire you, because there's always something new to learn, even from photos that you've seen many times. Those images that you look at and study repeatedly will fix themselves in your mind, and this will help you make better photos.

"Be patient and keep your fingers crossed: if you wait long enough something interesting is bound to happen."

TECHNICAL INFORMATION

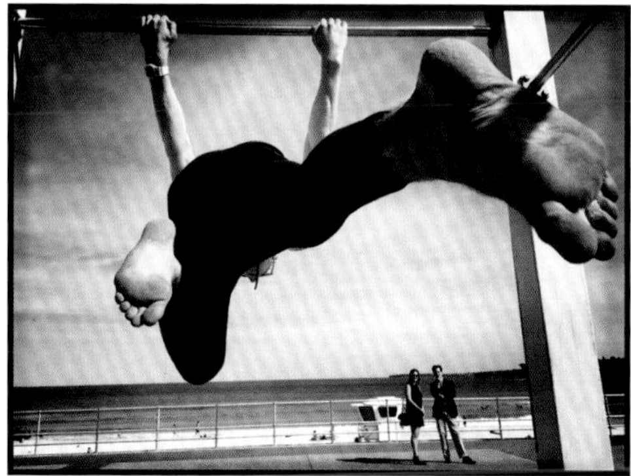

UNTITLED
BONDI BEACH, SYDNEY, AUSTRALIA

Camera: Apple iPhone 6s and Hipstamatic app
Lens/Focal length: 4.15mm f/2.2 (35mm equivalent: 29mm)
Aperture: f/2.2
Shutter speed: 1/1923 sec.
ISO: 25

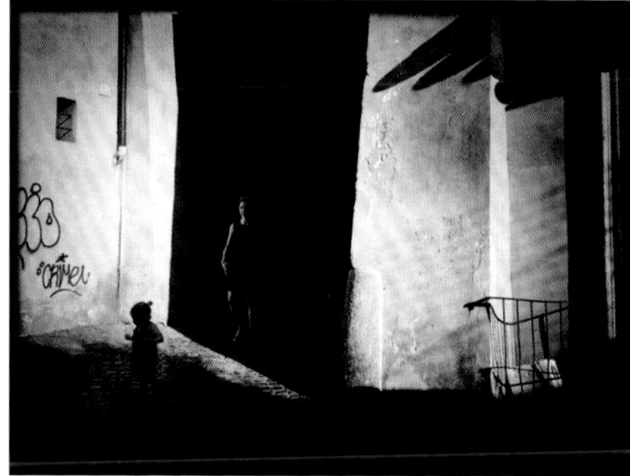

LOOKING BACK
ROME, ITALY

Camera: Apple iPhone 6s and Hipstamatic app
Lens/Focal length: 4.15mm f/2.2 (35mm equivalent: 29mm)
Aperture: f/2.2
Shutter speed: 1/674 sec.
ISO: 25

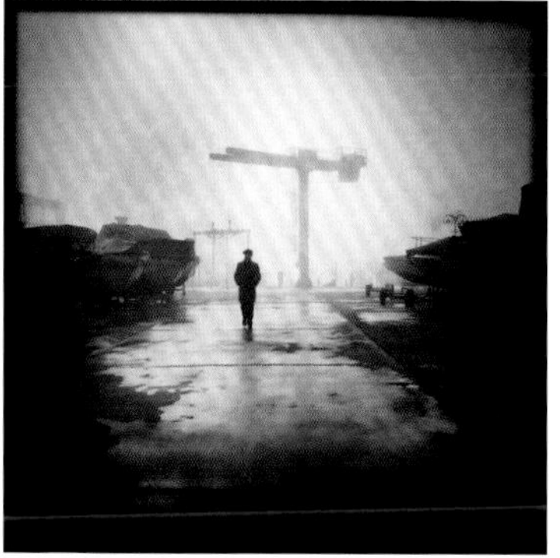

A COLD MORNING
VENICE, ITALY

Camera: Apple iPhone 6s and Hipstamatic app
Lens/Focal length: 4.15mm f/2.2 (35mm equivalent: 29mm)
Aperture: f/2.2
Shutter speed: 1/3846 sec.
ISO: 25

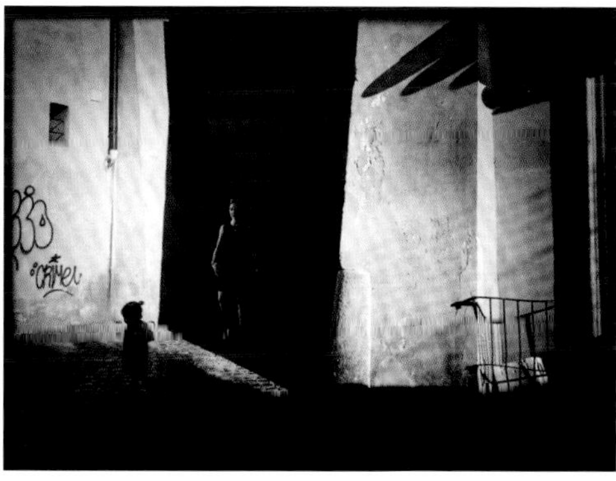

LITTLE STEPS
ROME, ITALY

Camera: Apple iPhone 6s and Hipstamatic app
Lens/Focal length: 4.15mm f/2.2 (35mm equivalent: 29mm)
Aperture: f/2.2
Shutter speed: 1/1789 sec.
ISO: 25

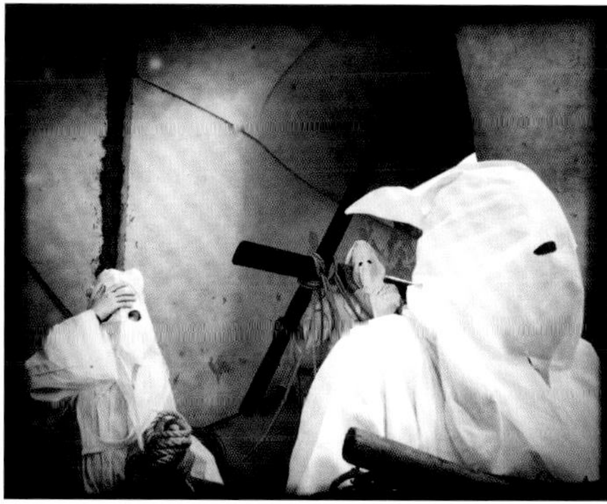

GOOD FRIDAY
POSITANO, ITALY

Camera: Apple iPhone 6s and Hipstamatic app
Lens/Focal length: 4.15mm f/2.2 (35mm equivalent: 29mm)
Aperture: f/2.2
Shutter speed: 1/273 sec.
ISO: 25

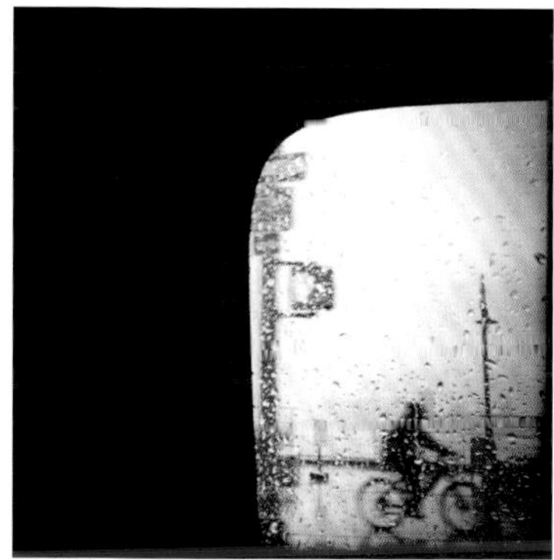

DELUGE
NEW YORK CITY, NEW YORK, USA

Camera: Apple iPhone 6s and Hipstamatic app
Lens/Focal length: 4.15mm f/2.2 (35mm equivalent: 29mm)
Aperture: f/2.2
Shutter speed: 1/120 sec.
ISO: 32

ALEXEY TITARENKO

Alexey Titarenko was born in Leningrad (now St Petersburg), in Russia, in 1962. He started taking pictures in 1971, at the age of nine; graduated from Leningrad Public University of Society-related Professions in 1978 with a degree in Photojournalism; and received a Master's degree in Cinematic and Photographic Arts from the Leningrad Institute of Culture in 1983. After serving in the military, Alexey began work on *Nomenklatura of Signs*, a series of collages and photomontages that served as a commentary on the Communist regime as an oppressive system. By 1989, he had his first solo exhibition in Western Europe, in Paris, France, and *Nomenklatura of Signs* was also included in Photostroyka, a major show of new Soviet photography that toured the USA.

After the collapse of the Soviet Union in 1991, Alexey produced several series of photographs about the human condition of the Russian people during this time and the suffering they endured throughout the 20th Century, including his most well known—*City of Shadows*. His St Petersburg body of work from the 1990s has won him worldwide recognition. In 2002, the International Photography Festival at Arles, France, presented this work at the Reattu Museum; and, in 2005, the French-German TV Channel Arte produced a 30-minute documentary entitled *Alexey Titarenko: Art et la Manière*. Alexey's works are now in the collections of many major European and American museums.

VASILEOSTROVSKAYA METRO STATION
(VARIANT CROWD 2),
FROM *CITY OF SHADOWS* (1992)

The image was taken at the entrance to the Vasileostrovskaya Metro station, on Vasilyevsky Island, during the collapse of the Soviet Union. The Metro was the only reliable means of transport at that time, and many people used it to commute to and from work. Once you are inside the station, you have to pay, passing the turnstiles with a pass or a coin, and then take a long escalator deep underground to the platforms. This was quite a long exposure, as the crowd was moving very slowly and erratically—many people were trying to jump the line, creating chaos, sometimes losing their clothes and shoes, if not lives.

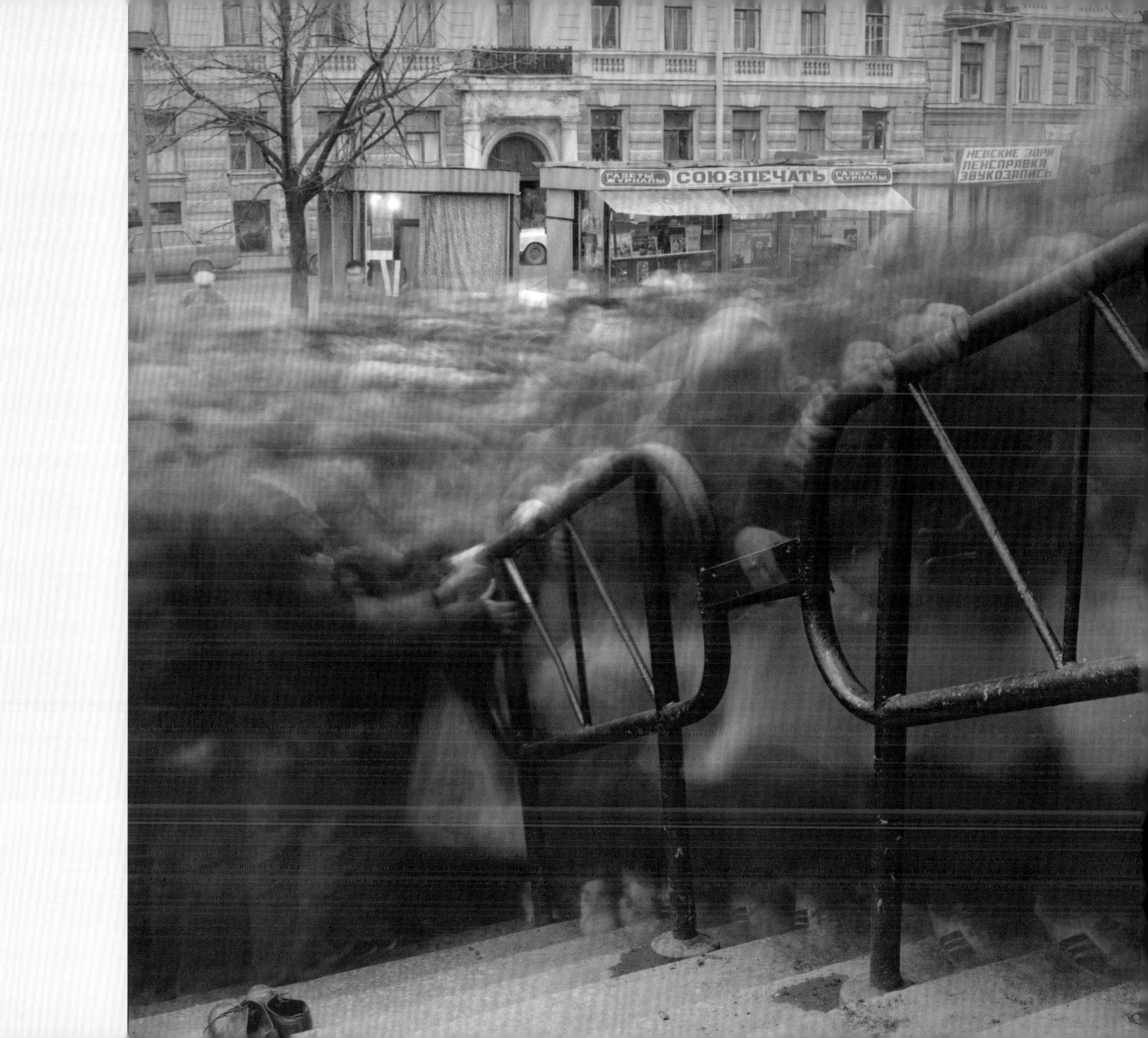
ГАЗЕТЫ ЖУРНАЛЫ
СОЮЗПЕЧАТЬ
ГАЗЕТЫ ЖУРНАЛЫ
НЕВСКИЕ ЗОРИ
ПЕНСПРАВКА
ЗВУКОЗАПИСЬ

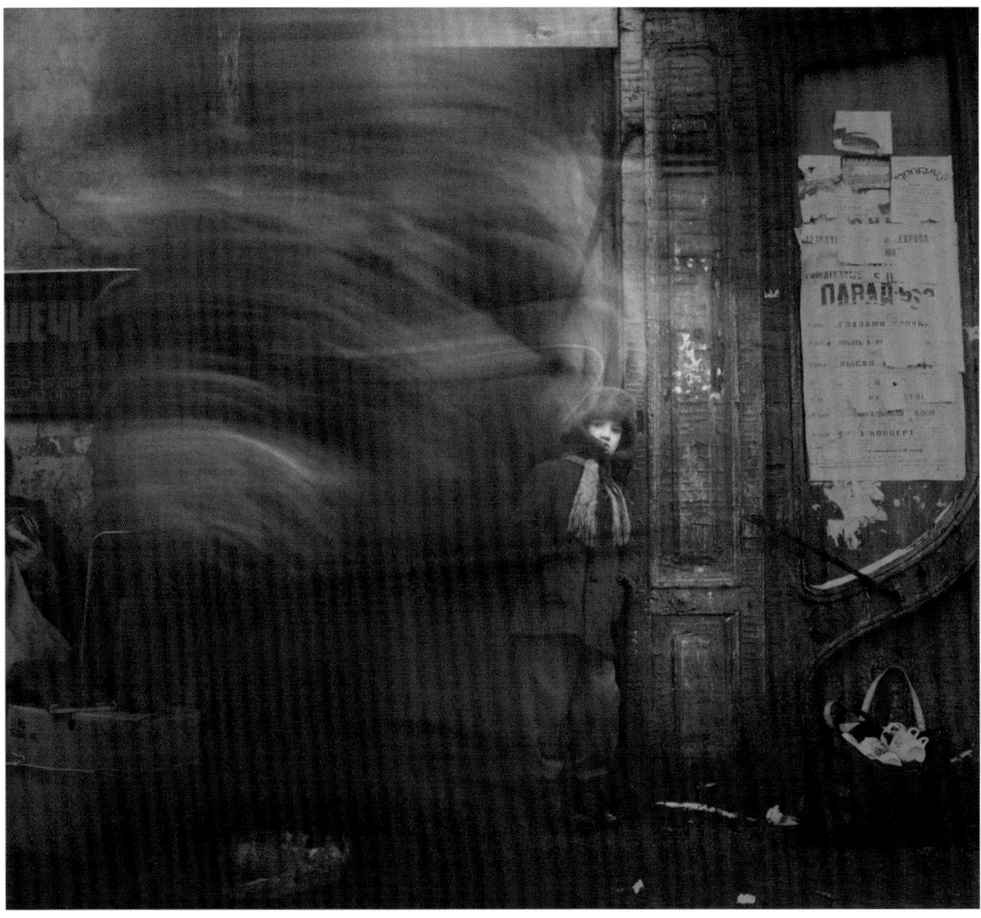

HOMELESS BOY, BLACK MARKET
NEAR HAY MARKET SQUARE,
FROM *CITY OF SHADOWS* (1993)

With the collapse of the Soviet Union, many
institutions, such as orphanages, were unable
to provide basic services. Often, they were
totally abandoned by the staff. Children, like
this homeless boy at the black market, weren't
getting any food and were forced to live on
the street to survive.

GRANDMA WITH GRANDCHILD,
FROM *CITY OF SHADOWS* (1992)

This was a mother, or a grandmother, with her
child. This is the only shot I took with a 180mm
lens for the *City of Shadows* series. It was taken
in a residential neighborhood, with relatively
few passersby. The telephoto lens has the ability
to "compress" space, and make it seem more
"populated." The tripod had to be extremely
stable, and this needed preparation and
care. The print was solarized.

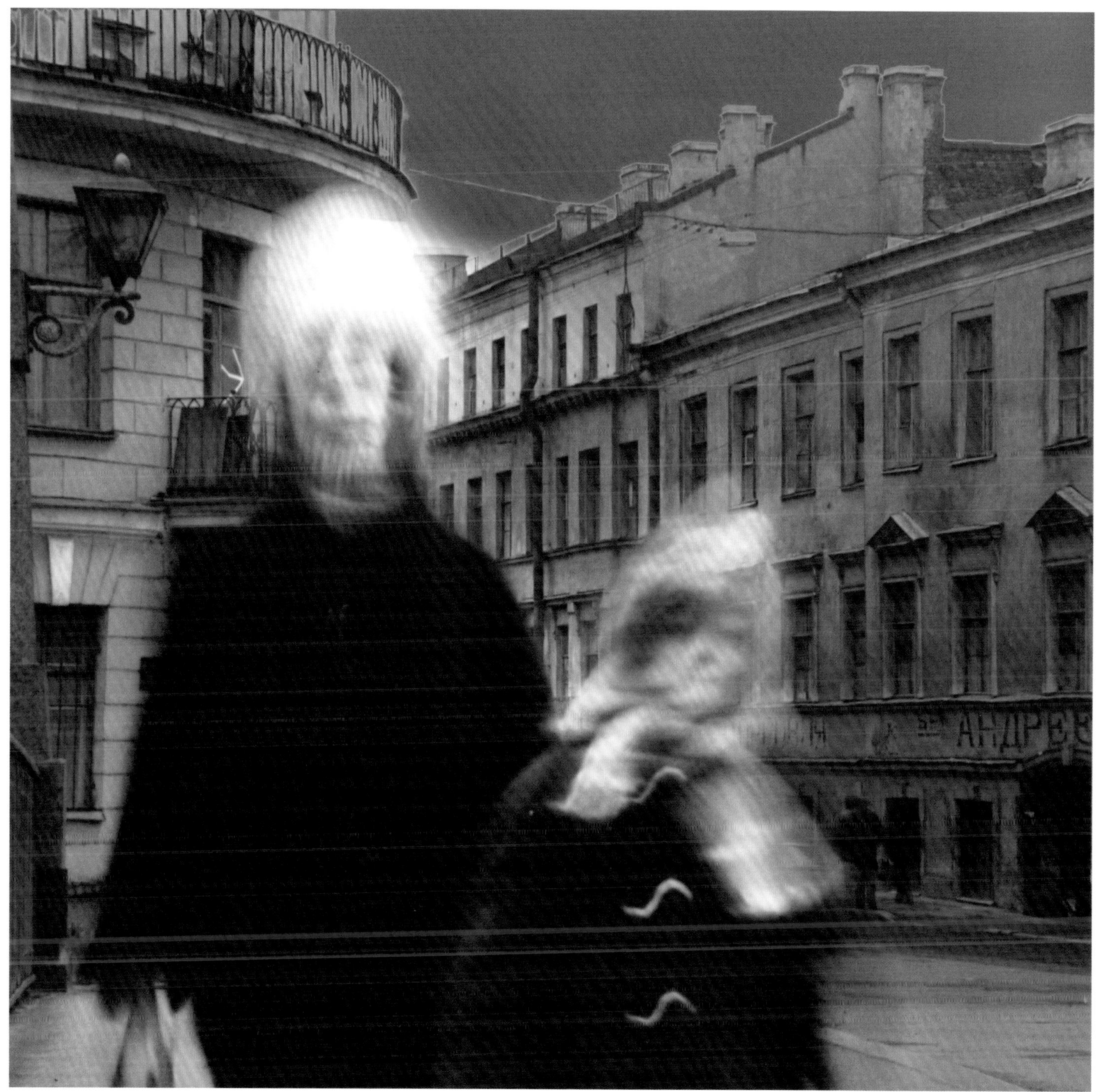

Q + A

How did you get started in street photography?

As a young boy I loved French culture, literature, and art—including photography. When my parents gave me my first camera, I hoped that photography would enable me to express my vision, my thoughts, my emotions, but I was deeply disappointed—my images did not reflect any of it. So I dropped photography and started to create collages instead, starting what would become the *Nomenklatura of Signs* project. This enabled me to express my vision and my feelings about the communist regime, and I also felt happy doing it. The project took me out onto the streets, in order take pictures of the propaganda, buildings, walls with slogans, communist sculptures, monuments to Soviet leaders, and so on. In the end, I found myself spending almost all of my time on the streets of Leningrad, walking from one neighborhood to another, which created a very different spiritual and emotional background in my mind and changed my vision, pushing me in a completely different direction.

What have been the main creative influences on your work?

There have been many influences, mostly unconnected to photography, but something that I really didn't like and tried to distance myself from was official Soviet photo reportage—a style called "socialist realism." This kind of "official" street photography was boring, alienating, and so far from what I was aspiring to that it kept me away from taking pictures for many years. Despite that, from the 1920s onward, the USSR was rather productive in introducing new ideas to the visual arts in general and to photography in particular. Even though the Constructivist style was already condemned as being "formalist" by the time I was born in 1962, it was easy to find old papers or magazines with Aleksandr Rodchenko's photographs, Gustav Klutsis's collages, and so on, which were very interesting. I had also admired the paintings, sculptures, and architectural projects of the early revolutionary age of 1917 to 1924 as a kid during visits to the State Russian Museum. Suprematism, Constructivism, and the works of Kazimir Malevich, Marc Chagall, El Lissitzky, and Vladimir Tatlin were also extremely inspiring.

You took your most famous images of St Petersburg during a period of change and uncertainty—why was this important to you?

How could I not take pictures? The collapse of the USSR for the inhabitants of provincial cities like Leningrad (now St Petersburg) was quite similar to life in wartime: not so much a life, but a long and painful survival that was lethal for many. At some point, many of us ordinary Petersburgians realized that we were also citizens that should care about the country we're living in, especially during this harsh and difficult time. Being a citizen means caring about what is going on, and doing what is best. I felt it was my mission to take pictures on the streets of my city, to document everything. Through those images I tried to express my feelings and emotions about what was happening, which I described in my book, *The City is a Novel*.

What challenges has using long exposures presented?

For long exposures—even relatively brief ones—you need to work with a tripod. Shooting with a tripod in the street may get you into jail even in New York (I have been threatened with arrest several times by the NYPD because of my tripod), so it was certainly a problem shooting in a country that was experiencing shortages in everything, as well as an explosion of criminality and gang-related violence. Every day, when I went out to take photographs, I felt as if I was going to the front line, risking injury or death. Did I have any fear? Of course—huge fear! The situation was completely unpredictable and anything may have happened. I developed strategies for keeping a low profile, for example, pretending to sell the camera at the black market. But this only worked for a very brief moment before people realized what I was doing. It took all my courage just to approach some places where tens of thousands of angry people were gathering, such as near the subway stations, and there were many moments I will never forget. I was often followed and attacked, and had to defend myself, sometimes using my Hasselblad as a weapon!

UNDER WOODEN SCAFFOLD, FROM *CITY OF SHADOWS* (1992)

I don't look at my watch when I take the photograph—I close the shutter by feeling—but this exposure lasted more than 10 seconds (Soviet films had reciprocity problems with exposures longer than 1 second). This print was slightly solarized. The effect of light coming through the wooden beams was created by the movement of people.

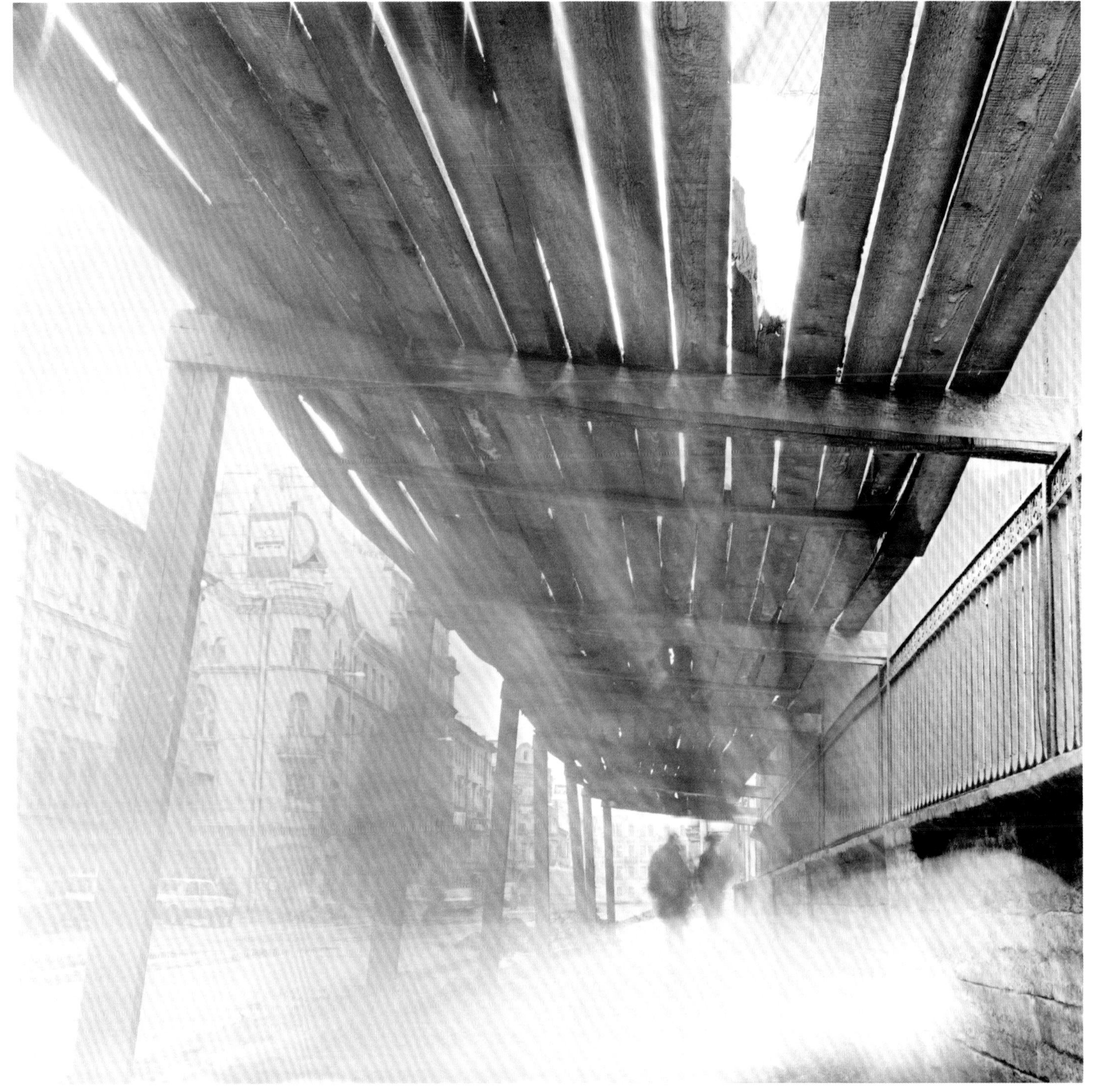

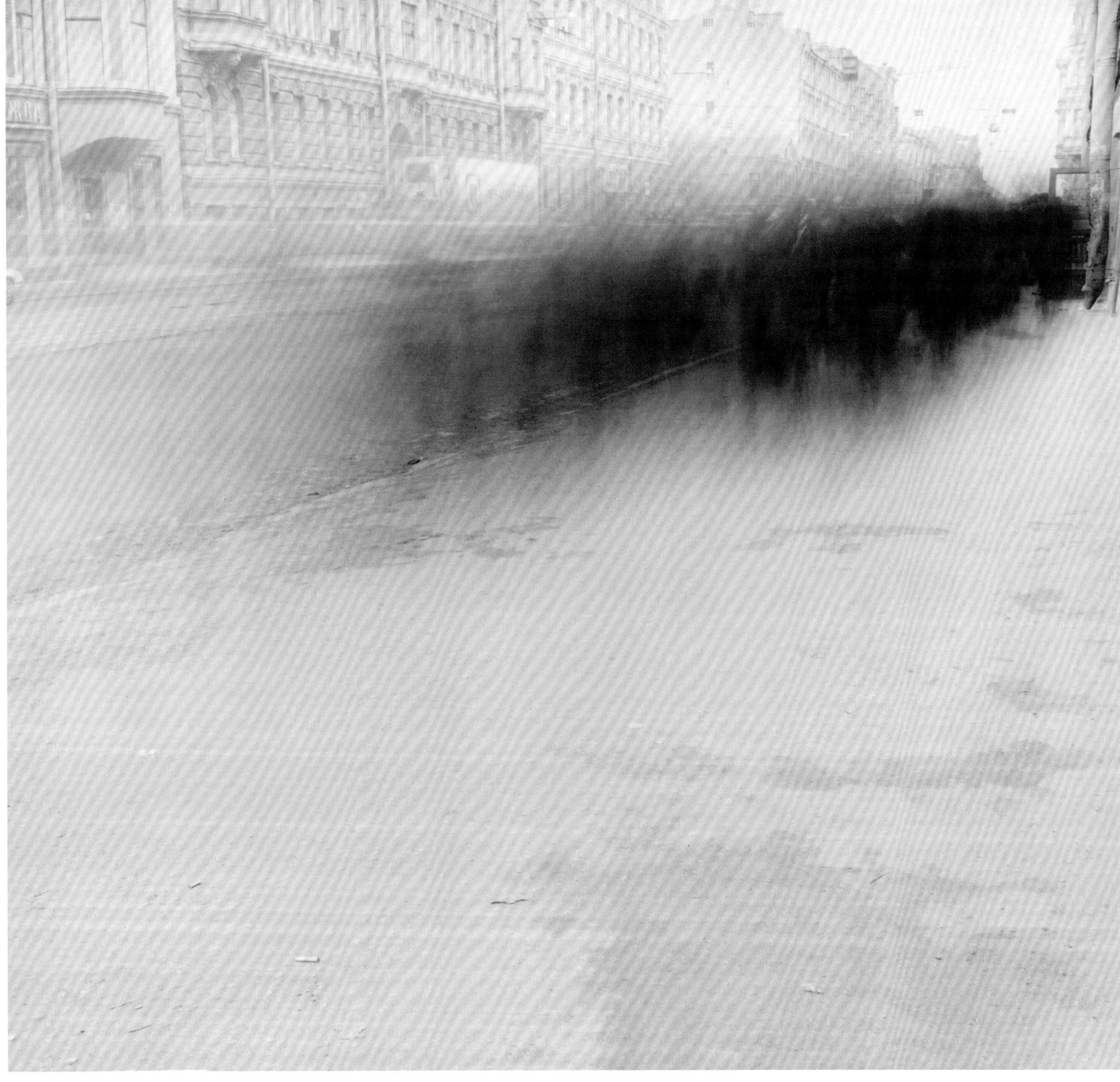

CROWD ON SREDNIY PROSPECT (CROWD 3), FROM *CITY OF SHADOWS* (1992)

This is a busy area on Vasilyevsky Island, called Sredniy Prospect, which is a part of the historic city center. It is also an industrial area with many factories and shipyards. I lowered the tripod almost to knee-level for this long-exposure shot.

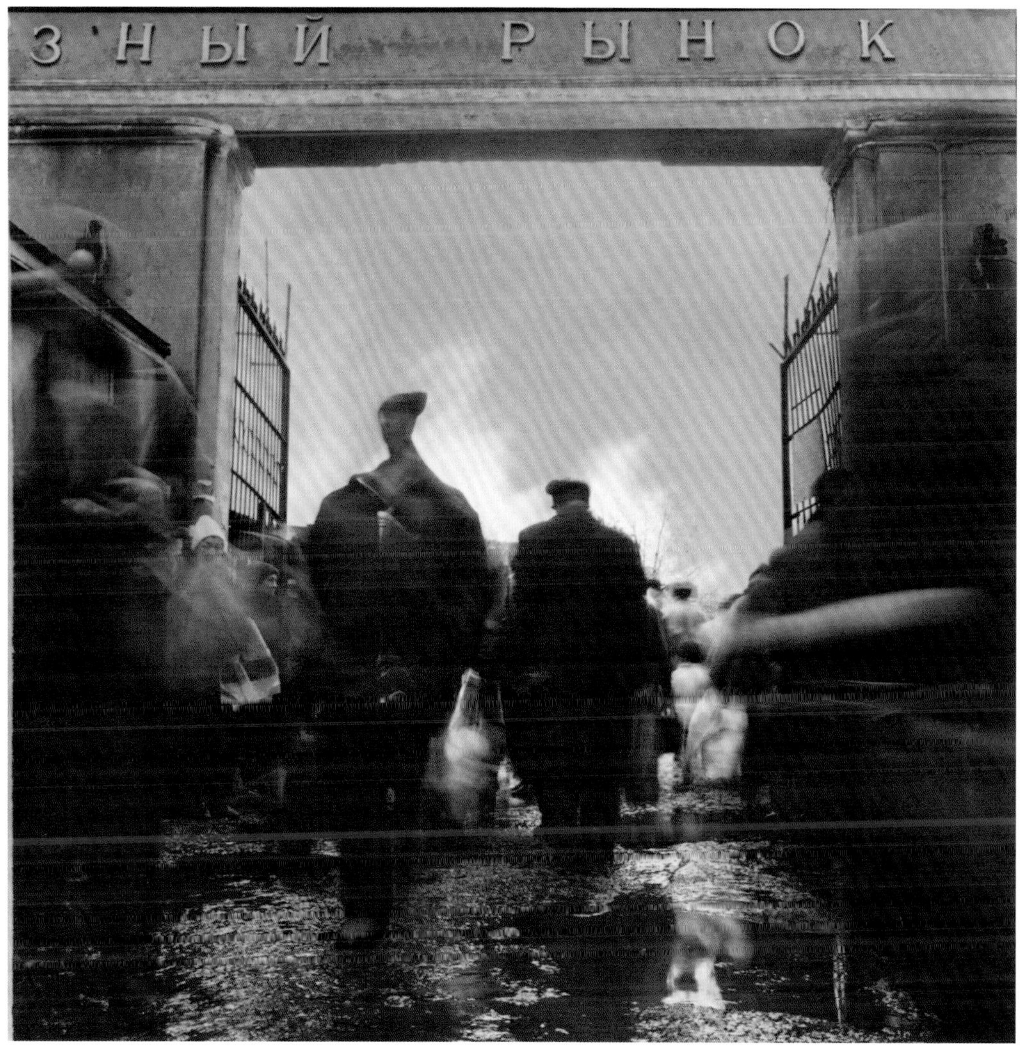

BLACK MARKET, FROM *CITY OF SHADOWS* (1993)

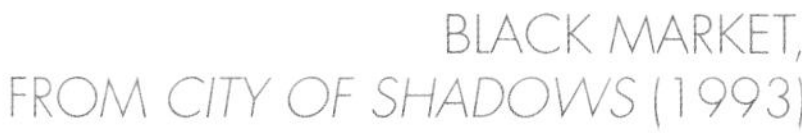

This is the entrance to the open market near Sennaya Square, in St Petersburg's historic city center. At the time it was also our main black market where people traded everything. The exposure wasn't that long.

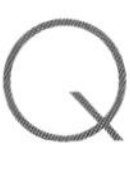

Q

+

A

How do you typically compose your images—what attracts you to a particular shot?

In St Petersburg, I usually chose to head to the most dangerous or busiest place—for instance, the black market in the city center, the subway station, or Nevsky Prospekt. Once there, I had only a few seconds to figure out the subject, composition, distance, exposure, aperture, and so on. If I detected anything that concerned me after I'd taken the first shot I left straight away. If all seemed okay, then I tried to calm myself and took a little bit more time crafting the composition, choosing a different position, and adjusting the exposure or aperture. There is no special light to look for in St Petersburg during fall and winter— it is usually cloudy—and, because of the high latitude (on the 60th parallel north, the same as Alaska) there is only "twilight" for a few hours in the middle of the day, so the light was usually the same every day. However, for safety, I changed the location each time—never returning to the same place until a number of days had passed.

Why do you use intentional camera movement to create your images?

The idea of intentional camera movement came when I started to create a photo series around Dostoevsky's novels. I had to shoot residential locations that didn't have many people during the daytime. There were a lot of nice, old, beautiful buildings, but no passersby to create the movement I wanted in the images. So I said to myself, if buildings don't move, maybe I can move my camera during the long exposure time? That's how it started. The type of movement and timing were difficult to set up, as it was difficult to predict what the effect would be on the film. I had to return to my darkroom, develop the film, look at the result, and then go back to retake the shot, making any necessary adjustments, and go through the process again. It was very time-consuming, often taking months for just a couple of successful shots.

What darkroom techniques do you use to create your prints?

Camera movement creates traces of light on the negative that have to be printed differently on the paper to create the right effect. That taught me to make changes in the printing process and to start to use partial bleaching and toning for the effects I wanted. Although they are passing out of use with digital photography, darkroom techniques are very exciting artistic tools. For example, reducing the silver adds depth or light; toning, if used properly, can change an image to what you'd call in music a major or minor key. And it's the same for density and contrast. But the process was very intuitive—I chose to use each technique as I felt appropriate to create the effect I wanted for each image.

What tips would you give to those who wish to master street photography?

When I started to take photographs, a long time ago, I often felt terribly bored and tired, as if I was wasting my life without any meaningful purpose. I even felt somewhat guilty—the same feeling that many creative people might experience when killing time or deferring their projects until another day. Perhaps this was the most important lesson I learned—the understanding that you need to approach every work in a creative manner, using all your skills to express yourself. In this way, a photographer will experience the true joy of creativity, and learn through their photography the meaning of life itself.

"There were a lot of nice old beautiful buildings, but no passersby to create the movement I wanted in the images. So I said to myself, if buildings don't move, maybe I can move my camera during the long exposure time? That's how it started."

TECHNICAL INFORMATION

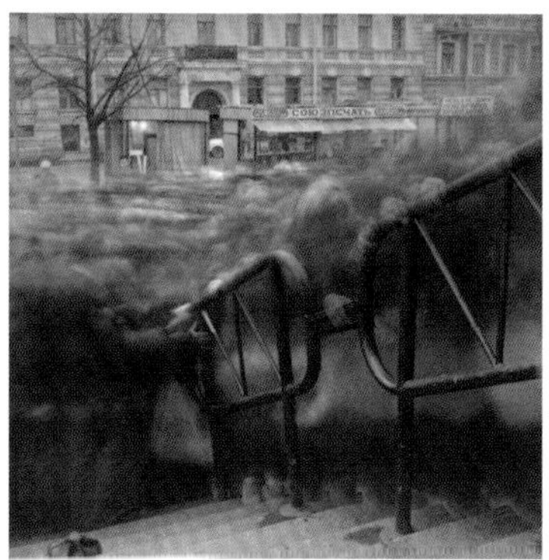

VASILEOSTROVSKAYA METRO STATION
(VARIANT CROWD 2)
FROM *CITY OF SHADOWS* (1992)
ST PETERSBURG, RUSSIA

Camera: Hasselblad 500CM
Lens/Focal length: Planar 80mm f/2.8
Aperture: In the range f/16–f/22
Shutter speed: "Bulb" mode, exposure time unrecorded
Film: Svema 64 (64 GOST/ISO 50)

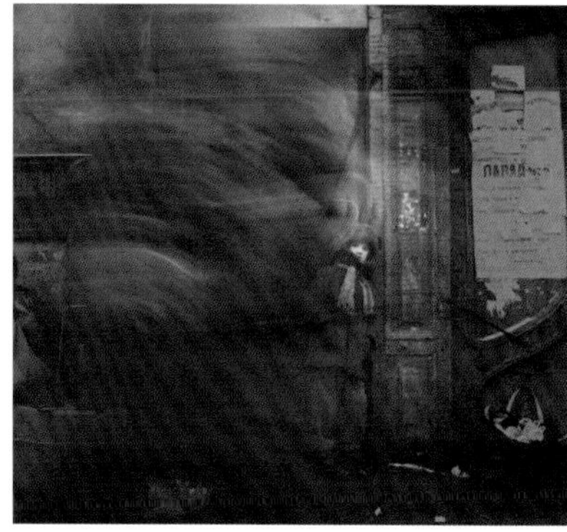

HOMELESS BOY, BLACK MARKET
NEAR HAY MARKET SQUARE
FROM *CITY OF SHADOWS* (1993)
ST PETERSBURG, RUSSIA

Camera: Hasselblad 500CM
Lens/Focal length: Planar 80mm f/2.8
Aperture: f/11
Shutter speed: "Bulb" mode, exposure time unrecorded
Film: Svema 64 (64 GOST/ISO 50)

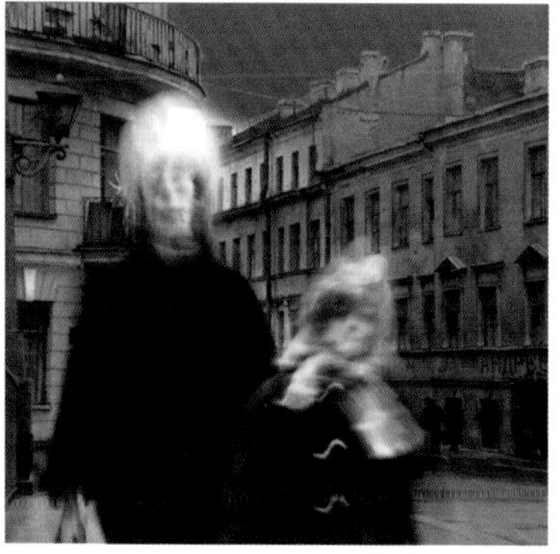

GRANDMA WITH GRANDCHILD
FROM *CITY OF SHADOWS* (1992)
ST PETERSBURG, RUSSIA

Camera: Pentacon Six TL
Lens/Focal length: 180mm f/2.8
Aperture: Unrecorded
Shutter speed: "Bulb" mode, exposure time unrecorded
Film: Svema 64 (64 GOST/ISO 50)

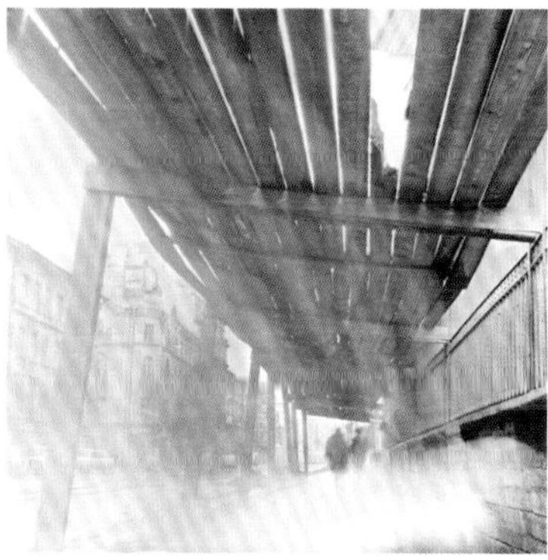

UNDER WOODEN SCAFFOLD
FROM *CITY OF SHADOWS* (1992)
ST PETERSBURG, RUSSIA

Camera: Hasselblad 500CM
Lens/Focal length: Planar 80mm f/2.8
Aperture: In the range f/16–f/22
Shutter speed: "Bulb" mode, more than 10 sec.
Film: Svema 64 (64 GOST/ISO 50)

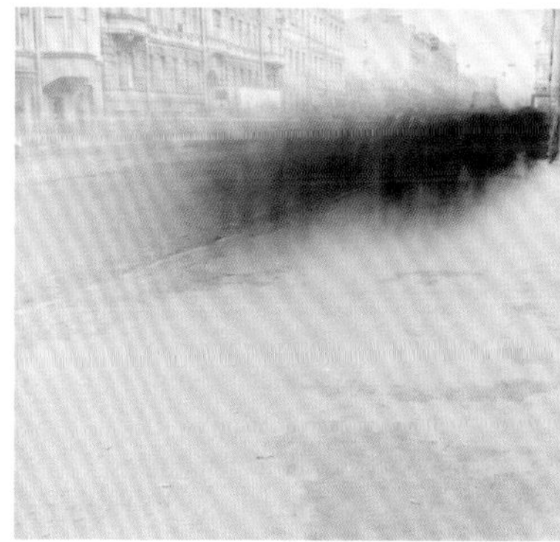

CROWD ON SREDNIY PROSPECT
(CROWD 3)
FROM *CITY OF SHADOWS* (1992)
ST PETERSBURG, RUSSIA

Camera: Hasselblad 500CM
Lens/Focal length: Planar 80mm f/2.8
Aperture: In the range f/16–f/22
Shutter speed: "Bulb" mode, more than 10 sec.
Film: Svema 64 (64 GOST/ISO 50)

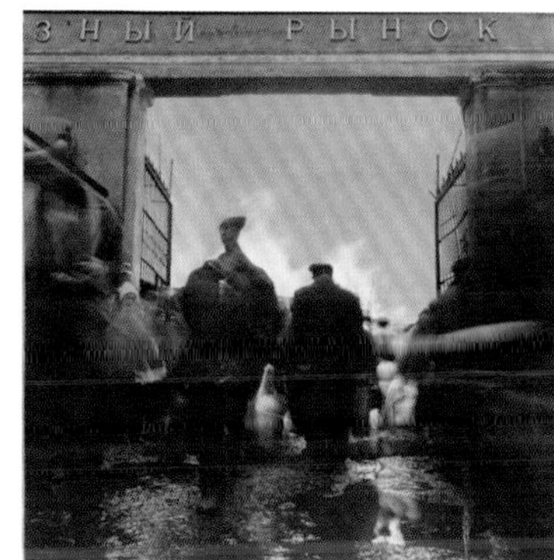

BLACK MARKET
FROM *CITY OF SHADOWS* (1993)
ST PETERSBURG, RUSSIA

Camera: Hasselblad 500CM
Lens/Focal length: Planar 80mm f/2.8
Aperture: In the range f/11–f/22
Shutter speed: "Bulb" mode, exposure time unrecorded
Film: Svema 64 (64 GOST/ISO 50)

MARTIN U WALTZ

Martin U Waltz works as a photographer, educator, and writer in Berlin. He is a founding member of the Berlin1020 Street Photography Collective and editor of the German Street Photography website, and has written and co-authored several books on street photography. As a passionate photography teacher, he offers personal street photography coaching and workshops in Berlin.

Martin has won numerous awards at international photography competitions, and his work has been shown at exhibitions in New York, London, Dublin, Rome, Budapest, Bucharest, and Berlin. His work is a reflection on the human condition in urban space, exploring the underlying emotions of the city between existential angst, boredom, and joy. Berlin plays a crucial role in Martin's images, and his view on contemporary Berlin is both poetic and analytical at the same time. He is a keen observer of the fragility and transiency in urban life, and his photography emphasizes the contrast between the soft, fluid human shape and the hard, static fabric of city infrastructure.

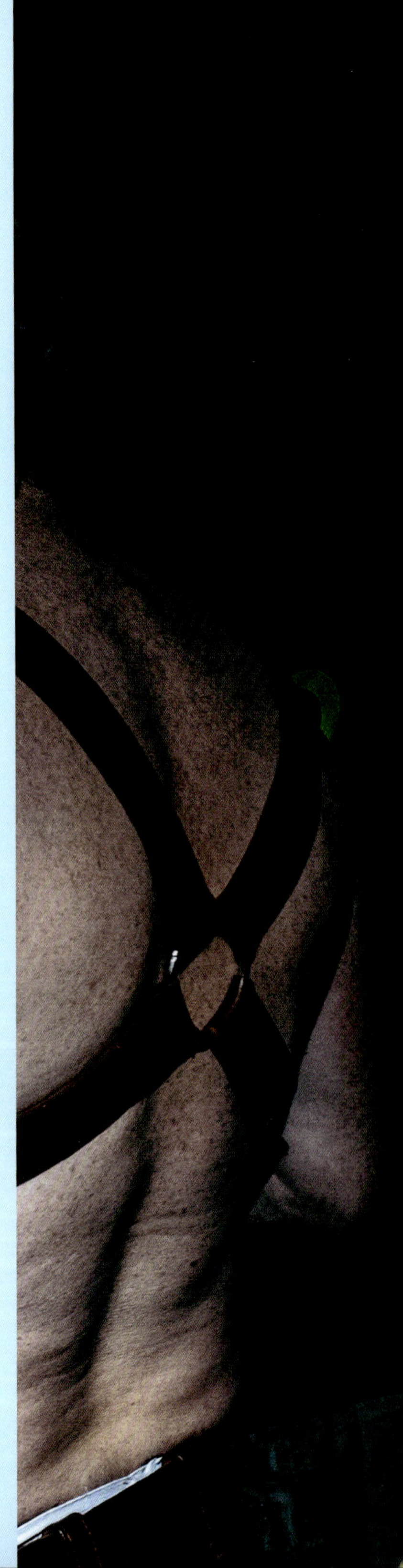

A SIMPLE STREET PORTRAIT

I rarely do street portraits, but I liked this subject in combination with the naked torso in the background. Using external flash from above allowed me to create the shadow over his eye.

Are street portraits still considered street photography? That is certainly open for debate.

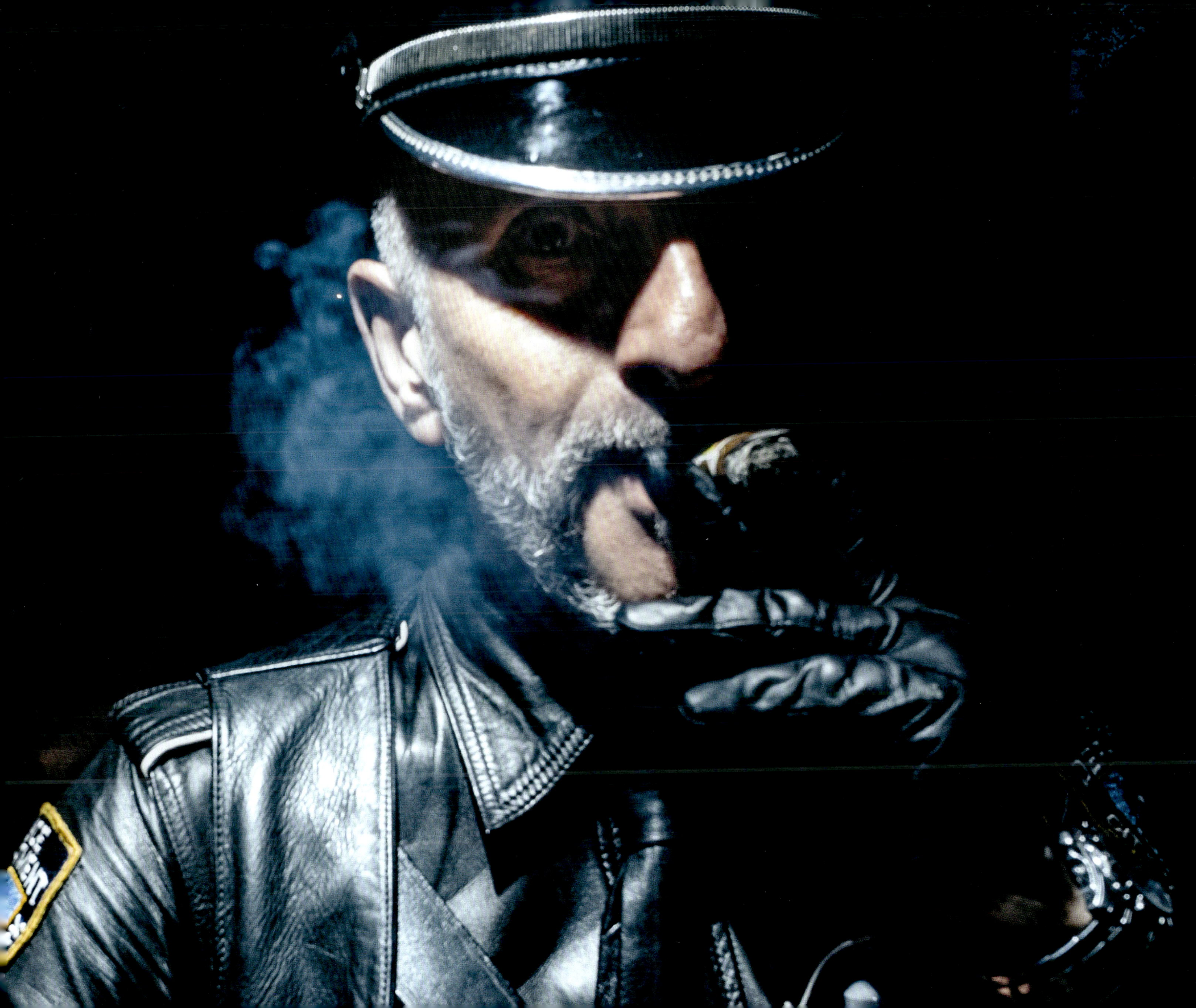

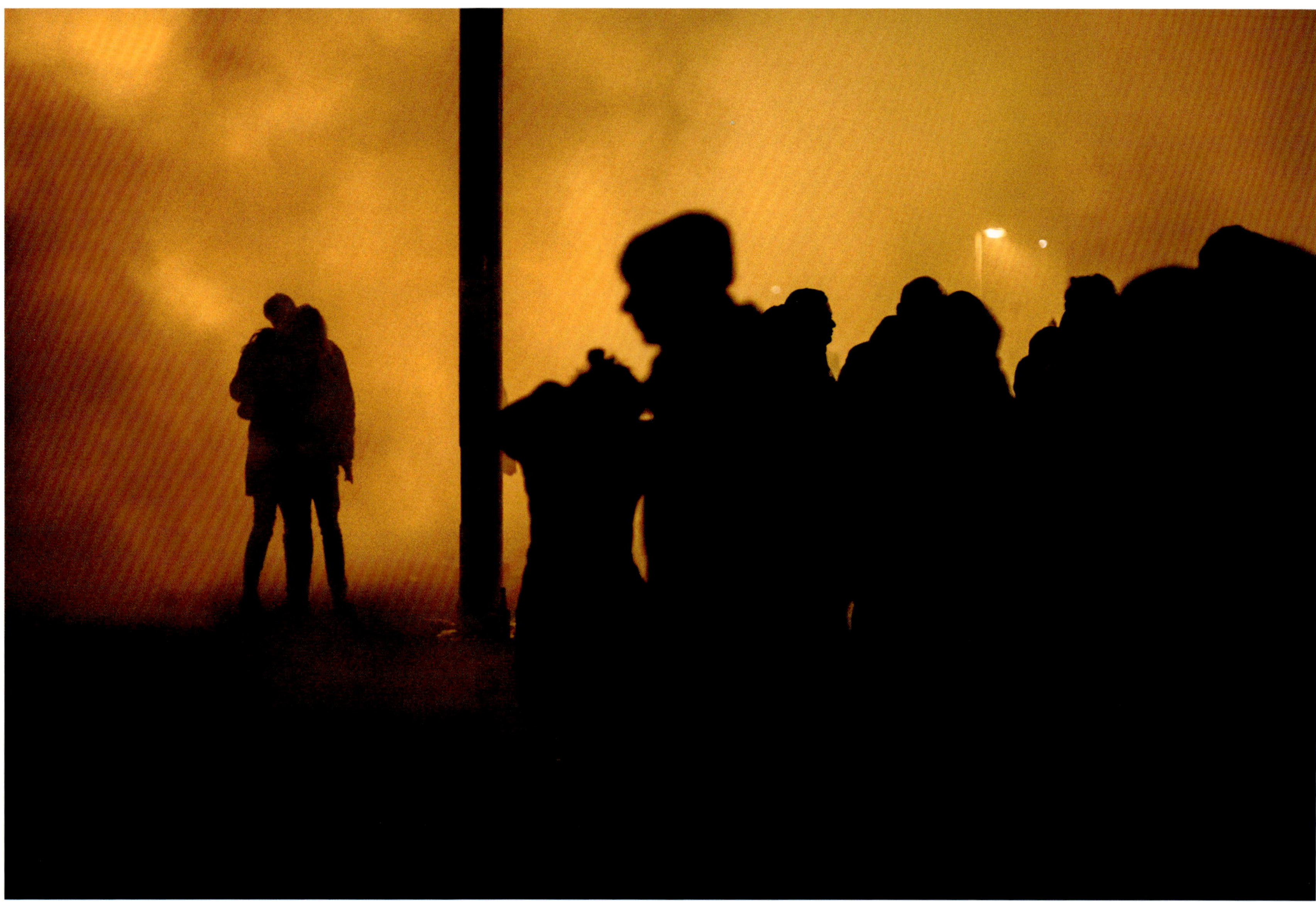

ORANGE

An illegal rave in the first hours of New Year's Day in Berlin and somebody threw a smoke grenade. There was orange smoke everywhere—a scene of surreal beauty. At that moment, I looked for an image, and found it when I saw the couple alone and separated from the dancing masses. The smoke was gone only seconds later.

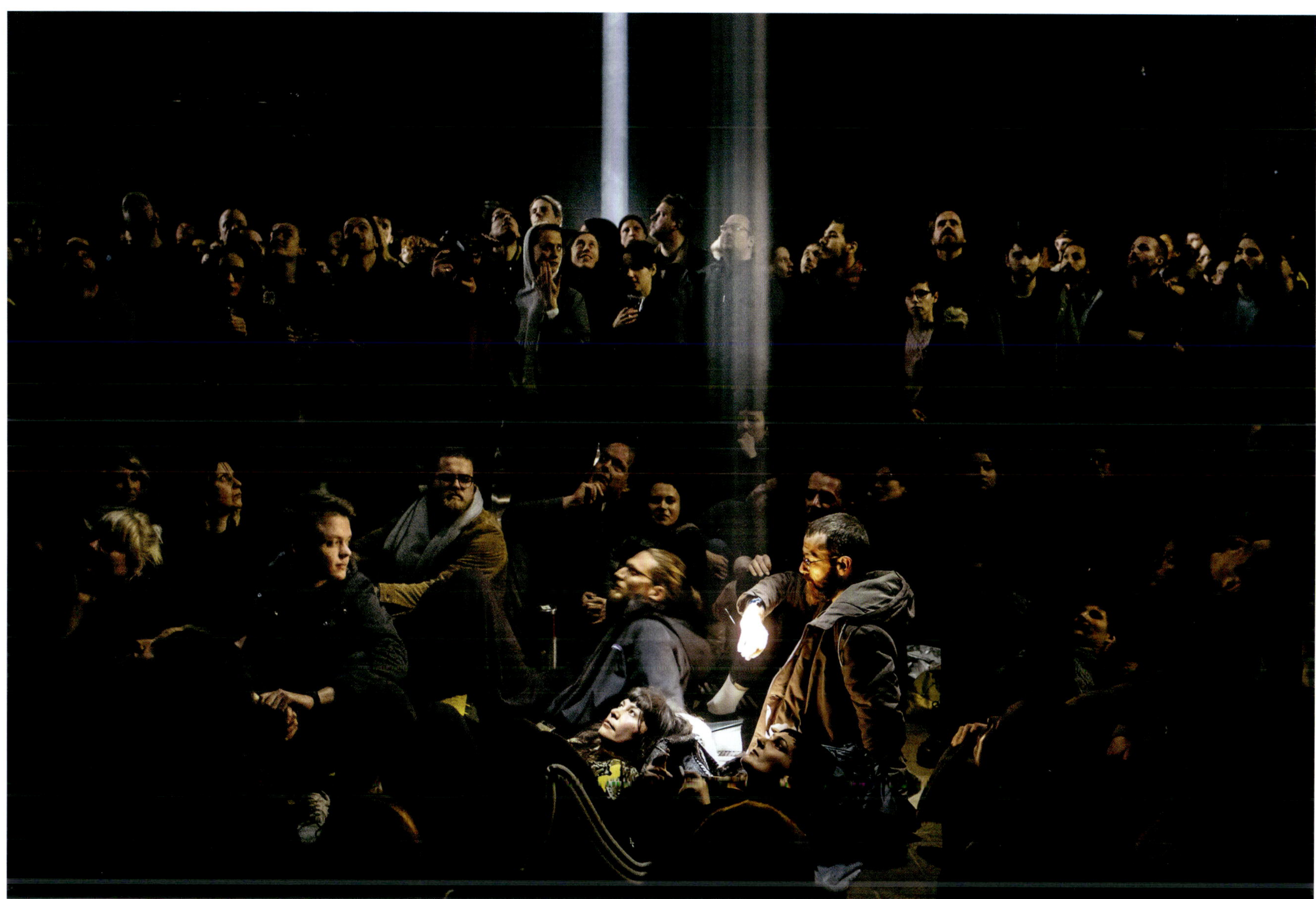

CHIAROSCURO

Chiaroscuro refers to the strong contrast between light and dark, a technique developed in the Renaissance era. This image reminds me of a Renaissance painting, with the single ray of light touching the hand—it almost feels like a religious scene. The reality of this photograph was quite mundane and worldly, though: it is a sound and laser performance in a former power plant. As always in street photography, it is more about the vision of the photographer than the reality being photographed.

Q

+

A

How do you assess a location or situation for potential images?

I like to scout a location before I start shooting. What kind of people are around? What is the vibe of the place? Is it busy? What is the quality of the light? Only then will I start shooting. I like to know the place where I'm going to shoot. In Berlin, I find myself returning to the same locations again and again over the course of many years. I very much like the government district and the Holocaust Memorial in Berlin, as both are defined by interesting abstract architecture. Geometry plays a big role in my images. On the other hand I like Alexanderplatz, which is a huge square in the very center of Berlin. The place is an ugly mess, but with 200,000 people crossing it every day there is always something going on. I choose to go to places where I feel safe on the streets and simply focus on shooting. That means I might be oblivious to anything else around me—not recommended in an unsafe neighborhood. While I like to return to some places again and again, I also try to find new locations. Sometimes I just get off the subway at a stop I don't know, and the place finds me. Situations change and evolve rapidly on the streets. Taking a shot is often a decision made in a split second. When something appeals to me, I will shoot—and most likely delete it later. I try to avoid overthinking when something happens, and prefer to focus on getting the shot.

How do you start to compose an image? What sort of features or light do you look for?

It rarely happens that I see a perfect image on the streets just waiting to be taken as it is. Usually when composing an image, I start somewhere—it may be the subject, the background, some urban structure, or the light. Starting from that one element, I will try to find something to add to and complement it. So, something needs to grab my attention—it doesn't have to be anything special at all. It can even be an abstract thing like "the light is great here," or "these lines in the background are really interesting." At times, that is enough. Like many photographers, I like the sunny morning or evening hours, because of the distinctive light and wonderful transitions into the shadows. With great light, the most mundane scenes look extraordinary. Many modern street photographers rely on strong directional light—from the sun or flash—and it is easy to understand why. The colors will pop, the contrasts are great, and everything uninteresting can be hidden in the shadows. Yet I'm also happy with a cloudy sky, because this means I have a nice indirect light everywhere and I can simply work on finding something interesting to fill the frame. Whenever I look at Henri Cartier-Bresson or Robert Frank, I'm amazed by how little they work with strong light. They use light in very subtle ways and still their work has stood the test of time.

What do you think makes a successful street photograph?

How do you define success? Many likes on social media, cheers from the street photography in-crowd, winning awards, selling well as a print, being selected by exhibition curators? There are several elements to a successful photograph. For me, the emotional impact is the most important one. If an image relates to the viewer in a way that triggers a strong emotional response, you have succeeded in capturing a glimpse of humanity. It really depends on looking into myself— if I react to something strongly and in an emotional way, then I feel there is a foundation for an image that is interesting and has an emotional impact. Then, for that to come across, the image needs to be well composed, allowing the content to unfold easily and have its desired effect. My work is really about the human condition, and what we are doing in our daily urban lives beyond the few great moments of love, kids, sex, and professional success—what are we doing the other 99 per cent of the time? Another question for me is whether the image is original or have I seen it lots of times. Everything has been photographed before, but what's my view on it, and how can I show it in a different way?

What are the technical challenges faced by a street photographer?

The challenge in street photography is mostly a creative one—finding an interesting frame in a sea of urban chaos, where you have zero control over your environment. From a technical point of view, shooting in broad daylight presents no challenge to the modern cameras most of us use. Even a smartphone will do a decent job in nailing the focus and the exposure. In night photography, things are a bit more complex. One of the challenges is balancing out the contrast of light and darkness. We often think of night photography as being in the dark, but for most of the time that is simply not true—there are very strong light sources, like street lights. And, it's more difficult to align light and subject matter. Finally, because of the overall scarcity of light, I will have to work with high ISO (which makes the image grainy or noisy), wider apertures (which means I lose depth of field), and slow shutter speeds (which can cause camera shake and unwanted motion blur). Modern autofocus systems usually work great in daylight, but autofocus will work considerably more slowly at night, or sometimes not work at all. Long story short: you have to work more diligently in night photography.

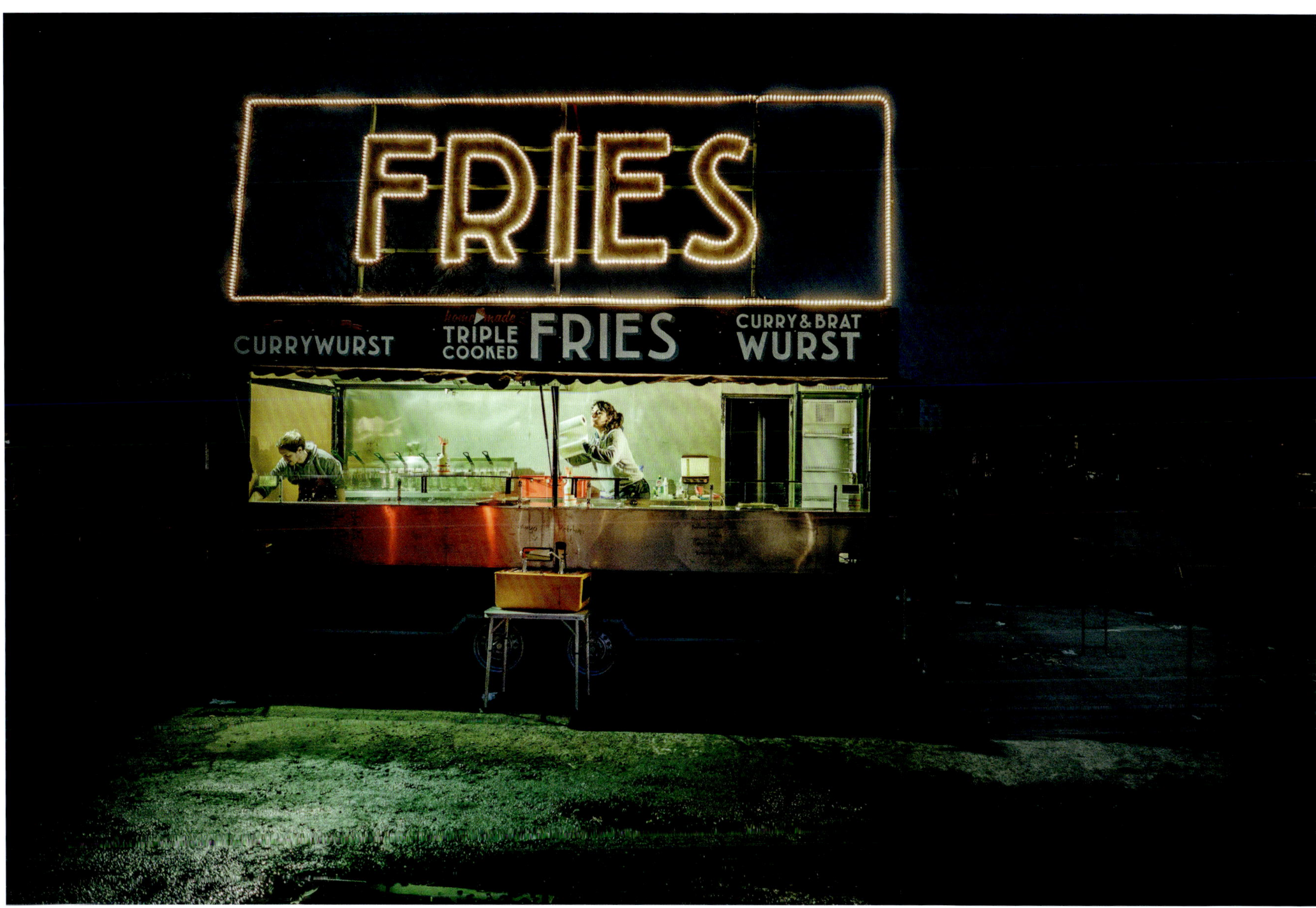

FRIES

I shot this at the end of a market day in winter. Can you imagine the same shot during daytime with a crowd waiting to order their fries? It would have been a rather ordinary image. This photo is defined by absence: the absence of daylight and the absence of any people around. Those absences, together with the electric lights, create this melancholic Edward Hopper feeling, which makes this image interesting.

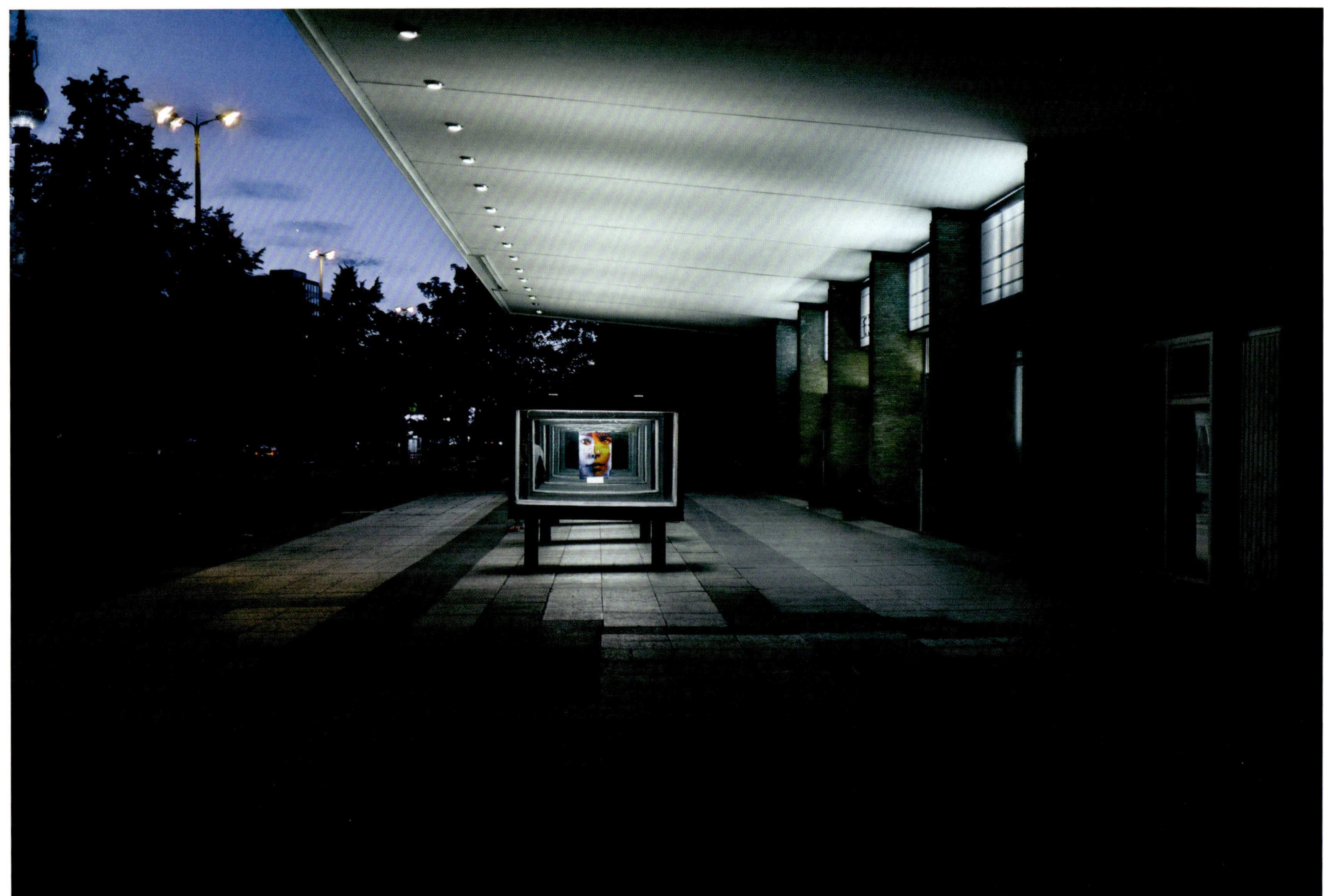

JULIA

Street photography is about the human condition, but it does not need people in it. In this case, a movie poster displaying a single face is enough. I had gone to see a movie (called *Julia*) and it was still daylight when I entered the cinema. I hadn't seen anything that was interesting to photograph. But when I left it was dark, and I immediately saw this shot. Mundane scenes during the day can turn into the most exciting ones at night, so it is good to always have a camera with you, even if you're just going to the movies.

GREEN

Here I employed a classic method of modern street photography. By combining two unrelated elements—the traffic light and the woman—I created a new, surreal reality: the green-headed woman. It is interesting to see how the mind operates, because even though we immediately understand the concept of the optical illusion, we still see a green-headed woman and react to that.

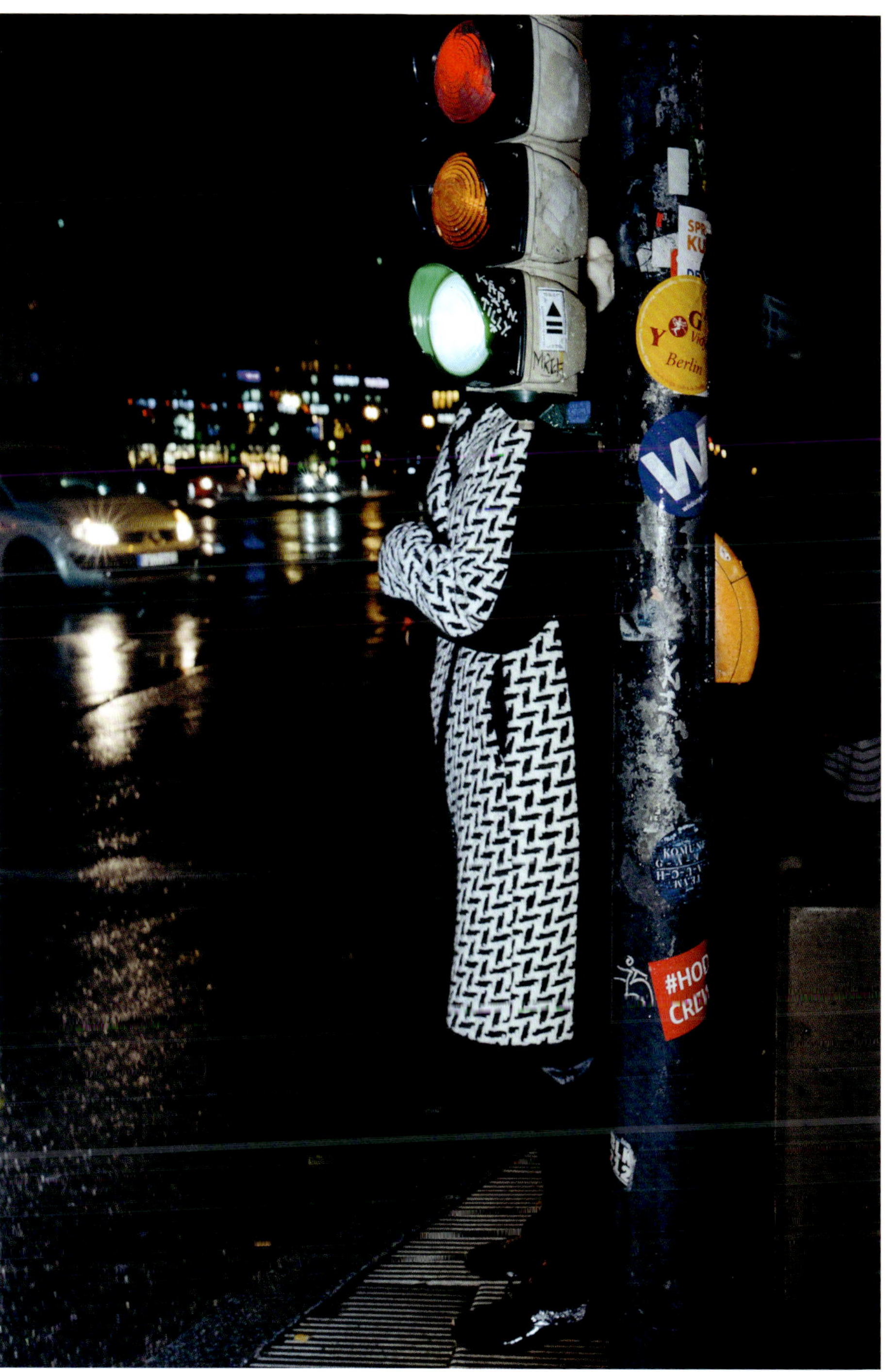

Q + A

Do you have a problem with white balance when shooting at night?

White balance in night photography can be tricky when you have several artificial light sources, all with different light temperatures. It can be quite a task to get all that aligned and it's a challenge but it's also an opportunity. The different light temperatures allow for certain effects that are not visible to the human eye. When shot with a camera, those can be quite interesting.

Do you do a lot of post-processing to your images?

It depends. I shoot in RAW format, which gives me a tremendous amount of leeway in terms of exposure, contrast, local dodging and burning—and I might use all of those if need be. Some night shots need a bit more work. Having said that, I will spend less than a minute in post-processing on most images. When it comes to building a series, I will go for an overall consistent look, which in turn might result in some additional post-processing work. And preparing an image for print is, of course, a completely different matter that requires additional work in post.

Do you ever feel you are invading a person's privacy?

That is an interesting ethical question. Basically, I try to behave like a decent human being on the streets. There are certain things I stay away from. I don't shoot people in physical or emotional distress, in their private homes, or photograph anything that looks undignified. I do not jump people when shooting close. I prefer to get close in a way that doesn't scare them into panic. Still some people do not like to be photographed, and they might very well feel that I invade their privacy when taking their picture.

What tips would you give to those who wish to master street photography?

The most important thing is to practice. There is no other way to get great images than to do it over and over again. The second tip would be to educate yourself visually. Learn from the masters of street photography and familiarize yourself with their work. Have a look at the classic images of Henri Cartier-Bresson, Elliot Erwitt, William Klein, Joel Meyerowitz, Gary Winogrand, René Burri, Robert Frank, Diane Arbus, and Mary Ellen Mark. Look at modern street photographers like Martin Parr, Trent Parke, Alec Soth, Bruce Gilden, Alex Webb, David Alan Harvey, and Daido Moriyama. Also, street photography is just another form of visual art. So, go to the museums— see how Rembrandt dealt with light, how Monet caught fleeting moments, and what Hopper had to say about human isolation. The third tip would be to evaluate an image across the whole frame. Everything in an image needs to work together: primary subject, secondary subject, background, light, and composition. And be ready to fail: most street photographs are crap. That is true for every street photographer. Simply be determined to edit out all the weak shots. For me, this means I delete 95–99 per cent of all the images I took during an outing. Sometimes, I delete everything. Finally, listen to qualified feedback on your work. Try to learn from critical comments.

"Street photography is just another form of visual art. So, go to the museums—see how Rembrandt dealt with light, how Monet caught fleeting moments, and what Hopper had to say about human isolation."

TECHNICAL INFORMATION

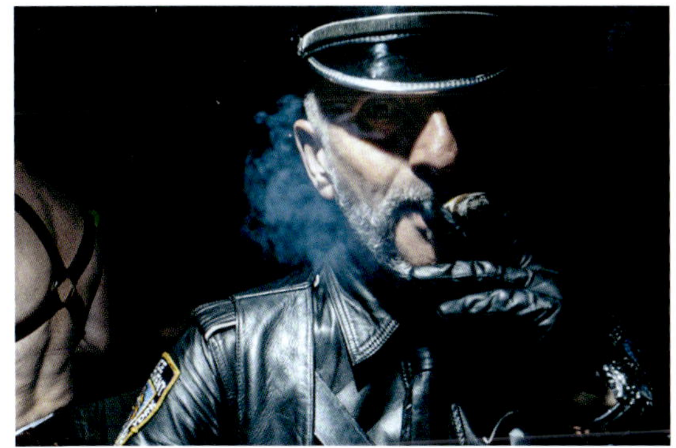

A SIMPLE STREET PORTRAIT
BERLIN, GERMANY

Camera: Fujifilm X70
Lens/Focal length: Fixed 18.5mm f/2.8 (35mm equivalent: 28mm)
Aperture: f/8
Shutter speed: 1/60 sec.
ISO: 1600

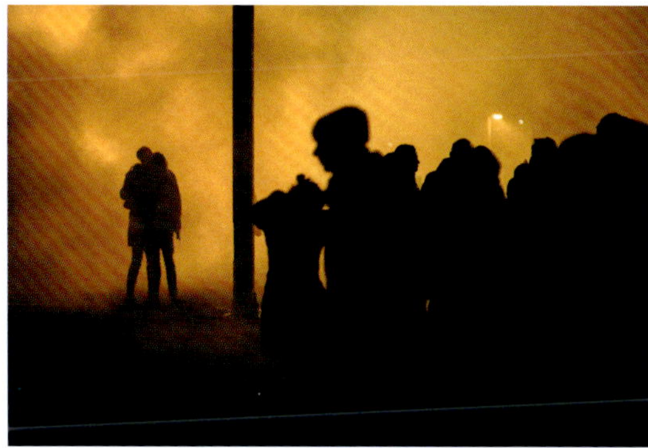

ORANGE
BERLIN, GERMANY

Camera: Sony a7R
Lens/Focal length: 50mm f/0.95
Aperture: f/0.95
Shutter speed: 1/125 sec.
ISO: 6400

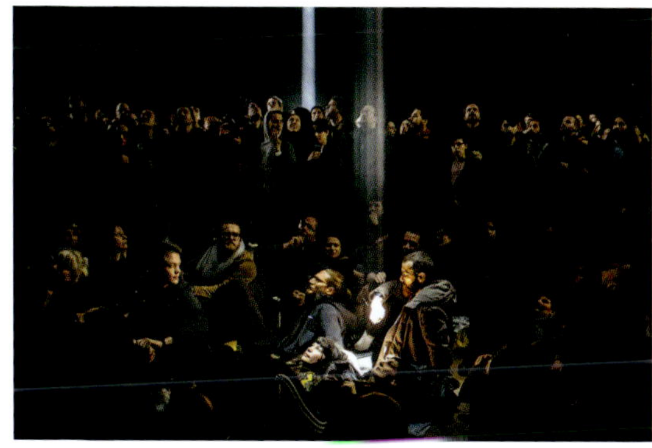

CHIAROSCURO
BERLIN, GERMANY

Camera: Fujifilm X100F
Lens/Focal length: Fixed 23mm f/2 (35mm equivalent: 35mm)
Aperture: f/2
Shutter speed: 1/13 sec.
ISO: 6400

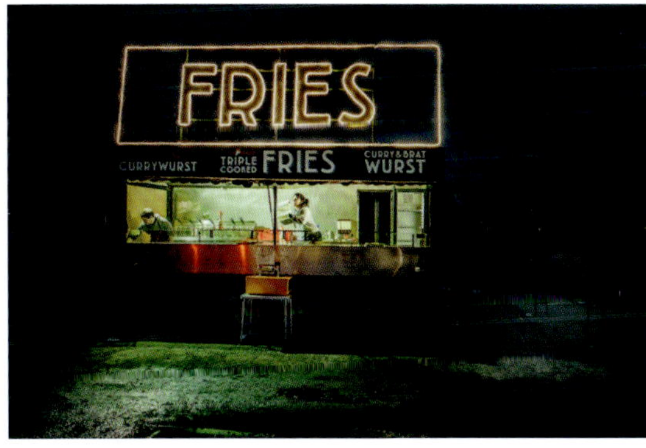

FRIES
BERLIN, GERMANY

Camera: Sony a7R
Lens/Focal length: Model E 25mm f/2
Aperture: f/2
Shutter speed: 1/80 sec.
ISO: 800

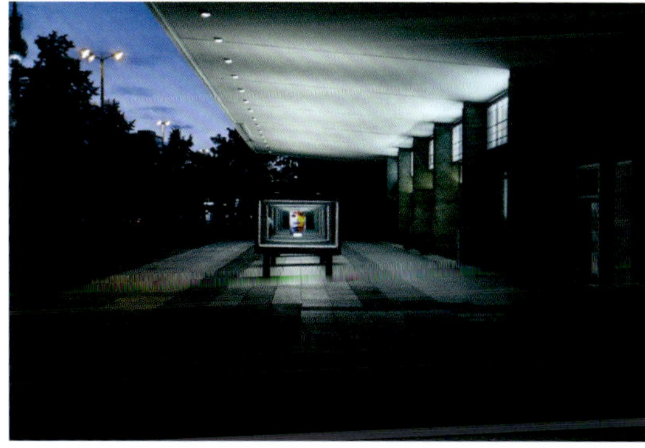

JULIA
BERLIN, GERMANY

Camera: Sony a7R
Lens/Focal length: Model E 35mm f/2
Aperture: f/2
Shutter speed: 1/60 sec.
ISO: 250

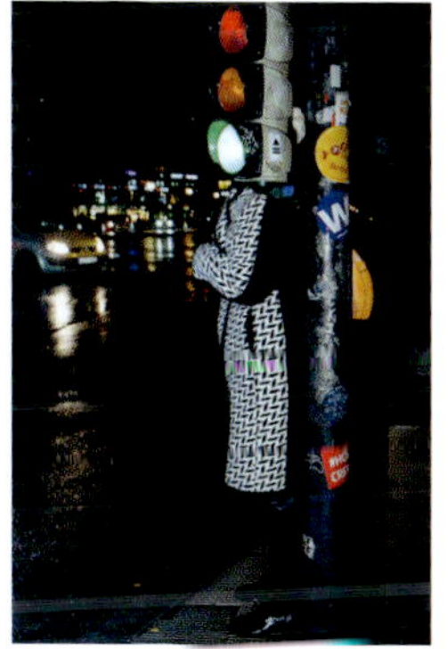

GREEN
BERLIN, GERMANY

Camera: Fujifilm X-T2
Lens/Focal length: XF23mm WR f/2 (35mm equivalent: 35mm)
Aperture: f/8
Shutter speed: 1/30 sec.
ISO: 1600

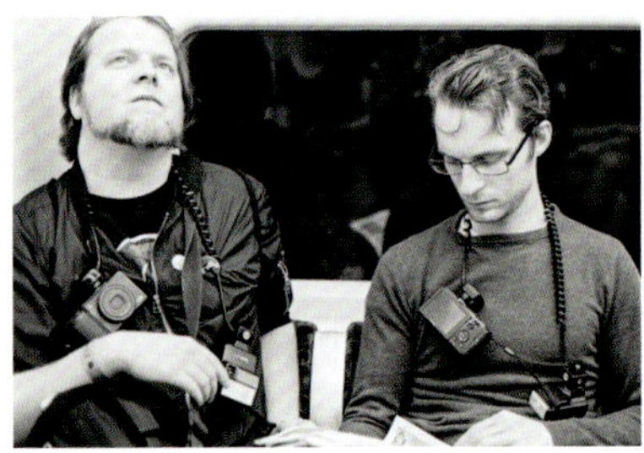

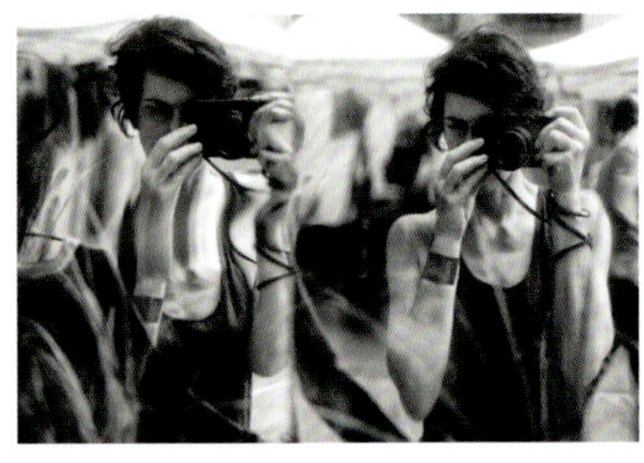

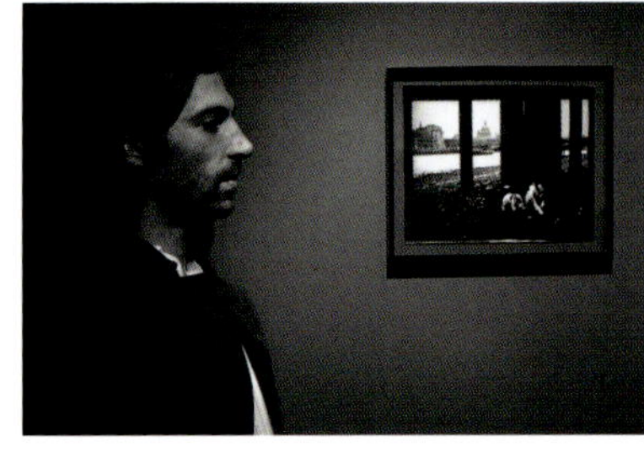

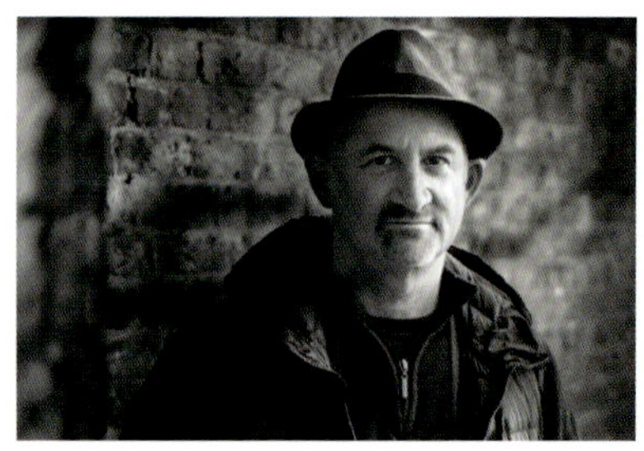

THE BRAGDON BROTHERS
MASTERS OF FLASH

www.bragdonbrothers.com

The Bragdon Brothers are based in Scotland, and their work has been exhibited at Out of The Blue, Drill Hall, Edinburgh, 2015/17; Emerging Talent, Retina Photography Festival, Edinburgh, 2016; London Street Photography Symposium (talk with Full Frontal Flash), London, 2016; Street Sans Frontières, Paris, 2017; Free Range 2017, London, 2017; Future Proof 2017, Street Level Photoworks, Glasgow, 2017; SFSP Festival, San Francisco, 2017/18; and BSPF, Brussels, 2017.

Instagram: @the_bragdon_brothers

MELISSA BREYER
MASTER OF HIDDEN STORIES

www.melissabreyer.com

Melissa Breyer lives and works in New York City, and her photographs have been published in *The New York Times* ("The 'Quiet Moments' of Waitresses at Work," April 28, 2017). A photobook of her work will be published in 2019 by Peanut Press. Her images have been exhibited at Home: An Exhibition of Candid Photographs, SFC, San Francisco, 2018; First Look, Panopticon, Boston, 2018; and Street Sans Frontières, ImageNation, Paris, 2018. Her *Steam Systems* won the Grand Prize in Photoplus Expo 2017.

Instagram: @melbreyer

GIACOMO BRUNELLI
MASTER OF NOIR

www.giacomobrunelli.com

Giacomo Brunelli was born in Perugia, Italy, and lives and works in London. His work is in the Museum of Fine Arts, Houston, and has been exhibited at The Photographers' Gallery, London; Galerie Camera Obscura, Paris; and Strange and Familiar, curated by Martin Parr, The Barbican, London. His photographs have won the Magenta Foundation's "Flash Forward 2009"; and the Sony World Photography Award, Nature, 2008.

Selected Publications: *Self Portraits* (Editions Bessard, 2017); *Eternal London* (Dewi Lewis Publishing, 2008).

Instagram: @brunelligiacomo

PAUL BURGESS
MASTER OF URBAN POETRY

www.paulburgessphoto.com

Paul Burgess has spent his professional career working in TV, editing and directing documentaries for a variety of international broadcasters including the BBC, ARTE, and PBS. Photography has always been his personal passion, in which he loves the freedom of being able to work alone. In his street photography, he tries to leave behind the gritty realism of documentaries and instead aims to capture the strangeness, drama, and poetry of the urban landscape.

Instagram: @paulburgessphoto

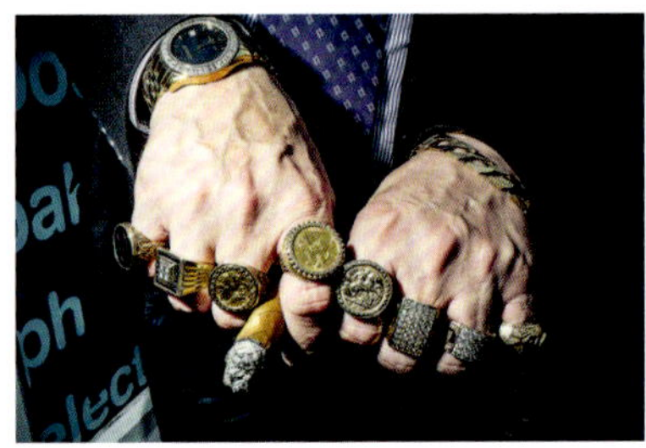

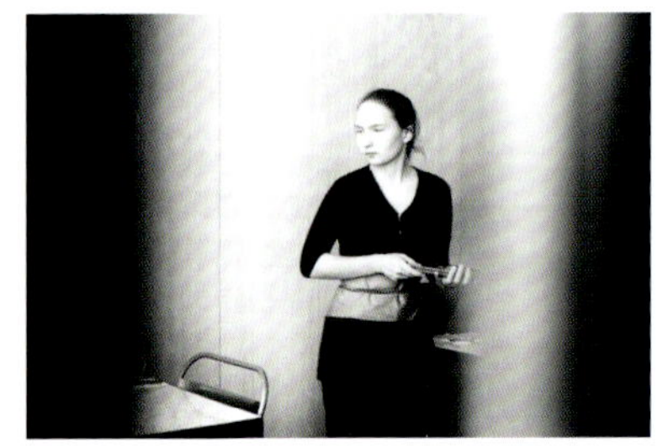

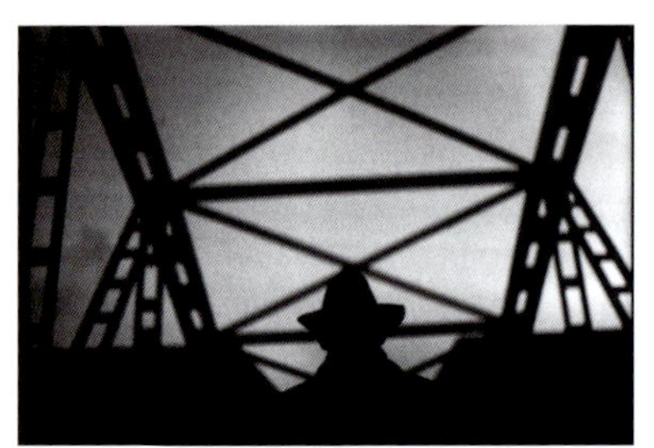

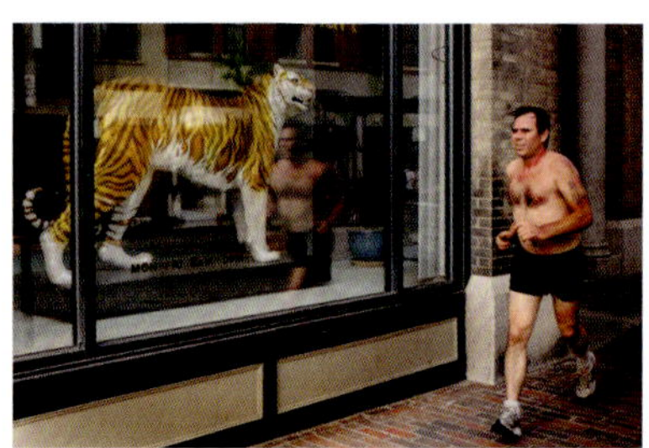

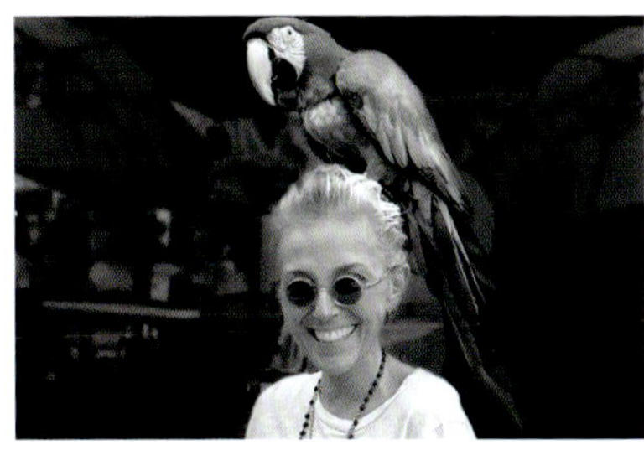

SALLY DAVIES
MASTER OF URBAN LANDSCAPE

www.sallydaviesphoto.com

Sally Davies has been photographing New York City since 1983, and her digital archive has recently been acquired for the Downtown Collection at the NYU Fales Library. Her images are in the permanent collections of The Museum of the City of New York; Harvard Business School; Museum of Fine Arts, Houston; and the 9/11 Museum, NYC. Sally's solo exhibitions have included "New York at Night," 2015, and "Photographs of the Lower East Side," 2014, both at the Bernarducci Meisel Gallery, New York.

Instagram: @sallydaviesphoto

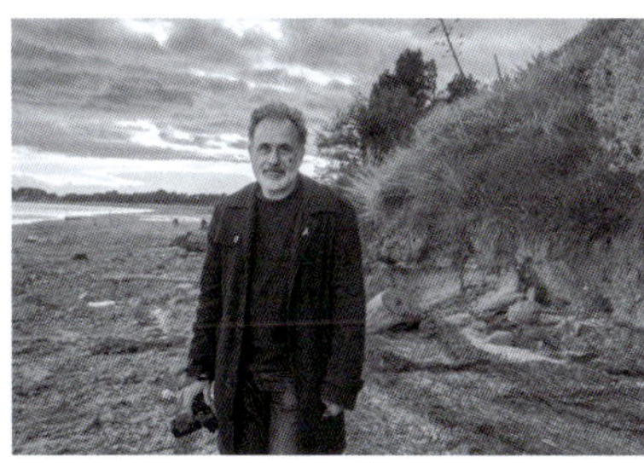

GEORGE GEORGIOU
MASTER OF COMMUNITY

www.georgegeorgiou.net

George Georgiou's work is in collections including the Museum of Modern Art (MOMA), New York, and the Elton John collection. He has won awards including *The British Journal of Photography* project prize, 2010; two World Press Photo prizes, 2003 and 2005; and Pictures of the Year International, first prize, 2004.

Selected Publications: *Last Stop* (Masa, 2015); *Fault Line/Turkey/East/West* (Schilt Publishing, 2010).

Instagram: @georgiou17

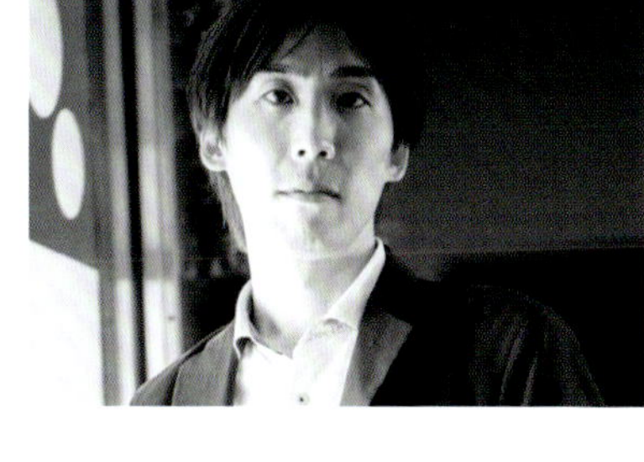

ASH SHINYA KAWAOTO
MASTER OF EXPRESSION

www.ashphoto.jp

Ash Shinya Kawaoto lives and works in Tokyo, and is a member of the street collective Void Tokyo. His images have featured in international magazines including *LensCulture* and *Szerokikadr*, and on the websites 1x.com and asiaphotoreview. His international awards include Sony World Photography Awards 2017 (shortlisted); Gold Prize, Moscow International Fotography Awards 2017; finalist, Magnum Photography Awards 2017; 2nd place, International Photography Awards 2017; first place, International Photography Awards 2018.

Instagram: @ashley_designing
Twitter: @ash_photos

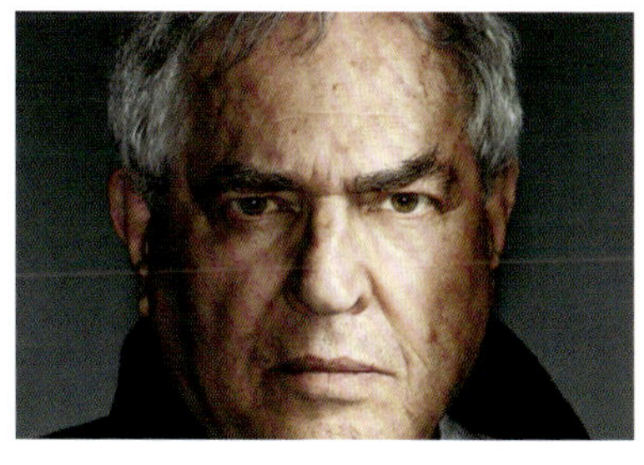

JAY MAISEL
MASTER OF GESTURE

www.jaymaisel.com

Jay Maisel's portfolio includes five *Sports Illustrated* swimsuit covers and the cover of Miles Davis' Kind of Blue. Among his many awards are Lifetime Achievement Award, PSW, 2015; Lifetime Achievement Award, PPA, 2003; Lifetime Achievement Award, ASMP, 1996; The Art Director's Club Hall of Fame, 1995. His exhibitions include "Blazing Editions, Jay Maisel: 60 Years of Photography," NY and LA, 2016/17; and "On Seeing," Maine Media Gallery, Rockport, ME, 2015.

Selected Publications: *New York in the '50s* (Nazraeli, 2014); *Light, Gesture & Color* (New Riders, 2014).

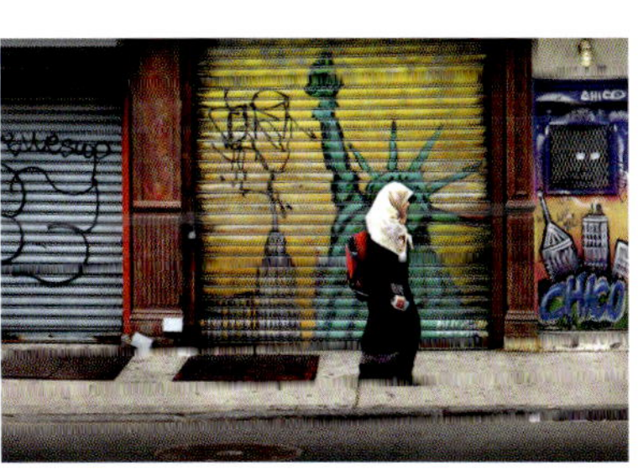

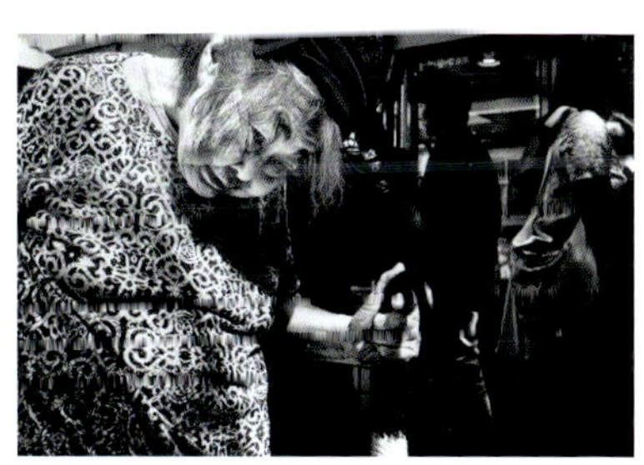

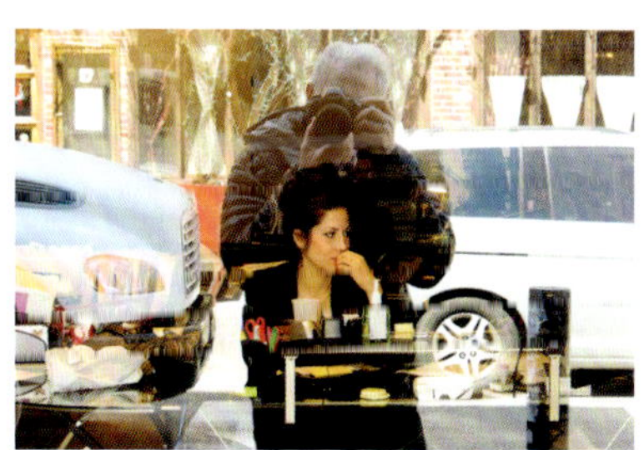

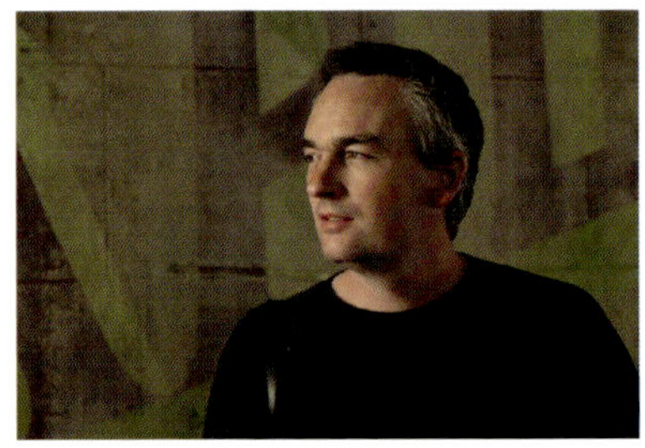

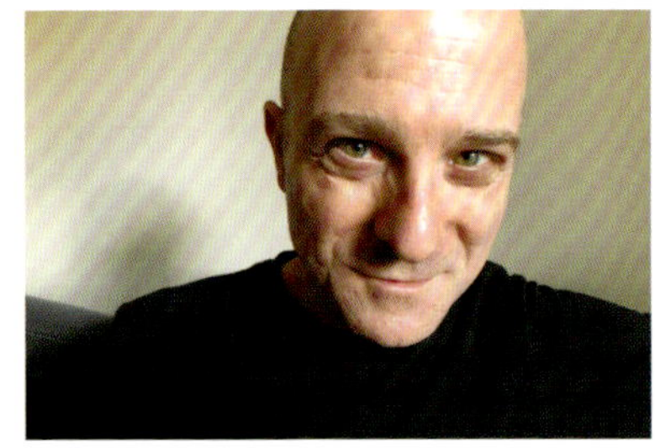

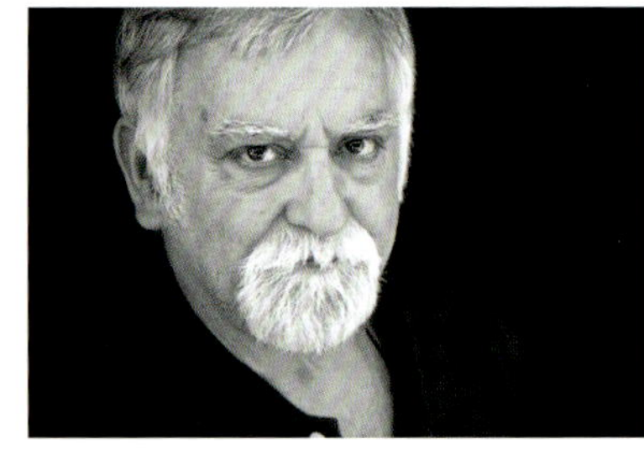

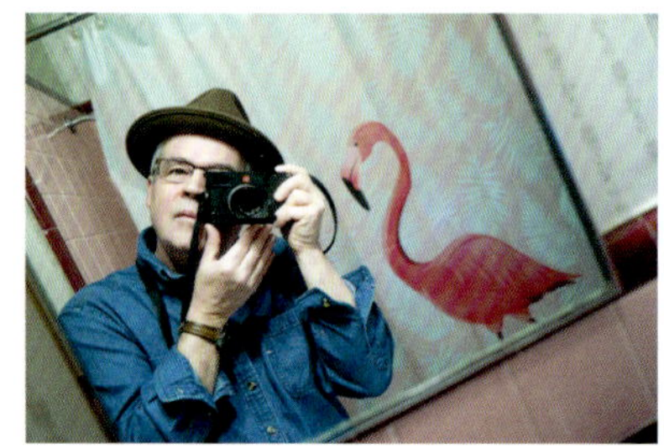

JESSE MARLOW
MASTER OF ABSTRACT

www.jessemarlow.com

Based in Melbourne, Australia, Jesse Marlow has his work in collections including the National Gallery of Victoria. He won the International Street Photography Prize, 2011, and the MGA Bowness Prize, 2012. Jesse is a Leica Ambassador and is a member of the international street photographer's collective iN-PUBLIC (in-public.com).

Selected Publications: *Don't Just Tell Them, Show Them* (M.33, 2014); *Street Photography Now* (Thames & Hudson, 2010); *Wounded* (Sling Shot Press, 2005).

Instagram: @jessemarlow

DIMITRI MELLOS
MASTER OF CHIAROSCURO

www.dimitrimellos.com

Dimitri Mellos was born in Athens, Greece, and lives in New York City. He has been photographing consistently since around 2007. His work has been featured in *The New York Times* and other international publications, and has been exhibited in the USA, UK, Greece, Australia, Germany, Poland, Spain, and Portugal. Among other distinctions, he won 1st place in the 2018 Pollux Awards and has been a Finalist for the Visura Grant, the Renaissance Photography Prize, the Magnum Expression Award, and the LensCulture Street Photography Awards.

Instagram: @dimitrimellos

RUI PALHA
MASTER OF ATMOSPHERE

www.ruipalha.com

Rui Palha lives in Lisbon. Since 2001, he has been passionate about street photography. He loves the freedom of being in the streets in the middle of people, the main subject of his photographs. He has won several awards including Best Work of Photography with his book *Street Photography*. His recent exhibitions include Hang Around..., 2018 Spazio Edit, Milan, Italy (invited by Leica Akademie Italy), and Wandering in Portugal, 2018, House of Lucie, Bangkok, Thailand.

ED PETERS
MASTER OF COMPLEXITY

www.epetphoto.com

Ed Peters is based in New York. He has worked as a staff photographer recording topical news stories including the plight of Burmese refugees, war in the Balkans, and famine in Somalia. As a street photographer, he has created long-term projects in the USA, Mexico, and India. Ed is a member of the photography collective VIVO, and galleries of his latest work can be found on their website:

street-photographers.com/author/ed-peters

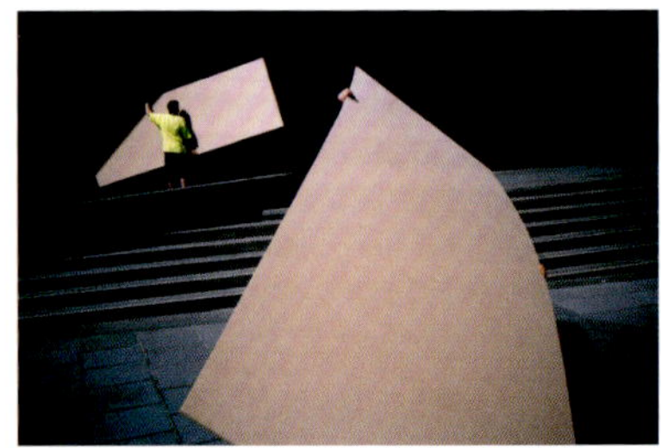

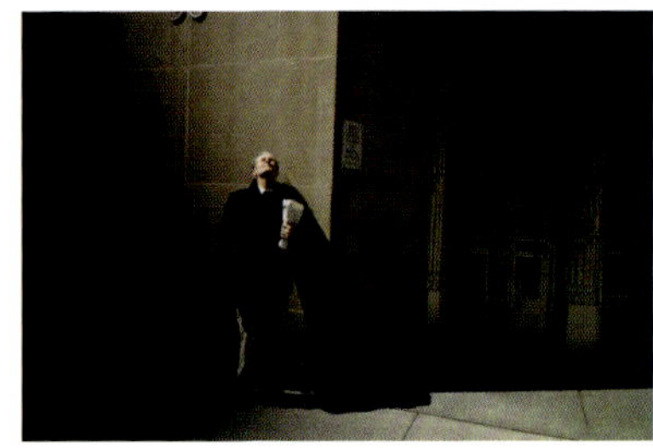

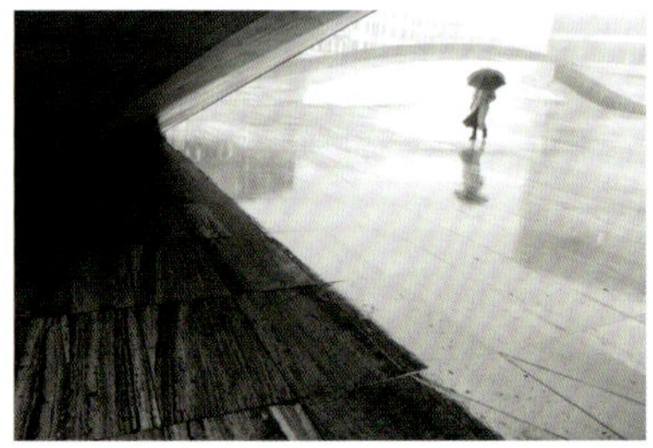

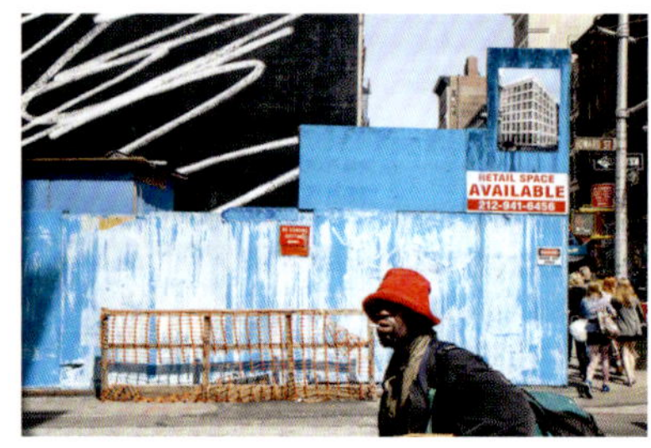